Unyielding Courage:

The Northeast United Resistance Army

Li Fasuo

Translated by Wu Laibao, Fan Jiaojiao and Wang Zhongsheng

Unyielding Courage: The Northeast United Resistance Army
Author: Li Fasuo
Translator: Wu Laibao, Fan Jiaojiao and Wang Zhongsheng
Language: English
Word Count (for space of all pages): 416 thousand words
Publisher: Chicago Academic Press
Number of Pages: 474
ISBN: 978-1-965890-73-8

Publishing	Chicago Academic Press
	5923 N Artesian Ave
	Chicago IL 60659
Email	contact@chicagoacademicpress.com
Website	http://chicagoacademicpress.com/
Book Size	6X9 inches
First Edition	

Translator's Profile

Wu Laibao (born in December 2000, Haikou, Hainan), holds a Bachelor Degree (City University of Wuhan) and an MA (Jilin International Studies University).

Served as a volunteer translator for the Wuhan Military World Games and the World Conference on Biosphere Conservation and Sustainable Development in Changbai Mountain. Won the second prize in the National Belt and Road Translation Competition for Chinese-English translation; the second grade in the final of the Hubei Province Translation Competition; the third prize at the provincial level in the National College Students' English Translation Competition.

Fan Jiaojiao (born in February 2000, Zhoukou, Henan), holds a Bachelor of Arts in English Translation from Guangdong Ocean University and is currently pursuing a Master of Arts in English Interpreting at Jilin International Studies University. She has demonstrated outstanding competence in translation and interpreting by winning multiple awards in national and provincial competitions, including the National Third Prize in the 4th "Peace Cup" China Legal and Diplomatic Translation Competition (2024), the Provincial Third Prize in the National College Students' English Translation Competition (2023), the Third Prize in the 2nd National College Students' Classic Literary Translation Competition (2023), the Third Prize (Jilin Division) in the 13th National Interpreting Contest (English) (2024), and the Excellent Award in the 6th National Patent Translation Competition (2023).

Her significant interpreting experience includes providing professional simultaneous and consecutive interpretation services for a visiting delegation from St. Petersburg University (USA) to facilitate academic exchange and campus tours (December 2024), serving as the on-site interpreter for international athletes and officials at an international skiing event to ensure seamless communication during trials and competition (January 2025), and acting as a cultural communication volunteer to provide language support and introduce Chinese cultural heritage to foreign visitors (December 2024). She is engaged in research on the application of AI technology in translating Chinese-specific discourses, exploring whether artificial intelligence can replace human translators in specific text types, aiming to provide reference for the development of translation in the era of artificial intelligence.

Wang Zhongsheng

Associate Professor, Master's Supervisor, Jilin International Studies University.

Research Interests: Translation Theory and Practice

Over the past five years, she has presided over a total of 5 research projects. Additionally, she has led 2 university-level research and teaching reform projects, published more than 10 academic papers in journals.

Contents

Chapter 11

The Puppet Regime

35. Puyi, Obedience or Death

Generally speaking, traitors to their country are seldom virtuous. The very essence of their existence is betrayal. They betray their fellow countrymen of the same nation to satiate their personal avarice and indulge in hedonistic pursuits. This very feature serves as a fertile soil and breeding ground for the Japanese to manipulate and exploit traitors. As the incisive and profound saying among the common people in Northeast China goes, "Rotten meat attracts flies."

In this regard, when it came to bribing and recruiting traitors, the Japanese spared no expense and were extremely precise in their targeting of specific individuals.

In Puyi's memoirs, during Japan's complete colonization of Northeast China, the traitors reaped substantial benefits. Each time a decree was issued and enforced, it presented an opportunity for them to amass wealth, with a "bonus" distribution ensuing. From the prime minister down to the local baojia heads, nearly everyone had a share.

Certainly, the Japanese Kwantung Army, following the "war to support war" strategy, would not contribute a single cent of this colossal sum. All of it was wrung from the hard-earned blood and sweat of the 30 million common people who could only subsist on acorn flour. In an era when one yuan could purchase five catties of pork, the publicly known monthly salaries of major traitors were as follows: Zheng Xiaoxu, the prime minister of the puppet state, had a monthly salary of 10,000 yuan; several "bigwigs" such as Zhang Jinghui, Zang Shiyi, and Xi Qia received 8,000 yuan each. And Puyi, the so-called "ruler" and "emperor", had an annual imperial household expense of 800,000 yuan.

The above are merely the overt accounts. The covert ones refer to the "illicit payments" for each large-scale event, as Puyi mentioned. The Japanese termed it the "special confidential funds", which were hefty rewards bestowed upon those major traitors who wholeheartedly defected. On March 1, 1932, after the formal establishment of the puppet Manchukuo, the Japanese distributed the "Founding Bribery Funds". Zheng Xiaoxu, the prime minister of state, received the largest amount, reaching 1 million yuan. [1]

In September of that year, Mutō Nobuyoshi, Japan's "first ambassador to Manchuria" and the newly appointed commander of the Japanese Kwantung Army, publicly inked the Japan-Manchukuo Protocol with the puppet "Manchukuo." Through this act, Japan arrogated to itself all the rights and interests in Northeast China. Zheng Xiaoxu, in his capacity as the prime minister of the puppet state, signed the Japan-Manchukuo Protocol with Mutō Nobuyoshi. Subsequently, he requested Puyi to "ratify" it (even though Puyi was displeased). Owing to such "merits" of "taking action first and then reporting," he received an additional 600,000 yuan as "Founding Merit Funds."

It should not be thought that the traitors were merely decorative figures.

The Japanese invariably contrived excuses for every heinous act they perpetrated, particularly major economic plundering and political suppression and control measures. For instance, "grain delivery" (military grain requisition), "devoting oneself to the country," the confiscation of the assets of the four major banks in Northeast China, and the establishment of the puppet Central Bank of Manchukuo. Moreover, the formulation and promulgation of so-called laws such as the Public Security Police Law, the Baojia Correction Law, and the National Military Service Law, as well as the implementation of the "village merger and settlement combination" policy and the establishment of "group tribes," all necessitated the issuance of decrees through the puppet "state" (the puppet Manchukuo). In other words, all the hardships endured by the people in Northeast China had been approved and consented to by the traitors. This is the primary reason why the major traitors of the puppet Manchukuo were unforgivable for their crimes.

Within the puppet "Manchukuo," Japanese individuals occupying positions in the so-called cabinet, as well as in counties and towns, were also on the payroll. Despite serving in deputy roles, their salaries far exceeded those of their Chinese counterparts holding the principal positions. This blatant disparity frequently stirred discontent and murmurs among the top-tier traitorous officials.

Koki Tadao, the personnel section chief, offered a preposterous explanation as follows: "We Japanese possess superior capabilities. Naturally, our salaries ought to be higher. Additionally, the Japanese maintain a higher standard of living. We are accustomed to consuming rice from birth, unlike the Manchus, who are used to sorghum. Allowing the Japanese to receive more in salary is an act of amity on our part."

Komai Tokuzo, the director of the General Affairs Hall, adopted an even more brazen stance. He snarled, "You've pocketed the money. Do you think you can shirk your duties? Among all of you here, who hasn't received confidential funds from the Kwantung Army? You're being well-provided for, yet you still dare to stir up trouble. You'd better wise up!"

In reality, Komai was the most influential and highest-ranking official within the "cabinet" of the puppet Manchukuo. His intimidating words promptly hushed everyone present. [2]

The Japanese were far from lenient towards traitors who dared to defy their commands. Mere reprimands were out of the question; they resorted to drastic measures to enforce their authority.

Ling Sheng, the scion of Gui Fu, a former Mongolian military governor during the Qing Dynasty, held the position of governor in the puppet Xing'an Province. When Pu Yi journeyed to Lushun, Ling Sheng hastened to offer his "imperial welcome," harbouring deep-seated hopes for the restoration of the "Great Qing Dynasty." At the inauguration of the puppet "Manchukuo," Ling Sheng's choice to don the traditional Qing official robes was a clear indication of his reluctance to acknowledge this new Japanese-sponsored regime. Recognizing his loyalty, Pu Yi arranged a betrothal between his fourth sister and Ling Sheng's son, thus forging an in-law relationship between the two families.

In the spring of 1936, Ling Sheng travelled to the "New Capital" to participate in a governors' joint meeting. During the gathering, he voiced his discontent, stating that Xing'an had long been a unified administrative region and questioning why it had been fragmented into four smaller provinces. He also lamented his own position as governor, complaining that he was "in office yet powerless," with every decision ultimately resting in the hands of the Japanese. Little did he know that his words would seal his fate! Immediately upon his return to Hailar following the meeting, the Japanese military police arrested Ling Sheng, accusing him of "colluding with the Soviet Union." In a matter of weeks, he was executed.

Simultaneously, Ling Sheng's younger brother, Fu Ling, who served as the colonel chief of staff of the puppet Xing'an North Province Garrison

Army, his brother-in-law Chun De, the director of the puppet police department, and his secretary Hua Lintai, were also put to death. Several others were handed down sentences of over 10 years in prison, and the majority of them perished behind bars. [3] This series of events vividly demonstrates the Japanese penchant for eliminating any potential threats completely, leaving no loose ends.

Despite his titular status as the "emperor" of the puppet state, Pu Yi was powerless to save his in-laws from the clutches of the Japanese. Once he learned of Ling Sheng's execution, his first act, as directed by the Japanese, was to promptly annul the engagement between his fourth sister and Ling Sheng's son.

The Japanese clearly grasped the Chinese strategy of "capturing the ringleader first when catching thieves." They knew that to control and manipulate a group of lackeys, one must first subdue the leading one. Thus, they went to great lengths regarding Pu Yi. Ever since Pu Yi set foot on the land of Northeast China, he gradually came to realize that he had become a puppet of the Kwantung Army, feeling like a "porcelain figure," constantly thinking that "he might be shattered into pieces at any moment." Consequently, his physical demeanor underwent changes: he walked on tiptoe, spoke in a hushed voice, and more significantly, he became completely subservient to the Japanese in political and administrative affairs. All the decrees and policies issued by the puppet State Council to persecute and plunder the people of Northeast China had passed through Pu Yi's "approval," which was a serious crime he committed against the people. Although some of these were merely perfunctory acts carried out under the intimidation of the Japanese.

The author of The Tokyo Trial stated, "There should be a limit to the degradation of a person who bears the title of emperor." [4] This holds true.

Not only for an emperor but for anyone, there ought to be a minimum threshold for degradation. What we need to explore now is why the last descendants of the powerful and influential Kangxi, Yongzheng, and Qianlong emperors lost the mettle and courage of their ancestors and turned out to be so cowardly.

Some people firmly believe that Pu Yi's unyielding ambition to restore the Qing Dynasty was his primary impetus, leading him to compromise with the Japanese. Pu Yi himself once said, "On the scales of my heart, on one side is false dignity (restoring the dynasty), and on the other side is my personal safety." [5] However, most scholars maintain that Pu Yi was mainly concerned about his "personal safety," and the restoration of the Qing Dynasty was merely his "main motivation" when he went to Northeast China recklessly at that time.

Over 80 years ago, an English journalist named Edward Bell managed to pass through the Chengguang Gate, ascend the narrow stairs, and enter the living room of the Puppet Manchurian Imperial Palace, which "smelled as if it hadn't been inhabited for a long time," and met the legendary Pu Yi. At that time, Pu Yi was 20 years old, only six months away from his third coronation and becoming the emperor of the Puppet Manchurian State, and he had been in the hands of the Japanese for over two years. Edward Bell described in his book The Last Emperor of China, "Pu Yi, who was tall and thin, short-sighted, timid, and extremely distracted, was vastly different from his rugged Manchu ancestors."

Edward Bell revealed a truth to us. The Aisin Gioro ancestors, who had been full of vitality and courage starting from Nurhachi, by the time of Pu Yi's generation, had completely decayed and degenerated, just like the crumbling Qing Dynasty.

Initially, the Japanese meticulously contrived a situation where the emperor of the puppet Manchukuo, Pu Yi, was rendered bereft of any real administrative duties. Conventionally, the issuance of imperial edicts commencing with "By the grace of Heaven, the emperor decrees..." was an integral part of an emperor's routine. An assiduous emperor could even promulgate one or multiple edicts daily. Nevertheless, from March 1, 1934, when Pu Yi ascended the throne, until his abdication on August 18, 1945, during his so-called reign spanning 11 years, 6 months, and 18 days, he issued a mere six imperial edicts in total. Notably, two of these were the edicts for his accession and abdication respectively.

The Japanese imprisoned Pu Yi within the "imperial palace" just like caging a canary, transforming him into a veritable "Son of Heaven in a cage". Not only was he stripped of his power to conduct state affairs, but he also forfeited his basic freedom of movement.

Moreover, through their all-encompassing and intrusive control mechanisms, the Japanese incessantly probed into Pu Yi's loyalty and utility value to the Kwantung Army. Their ulterior motive was to utilize Pu Yi as a crucial "trump card" in the high-stakes game of major international relations.

After the September 18th Incident, Chiang Kai-shek, who had risen to prominence with the backing of Anglo-American financial conglomerates and commanded an army of millions, opted for a policy of "non-resistance." Instead of confronting the Japanese aggression directly, he pinned his hopes of curbing Japan on Western powers, believing that they would act as his bulwark against Japanese expansion. His rationale for this strategy was as follows: "China today is a shared colony of the world's major powers. Therefore, if Japan wishes to transform China into its exclusive colony, it must engage in a decisive conflict with these global powers. Without such a confrontation, Japan cannot succeed in its attempt to annex China." [6]

Rather than taking up arms against the invaders himself, Chiang placed his country's security in the hands of foreign powers, hoping they would fight Japan on China's behalf. Even Jiang Menglin, a prominent intellectual and then President of Peking University (later the first Minister of Education in the Kuomintang government), recognized the ineffectiveness of the League of Nations. He aptly described it as "all bark and no bite," and noted that when faced with Japan's aggression, the organization lacked even the courage to issue a strong condemnation. [7]

In a puzzling move, on September 21, 1931, the Kuomintang government formally appealed to the League of Nations for assistance. This decision seemed at odds with the geopolitical realities of the time.

At that period, both Britain and the United States viewed Japan as a potential "anti-communist sentinel" in the Far East, hoping that it would engage the Soviet Union in Northeast China. However, after capturing Qiqihar, the capital of Heilongjiang Province, on November 19, 1931, the Japanese army defied Western expectations. Instead of advancing towards the Soviet Union, they turned southward, seizing Jinzhou in January 1932 and completing their military occupation of Northeast China. Meanwhile, the Soviet Union had no interest in intervening in the Sino-Japanese conflict. On October 29, 1931, the Soviet government announced a "strict non-intervention policy" towards the ongoing hostilities, signaling a tacit understanding between the two nations.

The Western powers, whose interests had been impinged upon, gradually altered their stances and began to level criticisms against Japan one after another. As Chiang Kai-shek later realized, "What the great powers term as aid to me is merely a rebuke to Japan. However, Japan will certainly retaliate with a lethal strike." [8] Although the Western powers' reproaches hardly reached the crux of Japan's actions, they did prompt the formation of the "League of Nations Investigation Commission." Among the principal individuals under the commission's scrutiny was Pu Yi, the puppet ruler of the sham "Manchukuo."

The investigation commission was constituted by representatives from five countries. These included Sir Victor Alexander George Robert Lytton from the United Kingdom, Major General Frank Ross McCoy from the United States, Lieutenant General Henri Claudel from France, Count Aldo Agostino Gudi from Italy, and Dr. Heinrich Schnee from Germany. Since Lytton headed the commission, it was commonly known as the "Lytton Commission."

The objective of this five-nation investigation commission was never to redress the Japanese army's flagrant acts of aggression and the establishment of the puppet regime. Instead, it aimed to convert Japan's exclusive occupation into joint control by all participating countries, to attain an equitable sharing of the spoils. Thus, Pu Yi's testimony was of pivotal importance. If it were conceded that the "Manchukuo" was spontaneously formed by the five ethnic groups in China, the Japanese would not only be exonerated from guilt but also lauded for their role in "nation-building." Conversely, if it were disclosed that he had been lured and coerced into becoming the "ruler," the Japanese would be held responsible for their aggression against China and the establishment of the puppet government.

The Japanese, eager to elude isolation in the arena of international politics and diplomacy, especially when the Japanese government had yet to officially recognize "Manchukuo," were in a state of extreme nervousness. Prominent figures such as Hideki Tōjō and Seishirō Itagaki of the Japanese Kwantung Army, who had taken the initiative to set up the "Manchukuo" without proper authorization, closely monitored this investigation. Before the commission's arrival, Zheng Xiaoxu and his son, equally on edge, tried to sway Pu Yi.

On May 3, 1932, the five members of the investigation commission held a brief 10-minute meeting with Pu Yi. They posed just two questions: how Pu Yi had come to Northeast China and how the "Manchukuo" had been established.

Years later, Pu Yi recalled that as he beheld the five ostensibly courteous gentlemen, he remembered his English teacher in Tianjin, Reginald Fleming Johnston, stating that the doors of London were open to him. A thought suddenly flashed through his mind. What if he informed Sir Lytton, the British head of the investigation commission, that he had been deceived by Kanji Ishiwara and intimidated by Seishirō Itagaki into becoming the "head of state of Manchukuo" and requested that they take him to London? Would they agree?

Regrettably, as soon as this thought crossed his mind, Pu Yi shuddered. Seated beside him were Hashimoto Toranosuke, the chief of staff of the Kwantung Army, and the senior staff officer Seishirō Itagaki. In particular, when he stole a glance at Itagaki, whose face assumed a bluish-white tint after shaving, he had no alternative but to recite the lines pre-arranged by Itagaki. "I came here because I was supported by the people of Manchuria, and Manchukuo was voluntarily established by the people of Manchuria..." [9]

The members of the investigation commission all nodded and smiled at Pu Yi. Subsequently, they took photographs with him and shared a glass of champagne. After their departure, a broad smile spread across Itagaki's bluish-white face as he repeatedly commended, "Your Excellency, the Ruler's speech was extremely impactful, and your demeanor was remarkable."

As the Taiwanese scholar Qiu Shuping metaphorically described, Pu Yi's situation at that moment was similar to the scene in the ancient Japanese folk song: "Cuckoo, will you sing? If you don't, I'll slay you."

Please note that there might be certain inaccuracies in the original text concerning historical details. You can further verify and rectify them based on more reliable historical sources. Also, this translation is for reference only, and you can make adjustments according to your actual requirements.

Some people feel profound sympathy for Pu Yi, who was ensnared by the Japanese invaders. They argue that his actions were the result of coercion, driven by circumstances beyond his control. In contrast, others hold Pu Yi in disdain, drawing a sharp contrast with Zhu Youjian, the last emperor of the Ming Dynasty. When the nation crumbled and the capital was overrun, Zhu Youjian chose a noble and commendable path, sacrificing himself for the country. Despite having the chance to escape, he resolutely remained, upholding his imperial dignity to the end.

Zhu Youjian, the last emperor of the Ming Dynasty, with the reign title Chongzhen, reigned for 17 years. In 1644, when Li Zicheng's army captured Beijing and the fall of the Ming Dynasty was imminent, Zhu Youjian handled the "matters after the event." He went to Meishan (Coal Hill), wrote a letter of self-reproach on his robe, removed his imperial crown, covered his face with his disheveled hair, and resolutely hanged himself at the age of 34. It is said that in the suicide note, there were words stating that others could butcher his body as they pleased, but they should not harm the innocent officials and common people.

Regarding Emperor Chongzhen, Zhu Youjian, Mr. Guo Moruo provided a relatively detailed and objective evaluation in his work "Commemoration of the 300th Anniversary of the Jiashen Year (1644)." Mao Zedong once regarded this famous historical treatise as a document for the rectification movement within the Party. [10] Setting aside Zhu Youjian's imperial conduct and political stance, in terms of his courage and backbone, it is far superior to Pu Yi's actions that brought shame to his ancestors.

What would be the result if Pu Yi had the courage and backbone of Zhu Youjian and publicly revealed the truth to the international investigation team? The fig leaf covering the dirty conspiracy of the Japanese invaders would surely be torn off resolutely. Would war maniacs like Hideki Honjō and Seishirō Itagaki, who had brought great shame to the Japanese military and the political establishment, become victims of the Japanese military and government's attempt to cover up their crimes? Of course, Pu Yi's life might come to an end, but history would always remember a heroic and nationalistic emperor.

Please note that there may be some inaccuracies in the original text in terms of historical details, and you can further verify and correct them according to more reliable historical materials. Also, for the names of Japanese figures, the above translation is for reference, and you can adjust it according to the standard translation.

Pu Yi's lack of a son sent ripples through the power dynamics of the puppet state of Manchukuo. The Japanese Kwantung Army, seeing an opportunity to further tighten its grip on the region, rejoiced at this void in the imperial succession. Meanwhile, Pu Yi himself was consumed by a gnawing sense of dread, acutely aware of the sinister intentions lurking behind the Japanese military's interest.

In Changchun, Pu Yi's only biological younger brother was Pu Jie, a graduate of the prestigious Imperial Japanese Army Academy. Upon his return to Changchun, the Japanese Kwantung Army promptly appointed Pu Jie as a second lieutenant in the "Imperial Guard," a seemingly honorary position that was, in reality, a means of control. When Pu Yi caught wind of the Kwantung Army's plan to marry Pu Jie off to a Japanese woman, he desperately attempted to intervene. He hastily arranged a match between Pu Jie and the daughter of a relative of his consort, Wanrong, hoping to keep his brother out of the Japanese clutches. Pu Jie initially agreed, but the course of events would soon take a drastic turn.

No sooner had the match been arranged than the Japanese authorities swooped in to assert their dominance. They bluntly informed Pu Jie that the Kwantung Army strongly desired him to marry a Japanese woman, making it clear that this was not a request but a command-"This is the will of the military," they declared. Having spent years in Japan, Pu Jie had become enamored with Japanese military might, political ideology, and even the prospect of a Japanese wife. Seduced by the allure of his adoptive culture, he quickly reversed his decision, much to Pu Yi's dismay.

Pu Yi understood all too well that this was a carefully orchestrated conspiracy, yet he was powerless to stop it. The two figures spearheading this arranged marriage were none other than General Jirō Minami, a former Minister of War of Japan, and General Shigeru Honjō, the ex-commander of the Japanese Kwantung Army. The prospective bride, Hiro Saga, came from an esteemed Japanese noble family; her father, Marquis Saga, was a member of the Japanese aristocracy and a distant relative of the Emperor.

On April 3, 1937, Pu Jie and Hiro Saga tied the knot in a lavish ceremony in Tokyo, Japan. Before the newlyweds could even fully enjoy their honeymoon, the puppet "Constitution-making Assembly" of Manchukuo, acting on the orders of the Kwantung Army, hastily passed a "Law of Imperial Succession." The law stipulated a hierarchical order of succession: the emperor's son would inherit the throne upon his death; in the absence of a son, the grandson would succeed; if there were no sons or grandsons, the younger brother would take the throne; and if there was no brother, the brother's son would inherit. Beneath the seemingly bureaucratic language of the law lay a dark design---it was deliberately crafted to pave the way for a Japanese-blooded heir, specifically a son born to Pu Jie and Hiro Saga, to ascend the throne of the puppet state.

This development plunged Pu Yi into an abyss of unending fear. When Pu Jie and Hiro Saga returned to Northeast China after their marriage, Pu Yi resolved to keep his guard up around his brother. He refused to confide in Pu Jie, fearing that any slip of the tongue could prove fatal. He point-blank refused to eat any food sent by Hiro Saga. Even when dining with Pu Jie, if there were dishes prepared by Hiro Saga on the table, Pu Yi would wait for Pu Jie to take the first bite and then, ever so cautiously, take only the tiniest of tastes, never daring to have more. [11]

The most harrowing period for Pu Yi came when Hiro Saga became pregnant and Pu Jie was on the verge of becoming a father. Understanding the true intent behind the "Law of Imperial Succession"---that it was designed to elevate a nephew with Japanese blood to the throne-Pu Yi lived in constant fear for his own life. At the same time, he worried deeply about Pu Jie, recognizing that both of them could easily be sacrificed to the Japanese military's ambitions. Only when he learned that Hiro Saga had given birth to a daughter did Pu Yi experience a momentary respite. For now, at least until Pu Jie and his wife had another child, he felt that his position on the throne was, if not secure, then at least not immediately threatened.

This historical episode serves as a poignant reminder: in the face of overwhelming power, those who cower and submit only invite further subjugation. Their weakness is exploited, and their oppression intensifies, a tragic cycle that Pu Yi and countless others under Japanese occupation during World War II were all too familiar with. As with any historical account, it's crucial to approach these events with an open mind, cross-referencing multiple sources to gain a more nuanced and accurate understanding of the complex web of power, politics, and human drama that unfolded during this dark chapter of history.

History, an impartial arbiter, has time and again borne witness to a grim truth: those who defected and embraced the ignoble path of treason throughout the annals of time seldom met with a fortunate demise. Even the very forces that exploited these traitors secretly held them in contempt. Once their utility had waned, they were discarded without a second thought, much like worn-out footwear.

Zheng Xiaoxu was among the early traitors to fall from grace. In May 1935, General Jirō Minami, the commander of the Japanese Kwantung Army, subtly "suggested" to Pu Yi, the so-called "emperor," that Zheng Xiaoxu should "retire to enjoy his twilight years." After stepping down, Zheng Xiaoxu expressed a desire to relocate to Beijing. However, the Kwantung Army firmly barred his departure from "Manchuria." Adding insult to injury, the one-million-yuan "confidential funds" he had stashed in the bank were never disbursed. Consumed by rage, he breathed his last in 1938. [12]

With Japan's surrender in 1945, Zhang Jinghui, Zang Shiyi, and Xi Qia were apprehended by the Soviet Red Army and transported to the frigid expanse of Siberia in the Soviet Union. Subsequently, Zhang Jinghui and Zang Shiyi were extradited back to China, only to meet their ends due to illness within the confines of the Fushun War Criminals Management Center. Zang Shiyi preceded Zhang Jinghui in death by three years, passing away in 1954, while Zhang Jinghui succumbed in the winter of 1957. Xi Qia's life came to an end four years before Zang Shiyi's. He died of illness in the 45th Detention Center in Khabarovsk, Soviet Union, in the summer of 1950, leaving his mortal remains in a foreign land.

In 1951, during the nationwide campaign to suppress counter-revolutionaries, Zhang Haipeng was unmasked and sentenced to death. His eldest son, Zhang Junzhe, a major general in the puppet Manchukuo army, was arrested by the Soviet Red Army following Japan's surrender on August 15th and whisked away to Siberia. Throughout his captivity, he feigned deafness and muteness. After being extradited back, he was set free and eventually settled in Changchun. There, in a small room on Chongqing Road (now in Chaoyang District), he eked out a living by mending shoes.

The tragic fates of these once-powerful traitors should serve as a resounding and cautionary tale for the handful of individuals harboring a "traitorous inclina

36. The Diary of an Imperial Household Aide-de-Camp

Punishing war criminals and unearthing the root causes of war are essential for mending the scars of conflict, soothing those wounded by hostilities, and warding off future wars. It is both a just imperative and a fundamental principle.

Mussolini, the prime instigator of World War II, met his end on April 28, 1945, when he was executed by firing squad. His body was then publicly displayed in Milan Square as a symbol of justice served. Just two days later, on April 30, Hitler took his own life at the German military headquarters in Berlin, escaping the consequences of his actions through self-annihilation.

Nevertheless, what has incensed the world, particularly the people of Asia, is the fact that Emperor Hirohito, the supreme commander of the Japanese army, navy, and air force and the preeminent war criminal of

Japanese militarism, remained untouched by retribution. From the moment he launched the brutal war of aggression against China at the age of 30 until his passing in 1989, Hirohito lived to the ripe old age of 88. His longevity in the face of the atrocities committed under his rule makes him an anomaly, a political malignancy that defies understanding.

During World War II, Japanese militarism brought about the tragic deaths and injuries of tens of millions of military and civilian individuals in other countries. The Japanese people themselves also endured millions of casualties. Countless families were torn asunder, their lives reduced to penury. Amidst this widespread devastation, one often-overlooked truth persists: Emperor Hirohito emerged as the greatest beneficiary of Japan's actions during World War II.

Prior to the war, Hirohito held 23.7% of Japan's total land and boasted $6 billion in capital. As the war of aggression unfolded, his personal wealth swelled by a staggering 275%. [13] On October 30, 1945, following Japan's surrender, the General Headquarters of the Supreme Commander for the Allied Powers in Japan (GHQ) released the total assets of the imperial family, figures that were likely understated, as they were provided by the Imperial Household Ministry. Only then did the Japanese people realize that their emperor possessed assets worth over 16 billion yen. This included vast forests, extensive pastures, substantial company stocks, a significant amount of national bonds, and numerous prefectural and local bonds. These holdings generated massive revenues for him. When combined with the large quantity of gold bars and cash in his possession, Hirohito was indisputably Japan's largest landowner and wealthiest individual, far surpassing all others in affluence. [14]

As Masashi Nezu revealed in "The Emperor and the History of Showa" (Volume II), "The values announced at that time were based on the currency worth in the immediate aftermath of surrender. Subsequent re-evaluations showed that the total value of the imperial family's assets skyrocketed." [15]

Actually, alongside Emperor Hirohito, the American plutocrats emerged as the true heavyweights reaping staggering profits from the war. Tens of thousands of American soldiers endured the bloodshed and strife on the battlefields of Europe and Asia, as the world was torn asunder by the ravages of war. Astonishingly, the American mainland remained entirely unscathed. The colossal arms trade ushered in an inundation of capital into the United States. As the nation transformed into a military-industrial powerhouse, it simultaneously amassed three-quarters of the gold reserves across the entire capitalist world. In July 1944, on the cusp of World War II's end, through the Bretton Woods Agreement, the United States firmly established the US dollar's hegemonic status in the international currency arena. Driven by the pursuit of greater economic and political gains and the aspiration to occupy Japan, the United States deliberately crafted Emperor Hirohito's image as a peace-loving monarch and a puppet-like commander of the Japanese army, allowing him to elude the clutches of war accountability.

Back in the 1940s, this flagrant act of flouting the global will incited widespread discontent among the governments and populaces of the victimized nations, including those within the United States and Japan. Over the ensuing decades, the quest to expose this concealed truth has persisted unabated.

Professor Herbert P. Bix, a Japanese historian affiliated with the State University of New York, dedicated a decade to penning the book Hirohito and the Making of Modern Japan. The publication triggered a profound reaction and was honored with the Pulitzer Prize in the United States in 2001. The award-conferring committee lauded the book for upending conventional perspectives, unearthing the genuine historical narrative, and serving as an exemplary work with weighty historical cautionary implications for Japan.

Considering the contemporary social milieu in Japan, right-wing intellectuals and conservative media outlets typically do not tolerate such critiques of the emperor. However, this particular book left them at a loss for words. The reason lies in the fact that the author's insights were gleaned from firsthand sources within the Japanese imperial palace. Spanning over 500,000 words, the book contains 120,000 words of reference notes.

There exists a divergence in global perspectives regarding the onset of World War II. Americans typically mark December 8, 1941, as the war's commencement, commemorating the Japanese surprise attack on Pearl Harbor. Europeans trace it back to September 1, 1939, when Germany launched a sudden invasion of Poland. Africans consider 1935, when Mussolini dispatched troops to invade Ethiopia, as the starting point. Asians, especially the Chinese, firmly believe that World War II began with the September 18th Incident in 1931. Significantly, the book Hirohito and the Making of Modern Japan aligns with the Chinese stance.

Irrefutable historical evidence incontrovertibly demonstrates that Emperor Hirohito functioned as a powerful patron for the fanatical soldiers during the September 18th Incident and was a driving force in expediting the aggression in Northeast China.

It's important to note that the original text may contain certain historical inaccuracies. Readers are encouraged to cross-reference with more reliable historical sources for verification and refinement.

The September 18th Incident, brazenly instigated by the Japanese Kwantung Army without the authorization of the military high command and the cabinet, ignited a furious feud between the two. On September 21st, Prime Minister Wakatsuki Reijirō chaired a six-hour meeting and ultimately decided against approving the reinforcement of troops in Northeast China. This decision effectively nullified the legitimacy of the September 18th Incident. Nevertheless, Lieutenant General Hayashi Senjūrō, the right-wing radical commander of the Korean Army, despite having his request for troop deployment rejected just two days prior, defiantly ordered the Korean Mixed Brigade to cross the border and enter Northeast China on September 21st. This blatant act directly challenged the Emperor's supreme command authority as the head of the army, navy, and air force.

In truth, Hirohito had a prime opportunity at that time to back the Wakatsuki cabinet, rein in the military high command, and prevent the situation from spiraling further out of control. Given the diverse views on the "Manchurian Incident" within Japan at the time, the military high command was in a politically vulnerable position. Had Hirohito chosen to restrain the military and correct the fanatical Japanese warlords, it would have been the opportune moment.

To the profound disappointment of the 30 million people in Northeast China, Hirohito did not take that path. The Chief of the Imperial Japanese Army General Staff, Nara Takeji, recorded that when faced with the military high command's "plea for retroactive approval of the Korean Army Mixed Brigade," "His Majesty instructed that there was no alternative this time, but in the future, utmost attention must be paid." [16]

In the subsequent years, Hirohito sanctioned the conferment of honors and promotions for nearly 3,000 military and civilian officials. These individuals were all deemed "meritorious" in the "Manchurian War" (the Japanese invasion of Northeast China) and the "Shanghai Incident" (the January 28th Incident). Shigeru Honjō, the commander of the Japanese Kwantung Army, was bestowed the title of Baron. This so-called Japanese national war hero, who had achieved success just months before, also succeeded Nara as the Chief of the Imperial Japanese Army General Staff. [17]

The "Three Musketeers" of the Japanese Kwantung Army who were directly responsible for the September 18th Incident—Lieutenant Colonels Seishirō Itagaki, Kenji Doihara, and Kanji Ishihara—all received rapid advancements. Itagaki was promoted to major general less than a year after the September 18th Incident, to lieutenant general in 1936, joined the cabinet as Minister of the Army in 1938, served as Chief of the General Staff of the Expeditionary Army for the Invasion of China the following year, and was promoted to general in 1941.

Doihara's promotion was even swifter than Itagaki's. He was elevated to major general half a year after the September 18th Incident, to lieutenant general in 1936, and had reached the rank of general by 1941.

Owing to his "accomplishments" in the September 18th Incident, Ishihara entered the most glorious phase of his life in 1937. He was promoted to head of the First Department (Operations Department), just one step away from the position of Deputy Chief of the General Staff. However, the rational and clear-thinking Ishihara opposed the expansion of the war against China and advocated focusing all efforts on consolidating and governing Northeast China. This stance clashed with Emperor Hirohito's will after the Marco Polo Bridge Incident, and he was not promoted to lieutenant general until 1939.

Emperor Hirohito's favoritism and reliance on Hideki Tōjō vividly demonstrated his fanaticism for the so-called "holy war." Tōjō, who was the colonel in charge of the Mobilization Section of the Equipment Bureau of the General Staff Headquarters during the September 18th Incident, was demoted to the Imperial Japanese Army Academy after serving as head of the Military Investigation Department for merely four months in 1934.

The real stepping-stone that catapulted Hideki Tōjō to the center of power was his tenure as Commander of the Japanese Kwantung Army's Military Police. Through his endeavors, the Japanese Kwantung Army's Military Police Headquarters, which initially had a staff of only around 200 people, grew into a formidable and intimidating espionage and intelligence-gathering organization. This transformation brought this "Razor General" to the notice of the Japanese military high command and the Emperor. In 1938, Hideki Tōjō was promoted to lieutenant general and appointed Vice Minister of the Army. In 1940, he became the Minister of the Army of Japan. On November 17th, 1941, Emperor Hirohito personally summoned Hideki Tōjō, promoted him to general, and tasked him with serving as Prime Minister of the cabinet and forming a cabinet in his capacity as an active-duty officer, while also retaining his position as Minister of the Army.

Relevant materials clearly indicate that Hideki Tōjō was chosen by Hirohito despite widespread opposition. On October 16th of that year, the cabinet of Fumimaro Konoe announced its dissolution. According to the Japanese cabinet formation convention, as the former Prime Minister, Konoe's final official duty was to jointly recommend Prince Higashikuni Naruhiko as his successor with Hideki Tōjō, the Minister of the Army. However, Hirohito rebuffed this recommendation, turned down the army's request, and instead directed Tōjō to form a cabinet. This was because Tōjō was his favored candidate. At that time, he firmly believed that the person he had carefully selected could resolve the prevailing issues.

Although some prominent ministers, including the former Navy Prime Minister Okada, opposed Hirohito's decision, in the end, Tōjō, the most zealous advocate of war in the army and the main opponent of withdrawing troops from China, was still elevated to the position of new Prime Minister by Hirohito.

Hideki Tōjō, the 40th Prime Minister of Japan, set a record for holding the most concurrent positions as a Japanese Prime Minister. In addition to serving as Minister of the Army, he also took on the role of Minister of Home Affairs, and later concurrently held positions such as Minister of Education, Minister of Commerce and Industry, Minister of Munitions, and even Chief of the General Staff.

The warmonger Hideki Tōjō, who a decade earlier was merely a lowly colonel in charge of a section, was promoted to a high-ranking official second only to the emperor, amassing extensive powers in Japanese military, political, economic, and cultural arenas. Emperor Hirohito was his principal promoter and powerful backer. From then on, Hirohito and Tōjō, the two warmongers, were inextricably linked.

Even two days after Tōjō stepped down as Prime Minister due to his inability to maintain the position, Hirohito personally presented his favored general with an extremely enthusiastic (unpublished) imperial edict, exhorting him to continue to live up to the trust placed in him and to strive for military improvement in the future.

On December 23rd, 1948, Hideki Tōjō was sentenced to death by the Far East International Military Tribunal. A court attendant stated that upon learning of Tōjō's death, Hirohito entered his office and wept. [18]

In essence, Hideki Tōjō was Emperor Hirohito's shadow. Or, to put it another way, Tōjō was the fanatical performer on the war stage, while Hirohito was the behind-the-scenes director who hand-picked this actor.

It should be noted that there may be certain inaccuracies in the historical details of the above content. Readers are advised to cross-reference with more reliable historical sources for verification and correction.

Let's turn our attention back to the period after the September 18th Incident. Due to Inukai Tsuyoshi's slight delay in recognizing the

"Manchukuo," the "Blood Pact League," which had intricate connections with the Japanese Kwantung Army within Japan, brutally assassinated him. This presented Emperor Hirohito with another golden opportunity to rein in or distance himself from military fascism and act as a "constitutional monarch."

Regrettably, instead of blaming the rebellious military officers, Hirohito directed the spearhead of his criticism towards the cabinet based on political parties. He distrusted the parliamentary parties even more than the military rebels and aimed to strengthen the imperial power by weakening the party-based cabinet. This was originally an unshakable fundamental principle.

Since Inukai Tsuyoshi did not actively support the "Manchukuo" established by the Japanese Kwantung Army, Hirohito's solution was to select someone who was proactive as the prime minister, and this person had to be "absolutely loyal and obedient" to him. Sure enough, Admiral Saitō Makoto, the elderly prime minister personally chosen by Hirohito, officially recognized the "Manchukuo" a few months later and signed the "Japan-Manchukuo Protocol."

In this way—through the hands of Saitō Makoto—Hirohito completed the legal procedures for the Japanese government's recognition of the Japanese Kwantung Army's occupation of "Manchuria," while maintaining his own image as a "constitutional monarch" without war responsibilities behind the scenes.

However, a person's ideology, especially fanatical fascist ideology, will always be reflected in their actions. As the Japanese army's aggression against China progressed smoothly, Hirohito, who had been staying behind the scenes, would occasionally step into the spotlight.

Regarding Rehe:

On February 12, 1933, Hirohito approved the operation in Rehe once again, on the condition that "absolute caution should be exercised when crossing the Great Wall. If the order is not followed, the operation in Rehe will be cancelled." The invasion of Rehe in China began on February 23. More than 20,000 Japanese troops completed the occupation of Rehe in about one week.

Regarding North China:

On April 17, 1936, Emperor Hirohito approved the request of the Japanese army to triple the number of its small-scale troops stationed in China, increasing it from 1,771 to 5,774. He also agreed to establish a new garrison base in Fengtai, a railway junction in the southwestern suburbs of Beiping (now Beijing), not far from the Lugou Bridge. This set the stage for the continuous conflicts with the Chinese troops.

On July 7, 1937, the Lugou Bridge Incident occurred, and the Konoe Cabinet decided to send more troops to North China. Hirohito stamped his seal on the dispatch order for sending troops to North China. Two weeks later, the Japanese Kwantung Army, the Korean Army, and three divisions from the Japanese mainland gathered in Langfang near Tianjin.

In 1938, the Japanese army launched a war of annihilation against the base areas of the Hebei guerrillas, implementing the "scorched earth" policy. The imaginary enemy was "men aged between 15 and 60 among the residents who were considered hostile." On December 2, Hirohito issued Continental Order No. 241 for the implementation of the "no-man's land" operation. This policy was expanded to the entire North China during its continuous implementation.

On December 3, 1941, Hirohito once again approved Continental Order No. 575 of the General Staff Headquarters, dividing North China into "security zones, quasi-security zones, and unsecured zones, and the latter would be turned into no-man's lands." Japanese historian Mitsuyoshi Himeda believed that "more than 2.4 million" unarmed Chinese people (civilians) were killed in these operations. [19] Compared with the Nanjing Massacre, the planned "scorched earth" operations were of unparalleled destructiveness and lasted for a longer time.

Regarding Shanghai:

On August 13, 1937, the Japanese army brought the war to Shanghai. On August 18, when convening the chief of staffs of the army and navy, Hirohito proposed that at key locations, concentrated forces should be used to increase the intensity of the attack, and there should be a strategy to make "China" reflect. Hirohito's opinion was to concentrate forces in Shanghai and oppose the reinforcement of troops in Qingdao. According to Hirohito's opinion, the content of dispatching troops to Qingdao was deleted from the order.

In the following two weeks, Hirohito approved six troop deployments prepared to reinforce the Shanghai area where the battle had reached a stalemate. On September 4, in his imperial rescript to the Imperial Diet, Hirohito stated: "My troops are surmounting all difficulties and loyally and bravely defeating the enemy. This is only to urge the Republic of China to reflect and quickly establish peace in East Asia." [20]

Regarding Chongqing:

Capturing Chongqing, the wartime capital of the Nationalist Government, had always been an urgent wish of Hirohito. Since May 1938, the Japanese army had carried out savage and indiscriminate strategic bombings on Chongqing and other major cities, using not only conventional shells but also incendiary bombs. In the first two days of the air raids, more than 5,000 unarmed people (civilians) were killed.

In the middle of 1942, on February 19, March 19, and May 29, Hirohito urged Chief of the Army General Staff Hajime Sugiyama to study the possibility of a final "attack" on Chongqing at least three times. Under his urging, Sugiyama drafted a large-scale offensive plan ("Operation No. 5"), planning to use 15 divisions to completely eliminate Chiang Kai-shek's main forces in Sichuan and capture Chongqing.

Regarding Nanjing:

On November 20, 1937, Hirohito issued an imperial rescript to Kiyoshi Hasegawa, the commander of the fleet in the Chinese region, praising the officers and soldiers of the fleet for their cooperation with the army (that entered Nanjing), for controlling China's coastal areas, and for blocking China's sea transportation lines. At the same time, he admonished that there was still a long way to go and hoped that they would work even harder to achieve a complete victory.

On November 24, at the first imperial conference of the General Staff Headquarters, Hirohito retrospectively approved the major decision of General Iwane Matsui, the commander of the Central China Front Army, to attack and capture the capital of China. On December 1, Hirohito issued an official attack order to General Matsui, requiring the commander of the Japanese army invading central China to act in coordination with the navy to capture Nanjing.

On December 14, the day after the fall of Nanjing, Hirohito sent an imperial edict to the Supreme Command, expressing his satisfaction with the report of the capture and occupation of Nanjing. Later, when General Matsui returned to Tokyo, Hirohito bestowed an imperial rescript on him to commend his great military achievements. "Extremely satisfied," Hirohito even invited Matsui and Prince Asaka (commander of the Shanghai Expeditionary Army and general commander of the attack on Nanjing) to his summer palace and presented them with silver vases engraved with the imperial chrysanthemum relief. [21]

The cruel and beastly massacres by the Japanese army in Nanjing caused a great tragedy that shocked the world, with more than 300,000 Chinese military and civilian deaths. As the supreme commander who approved the capture of Nanjing, there is no record of any instruction from Hirohito to stop the crimes of the troops in advance. After the event, there is no documentary record of any order from him to investigate the atrocities in Nanjing. On the contrary, there are records of the fact that Hirohito remained silent about the criminal acts of the troops, as well as several imperial decrees and rescripts mentioned above that encouraged and commended the troops for punishing the victims.

Can you still come to the conclusion that Emperor Hirohito never participated in World War II and was actually a puppet supreme commander of the army, navy, and air force?

37. I don't know if I should say it or not

What the Japanese invaders have done that is most despised by the world is that they employed bacteriological warfare, poison gas warfare, and carried out live human dissections during the war, thus committing numerous crimes against humanity. Japan, an island country with scarce resources and a relatively small population, harbors the enormous ambition of swallowing up and ruling the entire East Asia. In order to implement the cheapest yet most effective means of killing with bacteria and poison gas, Japan has always refused to sign international treaties banning the use of bacteria and poison gas, and all of this is related to Emperor Hirohito and Shiro Ishii, a name that sends chills down the spines of people around the world.

Shiro Ishii was a lieutenant general in the Japanese army (the highest rank in the military medical service) and the head of the Epidemic Prevention and Water Supply Department (Unit 731) of the Japanese Kwantung Army. There were two reasons why Shiro Ishii, who was originally unknown, received the favor, and support of Emperor Hirohito. Firstly, as the renowned British historian Mark Felton described, Ishii "developed a revolutionary new water filtration device for the Japanese military and was invited to demonstrate it to Emperor Hirohito. Ishii urinated into the filtration device and invited the Emperor to drink the filtered liquid, which the Emperor of course refused. As a result, Ishii drank the cup of filtered urine in front of the Emperor. This act not only skyrocketed his popularity but also aroused the official interest in his secret research."

The second reason is that Ishii's "characteristics" of bacteriological and poison gas warfare conformed to the psychological expectations of the Japanese Emperor and the military headquarters. Ishii held the view of "economic" killing in bacteriological attack warfare. He believed that the first characteristic of bacteriological attack warfare was its extensive effectiveness. Not only could it spread from person to person and from village to village within the effective range, continuously expanding, but its toxicity could also penetrate deep into the human body, resulting in a much higher mortality rate than that caused by bombs. Moreover, once injured, it was very difficult to be cured, and it was hard to expect these people to return to the battlefield. The second characteristic of bacteriological attack warfare was that for Japan, which lacked iron and steel, it was the most suitable and least expensive form of warfare.

Ishii's initial bacteriological research received active assistance from the Baden-Baden Group and Major General Tetsuyama Nagata, one of the "Three Musketeers" and the Director of the Military Affairs Bureau of the Japanese Army Ministry. In the autumn of 1932, Ishii established an "Epidemic Prevention Research Laboratory" within the Tokyo Army Medical School. Struggling with the lack of "experimental materials" – living human beings – in the second year after the September 18th Incident, Ishii established a live experiment base in Wuchang, Northeast China, which Feng Zhongyun called "the killing factory at Beiyin River Station".

At first, there were five or six hundred "materials" in the factory, and soon, the number increased to more than 1,000. Later, more than 20 "materials" escaped, and the killing factory was relocated. Among the 12 people who escaped, they joined the Anti-Japanese United Army. One of them, named Wang Xueyang, later served as an acting division commander of the Third Army of the Anti-Japanese United Army and heroically died in battle in Mulan in 1937. [22]

In order to make the heinous killing experiments more covert, after closing the Beiyin River experimental base, the Japanese army leveled eight villages in the Pingfang area south of Harbin. On this 10-square-kilometer land, they built special airplane runways, railway tracks of the train station, barracks for military police, prisons for holding "live subjects" of the experiments, basements, dungeons, gas chambers, operating rooms, cremation grounds... In total, there were more than 150 buildings.

The Japanese army also built a cinema, a bar, and a Shinto temple for the experimental personnel. This place was also part of the military facilities of the Japanese Kwantung Army and was externally called the "Epidemic Prevention Squad", which was later renamed the "Epidemic Prevention and Water Supply Unit" or "Unit 731". One of the main tasks of Unit 731 was to manufacture and test the bacteria and viruses of plague, cholera, anthrax, and typhoid fever on living people.

In the plague research laboratory, there were the corpses of rats and humans everywhere. Yoshio Tamura entered the laboratory and took a look around. The rats that had been injected with the virus a few days ago were still wriggling exhaustedly. With a smile on his face, he ripped open the belly of a dead rat, took out the spleen and liver, and started culturing them.

In another room, on the stretcher were the cut-open bellies, and the "pieces of flesh" of Chinese people whose heads had been smashed and feet had been chopped off. Tamura walked into the room where the Chinese person he had injected with the plague bacteria was staying. The Chinese person was so uncomfortable that he was thrashing around all over his body, spitting blood while lying on the bed, and trying to resist and stand up. While cursing "beast", Tamura kicked the person to the ground, then poured disinfectant on him, preparing to cut his body into eight pieces. [23]

One of the most terrifying and cruel means of Unit 731 was the live dissection without using anesthetic. They believed that drugs might affect the research results, so they carried out inhumane physiological experiments. Or rather, these cold-blooded people with human faces and dressed in human clothes preferred to take pleasure in the extreme pain of their fellow human beings.

After the war, a 72-year-old former assistant to a medical officer of Unit 731 confessed when describing a 30-year-old Chinese victim: When I picked up the scalpel, he started screaming. In the Pingfang area, similar terrifying scenes were just everyday occurrences. I cut him open, from the chest cavity all the way to the abdomen. He kept screaming horribly, and his face was distorted with pain. I pulled out the bone saw, cut through the ribs, and exposed all the internal organs. Beside the dissection table, there were three people holding tremella for culturing bacteria and medical glassware, waiting for the internal organs... They started smearing vigorously on the culture medium. Twenty minutes later, the Chinese person's body was cut into pieces, and the bloody pieces of flesh were scattered on the dissection table.

During the experiments, the Japanese would deliberately let the "materials" be infected with the virus and then conduct live dissections to observe the damage of the disease to various parts of the human body. At the same time, they released countless fleas on the patients infected with the virus, aiming to cultivate the disease-carrying insects for filling bacteriological bombs. Japanese doctors would also rape women to make them pregnant, and a few months later, they would dissect these women and take out the fetuses from their uteruses. The Japanese would often cut off the limbs of the "materials" to observe the impact of blood loss on the human body. There were also freezing experiments, that is, after deeply freezing the limbs, they would cut them off, or sometimes they would let the frozen limbs thaw without cutting them off to observe the necrosis of the active fibers in the human body.

Sometimes, the Japanese would also inject air into the human blood vessels to observe the generation of fatal blood clots, and they would use a flamethrower to spray flames at the "prisoners" to determine the optimal firing range of this weapon.

Ishii was an enthusiast and leader of these physiological experiments. One day, when Ishii suddenly needed a human brain for an experiment, the military police guards grabbed a "prisoner", pressed him to the ground, split open his skull with an axe, quickly took out the brain inside, and sent it to Ishii's laboratory. Every experiment of Unit 731 was a blatant challenge to the conscience of the medical community.

The Japanese army's poison gas experiments on living Chinese people were also carried out under the unified leadership of Ishii. As early as 1934, the experimental field for killing people with poison gas and high-voltage electricity, under the sign of the "Epidemic Prevention and Water Supply Department of the Japanese Kwantung Army", was set up in a middle school building forcibly occupied in the western suburbs of Siping, Jilin Province.

On the night of November 10, 1934, the first batch of experimental materials (the so-called 30 "Maruta") were sent here. In the middle of the double-layer tent, which was 5 meters square in the central hall, the "Maruta" was tied to the central pillar. The poison gas rushed into the tent through a wriggling rubber tube like a snake. The person tied to the pillar struggled in pain and almost broke the pillar. Five minutes later, the "experimental subject" with his head hanging down remained motionless. The military doctors wearing gas masks rushed in from outside the glass window. Some shone a flashlight on his eyes, nose, and mouth, and some listened to his chest with a stethoscope. After a while, the repetition for the next person began...

Soon, 30 Chinese people were brought in for the second experiment. The person was locked into an iron box that could only accommodate his body, and then venom was injected into his head, face, back, and abdomen. The victims cried out in pain and despair, struggling so hard that they shook the large iron box. The military doctors opened the box at regular intervals to check the injected parts. The skin on those people's bodies festered like pomegranates, and their bodies decayed in a very short time. In about a week, the people completely rotted inside the box.

For the high-voltage electricity experiment, the person was made to stand facing the high-voltage electric wire mesh with 5,000 volts, which was 30 meters away. Iron plates connected to the power supply were buried under the ground on both sides of the wire mesh, and the person was driven into the electric mesh. As soon as the person took a step forward with his left foot, he fell towards the wire mesh in an instant. The 5,000-volt high-voltage current passed through his body, and a spark immediately flashed between his right heel and the ground. Then, the person would be dissected to study the changes in the internal organs of the human body under the high-voltage current. [24]

How many people were killed by the cruel means of Unit 731? After the war, according to Shiro Ishii's confession: "We used 3,850 logs, that is, living people, for bacteriological experiments. When we said 'logs', it was a code word. We used 2,450 living people for poison gas experiments. Among these people, only 562 were Russians, 254 were Koreans, and the rest were all Chinese... None of these more than 6,000 people survived." [25]

It is obvious that Ishii did not tell the truth. According to the analysis of Professor Sheldon Harris, an American historian who engages in the study of bacteriological warfare, the number of deaths in human experiments should be between 10,000 and 12,000. [26]British historian Mark Felton revealed that a former doctor of Unit 731 named Takeo Ueno said that he once saw a large glass jar 1.8 meters high, in which a Western male corpse soaked in formalin had been vertically cut in half. There were many similar human specimens.

In 1995, a man who requested anonymity said in an interview that he had seen similar jars in the camp of Unit 731, with labels reading "American", "British", "French", etc., but most of the specimens were of Chinese people.

After the war, the United States manipulated the Tokyo Trials, and Ishii did not dare to offend the Americans.

In fact, in 1949, during the war criminal trials in Khabarovsk, the Soviet Union unearthed some evidence of the Japanese using white people for human experiments. A Japanese military doctor named Kiyohito Morishita testified that among the "Maruta", he found the figures of Americans or British people and also heard some "Maruta" speaking English to each other. The diary of Australian army medical officer Brennan once recorded that 150 American POWs were forced to leave the Fengtian POW camp and never returned.

The above facts show that the Japanese bacteriological experiments targeted all mankind, including Americans. Strangely, the US government deliberately let go of the pursuit of the crimes of Unit 731.

The group that Unit 731 killed the most through experiments was the Chinese people. Ishii admitted that 90% of the victims were Chinese, and the vast majority were officers and soldiers who were unfortunately captured in the fight against the Japanese army, as well as the so-called "warmongers". To ensure the need for "logs" for the experiments, the Japanese Kwantung Army Military Police Headquarters required its subordinate units to carry out secret transportation tasks.

Sgt. Masai Narui of the Puppet Manchukuo Jiandao Military Police Detachment confessed that in August 1938, according to the order of Captain Kojima Masanori of the Jiamusi Military Police, five Communist Party members from Fujin County were escorted to the Ishii Unit in Harbin and brutally killed. After Narui was transferred to work in the Japanese Kwantung Army Military Police Headquarters, from December 1942 to November 1943 alone, he transported more than 30 anti-Japanese patriots to Unit 731. This is just one example of many "special transports". To solve the problem of "exhaustion of materials, and it is better to send more" put forward by Ishii, from July to September 1941, in less than three months, the commander of the Japanese Kwantung Army Military Police issued the "Special Transfer Report" (Kwantung Military Police High No. 120) for 500 people (times). Tens of thousands of anti-Japanese united army soldiers and patriots were thus sent to Unit 731 to be tortured and killed.

These inhumane experiments were for savage massacres. According to incomplete statistics from Chinese archives, as many as 270,000 innocent Chinese civilians died due to the bacteriological warfare implemented by the Japanese army, and the number of Chinese soldiers who died as a result cannot be accurately counted. The base areas controlled by the Communist Party in North China were the key areas of the Japanese army's bacteriological warfare, and 33 cases of bacteriological warfare have been discovered. [27]

Ishii confessed to several bacteriological wars he commanded during the pretrial of the Tokyo Trials. One of them was in April 1941, when the Japanese army dispatched six aircraft and dropped 400 kilograms of plague bacteria, causing several counties in the Shanxi-Hebei-Shandong-Henan and Shanxi-Suiyuan border regions to have 350,000 people infected with the plague, and more than 165,000 people died. For example, in July 1942, in two POW camps in Nanjing, the expeditionary team of Unit 731 distributed 100 kilograms of flatbread injected with typhoid and paratyphoid bacteria to 50 captives, and then released them, spreading the epidemic to most areas of eight provinces including Hunan, Hubei, Guangdong, Guangxi, Jiangxi, Anhui, Zhejiang, and Jiangsu. According to incomplete statistics, more than 187,000 people died. [28]

The pernicious influence of the Japanese army's bacteriological warfare was extremely far-reaching. From 1946 to 1954, in Harbin, where Unit 731 was located, the plague occurred six times. In 1947, there were more than

30,000 plague patients in Northeast China, and more than 12,000 people died in Tongliao alone.

Hirohito has an unshirkable direct responsibility for poison gas, chemical, and bacteriological warfare. Hirohito's first order authorizing the use of chemical weapons was issued on July 28, 1937, and was conveyed by Prince Kan'in Kotohito, Chief of the General Staff. The order stated that during the capture of Beiping-Tongzhou, "tear gas can be used at an appropriate time." This order approved the use of poison gas on a small scale. After gaining experience, during the offensive against Wuhan from August to October 1938, the General Staff Headquarters approved the use of poison gas 375 times. In 1939, it also approved that Yasuji Okamura could use more than 15,000 barrels of poison gas. In 1940, Hirohito approved the first experimental use of bacteriological weapons in China. After that, bacteriological attacks were carried out one after another, and the Japanese army formed a dependence on chemical and bacteriological weapons until the end of World War II.

On August 9, 1945, the Soviet Red Army launched a surprise attack on the Japanese Kwantung Army. The first thing the Kwantung Army and Ishii did was to blow up all the buildings in the Unit 731 camp. However, because the buildings were too sturdy, the powerful explosives could not destroy them, and the shells of the evidence of their crimes were preserved. However, before Unit 731 dispersed, Ishii specially held a meeting and ordered everyone to "take the secrets to the grave"; if anyone did not remain silent, someone would find him in Japan and kill him.

It is unbelievable that after the US authorities found Ishii and his subordinates, instead of pursuing the evidence of their crimes, they provided them with asylum and good job opportunities. The condition for General Douglas MacArthur, the Supreme Commander of the Allied Forces in Japan, to exempt Ishii and his subordinates was that they should hand over the data and results of the live experiments, as well as bacteriological and chemical warfare, to the US government. The Americans believed that this batch of experimental achievements was "invaluable".

Therefore, in the Tokyo Trials manipulated by the Americans, not a single word was mentioned about Unit 731. The Central Intelligence Agency of the United States (formerly known as the Office of Strategic Services) secretly "smuggled" Ishii and others to the United States. After that, Ishii has been living in Maryland, the United States, and has been engaged in the research of bacteriological weapons for the US military. [29] Later, the Americans used bacteriological weapons in the Korean War and the Vietnam War.

What is even more of a violation of the will of the world is that the Americans portrayed Emperor Hirohito as a puppet monarch and shifted all the war crimes to other war criminals such as Hideki Tōjō. The means was to destroy all the secret evidence materials, especially the evidence of the crimes against humanity of Unit 731.

However, man proposes, God disposes. Although the US government, through MacArthur's underhanded actions, so arrogantly "helped" Emperor Hirohito get rid of the charges, the dark curtain of Emperor Hirohito's crimes in Japan was still torn a big hole by a little man forty years later. The sunlight shone through this hole into the dark curtain, and Hirohito's dirty crimes were finally laid bare.

This great little man is James Godwin, a former captain of the Royal New Zealand Naval Air Service, a Japanese POW, and an Allied war crimes investigator in Japan.

His experience as an investigator and a POW gave Godwin an urgent desire and positive motivation to expose the crimes of the Japanese emperor and the army, which was completely at odds with the intentions of the

Americans who manipulated the Tokyo Trials. Conscience prompted him to make copies of a large number of original files in his possession and secretly brought them back to New Zealand from Tokyo in 1950, where they were kept in an unknown place for a long time.

In the mid-1980s, the first thing Godwin did after retirement was to sort out these memorandums, instructions, and intelligence. Unfortunately, he only completed a quarter of the planned work before suffering a sudden stroke, becoming paralyzed, and then developing Alzheimer's disease. Medical experts found that part of his skull and cervical vertebrae were shattered and dislocated, which should have been caused by being severely beaten with the butt of a rifle by the Japanese army when he was a POW.

According to Godwin's precious original files, James McKay continued to fulfill his last wish, sorted out and published the book "Betrayal from the Top: The Secret History of America's Selling Out of Its Allies", which "revealed many historical facts that had been hidden and not publicized in the past fifty years", [30] including the evidence of Hirohito's crimes against humanity.

During the investigation, Godwin was surprised to find that the biological and bacteriological warfare center in Pingfang, Harbin was jointly established by General Ishii and a member of the imperial family, a cousin of Emperor Hirohito. "It has been confirmed that Emperor Hirohito stamped his 'imperial seal' on the document approving the establishment of the biological and bacteriological warfare experimental facilities." [31]Unit 731 was also approved to be established by Hirohito, and "was also allocated 6 million yen as the first year's activity funds for the unit." [32] This was a large sum of money at that time.

There were 5,500 people in all branches of Unit 731, and the units in Harbin, Nanjing, and Guangzhou were confirmed to have carried out human experiments. In 1938, according to the Japanese military order "Army No. 50" issued by Emperor Hirohito on July 19, the Japanese military expanded 18 more "epidemic prevention and water supply" units and assigned them to each division, moving from one battlefield to another, enabling each division of the Japanese army to generally have the ability to carry out bacteriological and poison gas warfare. The network of the "Ishii Organization" (as called by the army) reached its peak, with a number of more than 12,000 people.

Godwin confirmed that "when requesting authorization to arrest the imperial prince and General Ishii through Colonel Alva C. Carpenter, a senior American officer attached to the Legal Department of the Supreme Commander of the Allied Powers, Major General Charles A. Willoughby, the head of the intelligence agency of the Supreme Commander of the Allied Powers, and General Douglas MacArthur personally intervened, resulting in the incomprehensible rejection of this request."

The subsequent investigation enabled Godwin to find the answer to the "incomprehensible" question. If the investigation continued, it would directly point to the imperial family and Hirohito himself. This would not only embarrass the Americans but also disrupt their plan to foster a new Japan within the scope of American capitalist influence. For the interests of the United States, the just trial stopped at the ugly politics.

Letting go of the pursuit of Emperor Hirohito's war crimes made MacArthur receive praises such as "divinely noble mercy" and "living savior" from Japanese public opinion. Japanese Prime Minister Shigeru Yoshida praised him as a "great benefactor". MacArthur reciprocated by calling Emperor Hirohito "the most gentlemanly man in Japan", which should be the respect and praise of Westerners for a man being "the best".

However, the evil consequences emerged. After the war, the Japanese government has never seriously reflected on the war and has hardly paid any compensation for the war crimes. As John W. Dower, an American history professor and author of the book "Embracing Defeat", said, the US government and MacArthur's exemption from holding the emperor accountable made the issue of "war responsibility" become a joke. Assuming that a person who handled Japan's imperial diplomacy, military, and politics in his name for as long as 20 years does not need to take the due responsibility for launching and leading this war, how can we expect ordinary people to think about these things or seriously consider their own personal responsibilities?

What is terrifying is that countless historical facts have proven that forgetting the past is doomed to repeat the mistakes.

So, we are shocked to see that some people often comment on Japan's aggression against China as: "I went to the front line not to fight the enemy but to go to China with the mood of comforting my brothers." "We must regard this war as a means to prompt the Chinese people to reflect on themselves. We do this not because we hate them. On the contrary, we love them deeply. It is like in a family, when an elder brother can no longer tolerate the misbehavior of a younger brother, he has to severely punish him to make him correct his ways." [33]

The above are the words of Iwane Matsui, the main commander of the Japanese army who caused the tragic death of 300,000 people in the Nanjing Massacre. Now, he is enshrined in the Yasukuni Shrine in Japan.

Notes:

[1].[5]. Pu Yi. *From Emperor to Citizen* (Complete Edition). Quanzheng Press, January 2007, 1st Edition, pp. 249, 241.

[2]. Qiu Shuping. *A 14 - year History of the Puppet Manchukuo*. Compiled by the Cultural and Historical Studies Committee of the Changchun Municipal Committee of the Chinese People's Political Consultative Conference, April 1984, pp. 155 - 156.

[3]. Zhang Zhenglong. *Cold Blood, Hot Snow* (Volume 2). Changjiang Literature and Art Press, April 2011, 1st Edition, p. 24.

[4]. (Soviet Union) L. N. Smirnov, E. B. Zaitsev. *The Tokyo Trial*. Military Translation Press, August 1987 Edition, p. 80.

[6]. [8] . Wang Yao. *The Love - Hate Relationship between Chiang Kai - shek and the Great Powers*. Taiwan Strait Press, July 2013, 1st Edition, pp. 129, 137.

[7]. Jiang Menglin. *The Autobiography of Jiang Menglin: The West Tide and the New Tide*. Tuanjie Press, October 2004, 1st Edition, p. 361.

[9]. 11. 12. Pu Yi. *From Emperor to Citizen* (Complete Edition). Quanzheng Press, January 2007, 1st Edition, pp. 254, 267, 258.

[10]. "Letter to Guo Moruo" (November 21, 1944), in *Selected Works of Mao Zedong* (Volume 3), compiled by the Party Literature Research Center of the Central Committee of the Communist Party of China. People's Publishing House, August 1996, 1st Edition, pp. 227 - 228.

[13]. Liu Jiachang, et al. *The Rehabilitation of Japanese, Puppet and Chiang Kai - shek War Criminals*. Chunfeng Literature and Art Press, March 1993, 1st Edition, p. 77; quoted from Zhang Fulin, et al. Historical Evidence: The Record of China's Education and Rehabilitation of Japanese War Criminals. Jilin People's Publishing House, September 2005, 1st Edition, p. 83.

[14]. (USA) Herbert Bix. Hirohito and the Making of Modern Japan. Xinhua Publishing House, September 2004, 1st Edition, p. 412.

[15]. (Japan) Nitsu Masashi. The Emperor and the History of the Showa Era (Volume 2). San - I - Shoin, 1976, pp. 265 - 266; quoted from (USA) Herbert Bix. Hirohito and the Making of Modern Japan. Xinhua Publishing House, September 2004, 1st Edition, p. 432.

[16]. Diary and Memoirs of the Chief of the Imperial Household Guard, Nara Takeji (Volume 3), p. 359, entry for September 22, 1931; quoted from (USA) Herbert Bix. Hirohito and the Making of Modern Japan. Xinhua Publishing House, September 2004, 1st Edition, p. 168.

[17]. (Japan) Aoyama Shomei. "Why Talk about Togo Heihachiro Now?" Cultural Review 346, Shin Nippon Shuppansha, 1989, p. 68; quoted from (USA) Herbert Bix. Hirohito and the Making of Modern Japan. Xinhua Publishing House, September 2004, 1st Edition, p. 172.

[18]. (USA) Herbert Bix. Hirohito and the Making of Modern Japan. Xinhua Publishing House, September 2004, 1st Edition, p. 456.

[19]. (Japan) Fujiwara Akira. "The 'Three - Alls' Campaign and the North China Front Army (2)", Quarterly Journal of War Responsibility Studies, No. 21 (Autumn 1998 issue), p. 73; quoted from (USA) Herbert Bix. Hirohito and the Making of Modern Japan. Xinhua Publishing House, September 2004, 1st Edition, p. 266.

[20]. (Japan) Chida Natsumitsu. The Emperor, the Imperial Rescript, and the History of the Showa Era. Shabunsha, 1983, pp. 257 - 258; quoted from (USA) Herbert Bix. Hirohito and the Making of Modern Japan. Xinhua Publishing House, September 2004, 1st Edition, p. 231.

[21]. 33. (USA) Iris Chang. The Rape of Nanking. CITIC Press, 2013, 1st Edition, pp. 175, 213.

[22]. Shi Yijun. A Long - form Chronology of Feng Zhongyun. National Library of China Publishing House, May 2019, 1st Edition, pp. 66 - 69.

[23]. (Japan) The Association of Returned Japanese. The "Three - Alls" Policy: The Self - Accounts of Japanese War Criminals' Crimes of Aggression against China. World Affairs Press, 1990; quoted from Zhang Fulin. Historical Evidence: The Record of China's Education and Rehabilitation of Japanese War Criminals. Jilin People's Publishing House, July 2005, 1st Edition, p. 486.

[24]. (Japan) The Association of Returned Japanese, Shin - Doshosha. Aggression: The Confessions of Japanese War Criminals. Shandong People's Publishing House, 1985, pp. 20 - 32; quoted from Zhang Fulin, et al. Historical Evidence: The Record of China's Education and Rehabilitation of Japanese War Criminals. Jilin People's Publishing House, July 2005, 1st Edition, pp. 513 - 514.

[25]. Huang Heyi. The Tokyo Trial. Beiyue Literature and Art Press, April 2010, 1st Edition, pp. 204 - 205; quoted from Zhang Fulin, et al. Historical Evidence: The Record

of China's Education and Rehabilitation of Japanese War Criminals. Jilin People's Publishing House, July 2005, 1st Edition, p. 501.

[26]. [28]. (Japan) The Quarterly of the Association of Returned Japanese No. 7, p. 71; No. 20, pp. 42 - 49; quoted from Zhang Yilin, et al. Historical Evidence: The Record of China's Education and Rehabilitation of Japanese War Criminals. Jilin People's Publishing House, July 2005, 1st Edition, pp. 483, 497.

[27]. People's Daily, November 29, 1999.

[28]. (UK) Mark Felton. The Secret History of the Japanese Kempeitai: Murder, Violence, and Torture on the Asian War Front. Chongqing Publishing Group, Chongqing Press, November 2017, 1st Edition, pp. 126 - 127.

[29]. [30]. [31]. (New Zealand) James Mackay. Betrayal from the Top: The Secret Story of America's Betrayal of Its Allies. China City Press, October 1998, 1st Edition, pp. 323, 182 - 183, 246.

Chapter 12

There can never be too much deception in war

38. Facing a strong enemy, the only way is to rise up

Following the failure of the Kuomintang (KMT) army's fourth "Encirclement Campaign" against the Central Revolutionary Base Area, Chiang Kai-shek grew increasingly restless and anxious. Since the September 18th Incident (Mukden Incident), public criticism of the "non-resistance policy" had intensified, with accusations of Chiang's passive stance against Japanese aggression and even rumors of collusion with Japan to betray the nation. Chiang understood that allowing such public sentiment to escalate would give the Communist Party a chance to survive. Yet, abandoning the "Communist suppression" campaign to focus entirely on resisting Japan would enable the Communists to expand their influence, directly threatening the KMT regime. In contrast, Japan posed no immediate threat to his rule in the short term.

Guided by the principle of "Internal pacification must precede resistance against foreign threats," Chiang launched the fifth large-scale "Encirclement Campaign" against revolutionary base areas in the latter half of 1933. He mobilized one million troops to attack Red Army forces across regions, with

500,000 troops advancing toward the Central Revolutionary Base Area in late September. To unify ideological alignment within the KMT, Chiang delivered a series of speeches in November at the Nanchang KMT headquarters, declaring: "Resisting Japan must begin with exterminating the bandits," "Anti-Japanese resistance cannot be discussed until the Communist scourge is eradicated," and "Anyone who prioritizes 'resisting Japan' over suppressing the Communists shall be deemed a coward and executed without mercy." [1]

In mid-to-late April 1934, KMT forces concentrated their assault on Guangchang, the northern gateway to the Central Soviet Area. Due to tactical errors, the Red Army suffered heavy losses after 18 days of fierce fighting, resulting in the fall of Guangchang. By October, the Central Committee of the Chinese Communist Party and the Central Military Commission led the main force of the Red Army—over 86,000 troops—to embark on the Long March, an unprecedented feat in world history. During the breakthrough of the KMT's fourth blockade line at the Xiangjiang River, the Red Army endured catastrophic casualties. After crossing the river, its numbers plummeted from 86,000 to just over 30,000.

The painful lessons compelled the Chinese Communists to make the correct choices regarding their revolutionary path and leadership. In May 1935, an enlarged meeting of the Central Politburo convened in Zunyi, Guizhou, where Mao Zedong was co-opted as a member of the Politburo Standing Committee, effectively establishing his leadership role within the Party Central Committee and the Red Army.

In December 1935, the Central Politburo held another enlarged meeting in Wayaobao, northern Shaanxi, adopting the *Resolution of the Central Committee on the Current Political Situation* and the *Party's Tasks*. Two days later, at a meeting of Party activists, Mao Zedong delivered the report *On the Tactics of Fighting Japanese Imperialism*, praising how "the anti-Japanese guerrilla warfare in Northeast China and eastern Hebei is answering the onslaught of Japanese imperialism." [2]

The resolutions of the Wayaobao Meeting and Mao Zedong's report explicitly outlined the Party's fundamental strategic task of building a broad anti-Japanese national united front, while criticizing the long-standing erroneous tendencies of "Left" opportunist adventurism and closed-door sectarianism within the Party.

By 1936, the anti-Japanese struggle of the Northeast Anti-Japanese United Army had flourished. On New Year's Day, brimming with optimism, Mao Zedong personally drafted a telegram to Zhu De, stating: "As Japan aggressively advances into North China, the Central Committee has dispatched numerous cadres to direct the anti-Japanese war, and the anti-Japanese resistance in the three northeastern provinces has achieved significant growth."

In truth, the Northeast Volunteer Armies and Anti-Japanese, who fought a bloody resistance in the northeast, had long held a pivotal place in his mind. As early as late 1933, during Mao Zedong's investigation in Changgang Township, Xingguo County, Jiangxi, he personally recorded the township's donations to support the Northeast Volunteer Armies:

"Aid to the Northeast Volunteer Armies (also during the Langmu Township period, when the population was 2,900 and membership about 800): over 40 strings of cash were donated. Contributions ranged from five copper coins to 100, 200, or even one string. Most gave 100 coins, accounting for about 60% of members. Only a few contributed five copper coins or one string." [3]

One string of copper coins (1,000 coins) could be exchanged for one silver dollar (dayang). The donation of over 40 strings by 2,900 people— under the dual military and economic blockades imposed by the Nationalist government, where even basic necessities like salt had to be self-produced through the bitter-tasting saltpeter salt made by leaching nitrate from old wall soil—represented an extraordinary effort of solidarity.

On January 22, 1934, the opening day of the Second National Congress of the Chinese Soviet Republic, Mao Zedong proposed in his opening speech that all delegates stand and observe three minutes of silence to mourn and honor the martyrs who had sacrificed their lives, including many who had led anti-Japanese guerrilla warfare in the Northeast and were killed by Japanese invaders. In this poignant address, he specifically mentioned Luo Dengxian, the wartime secretary of the Chinese Communist Party's Manchuria Provincial Committee, who perished on the front lines. Later, the Provisional Central Government of the Chinese Soviet Republic, under his chairmanship, issued an order to establish Dengxian County in the Central Soviet Zone in commemoration. [4]

On the opening day of the Second National Congress of the Chinese Soviet Republic ("Second Soviet Congress"), Mao Zedong issued a special message of solidarity in the name of the congress to the Northeast People's Revolutionary Army and the Anti-Japanese Volunteer Armies. The message began with the heartfelt address: "To the Northeast People's Revolutionary Army and Anti-Japanese Volunteer Armies, our dear comrades: The congress extends a fervent revolutionary salute to your warriors heroically resisting Japan! The congress expresses boundless sympathy for your persistent struggle in the anti-Japanese national revolutionary war. On behalf of the millions of revolutionary masses and the Red Army in the Soviet zones and White-controlled areas, the congress welcomes the representatives dispatched by the People's Revolutionary Army to attend this gathering…"

Moreover, during the congress, Mao Zedong personally received representatives from the Northeast and listened to their reports on the anti-Japanese resistance. On February 1, the congress elected the Second Central

Executive Committee of the Chinese Soviet Republic, with Yang Jingyu (using the alias Zhang Guanyi) becoming a member. The election of Yang Jingyu, the key leader of the Northeast Anti-Japanese armed forces, underscored the strategic significance of the Northeast resistance movement and its military forces in Mao's vision.

During the Wayaobao Meeting, under Mao's leadership, participants deliberated on the critical issue of coordinating operations between the main Red Army forces and the Northeast Anti-Japanese United Army. From February to May 1936, the First Front Army of the Red Army, commanded by Mao Zedong and Peng Dehuai, launched the Eastern Expedition, crossing the Yellow River into Shanxi Province and advancing toward Rehe, Chahar, and Suiyuan. On June 15, "Songshan" (Wu Ping) wrote to Zhou Baozhong and others, reporting on the Eastern Expedition:

> "Under the direct leadership of Comrade Mao, the Anti-Japanese Red Army has reached Shaanxi-Gansu and recently crossed the Yellow River into the heart of Shanxi. Advancing north beyond the Great Wall toward Suiyuan in Inner Mongolia, the Red Army is increasingly approaching a period of direct confrontation with Japanese invaders and the puppet 'Manchukuo' army… This has exerted a tremendously positive political influence on the Northeast anti-Japanese guerrilla movement, providing it with fresh momentum." [5]

Earlier, various units of the Northeast resistance had learned fragments of news about the Red Army's Eastern Expedition from Japanese-puppet newspapers. Yang Jingyu recognized that the Northeast Anti-Japanese forces occupied a dual position: they were both the rear base of Japan's aggression in North China and the forward outpost and vanguard of resistance efforts within China proper. After learning of the main Red Army's Eastern Expedition, Yang Jingyu organized two successive western expeditions into Rehe in late June and November 1936. Though these campaigns failed to achieve their objectives due to overwhelming enemy forces, historians later noted that the western expeditions constituted a bold attempt by Northeast anti-Japanese forces to coordinate with the Anti-Japanese Red Army, which was then advancing from northern Shaanxi toward the Great Wall.

To express his ardent aspiration toward the Party Central Committee and the main Red Army forces, Yang Jingyu composed the *Song of Victory for the Western Expedition* to rally the troops before their campaign. One verse proclaimed:

> "The Chinese Red Army has seized Rehe, advancing toward Fengtian;
> The Western Expedition launches a pincer strike—rally now to crush the
> Japanese invaders!"

Meanwhile, following the *Tanggu Truce*, the Nationalist government under Chiang Kai-shek assumed that Japan, having occupied the four northeastern provinces, would be satisfied. Seeking to ease tensions with Japan, Chiang concentrated all efforts on the Fifth Encirclement Campaign against the Soviet zones and the Red Army. During this period, Chiang published a convoluted essay titled *"Friend or Foe? A Reassessment of Sino-Japanese Relations"* (recorded by his secretary Chen Bulei).

After critiquing seven historical errors in handling Sino-Japanese relations, the essay emphasized the two nations' interdependence:

> Historically, geographically, and ethnically, the relationship between
> China and Japan transcends even the proverbial interdependence of lips and
> teeth—it is a mutually sustaining bond where survival and demise are
> inextricably intertwined. Their fates are so profoundly connected that they
> stand to prosper or perish as one. [6]

This lengthy treatise, less an address to the Chinese people than a plea to Japan, exposed Chiang Kai-shek's failure—as the nation's leader—to comprehend Japanese imperialist logic, even as four northeastern provinces had been turned into colonies. No matter how many conciliatory smiles China offered, Japan's iron-hoofed aggression would never halt at the Great Wall.

Ironically, Japan interpreted Chiang's essay as a display of "sincere goodwill". In January 1935, Japanese Foreign Minister Hirota Kōki announced a diplomatic principle of "no threat, no aggression" toward China, which Chiang immediately hailed as a reciprocal act of goodwill. Subsequently, Nationalist officials visited Tokyo to meet Japanese military and political leaders, while the regime issued nationwide bans on anti-Japanese activities, censored related media reports, and promulgated the *Order to Lift the Boycott of Japanese Goods.*

The Japanese cabinet, thoroughly satisfied, proactively proposed upgrading its Minister to China to an Ambassador to China. Shortly afterward, both China and Japan jointly announced the elevation of their diplomatic representatives.

In the spring of 1935, Sino-Japanese relations appeared to enter a phase of "friendship," yet a formidable force was overlooked: while officials from both governments exchanged frequent visits and naively celebrated this "friendship," the Japanese military establishment—particularly right-wing junior officers—was secretly orchestrating plans to invade North China.

Historical records later revealed that Japan's military leadership initially lacked a comprehensive strategy for occupying North China. The invasion essentially mirrored the September 18th Incident (1931), unfolding as a bottom-up initiative: frontline officers took the lead, the Army Ministry followed, and the General Staff Office retroactively sanctioned the aggression. The mastermind was Lieutenant General Yoshijirō Umezu, commander of the Japan's China Garrison Army and a core member of the Baden-Baden Group (a secret clique of 11 imperial army elites).

The Japanese military's rigid hierarchy, rooted in a deep sense of seniority, led the China Garrison Army to flaunt its status as the 'oldest' force in China, openly looking down on other Japanese units. Its presence in China dated back to 1901, the year following the Eight-Nation Alliance's suppression of the Boxer Rebellion. Under the *Xinchou Treaty* (Boxer Protocol), it stationed a permanent garrison of 1,117 troops in Beijing, Tianjin, and surrounding areas. By contrast, the Kwantung Army was not formally established until 1919—18 years later. Although its predecessors had entered China under the *Treaty of Portsmouth* of the 1905, they were merely railway guards along the South Manchuria Railway, with a sparse deployment of 15 men per kilometer.

The Kwantung Army's starring role in the September 18th Incident (1931), which earned it the honorific title "Flower of the Imperial Army," deeply provoked the rival China Garrison Army. This rivalry likely drove Yoshijirō Umezu to emulate Shigeru Honjō's Manchurian playbook by engineering a second "September 18th-style" crisis in North China. Umezu's orchestration of the North China Incident catapulted him to the rank of full general and eventually Chief of the Army General Staff—a career trajectory that ultimately led to his conviction as a Class-A war criminal after Japan's defeat.

The so-called "North China Incident" and "North China Autonomy Movement" aimed to establish Japanese-controlled puppet regimes across five northern provinces under the pretext of "anti-communism" and "self-rule." The goal was to sever these provinces from Nanjing's jurisdiction, transforming North China into a nominally autonomous region—effectively a second "Manchukuo"—under Tokyo's dominion.

Why did the overconfident Japanese military refrain from outright occupation of North China, as they had done in the Northeast? The answer lay in the tension between ambition and military capacity: even after two troop reinforcements, the China Garrison Army numbered only 8,400 soldiers, dwarfed by the 29th Army of Song Zheyuan, which boasted over 100,000 troops. To compensate, the Kwantung Army "loaned" its master schemer Kenji Doihara to the Garrison Army.

Doihara commanded Japanese forces to orchestrate a series of staged incidents. Under his orders, Garrison Army Chief of Staff Takashi Sakai arranged the assassination of two collaborationist publishers of the *Guoquan Bao* and *Zhen Bao* newspapers—falsely labeled as an "anti-Japanese Hebei Incident"—then deployed tanks and armored vehicles to stage a show of force outside the Hebei Provincial and Tianjin Municipal governments, while over a dozen Japanese warplanes circled over Beiping (Beijing). Umezu then issued an ultimatum to He Yingqin, chairman of the Beiping Office of the Nationalist Military Council: dissolve the Nationalist Party organizations in Hebei, Beiping, and Tianjin; withdraw all Chinese troops from Hebei; dismiss Yu Xuezhong, commander of the 51st Army in Tianjin; and remove and replace the Governor of Hebei and the Mayors of Beiping and Tianjin.

With Chiang Kai-shek's approval, He Yingqin, chairman of the Beiping Military Council Branch, sent a formal reply to Yoshijirō Umezu on July 6, 1935, stating: "All items proposed by Chief of Staff Sakai on June 9th are hereby accepted." [7]

He Yingqin's reply and Umezu's Memorandum became the infamous He-Umezu Agreement.

The Chiang-Faction's capitulation to Japanese demands nearly obliterated the Nationalist government's administrative authority in Hebei. Yet how could Japan's ambitions be sated by a single province? While seizing Hebei, Japanese forces simultaneously encroached upon Chahar Province. On June 27, Qin Dechun, acting chairman of Chahar, and Japanese representative Kenji Doihara finalized the "*Qin-Doihara Agreement*" through an exchange of notes, mandating the withdrawal of

Chinese troops from Guyuan, Baochang, Kangbao, and Shangdu, alongside the expulsion of Nationalist Party organizations from Chahar. [8]

Japan's strategy to dominate the five North China provinces was meticulously planned. Firstly, forced withdrawal: Demand the evacuation of Nationalist forces and Party institutions, creating a power vacuum—achieved via the "Qin-Doihara" and "He-Umezu" agreements. Secondly, puppet regimes: Install collaborationist administrations under the guise of "autonomy," controlled by Japanese advisors. Thirdly, formal subjugation: Coerce Nanjing into recognizing Japan's "guiding role" in North China, transforming Hebei, Shanxi, Suiyuan, Chahar, and Shandong into a second "Manchukuo."

Under Doihara's orchestration, Japan incited a puppet uprising in October 1935, seizing Xianghe County under the pretext of an "Anti-Communist Autonomy Movement." By late November, Yin Rugeng, the collaborationist Inspector of Jidong (Jixian-Miyun) Administrative District, declared the establishment of the "East Hebei Anti-Communist Autonomous Committee" in Tongzhou, proclaiming the "autonomy" of 25 counties in eastern Hebei and severing ties with the Chinese government.

Yin Rugeng, a notorious collaborationist who inflicted immense harm on the Chinese nation during the War of Resistance, studied at Waseda University and other Japanese institutions. His prolonged residence in Japan, coupled with his marriage to a Japanese woman, solidified his pro-Japanese sympathies and entrenched his ties to Japan's military-political elite.

Yin's brazen declaration of "autonomy" provoked both fury and embarrassment within the Nationalist government. While the Executive Yuan resolved to arrest him, Chiang Kai-shek argued that punishing this Japanese-protected traitor would risk direct conflict with Japan—a risk China, still militarily weak, could ill afford. Thus, Nanjing reluctantly tolerated his betrayal.

By year's end, to prevent the replication of such "autonomy" schemes, the Nationalist government dissolved the Beiping Military Council Branch and established the nominally sovereign but de facto semi-autonomous "Hebei-Chahar Political Council".

The council's chairman, Song Zheyuan, was a complex figure: as commander of the 29th Army, he had earned fame during the Great Wall Resistance by leading his troops in bloody hand-to-hand combat against Japanese invaders. Now, as North China's top military-political authority commanding 100,000 troops, Song straddled a precarious balance. His army—originally part of Feng Yuxiang's Northwest Army—had historically clashed with Chiang's forces and only recently secured control of Beiping and Tianjin. Determined to avoid being driven back to the impoverished Northwest, Song faced dual adversaries: the Japanese and Chiang's Central Army.

Song Zheyuan's strategy mirrored Chiang Kai-shek's approach: endure humiliation to deny Japan pretexts for war. A conflict would inevitably decimate his Northwest Army, and mutual destruction with Japan would only invite Chiang's Central Army—long coveting control of Beiping and Tianjin—to seize his hard-won territories, leaving him with no foothold. "It's not cowardice or fear of Japan," remarked Zhang Zizhong, a renowned anti-Japanese general, voicing the Northwest Army leadership's mindset: "War would serve the Nationalists' agenda—exploiting resistance to eliminate regional rivals. The Hebei-Chahar regime we've painstakingly built would collapse." [9]

In a China fragmented by warlordism, the mutual suspicion and power struggles between Chiang's central regime and regional militarists formed an intractable knot in modern Chinese politics.

This knot birthed the Hebei-Chahar Political Council—a political monstrosity. It was both a product of Chiang's compromise with Japan and his tactic to co-opt regional warlords, as well as Song's desperate bid to survive between Chiang's pressure and Japanese aggression.

Digging deeper: Chiang sought to use the council as a buffer in Sino-Japanese relations, while Song leveraged it to bargain with Nanjing. Their rivalry, however, played into Japan's hands, enabling Tokyo to effortlessly advance its first two steps in dominating North China.

He first publicly declared that 'Hebei and Chahar provinces maintain special relations with Japan,' then signed the *Sino-Japanese Anti-Communist Agreement for North China with the Japanese China Garrison Army*, and further negotiated the so-called "Four Principles and Eight Key Points"—a framework for economic collaboration designed to subordinate North China's resources to Tokyo. These actions marked perilous strides toward capitulation to Japanese domination.

Fortunately, China had the Communist Party and an enraged populace. Beiping students, declaring "North China is too vast to hold a single peaceful desk!" stormed into the streets, igniting the seismic December 9th Movement that shook the nation.

Mao Zedong remarked: "The youth and students were like the firewood of the December 9th Movement—everything was prepared, needing only a spark to ignite. And who was the igniter? It was the Communist Party." [10]

In other words, it was the Communist Party-led *December 9th Movement* and the surging public opinion it ignited that pulled figures like

Song Zheyuan—wavering between resistance and compromise—back to the side of the people.

In late December 1935, 14 social organizations in Shanghai cabled Song Zheyuan: "Immortal honor or eternal shame—you choose." By early January 1936, Song replied: "My devotion to the nation shall not lag behind others." A narrow escape!

War is not merely a clash of material forces (resources and military might) but a contest of spirit (willpower and wisdom). Why did central and regional warlords resist active anti-Japanese resistance? Was it due to inadequate strength (troops, equi p.ment, supplies)? Even a child could calculate the odds: 100,000 Chinese troops in North China versus Japan's 8,400-strong China Garrison Army—what overwhelming superiority!

The tragedy lay in China's warlords prioritizing factional self-interest over national survival, draining their armies of courage, soul, and fighting spirit.

Sun Tzu's Art of War states: "Know yourself and know your enemy— victory is assured." In the 1920s-30s, while Chinese leaders knew little of Japanese politics, Japan's military-political elite had mastered China's internal dynamics. A 1936 secret report by Takayoshi Matsumuro, head of Japan's Beiping intelligence agency, remains essential reading for all Chinese.

Matsumuro argued that China's "non-resistance doctrine" and "Japan-phobia" enabled Japan's outnumbered forces to prevail. The seizure of Northeast China was achieved through "victory without battle"—breaking Chinese morale. This "Japan-phobia" paralyzed Chinese officials:

"Now, 70% of North China's factions refuse unity, prioritizing self-preservation… These petty cliques, obsessed with immediate gains, crumble before Imperial assaults. Their selfishness grants us effortless conquest—no battle needed, mere words suffice…

Since the September 18th, China's reliance on the League of Nations and non-resistance allowed the Imperial Army's victories. Later, Chinese forces—ignorant of Sun Tzu's wisdom—succumbed to phantom fears under Imperial pressure. As Japan intensifies its heat, China's panic deepens, and official Japan-phobia worsens daily." [11]

It must be acknowledged that this intelligence chief possessed a bone-deep understanding of the Nationalist regime's internal dynamics. Once the Japanese discerned the pulse of the warlords and Chiang's government, their audacity—whether the Kwantung Army's 20,000 troops confronting 200,000 Northeastern forces, or the Garrison Army's 8,400 soldiers facing 100,000 in North China—becomes explicable, along with their bluffs like the Imperial Army's "independent actions."

As previously detailed, the September 18th Incident unfolded through a familiar script: junior field officers took the initiative, the cabinet hesitated, the Army Ministry equivocated, and the Emperor retroactively sanctioned the fait accompli. The North China Incident followed the same playbook. Even two days after the Marco Polo Bridge Incident (July 7, 1937), Prime Minister Fumimaro Konoe's cabinet resolved to "temporarily halt troop reinforcements to North China… and localize the conflict under the non-escalation principle."

Emperor Hirohito initially opposed the military's expansionist agenda, believing "compromise and delay are our only options with China"[12]. Yet China's shockingly bottomless concessions emboldened the Army to overturn the cabinet's restraint—ultimately swaying the Emperor himself.

Conversely, how well did China understand Japan?

In the 1920s-30s, Chinese warlords—Chiang included—knew perilously little about Japan's military-political machine, many crippled by a spineless fear of Japan. Had China struck decisively against Japan's early provocations, could 14 years of brutal occupation have ensued? History, alas, brooks no "what-ifs."

This is precisely why we hold in such high esteem the heroes of the Northeast Anti-Japanese United Army, who rose fiercely against Japan's brutality and fought with unyielding blood and resolve—embodying the national integrity and backbone of our people. The Communist leadership understood this deeply. Over three decades after the September 18th Incident, in 1965, when discussing national defense, a Communist leader remarked:

> We must not follow Chiang Kai-shek's path, allowing the Japanese to sweep unchecked into Nanjing, Wuhan, and Changsha. Nor should we repeat Stalin's mistake, letting Hitler storm to the gates of Moscow and Leningrad. …We must hold our ground where necessary… Holding ground buys time… to ultimately annihilate the enemy.[13]

To "hold ground" against a formidable foe demands the courage, tenacity, and indomitable spirit of Chinese Communists and the righteous defiance of the Anti-Japanese United Army's warriors. This is the spiritual force invaders fear most.

Even the same intelligence chief, Takayoshi Matsumuro, who dismissed Nationalist warlords with contempt, expressed grave concern about the Communists:

This (Communist force) cannot be ignored. Their Red Army is formidable in strength and combat prowess, their endurance unparalleled among modern armies. Their ideology deeply resonates with the masses…

> Having marched tens of thousands of miles from their Jiangxi base through Central and North China, enduring extreme material deprivation yet

unwavering in spirit… They exploit every opportunity, rallying the people with anti-Japanese fervor. Their future potency must not be underestimated.

Matsumuro posed a stark hypothetical:

> Had China's officials and citizens united in heart and mind to resist, Japan's dominance in Manchuria would have been encircled. Whether the supply of raw materials to the Empire could be sustained; whether Chinese markets could continue absorbing Japanese goods; whether Japan could maintain control over transportation hubs and resource-rich factories; whether vast territories and populations could be subjugated under Imperial rule—all would be thrown into grave uncertainty…[14]

Thus, this seasoned spymaster vehemently urged Japan to act swiftly while Chinese "Japan-phobia" still paralyzed resistance.

Yet clear-sighted Communists would never permit such schemes to prevail.

39. This is a deadly pheasant

Countless episodes of revolutionary history attest that all correct ideologies, actions, and policies originate from revolutionary praxis—often forged and cemented by the blood and lives of grassroots fighters.

One of the Chinese Communist Party's pivotal united front documents, the *Manifesto to All Compatriots for Resisting Japan and Saving the Nation* (commonly known as the *August 1st Declaration*), distilled the Party's anti-Japanese praxis, particularly lessons from the Northeast's bloody resistance against Japanese forces. Facing critiques like "collusion with elites" and "Right opportunism," grassroots Party organizations and anti-Japanese forces—including the Northeast People's Revolutionary Army, Allied Armies, and National Salvation Armies—unitedly demanded the formation of a consolidated Northeast Anti-Japanese United Army.

On May 11, 1935, the *Report from the Jidong Special Committee of the CCP to the Provincial Committee* outlined three key proposals: Organizing the Northeast Anti-Japanese United Army with the existing 1st, 2nd, 3rd, 4th, and 5th Armies as the backbone, integrating other volunteer forces, National Salvation Armies, and anti-Japanese mountain forest units; Abolishing all disparate names to unify under the designation of the Northeast Anti-Japanese United Army; Establishing a unified Northeast Anti-Japanese United Army Military Commission and General Headquarters, with subordinate military commissions and headquarters at local levels.

Subsequently, at the Lianghekou Politburo Standing Committee Meeting on June 29, 1935, confronting the crisis of the North China Incident, Mao Zedong noted: "Imperialist rivalries in China manifest as warlord conflicts. Japanese imperialism seeks total control over Chiang Kai-shek. The Party must respond to this juncture with public declarations." The meeting thus resolved to issue a Central Committee manifesto, publish articles, and dispatch operatives to Nationalist military units. [15]

At this time, Chen Yun had been dispatched by the Central Committee to the Chinese Communist Party delegation in Moscow. He approached Wang Ming, head of the delegation, arguing: "We still lack a correct political line on establishing the anti-Japanese national united front, but it is not too late to act now. The united front is absolutely necessary and the only correct policy at present."

This position, of course, was not merely Chen Yun's personal view but reflected the collective stance of the Party Central Committee under Mao Zedong's leadership following the Zunyi Conference. Chen Yun held dual significance, who was the first senior CCP leader from the Central Soviet Zone and the Long March to reach Moscow, and was one of the CCP's three formal representatives to the Comintern (Communist International), ranked after Wang Ming but ahead of Kang Sheng.

From July 25 to August 1, 1935, the Communist International convened its Seventh Congress in Moscow. During the proceedings on August 7, Wang Ming, aligning with the Comintern's strategic pivot and the Chinese delegation's consensus, delivered a speech declaring: "To establish, expand, and consolidate the anti-imperialist united front is the paramount task for Communists in colonial and semi-colonial countries." [16]

On July 14, the CCP delegation finalized the *Manifesto to All Compatriots for Resisting Japan and Saving the Nation* (jointly issued by the Chinese Soviet Central Government and the CCP Central Committee). Approved by the Comintern Executive Committee Secretariat on September 24, the manifesto was published on October 1 in the Paris-based *Jiuguo Bao* (National Salvation News). Dated August 1 for symbolic resonance, this pivotal document became immortalized as the *August 1st Declaration.*

The declaration vehemently condemned Japanese imperialist aggression and the Nationalist regime's capitulation under Chiang Kai-shek, while extolling nationwide resistance—particularly in Northeast China. It proclaimed: Under the leadership of national heroes like Yang Jingyu, Zhao Shangzhi, Wang Detai, Li Yanlu, Zhou Baozhong, Xie Wendong, Wu Yicheng, and Li Huatang, our people have fought courageously, wave after wave. Their sacrifices embody the indomitable spirit of national survival

Confronting national peril, the *August 1st Declaration* articulated the Chinese Communist Party's stance and policy: "Despite past or present differences in political views or interests among parties, disputes among compatriots of all walks of life, or historical hostilities between armies, all must embrace the sincere awakening of 'brothers quarreling at home yet uniting against external threats'. First and foremost, all must cease civil war to consolidate every national resource—human, material, financial, and military—for the sacred cause of resisting Japan and saving the nation." [18]

Acknowledging the ongoing civil war between the CCP and the Nationalists, the declaration solemnly proclaimed: "Provided that Nationalist forces halt attacks on Soviet zones, and provided any army engages in anti-Japanese resistance, the Red Army will not only immediately cease hostilities but willingly join hands in national salvation—regardless of past grievances or disagreements on domestic issues." [19]

The *August 1st Declaration*, drafted and advanced by the CCP delegation led by Wang Ming, received unequivocal endorsement from Mao Zedong—a leader who adhered lifelong to the principles of seeking truth from facts and judging merits and faults with clarity. It repeatedly publicized the manifesto in pivotal forums, underscoring its historical significance.

On March 1, 1937, during an interview with American journalist Agnes Smedley, Mao cited the *August 1st Declaration* (titled *Manifesto for*

Organizing the Anti-Japanese United Army and a National Defense Government) published two years prior, reaffirming the Communist Party's sincere willingness to form an Anti-Japanese National United Front with the Nationalists. In April 1945, the declaration was enshrined in the *Resolution on Certain Historical Issues* adopted at the Enlarged Seventh Plenary Session of the Sixth Central Committee of the CCP. Later, it was included in the *Selected Works of Mao Zedong.* [20]

Though the *August 1st Declaration* failed to alter Chiang Kai-shek's obstinate pursuit of annihilating the CCP and its Workers' and Peasants' Red Army, its impact proved transformative in Northeast China—where Nationalist forces were absent. The declaration effectively addressed the long-standing influence of the Left-deviationist "closed-door" policy, enabling the Northeast Anti-Japanese United Army to break free from ideological constraints. It united diverse resistance forces against their sole enemy—Japanese invaders—thereby expanding and strengthening both the Anti-Japanese National United Front and guerrilla warfare.

On October 11, guided by the principles of the *August 1st Declaration*, the CCP delegation, under the name of Yang Jingyu (as the lead signatory), Commander of the First Army of the Northeast Anti-Japanese United Army, and other Northeast resistance leaders, issued the *Open Telegram from the Northeast Anti-Japanese United Army Calling for United Resistance Against Japan*. The telegram stated: "For four years, Japanese invaders have occupied our Northeast, and for four years, the United Army has waged a bloody struggle. Daily, we await reinforcements from China proper, yet not a single soldier or bullet has been sent. Now, Japan openly plots to carve out a so-called 'North China State' across five provinces. Their policy is clear: to use Chinese hands to slaughter Chinese people." On behalf of 30 million Northeast compatriots and resistance forces, Yang Jingyu appealed earnestly to all political factions: "Immediately exchange representatives to begin negotiations. Let us jointly establish a National Defense Government and a unified Anti-Japanese United Army Command, reorganize resistance forces, and coordinate military strategies."

This open telegram was published in the inaugural issue of the *Jiuguo Shibao* (National Salvation Times) on December 9. As an appeal from frontline soldiers and officers bleeding for resistance in the Northeast, it resonated profoundly domestically and internationally, garnering widespread support across the Nationalist-Communist divide and among democratic parties.

On February 20, 1936, the CCP delegation, under the signatures of Yang Jingyu and other commanders of the 1st to 6th Armies of the Northeast Anti-Japanese United Army, issued the *Manifesto on the Unification of Military Structures of the Northeast Anti-Japanese United Army*. Henceforth, all CCP-led resistance forces in the Northeast were unified under the designation Northeast Anti-Japanese United Army or Anti-Japanese United Army Guerrilla Units.

The military unification held dual political and strategic significance: it absorbed willing anti-Japanese volunteer forces and guerrilla bands into the United Army while fostering a cohesive front—and even centralized command—among disparate resistance groups.

The term "Northeast Anti-Japanese United Army" was first proposed by Yang Jingyu in February 1934. The concept of integrating People's Revolutionary Army units with other forces was also advanced by him in October 1935. Despite his staunch party discipline, Yang persisted in allying with diverse anti-Japanese factions despite facing political pressure and accusations of "rightist tendencies". He understood deeply that against Japan's overwhelming force, resistance could not be achieved by the CCP alone; even with the Party's vanguard sacrifices, victory demanded a united front of all military and civilian forces. Without unity, there can be no victory; without unity, there can be no survival. Unity is our lifeblood.

The declaration greatly inspired Yang Jingyu. By the time he received the declaration, the 1st Army had already made strides in uniting resistance forces, establishing the South Manchuria Anti-Japanese United Army Jiangbei General Headquarters with Cao Guo'an, commander of the 1st Army's 2nd Division, elected as general commander. This headquarters integrated over 1,000 newly allied troops. These details were documented in a report by Xiao Luo (Zhang Wenlie), Standing Committee Member of the CCP Manchuria Provincial Committee and Secretary of the Provincial Youth League Committee, to the CCP delegation.

The report further stated: "Around the 1st Division headquarters, alliances with 500–600 mountain forest guerrilla units have been forged. Through the Army Command's active efforts, significant connections have also been established with the Korean Independence Army (a force composed entirely of Koreans, numbering around 300 troops, with a peak strength of 1,000; its commander, surnamed Zhao, previously clashed with a detachment of our forces). The Provisional General Headquarters of the South Manchuria Anti-Japanese United Army has been established, with Yang Jingyu unanimously appointed as commander".

Yang Jingyu's great implementation of the declaration and his efforts to consolidate the Anti-Japanese United Army alarmed the Japanese puppet authorities. They intensified espionage operations, as documented in the classified internal report *Study on Communist Bandits in Manchuria* compiled by the Military Investigation Department of the Puppet Manchukuo regime:

> "In the two guerrilla zones of South Manchuria and the Haidong region, previous attempts to build an anti-Japanese united front around the People's

Revolutionary Army repeatedly failed. However, since the Chinese Communist Party's August 1st Declaration advocated the establishment of a National Defense Government and an Anti-Japanese United Army, alongside the expansion of China's anti-Japanese popular front, these previously stagnant guerrilla zones have witnessed a consolidated and expanding united front movement." [21]

By the first half of 1936, the 1st Army's 1st Division had expanded by one and a half times, and the 2nd Division had doubled in size. To accommodate this growth and expand guerrilla zones, Yang Jingyu established the 3rd Division based on the Army's 2nd Training Regiment and Wang Renxi's Guerrilla Battalion, extending operations to six or seven counties, including Xingjing (Xing'an), Fushun, and Xifeng.

The rapid expansion of the Northeast Anti-Japanese United Army—particularly the South Manchuria forces centered on the 1st Army—solidified Yang Jingyu as the movement's iconic leader. Determined to extinguish the resistance by toppling its banner, the Japanese puppet authorities, after repeated failed military campaigns, deployed infiltrators from their military police intelligence agencies into the 1st Army's ranks—a tactic long favored and often effective for Japanese intelligence.

In the early autumn of 1935, a man claiming to be from the party organization within the Pass arrived at the headquarters of the First Army. He ripped open the lining of his clothes to retrieve a letter of introduction. After personally speaking with him, Yang Jingyu immediately led his troops to evacuate the current location and relocate to a rear base. Once the troops reached a secure area, they promptly subjected the man to an intensive interrogation. After several rounds of questioning, the man indeed revealed his true colors. It turned out he was a spy from the puppet police station in Gushanzi, aiming to infiltrate Yang Jingyu's forces. Once trusted, he intended to send back intelligence on troop movements, enabling the enemy to concentrate heavy forces for a surprise "decapitation strike" against the First Army headquarters.

After eliminating this infiltrator, everyone asked Yang Jingyu how he had discerned the man's deceit after just one conversation. Yang outlined three reasons that left them in awe: First, the letter of introduction was suspiciously pristine—given the long journey from within the Pass, it should have been worn. If truly sent by the party organization, he should have known internal protocols, rendering many written details unnecessary. Second, since it questioned about conditions inside the Pass, he couldn't provide any specifics. With extensive experience in underground operations, Yang was intimately familiar with their protocols, enabling him to expose spies who lacked genuine party training.

Yang Jingyu, with his extensive underground experience, was deeply familiar with covert protocols, enabling him to expose spies who lacked genuine party credentials.

At the time, Japanese intelligence agencies employed every conceivable scheme to eliminate Yang Jingyu, even nearly succeeding in assassinating him.

In the autumn of 1935, a "salt peddler" arrived at the First Army headquarters, claiming to join the People's Army to fight invaders. He was assigned to Training Company 3. Yang, suspicious of this recruit with no "sponsor" or verifiable background, ordered party members to monitor him. Over time, reports reached Yang: the man possessed advanced military knowledge, could operate various weapons, and had an opium addiction… Yang instructed company instructor Jin Guangxue to secretly surveil him and track his contacts—knowing saboteurs never act alone.

Indeed, the man frequently interacted with the Company 3 commander, Bugler Shi from headquarters, a platoon leader, and Trumpeter Guan—all in critical positions. Yang discreetly directed Jin to intensify surveillance while investigating the "salt peddler" through underground channels: he was a lieutenant in the puppet Manchukuo army, tasked with infiltrating the First Army to liaise with pre-planted agents like Bugler Shi, either to assassinate Yang or incite mutiny, aiming to decapitate the army's leadership.

After identifying all suspects and assigning monitors, Yang bided his time, waiting to strike once they acted.

As winter approached, the troops moved to the Huanren base area. One day, Bugler Shi purchased three pheasants for Yang's meal. According to Yang's bodyguard Wang Chuansheng, that evening, Yang and his commanders were guarded by over a dozen armed soldiers. Upon learning Shi had brought the pheasants, Yang remarked ominously: "These pheasants could cost us our lives!" Wang, smelling the stew and hearing Yang's words, was baffled—even the closest guards were kept in the dark, testament to Yang's meticulous secrecy.

Where there's smoke, there's fire.

Shortly after the pheasant dinner, Yang ordered the immediate arrest of the Company 3 commander, the "salt peddler", Bugler Shi, the platoon leader, and others. Interrogations revealed their plot: the spy had connected with Shi, Guan, and the platoon leader, corrupting the company commander. They planned a two-pronged attack at midnight—one group assassinating Yang and his staff, the other seizing headquarters with Company 3—then defecting to the Japanese.

Due to the rebellion led by the commander of the Third Company, which implicated many soldiers in the unit, Yang Jingyu decided to implement a policy of severely punishing the principal offenders while leniently treating those coerced or exploited. During this internal counter-espionage operation, seven principal offenders were executed. Shortly afterward, Yang Jingyu transferred a company from the First Division to form a new Third Instructional Company under the army headquarters. [22]

Yang Jingyu's repeated foiling of enemy sabotage conspiracies within the Anti-Japanese Allied Forces also served as a warning to other units. Zhou Baozhong, commander of the Fifth Army (which had experienced the defection of key cadres recruited by Japanese puppet intelligence agencies), praised Yang Jingyu as "resourceful and wise", noting that the enemy greatly feared him and constantly employed ruthless and underhanded tactics in attempts to eliminate him. However, as Comrade Yang remained vigilant, enjoyed strong popular support, and maintained solid internal cohesion within the First Army, none of the enemy's schemes succeeded.

Facing the pervasive infiltration of Japanese puppet spies, Yang Jingyu maintained not only personal vigilance but also established comprehensive counter-espionage systems within his forces. Military operational plans and Party membership status were strictly confidential within the First Army. Even ordinary members of the guard brigade addressed each other by code names, with no knowledge of each other's real identities or hometowns. Yang Jingyu himself typically used the alias "Commander Liu" from the First Army's battalion headquarters. Through thorough security education, soldiers understood that such measures were not only appropriate but essential given the brutal realities of their struggle.

Years of guerrilla warfare against the Japanese had taught Yang Jingyu that the most dangerous enemies were often Chinese traitors deeply familiar with China's internal affairs and terrain, particularly those who wholeheartedly served the Japanese invaders. Figures like Shao Benliang, a former bandit turned Japanese collaborator, acted as the "eyes and ears" of the Japanese army. To defeat the invaders, Yang believed it was critical to first "blind their eyes" and "deafen their ears", crippling their ability to operate.

A meticulous strategist, Yang Jingyu never engaged in battles without certainty. The First Army's repeated victories were closely tied to underground intelligence networks within enemy-occupied territories. In other words, covert operations were vital resources and an organic component of the Anti-Japanese Allied Forces. Yang often emphasized: "No matter how brilliant guerrilla tactics are, they will fail without coordination between the fighters and the masses". To establish bases in Huanren and Xingjing, Yang had long planted informants like Old Liu, a horse groomer.

In underground terminology, Old Liu was a "sleeper agent", remaining dormant for extended periods. To gather intelligence, Yang also dispatched Wang Deyu, a young company political instructor, to Tonghua County Middle School under the guise of a student for covert reconnaissance.

Old Liu informed Wang Deyu about Shao Benliang's forces: The Seventh Regiment under Shao Benliang was stationed in Reshuihezi with over 150 Japanese puppet troops, including a Japanese garrison of 30+ soldiers. The remaining 120+ troops consisted entirely of traitorous police and puppet militia, with Shao's own unit comprising over 70 puppet soldiers. At the town center stood a fortified watchtower dominating the entire street. "To attack the puppet regiment headquarters, it was imperative to first seize the fortified artillery tower".

In the early spring of 1936, Yang led a surprise force of over 300 men to Reshuihezi. Around 1:00 a.m., following the plan, Xu Guoyou, commander of the instructional regiment, guided a pistol squad cloaked in puppet army yellow overcoats toward the watchtower under Old Liu's direction. When a pistol was pressed against the sentry's head, he muttered: "Aren't you asleep? What's this joke…"

After seizing the watchtower, the machine gun squad swiftly aimed their weapons to control all streets. Yang and his main force stormed the enemy barracks, capturing over 60 puppet soldiers in their sleep. The primary target, Shao Benliang, however, had coincidentally traveled to Tonghua with his Japanese advisor.

The raid resulted in the capture of 60 puppet soldiers, the seizure of 40 Type 38 rifles, 20 Mauser pistols, 30,000 rounds of ammunition, and vast quantities of military uniforms, cloth, rubber shoes, and other supplies. [23]

In early April, an enraged Shao Benliang—whose regiment headquarters had been destroyed—gathered heavy reinforcements under the support of Man Liang (chief of staff of the Puppet Manchukuo Army's First Military District) and Japanese advisor Takeda, launching a multi-pronged pursuit to annihilate Yang Jingyu's forces. Yang ordered the First Division to maneuver in Xingjing and Benxi, while the Second Division operated in the Jiangbei-Huadian area, dispersing to pin down the enemy.

Yet Shao Benliang, with a hound-like instinct, deployed numerous scouts and spies. Whenever they detected Yang Jingyu's direct command unit, they immediately alerted Japanese puppet authorities to dispatch planes for tracking or bombing. No sooner had Yang Jingyu's troops set up camp than Shao Benliang would arrive with a large contingent of troops the very next day. One report noted: "After bandit leader Yang's forces passed through Huanren County, the punitive corps surrounded them. At around 1 p.m. on the 21st, aircraft (number 00) bombed Yang's base…" On one occasion, Yang's unit even shot down a low-flying plane with machine gun fire.

Frustrated by Shao's relentless pursuit, some Anti-Japanese Allied soldiers clamored to "teach him a lesson." Yang Jingyu, however, insisted on avoiding direct engagement. Instead, he aimed to exhaust Shao's forces by out-marching them, testing their stamina and resolve. Only when the enemy was fully drained would Yang deliver a decisive blow.

During this period, to prevent Shao's troops from slacking in their pursuit, Yang ingeniously executed three feints to continuously lure them into traps:

Provoking Engagement: At Xingjing's Danaozi Valley, Yang staged a controlled skirmish with Shao's forces, reigniting their dwindling enthusiasm for pursuit.

Feigning Entra p.ment: Yang fabricated the illusion of being trapped by enemy encirclement. Years later, Yang's messenger Wang Chuansheng recalled that even his own troops grew disoriented, zigzagging unpredictably. Enemy newspapers boasted: "Communist bandits flail north and south, yet cannot escape heaven's net".

Simulating Retreat: After days of attrition, Yang ordered his troops to discard broken equi p.ment, clothes, and shoes, feigning a "routed army" to bait Shao's forces into chasing them to annihilation.

By late April, after weeks of circling, Yang rendezvoused with the First Division headquarters and the Youth Battalion. The combined force of over 500 troops, armed with more than a dozen light and heavy machine guns, far outgunned Shao's 200-strong pursuers.

On April 30, after being lured into a month-long pursuit, Shao Benliang's forces finally fell into Yang Jingyu's prearranged ambush at Lishudianzi, Benxi County. The terrain heavily favored Yang's forces: two hills flanked a narrow passage, funneling the enemy into a death trap. Yang's troops lay in ambush on both hills, their light and heavy machine guns strategically positioned to cover every angle. As Shao's cavalry entered the kill zone, Yang gave the signal. Gunfire erupted from the hillsides in a coordinated barrage, catching Shao's troops completely off guard. The slopes were soon littered with the corpses of soldiers and horses, a scene of utter devastation. A post-battle sweep of the battlefield confirmed over 100 enemy casualties.

The battle yielded over 100 rifles, 20 pistols, a radio transceiver, and a mortar. Shao Benliang, ever the cunning bandit, narrowly escaped by stealing civilian clothes and fleeing. Humiliated, Japanese puppet authorities mobilized over 1,000 troops with heavy artillery for retaliation, but Yang had already dispersed his forces and vanished. After seven days of futile searches, the enemy found no trace of the First Army.

The ambush at Lishudianzi stands as one of Yang Jingyu's most successful examples of combining guerrilla tactics with mobile warfare.

During the battle, Shao Benliang suffered a shattered foot. After recovering, he redoubled his frenzied efforts to hunt down Yang's forces. However, Shao's movements were closely monitored by Communist underground operatives embedded in Japanese-occupied territories. By late July, Wang Deyu—who had infiltrated Tonghua County—obtained precise intelligence: Shao Benliang had departed Tonghua and was scheduled to garrison Badaojiang on the morning of August 4, accompanied by dozens of large horse-drawn wagons loaded with military supplies. Faced with the dual objectives of eliminating Shao and seizing the supplies, Yang Jingyu devised a tactical principle: "strike the middle, release both ends"— prioritizing the capture of the central supply convoy.

On the night of August 3, Yang Jingyu mobilized over 400 troops to deploy a heavily-armed ambush along Shao Benliang's predetermined route, flanking the kill zone with blocking forces. Around 10:00 a.m. on the

4th, Shao entered the ambush area under the protection of 20+ cavalrymen, trailing behind a vanguard of scouts. However, Yang held fire as Shao's supply wagons lagged behind, allowing Shao himself to pass unscathed. When the convoy finally arrived, Yang signaled the attack. A barrage of gunfire tore through the enemy ranks. Sensing danger, Shao fled into the dense woods, escaping pursuit even as a young soldier chased him for over half a kilometer.

Shao's Japanese advisor, Yingjun Zhi Xiong, was less fortunate. He played dead in a roadside ditch—a tactic he had used in previous ambushes—but was discovered and executed on the spot by cleanup troops. The ambush resulted in over 30 enemy casualties, more than 20 prisoners, and the seizure of critical supplies: 1 light machine gun, 50-60 rifles, and vast quantities of grain, uniforms, and ammunition—all desperately needed by the Anti-Japanese Allied Forces.

Despite his cunning as a seasoned bandit, Shao Benliang—who repeatedly escaped by sheer luck—met his match in the brilliant strategist Yang Jingyu, who vowed to eliminate this die-hard traitor. Not long after, Shao's forces were again encircled and annihilated by Yang's troops at Huitougou, leaving Shao wounded once more as he fled back to Badaojiang. Yang's consistent victories over Shao during their three-year rivalry stemmed not only from his exceptional leadership and the Anti-Japanese Allied Forces' combat prowess but also from effective intelligence operations. Yang had near-complete knowledge of Shao's troop movements, routes, and numbers, leading the Japanese to suspect collusion within Shao's ranks and ultimately withdraw their trust in him.

The Japanese had always treated their Chinese collaborators with ruthless pragmatism: they lavished resources on those proving loyal and productive, but demanded returns multiplied tenfold.

Over years of investment, Shao's failures and losses rendered him useless. The Japanese first confined him under guard at Fengtian Army Hospital under the guise of medical treatment. In the spring of the following year, on orders from Major Shimoyama of the Fengtian Kempeitai, Japanese doctors poisoned Shao to death within the hospital. [25]

Some argue that the Japanese killed Shao Benliang as a scapegoat for their failure to suppress "Bandit Commander Yang" (Yang Jingyu), using his death to shift blame to their superiors. Regardless of the motive, Shao—a notorious bandit who had roamed the mountains and terrorized the region for decades, even before the Fengtian warlord era—met his end at Yang's hands. This cemented Yang Jingyu and the First Army's legendary reputation as an indomitable force.

40. You can't afford it, give me the gun

For Zhao Shangzhi—a leader deeply scarred by the "Northern Conference", the Left-deviationist line that dismantled the Bayan Guerrillas, and the temporary loss of his Party membership—the desire and actions to unite diverse anti-Japanese forces burned fiercer and more urgently than in anyone else. Though he had not yet seen the Declaration, Zhao had long been actively advancing a united front against Japan. Indeed, the Declaration crystallized the blood-soaked struggles of frontline commanders like Yang Jingyu, Zhao Shangzhi, and Zhou Baozhong.

Li Huatang of the Self-Defense Army saw Zhao's intentions clearly. He urged Xie Wendong of the People's Salvation Army to seek Zhao's support for revival, confident that Zhao would back them precisely because Zhao wants as many fighters against the Japanese as possible.

At the time, the alliance between Zhao and the defeated remnants of Li's forces (down to 50 men) and Xie's (30 men) drew ridicule: "Crafty Old Li, Foolish Old Zhao, Xie Wendong tags along in chaos". The rhyme mocked Li's cunning, Xie's aimless scheming, and Zhao's "foolish" gamble on rebuilding their strength. While the criticism of Li and Xie's character held truth, Zhao dismissed it with a laugh. He knew their flaws but prioritized their hatred for the Japanese and their resolve to revive resistance.

The criticism of Li and Xie's character was not unfounded. Zhao Shangzhi merely laughed it off. He was well aware of their flaws, but what mattered was their burning hatred for the Japanese and their determination to revive resistance. Past attempts to unite anti-Japanese forces had failed precisely because the Communists had imposed their own standards on such allies. Zhao's approach was pragmatic: as long as they agreed to three conditions, they were acceptable: No surrender, no treason, fight Japan to the last. Confiscate all properties and lands of Japanese imperialists and their collaborators to fund the war effort. Safeguard civilian interests and permit armed popular resistance. These terms defined the non-negotiable bottom line and core principle of the united front, embodying the Communists' pragmatic tolerance for the sake of a greater cause.

In the spring of 1935, Zhao Shangzhi led the Political Security Battalion and Youth Company of the Third Army Headquarters from the Zhuxian County base area to Daluolemi, joining forces with the First Regiment. His primary goal was to meet with Li Huatang, Xie Wendong, and Qi Zhizhong to establish the Northeast Anti-Japanese Allied Army General Headquarters. Zhao was elected Commander-in-Chief, Li Huatang as Deputy Commander-in-Chief, Xie Wendong as Chairman of the Military Council, and Zhang Choujian—the political director of the First Regiment who had advocated for uniting with Li and Xie—as Director of the General Political Department.

The wisdom of Zhao's decision to ally with Li and Xie soon became evident. The anti-Japanese coalition, shattered a year earlier by the rebellions of "Jiujiang" and "Huangpao", was revitalized. The resurgence of Li and Xie's once-doomed forces sent shockwaves through other volunteer armies and mountain forest units.

Zhao knew that to solidify Li and Xie's resolve, a decisive victory was crucial. The Allied Headquarters thus planned to attack Fangzheng County, employing a tactical feint: they first created a diversion by maneuvering the newly formed Allied forces around Daluolemi and Xiaoluolemi for days, drawing enemy attention. Then, mobilizing over 450 soldiers from the Third Army and the units of Li, Xie, and Qi, they launched a surprise assault on Fangzheng. Under Zhao's command, the Third Army's Youth Company breached the eastern gate, allowing the Allied forces to storm the city, seize the puppet police station, kill or wound 6 enemy soldiers, capture 1, confiscate 15 firearms, burn down the Japanese advisor's residence, and arrest over 40 traitors. Over 200 Japanese puppet troops garrisoned in the city fled in disarray; even reinforcements, hearing Zhao himself led the attack, dared not enter.

The capture of Fangzheng stunned Japanese forces in Yilan and Boli. As news spread of Zhao's eastward advance, enemy "punitive forces" withdrew to defend key towns. Emboldened by the victory, Li and Xie's ranks swelled. Meanwhile, over 3,000 fighters from 60-70 volunteer and mountain forest units across Hedong flocked to the Third Army, seeking protection and integration into its ranks.

In late March, Zhao Shangzhi convened a meeting of over 40 volunteer army and mountain forest unit leaders at Laoheidingzi in Bin County, establishing the Anti-Japanese Allied Army Northern Route Command. The region was divided into 21 districts, each assigned a battalion commander tasked with protecting local anti-Japanese associations and peasant self-defense forces. Shortly after, the Southern Route Command and the Yan (Shou)-Fang (Zheng) Command were also formed.

On March 25, Zhao Shangzhi, Feng Zhongyun, Li Huatang, and Xie Wendong issued a joint proclamation from the Third Army Headquarters and the Allied Army General Headquarters, announcing that the Yan-Fang, Northern Route, and Southern Route Commands would be led by Liu Haitao, Wang Huitong, and Zhang Lianke respectively. These commanders were to "oversee all operational affairs," with all Allied units ordered to "submit to local command." Notably, Liu, Wang, and Zhang were all Third Army regimental commanders, ensuring that volunteer and mountain forest units in these zones operated under the core leadership of Communist forces. The Central Zhuxian County Committee of the Chinese Communist Party praised this as "a flexible application of united front tactics".

Zhao dedicated immense effort to organizing the Anti-Japanese Allied Army. Japanese puppet archives reveal that between April and June 1935, Zhao held four meetings with volunteer leaders to coordinate regional defense and joint operations. For example: April 16–17: At Qinglong Mountain north of Yianpo, Zhao and 24 insurgent leaders discussed territorial demarcations and methods for anti-Manchukuo resistance... Mid-June: Near Erdiaohezi, 20 li south, Zhao and 20 leaders planned a second assault on Maoershan Station and railway sabotage... [26]

The united front catalyzed the growth of the Anti-Japanese forces and intensified resistance. According to 1935 statistics from the Puppet Binjiang Provincial Police Department: First Quarter: Anti-Japanese forces launched 352 attacks across 9 counties (Weihe, Zhuxian, Yanshou, Wuchang, Binxian, Acheng, Shuangcheng, Hulan, Bayan), involving 42,208 personnel. Second Quarter: Attacks surged to 559, mobilizing 80,364 personnel. Alarmed Japanese reports noted: "Notorious bandits... persuaded by Zhao

Shangzhi, now unite under a single slogan, the Zhuxian region has become a communist stronghold". [27]

In leading the Allied forces in valiant combat, the Third Army set a pioneering example for other armed groups, earning widespread public support and rapid expansion—growing from three regiments to six. By 1935, the Third Army numbered approximately 790 well-disciplined troops: 75% were impoverished peasants, 60% were Party or Youth League members, and 60% were under 30.

These figures further highlight a crucial reality: with a core force of 790 troops, the Communists united and led thousands of anti-Japanese fighters, mobilizing 120,000 personnel engagements in combat during the first two quarters of 1935 alone. This exemplified the historic significance of the united front—the Anti-Japanese Allied Army's organizational approach—while also attesting to the outstanding operational achievements of Third Army leaders such as Zhao Shangzhi, Feng Zhongyun, and Li Zhaolin.

Zhao Shangzhi relentlessly focused on expanding the Communist Party's own military strength to solidify its role as the core leadership uniting and guiding other anti-Japanese forces.

Wang Yachen's volunteer force, operating under the codename "Double Dragon", grew significantly through joint operations with the Third Army, laying the groundwork for the eventual formation of the Tenth Army of the Anti-Japanese Allied Forces. As early as May 1934, Zhao dispatched liaison officer Xiao Yimin to establish communication with the "Double Dragon" unit. Wang reciprocated by sending representatives to coordinate with the Third Army's Third Regiment. After formalizing their alliance, the "Double Dragon" unit frequently supported the Third Regiment in combat. During the 1935 campaign to break through the Japanese puppet "large-scale punitive operations", Zhao personally led Third Army troops alongside the "Double

Dragon" unit to destroy the "collective hamlet" at Kangjialu in Shuangcheng's Eighth District—a key forced resettlement village.

Qi Zhizhong, leader of the volunteer force "Mingshan Unit", was deeply influenced by his interactions with the Third Army. He abolished bandit organizational practices ("huzi" traditions), improved civilian relations, and expanded his force to over 60 fighters, who often operated alongside the Third Army. Eventually, the "Mingshan Unit" evolved into the Northeast Anti-Japanese Allied Independent Division, later reorganized as the Eleventh Army.

The rapid growth of Zhao's Third Army and its alliances with Li, Xie, and Qi alarmed Japanese puppet authorities. From summer 1935, they launched "large-scale punitive campaigns" led by Japanese troops with Manchukuo support. Through forced "hamlet consolidation", they herded peasants into controlled "collective hamlets" to destroy Zhao's base areas. By September 1935, over two-thirds of the Southern Route guerrilla zone lay in ashes. In the Northern Route base, only the Dalianzhuhu plains remained intact; settlements like Dongqingchuan, Laoheidingzi, and Qiupidun were razed. Following summer campaigns, Kwantung Army Commander Minami Jiro personally organized autumn and winter offensives to crush the resistance.

To crush the enemy's "large-scale punitive campaigns" and establish new guerrilla zones and base areas, Zhao Shangzhi led two-fifths of the Third Army's main forces to advance into Yanshou and Fangzheng. Determined to annihilate the Third Army—the backbone of the Anti-Japanese resistance in Hedong—Kwantung Army Commander Minami Jiro deployed elite Japanese troops, primarily the Iwatsuki Division, along with puppet forces in riverside towns like Fangzheng, Yilan, and Tonghe on both banks of the Songhua River, aiming to block Zhao's expedition.

Facing overwhelming encirclement, Zhao remained composed, leveraging the combined strength of the Allied forces. In late July, he convened a Third Army headquarters meeting at Qingshanli in western Boli. The meeting resolved that Zhao would lead Li, Xie, and other Allied units across the Songhua River to Tangyuan, a relatively weakly defended area, to establish a new base.

During the northward march, Zhao met Li Yanlu, commander of the Fourth Army operating in Jidong. Previous friction between the two forces, caused by poor communication, dissolved into mutual respect. United as Communist commanders, they swiftly agreed to joint action: their main forces would flank the enemy rear, crossing the Songhua River near Daluolemi to break the siege.

The plan called for a breakout from Mengjiatun, with the Third Army spearheading the advance and the Fourth Army covering the rear. As dusk fell, Li rushed to the front, halting Zhao's progress. Pointing to a forested hill ahead, Li noted birds scattering—a sign of hidden enemy cavalry. Zhao, blind in his left eye and struggling in the fading light, confirmed the threat through binoculars. Therefore, they led the forces retreated to Xiaoluolemi to seek another crossing.

Though winter had set in, a 20-meter-wide stretch of the Songhua River remained unfrozen, forcing the troops to take cover in the mountains and wait. In a makeshift shelter of branches and straw, Zhao and Li shared stories of their struggles to build resistance forces, pondering Manchuria's future and the nation's fate. Their most pressing concern was the river's freeze—each day delayed heightened the risk for their men, already trapped for over ten days.

Finally, through local villagers, Zhao Shangzhi and Li Yanlu learned that the Zhuti River Estuary—a cold wind corridor—experienced earlier river freezing. That night, they laid wooden planks over the partially frozen section of the Songhua River. Under cover of darkness, the combined forces of the Third and Fourth Armies crossed the river, evading the Japanese puppet encirclement, and entered Tonghe County.

By December, soldiers still lacked proper winter uniforms, clad in tattered layers, with only sentries rotating a single roe deer hide waistwrap for warmth. On December 12, the Third and Fourth Armies outwitted the puppet garrison at Erdaohezi, killing Japanese advisor Motoki, counselor Haruta, instructor Akamatsu, and one puppet officer, while capturing over 60 puppet personnel. They seized 1 light machine gun, 57 rifles and carbines, 3 pistols, 10,000+ rounds of ammunition, and critically, nearly 300 sets of winter uniforms.

Mid-December saw Zhao and Li leading their forces through Tonghe and Yilan into Tangyuan County, trekking across snow-blanketed terrain against biting winds. They were warmly welcomed by Xia Yunjie, commander of the Tangyuan Guerrilla Brigade. Zhao revealed to Xia that a key purpose of their northern campaign was to assist in expanding the Tangyuan guerrillas into the Sixth Army of the People's Revolution.

To expand their forces, securing weapons was paramount. At the Liangzihe Gold Mine, a puppet garrison company—well-armed and led by a Commander Meng—had previously agreed with the Tangyuan Guerrilla Brigade to avoid conflict. Xia Yunjie, weighing the guerrillas' limited strength, accepted Meng's terms (including restricting the garrison to the mining zone and halting anti-resistance arrests) to buy time for growth. For a period, both sides maintained an uneasy truce.

Zhao Shangzhi deemed this garrison a "nail that must be pulled out." Dismissing prior agreements, he declared bluntly: "What camaraderie is there to speak of in revolution? If you can't act, we'll do it ourselves!"

The prudent Li Yanlu concurred.

Following a "courtesy before force" strategy, Xia enlisted Old Shan, a landlord with ties to Meng, to lure him to the Shan family compound.

With crisp efficiency, Li Yanlu first removed the pistol from Commander Meng's holster, then pleaded earnestly for him to lead his troops out to join the resistance. For hours, Li hammered home principled appeals to national duty and anti-Japanese solidarity, yet Meng remained silent. Under the flickering oil lamp, his sallow, cyanotic face glistened with beads of sweat.

Zhao cut to the chase: "Let's be clear: Choose now—will you be an anti-Japanese hero or a coward?"

Meng sighed: "I can't be a hero. My opium habit… I can't endure that hardship."

Zhao retorted: "Then hand your guns to us! We'll suffer gladly to fight the Japanese!" [28]

Cornered, Meng relented. That night, a joint force of the Third Army, Fourth Army, and Tangyuan guerrillas disarmed over 100 puppet garrison troops and 30 mine guards, seizing over 700 rifles, 2 light machine guns, nearly 100 taels of gold, and vast ammunition. At a rally in the mining bureau, they urged workers and defectors to join the resistance, providing travel funds for Meng, his family, and captives to return home.

Zhao Shangzhi and Li Yanlu agreed to transfer all captured weapons, ammunition, and equi p.ment to the Tangyuan Guerrilla Brigade, assigning defected mine workers and surrendered puppet police to Xia Yunjie's command. By February 1, 1936, the Tangyuan guerrillas had rapidly expanded to over 700 fighters, officially reorganizing as the Sixth Army of the Northeast People's Revolutionary Army. To strengthen its leadership,

Zhao reassigned Li Zhaolin—former political director of the Third Army's First Regiment—to serve as the Sixth Army's (acting) Political Director.

Zhao and Li exemplified the Communist commitment to uniting and empowering all anti-Japanese forces. Earlier, on January 26, key resistance leaders—including Zhao Shangzhi, Li Yanlu, Xia Yunjie, Li Zhaolin, Xie Wendong, Li Huatang, and Feng Zhigang—gathered in Jixinggou, Tangyuan County, to establish the Northeast People's Anti-Japanese Allied Forces General Headquarters. On January 28, Zhao was elected Commander-in-Chief, with Li Huatang as Deputy Commander-in-Chief and Li Zhaolin as Chief Political Commissar.

The evolution from the "Northeast Anti-Japanese Allied Army General Headquarters" (established March 1935) to the "Northeast People's Anti-Japanese Allied Forces General Headquarters" marked a pivotal leap, achieved through breakthroughs against the Japanese puppet regime's summer, autumn, and winter large-scale punitive campaigns of 1935. Amid relentless enemy offensives, forces under Zhao Shangzhi's Third Army catalyzed significant growth: Xie Wendong's People's Army and Li Huatang's Self-Defense Corps expanded their ranks. Coordinating with the Fourth Army, Zhao breached enemy defenses across the Tongjiang-Tangyuan frontier, aiding the Tangyuan guerrillas' expansion into the Sixth Army. After the Third Army's Zhuxian County base was destroyed, they established a new stronghold in the vast forests of the Xiaoxing'an Mountains.

The Japanese puppet regime assessed the Allied Headquarters as having "consolidated anti-Manchukuo and anti-Japanese forces, achieving temporary organizational and systemic unity. This transformed the fragmented resistance in northern Manchuria—where Communist-led forces dominated—into a centralized structure under the Allied command." The *Resolution of the Expanded Joint Military-Political Conference of the*

Northeast People's Anti-Japanese Allied Forces further emphasized the efficacy: "This united front has coalesced scattered, even transient forces into a formidable convergence of revolutionary struggle in Northeast China..." [29]

After Tang Yuan and Zhao Shangzhi parted ways, Li Yanlu never met him again. Years later, in his memoirs, he said that Zhao Shangzhi was indeed a lion like figure.

Notes:

【1】Zhou Haifeng. *Biography of Chiang Kai-shek*. Writer Publishing House, 2006, 1st ed., p. 157.

[2] Central Committee for Party Literature Compilation and Research, ed. *Selected Works of Mao Zedong* (Vol. 1). People's Publishing House, December 1993, 1st ed., p. 151.

[3] Central Party Literature Research Office. *Collected Works of Mao Zedong*. People's Publishing House, June 1993, 1st ed., p. 311; qtd. in Zhang Hongjun. *An Epic of Heroism: Mao Zedong and the Northeast Anti-Japanese United Army*. Central Party Literature Press, October 2013, 1st ed., p. 7.

[4] Zhang Hongjun. *An Epic of Heroism: Mao Zedong and the Northeast Anti-Japanese United Army*. Central Party Literature Press, October 2013, 1st ed., p. 11.

[5] Chen Guangxu and Wu Longfan. *Witness to History: Commemorative Essays on Yang Song*. 2002 ed., p. 166; qtd. in Zhang Hongjun. *An Epic of Heroism: Mao Zedong and the Northeast Anti-Japanese United Army*. Central Party Literature Press, October 2013, 1st ed., p. 38.

[6] Qin Xiaoyi. *Preliminary Compilation of Important Historical Materials of the Republic of China: The War of Resistance Against Japan Period* (Introductory Volume III). (Taiwan) Historical Committee of the Kuomintang Central Committee, 1981, pp. 613–637.

[7] Zhang Pengzhou, ed. *Chronicle of Sino-Japanese Relations over Five Decades 1932–1982* (Vol. 1). Culture and Art Publishing House, September 2006, 1st ed., p. 356; qtd. in Weng Youwei and Zhao Wenyuan. *Chiang Kai-shek's Entanglement with Japan*. People's Publishing House, January 2008, 1st ed., p. 132.

[8] Weng Youwei and Zhao Wenyuan. *Chiang Kai-shek's Entanglement with Japan.* People's Publishing House, January 2008, 1st ed., p. 133.

[9] Jiang Kefu. *Military History of Republican China* (Vol. 3, Pt. 1). Chongqing Publishing House, pp. 5–6; qtd. in Wang Shuzeng. *The War of Resistance Against Japan* (Vol. 1). People's Literature Publishing House, June 2015, 1st ed., p. 88.

[10] Mao Zedong. "The Great Significance of the December Ninth Movement." In *Collected Works of Mao Zedong*(Vol. 2), edited by Central Party Literature Research Office. People's Publishing House, December 1993, 1st ed., p. 256.

[11][14] Qin Xiaoyi. *Preliminary Compilation of Important Historical Materials of the Republic of China: The War of Resistance Against Japan Period* (Vol. 6, Pt. 2). (Taiwan) Historical Committee of the Kuomintang Central Committee, pp. 38–47; qtd. in Wang Shuzeng. *The War of Resistance Against Japan* (Vol. 1). People's Literature Publishing House, June 2015, pp. 63–64.

[12] (U.S.) Herbert Bix. *Truth: Emperor Hirohito and the War of Aggression Against China.* Xinhua Publishing House, September 2004, 1st ed., p. 227.

[13] Hu Zhefeng. *Mao Zedong's Military Strategies.* People's Publishing House, May 2001, 1st ed., p. 435.

[15] Central Party Literature Research Office. *Chronicle of Mao Zedong's Life* (1883–1949), rev. ed., Vol. 1. Central Party Literature Press, 2013, p. 460.

[16] Central Archives. *Selected Documents of the Central Committee of the Chinese Communist Party* (Vol. 10). Party School of the CPC Central Committee Publishing House, 1991, p. 733.

[17][18][19] Central Party Literature Research Office and Central Archives, eds. *Selected Important Documents Since the Founding of the Party (1921–1949)* (Vol. 12). Central Party Literature Press, June 2011, 1st ed., pp. 264–265; p. 266; p. 266.

[20] Central Committee for Party Literature Compilation and Research, ed. *Selected Works of Mao Zedong* (Vol. 3). People's Publishing House, June 1991, 2nd ed., p. 973.

[21] Puppet Manchukuo Military Affairs Department Military Investigation Division, ed. *Study on the Manchurian Communist Bandits*, p. 34; qtd. in Zhao Junqing. *Biography of Yang Jingyu.* Heilongjiang People's Publishing House, August 2015, 1st ed., p. 230.

[22] Wang Chuansheng and Hu Weiren. *Snowstorms on Changbai Mountain: Memoirs of Wang Chuansheng*. Jilin Education Publishing House, 1992, p. 33; Zhao Junqing. Biography of Yang Jingyu. Heilongjiang People's Publishing House, August 2015, rev. ed., p. 217.

[23][24] Central Archives; Liaoning Provincial Archives; Jilin Provincial Archives; Heilongjiang Provincial Archives, eds. *Compilation of Revolutionary Historical Documents in Northeast China* (Series A47), pp. 89, 95; qtd. in Zhao Junqing. *Biography of Yang Jingyu*. Heilongjiang People's Publishing House, August 2015, rev. ed., pp. 224, 261.

[25] Zhao Junqing. *Biography of Yang Jingyu*. Heilongjiang People's Publishing House, August 2015, rev. ed., p. 226.

[26][27] Puppet Manchukuo Military Affairs Department. Research on Manchurian Communist Bandits: Activities of the Zhuxian Central County Committee and the Third Army; qtd. in Zhao Junqing. Biography of Zhao Shangzhi. Heilongjiang People's Publishing House, August 2015, rev. ed., pp. 169, 170.

[28] Zhao Junqing. *Biography of Zhao Shangzhi*. Heilongjiang People's Publishing House, August 2005, rev. ed., pp. 193–194.

[29] *Expanded Joint Conference of the Northeast People's Anti-Japanese Allied Forces* (January 25, 1936). In Central Archives; Liaoning Provincial Archives; Jilin Provincial Archives; Heilongjiang Provincial Archives, eds. *Compilation of Revolutionary Historical Documents in Northeast China* (Series A47), pp. 89, 408; qtd. in Zhao Junqing. *Biography of Zhao Shangzhi*. Heilongjiang People's Publishing House, August 2015, rev. ed., p. 196

Chapter 13

A Paragon of Female: Virtue and Excellence

41. "Collective Hamlets" is the circle of people

During the 14-year resistance in Northeast China, no Japanese puppet policy proved more devastating to the Anti-Japanese Allied Forces than the "Collective Hamlets"—a sinister strategy of forcibly relocating villages into controlled settlements, imposing collective responsibility systems, and creating "civilians-guerrilla separation zones" to starve the resistance. This malicious policy severed the vital bond between the guerrillas (the "fish") and the people (the "water"), pushing the Allied Forces toward collapse. The architect of this atrocity was Kuniaki Koiso.

Kuniaki Koiso (1880–1950), a Japanese Imperial Army general and the 41st Prime Minister, hailed as a "versatile leader" in Japan, was sentenced to life imprisonment post-war and died in prison.

In August 1932, as Lieutenant General Chief of Staff of the Kwantung Army and Director of Intelligence, Koiso prioritized "security-first governance" to stabilize Japanese control over Manchuria. Unlike brute-force militarists, Koiso combined military suppression, pacification tactics, and political manipulation—a triad that birthed the "collective hamlets".

The ruthless "Collective Hamlets" scheme was proposed by two Japanese officials. In 1932, Araya Senji, the puppet advisor of Panshi County, and Takoi Motoyoshi, the puppet advisor of Emu County, put forward the plan to establish "collective hamlets." It was immediately approved by Koiso Kuniaki and implemented that same year in Panshi County, where Yang Jingyu's South Manchuria Guerrilla Unit operated. By the following year, it had expanded to Emu, Dunhua, Huadian, and other counties. In December of the same year, the puppet Ministry of Civil Affairs issued *Directive No. 969, Order on the Establishment of Collective Hamlets*, leading to the widespread enforcement of the policy across Northeast China.

The so-called "Collective Hamlets" involved forcibly relocating scattered residents from plains and mountains into consolidated settlements. Each hamlet housed "80 to 100 households" for easier control and resource extraction. Designed as "400-meter-perimeter squares or rectangles", they were strategically placed along "key supply routes or guerrilla-infested areas". Construction prioritized "barbed wire, earthen walls, and watchtowers" before public buildings, housing, or facilities. [1]

Within these hamlets, a collective responsibility system (Baojia Lianzuo) was enforced. Residents faced strict surveillance: Four guarded gates controlled entry or exit. Farming or firewood collection required registration and item inspections to prevent supplies reaching "bandits". Gates locked at sunset; latecomers risked interrogation as "collaborators". This system was euphemized as "fortress-concentration camps" by authorities, while locals called them "enclosed pens" (Weizi) or "human corrals" (Renjuan).

Structural Specifications: Walls: 10 feet high, 6 feet wide at the base, tapering to 2.5 feet at the top, topped with barbed wire. Outer trenches: 14 feet wide (top), 3 feet wide (base), 10 feet deep, with drainage ditches. All labor was extracted from relocated farmers, while Japanese and puppet officials supervised without lifting a finger. Housing for residents was built last.

The Japanese puppet authorities mandated that "Collective Hamlets" be constructed "preferably from mid-September to mid-November"—a schedule designed to prioritize Japanese agricultural operations over local farming. Once the walls, trenches, and watchtowers were completed, farmers were forced to hastily assemble makeshift A-frame shelters with wooden poles and straw for their own housing. The puppet Ministry of Public Security's *Compilation of Regional Public Security Reports* admitted:

> "Roofs were mostly bark and straw. Walls gaped with holes, offering no warmth. With no proper clothing, they huddled around fires. It's a wonder no one fell ill… You could see clouds through the roofs. Their suffering in this cold is unimaginable." [2]

Another architect who refined the "Collective Hamlets" to brutal perfection was Yasuji Okamura. As Major General Deputy Chief of Staff under Koiso's Kwantung Army command, Okamura—a core member of the Baden-Baden Group's "Three Crows" and a warlord notorious for cruelty—immediately enacted draconian "laws" like *the Provisional Bandit Punishment Act*, codifying policies that institutionalized the hamlet system. Later, as Commander-in-Chief of the North China Area Army, he exported Manchuria's barbaric experiments to northern China, implementing the "Three Alls" (Kill All, Burn All, Loot All) and "scorched-earth" policies.

Tragically, after Japan's surrender, Chiang Kai-shek secretly hired Okamura as a military advisor to strategize attacks against Communist forces. In early 1949, under public outrage, Chiang staged a sham trial that acquitted Okamura. Grateful, Okamura later accepted Chiang's 1950 invitation to serve as a senior instructor at Taiwan's "Revolutionary Practice Institute." [3]

The atrocities committed by Kuniaki Koiso and Yasuji Okamura through the "collective hamlets" inflicted catastrophic suffering on Northeast China's people. According to *the Japanese-authored History of Police in Manchukuo* (Volume 1), 12,565 defensive collective hamlets were established from the puppet state of Manchukuo's founding (1932) to the end of 1938.

At the time, mountain villages in the Northeast typically comprised a few to a dozen households, with 20–30 considered large. Yet each "Collective Hamlet" forcibly consolidated 80–100 households, meaning over 10 natural villages were destroyed per hamlet. Within years, conservative estimates indicate over 100,000 natural villages were obliterated.

The first step in establishing "Collective Hamlets" was burning houses. Yang Jingyu's early revolutionary base at Xianren Cave was burned down three times successively. Zhao Shangzhi's Zhuhe Base Area, considered an even more "Red" territory, suffered fiercer flames that left most village houses as empty shells. Smoke signals rose across the land amidst scorched earth. The Japanese not only burned houses but also felled trees and crops. All vegetation including trees and tall-stalked crops within 200 meters on either side of railway lines and national highways were cleared. This was implemented to prevent anti-Japanese guerrilla forces from launching surprise attacks from concealment provided by the tall crops.

Not all villages were burned during the forced relocation into "Collective Hamlets". Around 1934, the Japanese puppet regime carried out "border clearance operations" within 5 kilometers of China's borders, expelling locals to non-border regions. Those who resisted were accused of colluding with the Soviet Union. Unlike standard hamlet construction, these operations spared houses, wells, trees, and crops—resources reserved for the Japanese Pioneer Corps (Kaitakudan)—to enable Japanese settlers to occupy homes and land without payment upon arrival.

Why did Koiso and Okamura relentlessly push the hamlet system? Puppet authorities claimed it allowed Chinese to "live joyfully under the benevolent Kingly Way policy." Yet Anti-Japanese Allied Forces saw through the ruse: the hamlets aimed to sever the fish-water bond between civilians and guerrillas, starving resistance fighters of shelter, food, and intelligence to crush them without battle.

When reflecting on the immense suffering inflicted by the "Collective Hamlets" on Northeast China's people and the Anti-Japanese Allied Forces, history must document not only Koiso and Okamura but also Araya Chikatsugu and Takui   Motoyoshi—the   puppet sanjikan (advisors) who originated the policy.

As for civilian resistance: "No golden or silver nest compares to one's own earthen home." Few willingly entered these "human corrals". When initial burnings failed to force compliance, the Japanese resorted to mass killings. Villages linked to resistance faced dual horrors: hamlet construction preceded by "massacre villages", as seen in Laobeigou in southern Shulan County, Jilin Province.

Laohei Gully stretches 40 kilometers in length, with the Hulan River flowing through its valley. At its widest point, it spans 4 kilometers. Situated between Wuchang and Jiaohe counties, the gully is flanked by the undulating branches of the Zhangguangcai Mountain Range. This land of ancient trees towering to the sky, nestled between mountains and rivers, has long been a divinely bestowed sanctuary for human survival and prosperity.

In the spring of 1935, this earthly paradise was instantly transformed into a living hell. The harbinger of this catastrophe was the Nara Regiment – the 38th Regiment of the 16th Division of the Japanese Kwantung Army, a unit notorious for its heinous atrocities. While history primarily remembers this military force for its participation in the 1937 Nanjing Massacre, few are aware that two years prior to that infamy, they had already brutally slaughtered inhabitants in Laohēi Gully, northeastern China. This atrocity was locally known as "Sha Dagou" (The Great Gully Massacre) by the people of Manchuria.

The specific execution of "Sha Dagou" was carried out by 600 heavily armed Japanese soldiers from the 3rd Battalion of the 38th Regiment. This was a coordinated air-ground operation. Reconnaissance planes circled overhead, dropping leaflets and supplies, indicating the action was not solely the battalion's initiative. On April 22, Japanese troops initially searched for "bandits" but found none. A week later, on April 27, they turned their weapons on unarmed civilians. It was spring planting season, and men were working in the fields. The Japanese slaughtered indiscriminately—shooting those at a distance and bayoneting those nearby. Farmers, unfamiliar with steel-helmeted soldiers, fled in panic after witnessing three deaths. Those who escaped into the mountains survived, while villagers who ran toward their homes faced secondary attacks of gunfire and blades.

At Huaquliudingzi, Li Xianting's wife was nursing her child on the kang (heated bed) when Japanese soldiers barged in. She shielded her two-year-old behind her. The soldiers killed the mother, then bayoneted the child through the back and chest, impaling the toddler against an earthen wall. As the child writhed in agony, the soldiers laughed. Huaquliudingzi, located at the southern entrance of Laohei Gully, became a slaughter site. Captured civilians were forced to dig seven mass graves near a birch forest, each holding about 10 victims. The Li Kuijiang family lost nine of eleven members, all buried in one pit.

Near Qingdingzi Village on the northern bank of the Hulan River, a crescent-shaped lake became the largest massacre site. Over three days from

April 29 to May 1, more than 300 people were slaughtered here. On the first day, Japanese soldiers forced civilians to kneel at the lake's edge, machine-gunned them, and pushed the bodies into the water. The second day saw a different method: villagers were bound with poles thrust between their arms—about twenty people per pole—before being executed in succession by machine gun.

Jiang Tongbin, a rare survivor, witnessed another form of atrocity. At noon on the 30th, he was tied to a tree by the crescent lake. Japanese soldiers stripped his upper garment to expose his chest, then stepped back as screams filled the air. Luckily, fate intervened when a young-looking soldier botched the killing: the first bayonet thrust struck Jiang's ribs; the second glanced off his heavily patched cotton-padded jacket, leaving a long gash across his abdomen; the third pierced his neck... Subsequent stabs missed vital organs but left him bloodied. Mistaking him for dead, the soldiers departed. [4]

The Laobeigou Massacre was but one of countless atrocities committed by the Japanese military against civilians in Northeast China. On July 15, 1936 (the 27th day of the fifth lunar month), Captain Hachiro Nakayama, commander of the Kwantung Army garrison in Liuhe County, led troops into Baijiabaozi—a village labeled a "bandit zone"—and slaughtered every person in sight. All 368 villagers were bound together and marched to the foot of a mountain, where they were executed en masse amid desperate screams. Japanese forces then conscripted laborers to bury the bodies in nine mass graves and razed every home in Baijiabaozi, leaving no roof tile intact. [5]

That autumn, Japanese troops stormed Chaoyangmen in Hongmiaozi, Xinggao County. Yang Jingyu organized civilians to evacuate to the mountains. When some urged him to attack the Japanese troops gathered in a courtyard—a vulnerable target—Yang refused, explaining: "If we fight and withdraw, the civilians will suffer retaliation". Thereafter, the First Army even ceased painting slogans on village walls to avoid branding areas as "bandit zones" and triggering further massacres.

In mid-January 1939, Feng Zhigang, a commander of the Anti-Japanese forces, ambushed Japanese puppet troops at Tianjiachuankou in Dedao County. The battle resulted in the death of Shunichi Meguro, a Japanese military police officer overseeing puppet forces, and the capture of 25 puppet police officers. Prior to the attack, Feng strategically ordered the village chief to deliberately delay reporting the troops' arrival to the puppet police station—a move to prove the village was not "colluding with bandits".

Faced with Japanese atrocities that escalated from "family extermination"to "village annihilation"—acts of inhuman slaughter—Communist forces exhausted every possible strategy to protect civilians. However, the inherent contradiction between Japan's imperial ambition to conquer China and its crippling shortages of population, resources, and military capacity transformed its invasion forces into the most barbaric and bloodthirsty killing machine in the world. Massacres became habitual, exemplified by the treacherous slaughter of surrendered troops, with methods like "filling the rivers" —drowning victims en masse—epitomizing their savagery.

To counter the relentless resistance, Japanese puppet authorities combined punitive campaigns with surrender policies, coercing family members to plead with guerrillas in the mountains to return home. By late 1936, around 400 individuals in Huanren County alone had surrendered—mostly remnants of the Self-Defense Army and mountain forest units, alongside a small number of wavering fighters from the First Army.

Those who surrendered and disarmed were required to report to the County Police Department to provide fingerprints and have three indelible ink marks tattooed on their left wrist or the web of their hand. This was done by pricking the skin three times with bundled needles and rubbing ink into the wounds—a ritual of "submission" that permitted them to return home while awaiting notification to collect their "certificates": the Good Citizen Card.

On February 21, 1937 (the 11th day of the first lunar month), local police stations notified individuals to claim their certificates. The next day, February 22, these individuals were transported to Huanren County town and housed at the police training center and several inns. On February 23, over 300 people lined up to enter the Japanese garrison compound. When a name was called, the person would enter a building to "receive their certificate". Instead, each was immediately pinned down, bound, gagged, and dragged out the back door before being tossed with a thud into trucks waiting in the rear courtyard. Once loaded, the trucks departed straight for the West River.

A one-kilometer area along the riverbank had already been cordoned off. At the river's deepest section, Japanese soldiers had carved an ice hole the size of three houses. The bound captives endured the jolting ride to this site.

Overseeing the massacre at the river was Japanese military police captain Sugimori Hei, while garrison commander Noda, who had orchestrated the arrests and loading, arrived with the final truck. Victims were hurled from the trucks like livestock. Some, already weakened by suffocation and the brutal journey, were dragged or prodded with bayonets toward the ice hole by Japanese soldiers and puppet police. The slow current beneath the thick ice caused bodies to resurface after being pushed in, prompting the Japanese to use long wooden poles to force the submerged victims deeper. This atrocity, documented in numerous records, became known as the "West River Massacre".

Among the over 300 people subjected to the "filling the rivers" massacre, only one child escaped. That day, seven boys around ten years old were spared binding because their fathers or brothers were absent, forcing them to "represent" their families. Terrified, all but one froze in place. As Japanese soldiers and puppet police fixated on the ice holes, the boy bolted toward willow thickets along the riverbank. Guards fired but missed, and a search failed to locate him.

While the massacre unfolded in the county seat, townships began rounding up those who had not reported to collect "certificates". Guaimozi Township arrested 12 people, drowning them in the Fu'er River on the 15th day of the lunar New Year. Erhulai Township detained 11, Shajianzi Township seized 19, and others arrested varying numbers. Where no rivers were available, victims were summarily executed.

To call Japanese troops "beastly" is no exaggeration—their atrocities breached all human limits.

Suddenly, the squad leader thrust his left hand deep into the victim's ribs, twisting and probing. Moments later, he withdrew a dark, bloody mass—whether flesh or clotted blood was unclear—and sliced it free with his blade. It was a gallbladder, still pulsing. [6]

I witnessed this act during the massacre. Later, I joined Sergeant Abe Saburō in cutting open five corpses to extract their livers and gallbladders. When questioned about the purpose of harvesting human gallbladders, he explained that the Japanese held a superstitious belief that they could cure lung diseases. This led to widespread demand among Japanese soldiers, prompting our decision to collect them. The five of us—all Japanese— divided the organs, each taking one. [7]

Two prisoners, deemed "staunchly anti-Japanese," were beheaded by Ishida. He charred their heads, claiming brain matter could be medicated. He sent one to me in Harbin, which I consumed. [8]

Following the orders of Captain Sato, I, along with three patrolmen, took the victims to the dense forests of Dongtang and executed them by gunfire. Simultaneously, I used a dagger while the other patrolmen employed Japanese swords to slit open the victims' abdomens, extract their livers for medicinal use, and bury the bodies on-site. After bringing the livers home, I received a letter from Japan informing me that my younger sister had contracted peritonitis. I ground the livers into powder, mailed it to Japan, and had her consume it. [9]

In the global village, even most animals refrain from cannibalism. Those that do are driven by primal hunger, as they are mindless beasts. The Japanese have long proclaimed themselves the world's most civilized "nation of etiquette and propriety"—what bitter irony this is! Among the many countries invaded by Japan during World War II, a shared perception emerged: no force matched the savagery of the Japanese military. Even Indonesia, often regarded as pro-Japan, explicitly states in its high school textbooks: "Of all nations that occupied our country, Japan was the most brutal". [10] The Chinese share this sentiment. This, too, is one of the fundamental reasons why the Chinese resisted with blood and sacrifice.

42. The power and wisdom in a suicide note

In the autumn-winter transition of 1935, Zhao Shangzhi led the main force of the Third Army from their base in Zhuxian County on an expedition to Yanshou and Fangzheng, advancing further into Tangyuan. He left the Second and Third Regiments in areas north and south of the Zhuxian railway to counter Japanese puppet forces during their "large-scale punitive campaigns". The Second Regiment, commanded by Wang Huitong (also written as Wang Hui) and political director Zhao Yiman, operated between northern Zhuxian, Yanshou, Binxian, and Acheng, sustaining guerrilla warfare in old strongholds. During maneuvers, the regiment was once trapped in dense forests, cut off from supplies, surviving on hunted game. On November 14, Wang and Zhao led over 50 troops to Anshantun in Daobei's Fifth District, planning to reunite with the main force in Yanshou.

As the saying went: "A great nation like China was brought to ruin by traitors devoid of national conscience." No sooner had the troops settled than Zhu Jingcai, a collaborator, reported their location to Japanese puppet forces stationed at Wujimi.

On the morning of the 15th, over 300 Japanese puppet troops surrounded the Second Regiment. Wang Huitong directed his men to seize advantageous terrain, fighting a fierce six-hour battle. Over a dozen soldiers died; Wang, severely wounded, was captured and later executed. Zhao Yiman sustained a gunshot to her left wrist during the breakout. Only over 10 soldiers escaped the encirclement, with the rest martyred. The enemy also suffered heavy losses: the regiment killed or wounded Captain Kiyoichi Furuya (machine gun unit leader of the Yokoyama detachment), squad leader Serizawa, and some 30 others.

In the chaotic retreat, Zhao Yiman regrouped with wounded veteran Lao Yu, 16-year-old women's association member Yang Guilan, and courier Liu Fusheng. They supported one another to a makeshift shelter in Houlin Township's Xibeigou to recuperate.

Once again, traitorous collaborators sabotaged things. On November 22, the collaborators Lian Jiang and Mi Zhenwen discovered Zhao Yiman and others, and immediately informed Chief Japanese Instructor Keisuke Tōma, a police sergeant, and Zhang Fuxing, captain of the puppet police. Over 30 puppet police officers surrounded the small shack. In the fierce battle, courier

Liu Fusheng and soldier Lao Yu were killed. Zhao Yiman's left leg was severely wounded by a "Type 79" rifle shot, causing blood to gush out. She fell unconscious, hovering near death.

Da Ye Taizhi, head of the Foreign Affairs Unit in the Special Affairs Section of the Puppet Binjiang Provincial Police Department, was the primary culprit responsible for torturing Zhao Yiman. It was his two confessions, written during his reformation as a war criminal, that revealed— from a different perspective—the unwavering faith of a Communist Party member and the unyielding courage of an Anti-Japanese United Army warrior.

The two confessions by Da Ye Taizhi were written eight years apart. The first, dated November 10, 1954, only vaguely recounts how Zhao Yiman, despite two severe injuries, resisted his brutal torture. Having gained nothing, Da Ye ultimately sent her to Harbin:

> "Zhao Yiman's wrist was pierced by a bullet, and her thigh was also
> shot. She was on the brink of death... I felt deeply gratified to have captured
> such an extraordinary figure. While she was still defiant, I attempted to
> extract key information by squeezing her bullet wound with my hands or
> prodding it with a whip. For nearly two hours, I interrogated her about
> Communist Party organizations and connections. But from her obstinate
> demeanor, I concluded it would be impossible to extract anything..." [11]

Despite her "brink of death" state, Da Ye subjected her to "nearly two hours of interrogation." His 1954 confession admitted only to "squeezing and whipping" her wrist wound. It omitted the specific torture tools used during those two hours, as well as Zhao Yiman's "defiant words" or why he deemed it "impossible to extract anything."

After eight years of ideological reform, by 1962, Da Ye—kneeling in tears, repeatedly begging for "the hero in his heart" Zhao Yiman to "forgive his soul"—penned another confession. This account revealed, in harrowing detail, Zhao Yiman's extraordinary resilience and heroism 26 years prior, a story that moves readers to tears:

"This woman wore a black cotton coat, her lower body soaked in blood. Her face rested against the carriage platform, with an 18- or 19-year-old girl tending to her. The wounded woman's hair was disheveled, her pant legs utterly saturated with blood that continued to seep out."

Fearing she might die before interrogation, depriving us of potential intelligence, I rushed to her side and barked, "Get up!" She raised her head calmly, her gaze so piercing that I instinctively stepped back. I ordered Enma Shigetaro to find a suitable interrogation site. After consulting with the county office's interpreter, Guard Zhan, they chose a sorghum stack in the fodder shed. During questioning, she identified herself as Zhao Yiman, 27, a member of the Women's Anti-Japanese Association, from a wealthy family, and educated to the highest standard for Chinese women. She answered these questions with composure and clarity.

When asked about Zhao Shangzhi's forces, she replied: "I know nothing of the Anti-Japanese Allied Army."

Pressed on Communist Party ties, she denied any affiliation. "Why engage in resistance?" I demanded. Her voice sharpened, transforming her answer into an indictment: "I am Chinese. Japan's atrocities since invading cannot be captured in words. If you were Chinese, how would you feel about what your army has done in Zhuxian? Must we explain why we resist? For us, resistance is survival. You Japanese—honey-mouthed but dagger-hearted!" She dismantled Japanese propaganda—claims of "protecting China from foreign aggression" and "Japan-Manchukuo unity as brother nations"—with methodical fury. Her passion seemed superhuman for someone so gravely wounded. Though enraged, her arguments were lucid and persuasive. As the interpreter relayed her words, Zhao stared intently at his lips, as if ensuring no nuance was lost. Once translated, she resumed her torrent of condemnation—a master orator. Unwittingly, I had become her audience.

I prodded Zhao Yiman's wound again with a whip. Her body shuddered, and her face twisted into a pained yet furious expression. At that moment, the young girl beside her leapt up to shield her. I ordered a nearby officer to drag the girl away. "You seem angry," I sneered. "I'm not here to listen to your lectures. Whether you speak or not, I'll make you talk. Start by confessing your Communist Party identity!" Under this threat, she calmly replied, "I have no Communist identity. Forcing someone to confess to things they know nothing of is nothing but tyranny. If you claim I'm a Communist, show me the proof!" She admitted only to working with women's organizations and refused to say more. When I lashed her hands with the whip, she fell silent. [12]

Reading this historical account, readers will undoubtedly experience a profound moral awakening from their own perspectives. It further clarifies what it truly means to embody the unyielding resolve and indomitable national spirit of a Communist Party member—steadfast in righteousness and unbroken by cruelty.

Zhao Yiman, already frail, had been recuperating at the home of "Mother Lü" Liang Shulin in Houlin Village, Zhuhe, part of the Anti-Japanese United Army's territory. She suffered from pulmonary tuberculosis, contracted during her studies in the Soviet Union. Yet at Zhuhe, a frontline of resistance against Japan, she threw herself into organizing local anti-Japanese efforts despite her worsening illness, even as a carbuncle festered on the back of her neck.

One day, noticing a feverish flush on Zhao Yiman's gaunt face, Mother Lü realized she was burning with fever. She touched Zhao's forehead—burning hot—and her heart ached. Hoping to find eggs to nourish her, she could only manage to gather a few potatoes. She cooked them into a large bowl of soup and offered it to Zhao, saying: "Let's treat these potatoes as ginseng to nourish your body."

Tuberculosis patients desperately need nutrients to heal. During her time with Mother Lü in Houlin Village, Zhao Yiman at least had regular meals. But soon after rejoining her guerrilla unit, even a single proper meal became a rarity.

In the Northeast Martyrs' Memorial Hall, there is a coarse porcelain bowl inscribed with the character "Fu" (meaning "fortune"). It was borrowed from a local villager named Wen Xiliang during a meal in Houlin Village, given to Zhao Yiman by a messenger. When a full bowl of sorghum rice was placed before her, Zhao knew it had come from the soldiers' meager "sick rations"—the unit had long run out of grain, surviving on wild herbs and acorns. Without drawing attention, she poured the rice back into the pot and ladled herself half a bowl of wild vegetable porridge. The cook, Old Li, watched silently, his eyes brimming with tears.

It should be noted that the author has not personally verified the existence of the coarse porcelain bowl at the museum exhibition, nor confirmed whether this story was a fictionalized account based on the Anti-Japanese Allied Forces' hardships. In 1981, Lesson 9 in the fifth volume of the primary school Chinese textbook, titled *A Coarse Porcelain Bowl*, recounted this episode. What remains certain is that when Zhao Yiman joined the troops despite her illness, they were enduring extreme deprivation—struggling even to secure meals.

Imagine the resilience required for a frail, gravely ill woman—accustomed to the warm, humid climate of Sichuan (the land of abundance)—to survive each day in the freezing northern wilderness, with scant food, no medicine, and relentless fever and coughing.

Even more harrowing: After her capture, Japanese forces transported her by oxcart over rugged mountain paths to Zhuxian County, deliberately leaving her two wounds untreated to bleed freely, aiming to break her will. At the puppet police station, interrogators tortured her wrist injury—not just squeezing it but jabbing it with horsewhips—to extract confessions.

On July 25, 1954, survivor Yang Guilan testified in her affidavit: "Japanese puppet police subjected Zhao Yiman, Zhou Boxue (a local official captured with her), and me to daily beatings, forced water ingestion, leg-pressing torture, and other abuses. By late October (lunar calendar), Zhao and Zhou were transferred to Harbin."

At the Harbin Police Bureau's underground detention center, Zhao endured even more systematic and brutal interrogations—yet yielded nothing. With her festering gunshot wound in her thigh, she was transferred to a municipal hospital under the alias "Wang Shi" to keep her alive for further exploitation.

Today, we have no way to fully ascertain what specific tortures the brutal Japanese-puppet regime inflicted upon Zhao Yiman over the course of eight months—how many times, in what settings, or by what methods. Historical records indicate that Japanese military police alternately poured scalding chili water and cold gasoline down her throat and nostrils, yet she never uttered a single groan. To prevent her from losing consciousness during torture, which would diminish its effectiveness, they doused her with cold water, then used chemical fumes, and repeatedly injected her with large doses of stimulants and camphor tinctures. Once revived and lucid, the torture resumed.

From *the Puppet Binjiang Provincial Police Department's Report on Zhao Yiman*, we learn that Han Yongyi, a 16-year-old probationary nurse at Harbin Municipal Hospital, had previously "read about Zhao Yiman in the *Da Bei Xin Bao* and believed her to be a rare heroine." The secret agents, considering her young age, paid her little attention.

As Zhao Yiman's wounds gradually healed, a gentle smile flickered in Han Yongyi's eyes. Yet to her fury, the secret agents would drag Zhao off her sickbed at the slightest pretext to interrogate and kick her, trapping her injuries in a vicious cycle of bleeding and partial recovery—agonizing yet never fatal. Filled with reverence, Han resolved to snatch her hero from the tiger's jaws.

The report reveals that even in prison, with her body mutilated, bones exposed, and flesh charred in multiple places, Zhao Yiman never ceased fighting. As long as she breathed, she continued to propagate Communist ideals and the cause of anti-Manchukuo resistance and national salvation. Her words led Han Yongyi to recognize the true nature of the puppet regime: "They shared a common hatred for the world's evils."

Though the report is riddled with vilifying language, we can still discern Zhao Yiman's relentless efforts to awaken the national conscience of the young puppet-police guard Dong Xianxun—urging him to resist the enemy—as well as her awe-inspiring experience and prowess in clandestine operations.

Learning of Dong Xianxun's literary interests, Zhao Yiman wrote on medicine wrappers and scraps of paper about the atrocities she witnessed Japanese troops commit in Fengtian during the Manchurian Incident (1931), the sinister motives behind establishing Manchukuo, the plight of enslaved Chinese, and the imperative to overthrow Japanese imperialism and the puppet state to liberate the people. Using accessible, engaging fiction, she articulated the duty of every Chinese citizen. Zhao, a gifted writer, infused her accounts of Japanese puppet brutality with such visceral truth that any reader of conscience would seethe with hatred and resolve to resist. Dong, a principled young man, soon embraced her cause, becoming a committed anti-Japanese activist. A puppet police report later sourly noted that Zhao had "corrupted the officer in just 20 days."

old her two gold rings and overcoats, raising 60 yuan. Dong arranged a sedan chair and, on June 28 (a quiet Sunday evening at the hospital), enlisted a White Russian driver to transport the chair and five carriers to Wenmiao Temple in Nangang. After smuggling Zhao out, they rendezvoused at the temple and fled toward Acheng—a base for Zhao Shangzhi's forces—with Han carrying medical supplies. In the countryside, they hired a horse-drawn cart.

The puppet police discovered Zhao's escape during the June 29 shift change. Like a swarm of enraged hornets, they traced the White Russian driver, intercepting her near Lijiatun, Acheng, at 5 a.m. on June 30. In a moment of tragic calm, Zhao instinctively reached for a nonexistent pistol at her waist. Her serene, pale face broke into a smile—composed yet defiant.

A puppet Binjiang Provincial Police report reveals Zhao's unyielding resolve: hospitalized with severe injuries before the escape, she feared post-discharge execution or life imprisonment would doom her lifelong mission to "destroy Japanese imperialism and Manchukuo." Thus, she vowed to "overcome all odds, rejoin Zhao Shangzhi, and fight as a soldier." [13]

Facing the imminent onslaught of the enemy, Zhao Yiman calmly instructed her companions: "Stay calm! Remember your testimony—say I paid you to help me escape. None of this concerns you."

Though Dong Xianxun and Han Yongyi were understandably nervous, Zhao's composure steadied them. From the moment they had tied their fates to hers, they had steeled themselves for this.

These two passionate youths, driven by justice and patriotism, were neither Communist Party members nor Anti-Japanese United Army soldiers. Yet they risked their lives to save the heroic resistance fighter they revered.

Like the countless Anti-Japanese fighters who perished in the snow—slain, frozen, starved, or claimed by disease—they deserve our deepest respect and remembrance. Regrettably, history has obscured their inner struggles during Zhao Yiman's rescue. Only fragments survive in enemy archives, yet even these glimpses move us profoundly.

The enemy subjected Han Yongyi and Dong Xianxun to brutal torture: electric shocks, suspension from ceilings, searing their faces and mouths with burning charcoal. Frantic interrogations demanded why they aided Zhao's escape. Dong Xianxun, tortured beyond endurance, died in prison without uttering a word—a tragic loss. Han Yongyi, bearing a boyish name, defiantly declared her "deep-rooted anti-Japanese convictions" during her trial:

> "Though I reside in Manchukuo, walk its streets, ride its vehicles, use its currency, and consume its produce—these are mere necessities of survival. The blood flowing through my veins is that of the Republic of China. I yearn for the day when our resistance expands, drives the Japanese from the Northeast, and raises the flag of the Republic of China once more." [14]

Han Yongyi, the 16-year-old girl who earned widespread admiration, saw her charges reduced from "political criminal" to "aiding a fugitive" through relentless advocacy. She was sentenced to four months imprisonment, but enemy torture left her with pleurisy, empyema, and other ailments. She passed away before the founding of New China.

Zhao Yiman, a severely wounded and frail woman, came agonizingly close to escaping the demonic lair with the aid of these two youths—humiliating and ridiculing the seemingly invincible 'state' machine that delusionally sought to dominate every inch of human flesh. Her defiance struck a profound psychological blow against the Japanese-puppet regime, compelling them to issue three self-criticisms in their report. One of these admissions reluctantly acknowledged: "Our propaganda efforts to eradicate communist and anti-Japanese ideologies under the guise of 'benevolent rule' have been overly theoretical and perfunctory. Immediate reform is imperative."

War is not merely a contest of material strength but a battle of spiritual resolve—a truth proven by countless historical episodes, from the War of Resistance against Japan to the Liberation War and the Korean War. In her struggle against Japanese invaders like Ōno Yasuji, Communist fighter Zhao Yiman, despite her broken body, triumphed over the ruthless machinery of imperialist violence.

The enemy's torture could not shatter Zhao's unyielding faith, for the "bones" of her convictions were indestructible, her spiritual fortitude invincible. In this clash of wills, the Japanese were utterly defeated: their fury reduced to destroying a frail woman's flesh. Who was the true warrior? Zhao Yiman!

This is the priceless legacy left by the Anti-Japanese Allied Forces heroine and Communist Party member—an unbreakable national spirit that chooses death over surrender.

On August 2, 1936, Japanese puppet forces returned Zhao to Zhuxian County, where she had once fought, aiming to terrorize the people of Communist strongholds with her execution. Unshaken, Zhao declared: "To die for resisting Japan is my honor." Yet she was also a woman of flesh and blood—a mother and wife. In her final hours, her deepest regret was surely the six-year separation from her seven-year-old son and the husband she had known for mere months before parting for the revolution. En route to her execution, she requested pen and paper, writing two farewell letters:

To My Beloved Ning'er:

My greatest regret is failing to fulfill my duty as your mother.

By steadfastly resisting the puppet Manchukuo regime and Japanese imperialism, I now face martyrdom.

We will never meet again in this life. Oh, Ning'er! Grow quickly, and comfort your mother in the afterlife! My dearest child—I need no words to teach you; my actions will be your lesson.

When you are grown, never forget: your mother died for her country.

August 2, 1936
Your mother, Zhao Yiman
(Written in the prison cart)

162 characters. Seven mentions of "mother." Four exclamation marks. The heartrending "Oh, Ning'er!" and "My child!"As I transcribe these words, tears blur my vision.

The second farewell letter, more to her husband Chen Dabang than her child, reads:

To My Poor, Beloved Child:

Mother came to Northeast China seeking work. Who could foresee such a tragic end?

My death matters little, but my heart breaks for you—deprived of a mother's guidance. After I am gone, you must continue my struggle, grow strong, and comfort me in the netherworld! Your father died here in the Northeast, and now I follow. Oh, my child—my poor, dear child!

I have no more words. Study well—this is your mother's final hope.

August 2, 1936
Your Mother on the Brink of Death [15]

This letter—nine "mothers," six "children"—is another testament to unbearable sacrifice.

Shackled and mutilated, Zhao Yiman fell on the soil of Zhuxian County where she once fought. The enemy obliterated her 31-year-old life but could not extinguish her spirit, which endured to inspire countless others to strike back.

Faith, above all, meant believing in the revolution's inevitable victory. Many faltered or betrayed the cause, doubting the Communists' ability to triumph against overwhelming odds—a recurring tragedy in the Anti-Japanese Allied Forces.

A careful reader might note: in both letters, Li Kuntai (her birth name) signed as Zhao Yiman, a necessary deception. Could her son Ning'er ever know "Zhao Yiman" was his mother? For decades after liberation, even as the film *Zhao Yiman* screened nationwide, he remained unaware.

Yet Zhao Yiman held unshakable faith: her conviction stemmed from the bedrock belief that the Communist Party would inevitably achieve nationwide victory. She trusted that after this triumph, the Party would ensure Ning'er discovered his mother's true identity—Li Kuntai, who had "resolutely resisted the puppet Manchukuo regime and Japanese aggression" and "sacrificed her life as a martyr of the Anti-Japanese Allied Forces for her country."

As expected, after the nation's liberation, the Party organization's long search for "Ning'er" and Ning'er's own quest to find his mother, Li Kuntai, finally bore fruit on November 12, 1955. On that day, "Ning'er" Chen Yexian joyfully wrote to Zhao Yiman's elder sister, Li Kunjie: "It was only this year, when Cigu met Comrade Feng Zhongyun, who had worked with my mother, that I learned my mother was Zhao Yiman. Then your correspondence with Cigu further confirmed it." [16] The "Cigu" mentioned by Chen Yexian was Chen Congying, sister of Zhao Yiman's husband Chen Dabang and wife of Ren Bishi. As his elder aunt by family hierarchy, Chen Yexian respectfully addressed her as "Cigu" ("Kind Aunt").

Zhao Yiman, seasoned in underground struggle, yearned in her final moments to inform her beloved husband Chen Dabang of her fate—yet dared not speak plainly. For not only the Japanese but also the Nationalists were hunting and executing Communists. In her letter, she could only hint to "Ning'er": "Your father went to the Northeast and died there; your mother followed his path." Thus, she revealed that his father had been a Communist, too.

Let us reiterate: The revolutionary faith of Communists lies in one unshakable core—no matter how formidable the enemy or how insurmountable the odds, they remain steadfast in the certainty of ultimate victory!

For the cause Communists pursue aligns with the fundamental interests of the people. It is the most historically inevitable, morally just, and vitally enduring great undertaking in the world. For this faith, Communists willingly shed their blood and lay down their lives before others.

Why does Zhao Yiman command such profound reverence? Because throughout the 14 grueling years of the Anti-Japanese War, she was not merely a singular hero but a symbol of an entire heroic generation. Just one month and one day after Zhao Yiman's martyrdom, another heroine, Li Qiuyue, sacrificed her life in Tonghe County, adjacent to where Zhao fell.

Li Qiuyue, born Kim Geum-ju in 1901 to a poor family in South Pyeongan Province, Korea, adopted the alias Zhang Yizhi. In the winter of 1924, she crossed the frozen Yalu River into China to reunite with her husband Yang Lin, who had arrived four years earlier and become an instructor at the Whampoa Military Academy. Yang Lin, originally named Kim Hun, had used aliases such as Bi Shidi and Yang Ning.

In 1925, Li Qiuyue and Yang Lin both joined the Eastern Expedition of the Guangdong Revolutionary Army. Amid the crucible of the Great Revolution, they became members of the Chinese Communist Party that same year. In 1927, Li Qiuyue enrolled at the Wuhan branch of the Whampoa Military Academy for further study. In August of that year, the Party arranged for the couple to travel to the Soviet Union for advanced training. By 1930, they had returned to China and were assigned to work in the Beiman Prefectural Committee.

Following the September 18th Incident, Yang Lin was appointed Secretary of the Military Commission of the CCP Manchuria Provincial Committee. Shortly thereafter, he moved to the "Red Base" of Panshi to organize anti-Japanese guerrilla forces, becoming a key founder of the Panshi Guerrilla Unit—the precursor to the First Army of the Anti-Japanese United Army. In the autumn of 1932, Yang Lin was transferred to the Central Soviet Zone.

Concurrently, Li Qiuyue was dispatched to the frontline of resistance in Zhuhe, where she served successively as a county committee member, head of the women's department, and secretary of the Tiebei District Committee. In the Zhuhe guerrilla zone, Li Qiuyue collaborated with Zhao Yiman to mobilize local communities, organize armed units, supply ammunition and uniforms to Zhao Shangzhi's Hadowng Detachment, and tend to wounded soldiers. These two heroines earned immense reverence among the people.

During her severe illness, Zhao Yiman was sent by the Party to recuperate in Houlin Township. To evade enemy checkpoints, Li Qiuyue and Liang Shulin (affectionately called "Mother Lü") risked their lives to escort her, disguising Zhao as a mute to bypass scrutiny.

Li Qiuyue, a woman of exceptional courage and organizational prowess, faced sudden tragedy amid her achievements: her only child—born during her and her husband's hardships and left with a rural family—tragically passed away. Grief and exhaustion led to tuberculosis, yet Li buried her sorrow with remarkable resilience, persisting through her illness to devote herself even more fiercely to the perilous struggle.

In early 1934, during the Second National Soviet Congress, Mao Zedong met with He Chengxiang, a representative from Northeast China and responsible comrade of the Communist Party of Manchuria Provincial Committee, and learned that Li Qiuyue was still fighting in Northeast China. He immediately instructed He Chengxiang to organize the transfer of Li Qiuyue to work in the Central Soviet Area after returning to Northeast China, in order to reunite them as a couple. Li Qiuyue expressed deep gratitude for Mao Zedong's care and expressed his willingness to continue working in Northeast China. [17]

It is said that a child is the flesh of a mother's heart. The agony of having that flesh torn away is something no man can ever fully comprehend. For most women who lose a child, the deepest solace lies in leaning on their husband's shoulder. Yet Li Qiuyue's decision to forgo reuniting with her husband in the Soviet Zone was borne of a resolve far beyond ordinary strength. Was she heartless? Of course not! When her child died, she fell gravely ill. To this day, no records survive to explain Li Qiuyue's determination to remain in the Northeast—a historical void that leaves us longing.

One thing is certain: Li Qiuyue must have witnessed countless families destroyed, parents writhing in the same anguish she endured. Moreover, had Japanese invaders not obliterated the basic conditions for survival in the Northeast, her own child—a product of her and Yang Lin's love—might not have perished from malnutrition and lack of medicine. This fueled her undying hatred. To flee to the Soviet Zone, where in 1934, only Nationalists—not Japanese—posed a threat in Ruijin, before avenging this injustice would have been unthinkable. She believed her work in the Northeast could spare other mothers' children-lost torment.

This interpretation, admittedly, is based on the author's speculation due to the lack of primary sources. For understanding a hero's inner journey—arguably more vital than chronicling their deeds—we invite readers to contribute insights and analyses.

In February 1936, the CCP Zhuhe Central County Committee appointed Li Qiuyue Secretary of the Tonghe Special Branch. Over six months, she achieved remarkable progress: expanding the Anti-Japanese Association membership to over 300 and establishing nine resistance cells. Alarmed, Japanese-puppet authorities declared Tonghe "incurably rebellious," offering hefty rewards for the capture of "Zhang Yizhi" (Li Qiuyue's alias). Once again, traitorous collaborators betrayed her: in late August, while organizing villagers to sew military boots for troops, Li was arrested by Sun Fengzhou, chief of the Xiangshun puppet police.

After enduring brutal torture, Li Qiuyue was murdered on September 3, 1936, in a desolate field west of Tonghe County's city gates. She was 35.

As she walked to her death, did Li Qiuyue think of Yang Lin, her beloved far away in the Soviet Zone? Unbeknown to her, Yang Lin had already sacrificed his life six months earlier during the Red Army's Eastern Expedition across the Yellow River.

Li Qiuyue's martyrdom was one of unparalleled brutality. Recognizing her pivotal role and influence, Japanese forces decapitated her and displayed her severed head above Tonghe County's city gate to terrorize anti-Japanese civilians. She is believed to be the first woman in Northeast China's resistance movement to suffer such desecration.

In 1934, the renowned writer Xiao Hong captured this unyielding spirit in her seminal work *The Field of Life and Death*: "We'd rather have our heads hung from every treetop in the village than live as slaves of a conquered nation." Zhao Yiman, Li Qiuyue, and countless others embodied this vow— national heroes who chose death over subjugation.

43. The backbone is the leadership of the Party

In accordance with *the Unified Military Structure Declaration of the Northeast Anti-Japanese United Army*, all Communist-led anti-Japanese forces underwent reorganization into the Northeast Anti-Japanese United Army (NEAJUA) beginning in February-March 1936.

The reorganization proceeded as follows: NEAJUA 5th Army (formerly the Suining Anti-Japanese Allied Army), led by Zhou Baozhong, was reorganized into the NEAJUA 5th Army. Shortly after, the Northeast People's Revolutionary Army 2nd Army and the Northeast Anti-Japanese Allied Army 4th Army were restructured into the NEAJUA 2nd Army and 4th Army, respectively. Yang Jingyu's Northeast People's Revolutionary Army 1st Army completed its reorganization into the NEAJUA 1st Army in July 1936. The 3rd and 6th Armies finalized their restructuring in August and September of the same year. By late 1936, the full reorganization of all 11 NEAJUA armies was completed. The organizational structure of the reorganized forces was as follows:

Northeast Anti-Japanese Allied Army 1st Army (July 1936)

Yang Jingyu served as Army Commander and Political Commissar, An Guangxun as Chief of Staff (later defected), and Song Tieyan as Director of the Political Department. The entire army comprised over 3,000 personnel, consisting of the 1st, 2nd, and 3rd Divisions, as well as a Training Regiment.

Northeast Anti-Japanese Allied Army 2nd Army (March 1936)

Wang Detai served as Army Commander, Wei Zhengmin as Political Commissar, Liu Hanxing as Chief of Staff, and Li Xuezhong as Director of the Political Department. The entire army comprised over 2,000 personnel, consisting of the 1st, 2nd, and 3rd Divisions, as well as a Training Regiment.

Northeast Anti-Japanese Allied Army 3rd Army (August 1936)

Zhao Shangzhi served as Army Commander, and Li Zhaolin as Director of the Political Department. The entire army comprised over 6,000 personnel, consisting of the 1st, 2nd, 3rd, 4th, 5th, and 6th Divisions, along with the 7th, 8th, and 9th Divisions (established in the autumn of the same year), and the 10th Division (established in July of the following year).

Northeast Anti-Japanese Allied Army 4th Army (March 1936)

Li Yanlu served as Army Commander (officially succeeded by Li Yanping in 1937), Hu Lun as Chief of Staff, and Huang Yuqing as Director of the Political Department. The entire army comprised over 2,100 personnel, consisting of the 1st, 2nd, and 3rd Divisions, as well as the 4th Division (established in August of the same year).

Northeast Anti-Japanese Allied Army 5th Army (February 1936)

Zhou Baozhong served as Army Commander, Chai Shirong as Deputy Army Commander, Zhang Jiandong as Chief of Staff, and Hu Ren as Director of the Political Department (did not assume the position). The entire army comprised over 700 personnel, consisting of the 1st and 2nd Divisions, as well as the Army Headquarters Training Unit. By July 1937, the army expanded to over 3,000 personnel.

Northeast Anti-Japanese Allied Army 6th Army (September 1936)

Xia Yunjie served as Army Commander, Feng Zhigang as Chief of Staff, and Li Zhaolin as Acting Director of the Political Department. The entire army comprised over 1,500 personnel, consisting of the 1st, 2nd, 3rd, 4th, 5th, 6th, and 7th Regiments. By February 1937, Dai Hongbin succeeded as Army Commander, and Lan Zhiyuan served as Director of the Political Department (later defected). The army totaled 2,000 personnel, consisting of the 1st, 2nd, 3rd, and 4th Divisions, as well as the 5th Division (formed in April of the following year).

Northeast Anti-Japanese Allied Army 7th Army (November 1936)

Chen Rongjiu served as Army Commander (later succeeded by Li Xuefu), and Cui Shiquan as Chief of Staff. The entire army comprised over 700 personnel, consisting of the 1st, 2nd, and 3rd Divisions. By the summer of 1938, the army expanded to over 880 personnel.

Northeast Anti-Japanese Allied Army 8th Army (September 1936)

Xie Wendong served as Army Commander (later defected), Teng Songbai as Deputy Army Commander (later defected), Yu Guangshi as Chief of Staff, and Liu Shuhua as Director of the Political Department. The entire army comprised over 300 personnel, consisting of the 1st, 2nd, and 3rd Divisions. By June 1937, the army expanded to 6 divisions and 1 training battalion, totaling over 1,000 personnel.

Northeast Anti-Japanese Allied Army 9th Army (January 1937)

Li Huatang served as Army Commander (later defected), and Li Xiangyang as Chief of Staff. The entire army comprised over 800 personnel, consisting of the 1st, 2nd, and 3rd Divisions.

Northeast Anti-Japanese Allied Army 10th Army (September 1936)

Wang Yachen served as Army Commander, Qi Yunlu as Deputy Army Commander (succeeded by Zhang Zhongxi after Qi was executed for defection), and Wang Weiyu as Director of the Political Department. The entire army comprised over 1,000 personnel, consisting of more than 10 regiments.

Northeast Anti-Japanese Allied Army 11th Army (November 1937)

Qi Zhizhong served as Army Commander, Bai Yunfeng as Chief of Staff (later defected), and Jin Zhengguo as Director of the Political Department. The entire army comprised over 1,500 personnel, organized into 1 division with subordinate 1st, 2nd, and 3rd Brigades. [18]

The practice of the Northeast Anti-Japanese War demonstrated that strengthening the Chinese Communist Party's (CCP) leadership over military forces was the lifeline for the survival and develo p.ment of the Northeast Anti-Japanese Allied Forces. The stark contrast between 300,000 volunteer armies collapsing within two years and 30,000 Allied troops enduring over a decade undefeated serves as a definitive testament.

The Chinese Communist Party's leadership over anti-Japanese armed forces was manifested in the Party's lines and policies (such as correctly distinguishing enemies, allies, and core supporters within the united front), also in the Party's timely formulation and issuance of policies and strategies tailored to the realities of the war (such as policies addressing "Collective Hamlets"), further in the Party's establishment of organizations at all levels (provincial and prefectural committees) and its deployment and allocation of cadres, and most significantly in the exemplary vanguard role played by Communist Party members within various anti-Japanese armed forces, among other critical aspects.

Throughout the war, the successes, failures, setbacks, and advancements of regional forces directly correlated with the accuracy or errors of Party leadership. Key leaders like Yang Jingyu, Zhao Shangzhi, and Zhou Baozhong actively sought and relied on the Party's guidance—a defining feature distinguishing the Anti-Japanese Allied Forces from other volunteer armies and mountain forest units.

Prior to September 1934, the Northeast resistance operated under dual leadership from the CCP Central Committee and the Chinese Delegation to the Comintern. On September 16, 1934, Wang Ming and Kang Sheng of the delegation wrote to the CCP Politburo: "We are drafting new directives for Manchuria. Until these are finalized, the Central Committee should refrain from issuing strategic guidance to the Manchurian Provincial Committee on guerrilla warfare." [19]

The "new directives" mentioned by Wang Ming and Kang Sheng in their letter to the CCP Central Committee's Politburo—intended to align with the spirit of the Seventh Congress of the Comintern—were delayed in finalization due to the Congress's postponement, which left overarching strategic policies undetermined. Consequently, the Chinese delegation's directive to Northeast Party organizations was not finalized until June 1935. Subsequently, the directive, titled *Secret Letter to Comrades in Charge of Jidong* (abbreviated as *the Wang-Kang Directive*) and signed by Wang and Kang, was issued by the delegation to the Jidong Special Committee. In August of the same year, the Jidong Special Committee circulated copies of the directive to Party organizations and anti-Japanese units across Northeast China.

It should be acknowledged that the fundamental spirit of *the Wang Kang Directive* aligns with *the August 1st Declaration*. For instance, policies such as "absorbing all elements willing to participate in armed anti-Japanese resistance to expand guerrilla forces," "implementing a nationwide anti-Japanese united front," "establishing general headquarters for the Northeast Anti-Japanese United Army in various regions," and "upper-level united fronts... being more conducive to grassroots mass work" played a positive role in correcting the Left-deviationist closed-door sectarianism, developing the anti-Japanese united front, organizing the Northeast Anti-Japanese United Army, and advancing anti-Japanese guerrilla warfare.

During the implementation of these two documents, the Zhuxian Central County Committee and the Third Army Headquarters successively received three additional letters: *Letter from* the *Jidong Special Committee* to the *Zhuxian Central County Committee* and *Comrades* in *Charge* of the *Third Army* (abbreviated as *the Jidong Supplementary Letter*); *Letter* from the *Central Committee's Northeast Representative* to the *Zhuxian Party-Youth League County Committee* and the *Third Army Headquarters*, (abbreviated as *the Central Representative Letter*); *New Political Front*. These letters supplemented and elaborated on *the Wang-Kang Directive*, providing further strategic and operational clarifications.

While *the Wang-Kang Directive* and its supplementary letters had positive effects, they also contained elements of dogmatism and subjectivism, with some policies being inappropriate or erroneous. For example: The directive misinterpreted the Party's policy of "not equating resistance against Japan with opposition to Chiang Kai-shek" (applicable in mainland China) as "do not equate resistance against Japan with opposition to Manchukuo." It advocated "alliance or neutrality, rather than confrontation" toward puppet self-defense groups.

The policies on countering the enemy's "collective hamlets" were also unrealistic given the actual conditions of the struggle. *The Jidong Supplementary Letter* instructed: "Residents under our influence should not remain isolated in the mountains but relocate to the large settlements alongside other civilians." Shockingly, *the Central Representative Letter* even proposed avoiding public opposition to the enemy's forced resettlement policy. [20]

The reality of the anti-Japanese struggle served as a rigorous test of policy correctness. The "Collective Hamlets" dealt a devastating blow to the rural foundations of the Northeast Anti-Japanese United Army—the vast countryside of Northeast China. In the Taipingchuan base areas of the Third and Sixth Armies, over 120 villages were destroyed during the "resettlement and consolidation" campaign, with more than 24,000 houses demolished, 13,000 people killed or dead from starvation and cold, and 2,100 shang (approx. 14,000 acres) of farmland abandoned. In Xingjing County, where Yang Jingyu's First Army operated, cultivated land plummeted from 840,000 mu (approx. 138,000 acres) to 390,000 mu by 1937, leaving 450,000 mu barren and overgrown with weeds.

Over 70 years later, the editorial team compiling *The History of the Northeast Anti-Japanese United Army* concluded that approximately 5 million peasants across Northeast China suffered under the "resettlement and consolidation" policy. At the time, the Japanese-puppet authorities boasted that these "Collective Hamlets"terrified "bandits" (a derogatory term for anti-Japanese forces), vowing to "bankrupt rural areas if necessary to completely sever ties between guerrillas and civilians."

In May 1936, facing the relentless encroachment of "Collective Hamlets"on guerrilla bases, Zhao Shangzhi openly criticized the directive of *the Jidong Supplementary Letter* that "residents under our influence should relocate to large settlements." He bluntly warned: "If the entire Northeast follows the forced resettlement model of Bayan and Mulan, all guerrilla movements will collapse within two years." May 13, 1936: Zhao led troops to raid the Taipinghe Tun collective hamlet in Mulan County, destroying nearby communication lines and bridges. June 9, 1936: His forces disarmed the puppet self-defense group at the Qianjiadian collective hamlet. June 12, 1936: They attacked the Taipingqiao collective hamlet, seizing 13 firearms.

Following the September 18 Incident (1931), the Manchurian Provincial Committee of the Chinese Communist Party spearheaded heroic resistance against Japanese aggression, establishing Party-led anti-Japanese guerrilla units, the People's Revolutionary Army, and multiple guerrilla bases. However, the Committee—based in major cities under strict Japanese surveillance—struggled to effectively lead remote rural guerrilla zones and their armed forces. Consequently, proposals to restructure Northeast Party organizations had emerged as early as *the January 26 Directive* (1933).

In September 1935, after the Communist International's Seventh Congress, the CCP Delegation convened the Second Manchurian Work Conference to address Party reorganization and the formal creation of the Northeast Anti-Japanese United Army. Key decisions included: Abolishing the Manchurian Provincial Committee Establishing four new provincial committees (SouthManchuria, East Manchuria, Jidong, Songjiang) and two special committees (Harbin, Fengtian/Dalian). Placing these directly under the CCP Delegation's leadership. On November 26, 1935, the CCP Delegation notified the Vladivostok Liaison Station (responsible for domestic communications) of these decisions and their implementation procedures.

In practice, the CCP Delegation's decision to establish four provincial committees underwent significant changes during implementation, primarily due to incompatibility with local realities. Ultimately, three provincial committees were formed: the South Manchuria Provincial Committee, the Provisional North Manchuria Provincial Committee, and the Jidong Provincial Committee.

The first to be established was the South Manchuria Provincial Committee. In July 1936, Wei Zhengmin Secretary of the South Manchuria Special Committee and Yang Jingyu jointly presided over a pivotal meeting of the South Manchuria and East Manchuria Special Committees, along with senior leaders of the First and Second Armies of the Northeast Anti-Japanese United Army. Held in the Heli area of Jinzhou, South Manchuria, this gathering became historically known as the "Huli Conference".

After discussions, considering that the anti-Japanese struggles in East Manchuria and South Manchuria were inseparable, and that the First and Second Armies had already formed the First Route Army, it was decided not to establish a separate East Manchuria Provincial Committee of the CCP. Instead, the Party organizations of South Manchuria and East Manchuria were merged to form the South Manchuria Provincial Committee of the CCP, which would uniformly lead Party organizations in East and South Manchuria as well as the First and Second Armies of the Northeast Anti-Japanese United Army. The meeting elected Wei Zhengmin as Secretary of the South Manchuria Provincial Committee, with Yang Jingyu, Wang Detai, and 10 others appointed as provincial committee members.

Subordinate Party organizations under the South Manchuria Provincial Committee of the CCP included the East Manchuria Special Committee, the Panshi Central County Committee, county committees in Liuhe, Changbai, Fusong, Huanren-Xingjing, and Fushun, as well as the Party committees of the First and Second Armies of the Northeast Anti-Japanese United Army. Subsequently, the headquarters of the South Manchuria Provincial Committee relocated from the Huli area of Jinchuan County (now incorporated into Liuhe and Huinan) to Huanren County.

Born Guan Youwei in 1909 to a peasant family in Tunliu County, Shanxi, Wei adopted numerous aliases—Wei Minsheng, Zhang Da, Feng Kang—during his underground work. Joining the CCP in 1927, he was dispatched to Northeast China in spring 1932, holding key roles: Secretary of the Harbin Municipal Party Committee. Secretary of the East Manchuria Special Committee. Political Commissar of the Second Army. Secretary of the South Manchuria Provincial Committee. Deputy Commander and Political Director of the First Route Army On March 8, 1941, despite severe illness, he led troops in combat against Japanese forces until his heroic death at age 32.

Following the establishment of the Communist Party of China's South Manchuria Provincial Committee, the Provisional North Manchuria Provincial Committee was subsequently formed. On September 18, 1936, a meeting of the Zhuhe and Tangyuan Central County Committees and the Third and Sixth Army Party Committees was convened at the Third Army Uniform Factory in Tangyuan's Mao'ershan, later abbreviated as "the Zhu-Tang Joint Meeting".

Prior to the decision to establish four new provincial committees, the CPC delegation learned that the Shanghai Central Bureau had been compromised, with key leaders Li Zhusheng and Sheng Zhongliang successively arrested and defecting. Consequently, Wang Ming and Kang Sheng arbitrarily concluded that Yang Guanghua, the Secretary of the Manchuria Provincial Committee (who had been dispatched to Northeast China by the Shanghai Central Bureau), was "suspected of being a mole." They transferred him to Moscow for investigation (it was later proven that Yang Guanghua was innocent). Most egregiously, when issuing the directive to abolish the Manchuria Provincial Committee and establish four new provincial committees, Wang and Kang demanded that all party organizations and military units in Northeast China immediately sever ties with the Manchuria Provincial Committee, citing the presence of "infiltrators" within its ranks. This abrupt order caused significant turmoil and distrust among party organizations and military forces across Northeast China, particularly in North Manchuria and Jidong regions.

The Zhutang Joint Conference was convened against the backdrop of confusion caused by alleged "saboteurs" within the Manchurian Provincial Committee of the CCP, as reflected in *the Resolution on the Organization of the Beiman Provisional Provincial Committee*: "Given the dissolution of the Manchurian Provincial Committee, the organizational chaos, and severe strategic errors, we must—from the standpoint of consolidating the Party— denounce both the former Manchurian Provincial Committee and the Jidong Special Committee, as well as the 'Central Committee's Northeast Representative'."

With this denouncement, the absence of Party leadership—equivalent to losing a "backbone"—was deemed unacceptable. The conference resolved to establish the Beiman Provisional Provincial Committee to temporarily lead all Party organizations in northern Manchuria while seeking directives from higher authorities.

The decision to establish the Provisional North Manchuria Provincial Committee instead of following the Central Delegation's directive to form a Songjiang Provincial Committee stemmed from another key reason: the Party's work in North Manchuria had already expanded across regions including Eastern Harbin, Southern Harbin, the Songjiang area, the Nen River Basin, the Huhai Railway corridor, and the Qike Road zone. The Songjiang Provincial Committee was deemed inappropriate because it failed to reflect the actual geographic reach of the Party's operational activities.

The conference elected the Beiman Provisional Provincial Committee, with: Zhao Shangzhi as Chairman of the Executive Committee. Feng

Zhongyun as Secretary. Seven Standing Committee members, including Li Zhaolin, Xia Yunjie, and Zhu Xinyang. The committee oversaw eight county committees (e.g., Hadong, Xiajiang, Tangyuan, Yilan) and Party organizations within the Third, Sixth, Ninth, and Eleventh Anti-Japanese Armies.

This decision significantly diverged from the Central Delegation's directives. Years later, Secretary Feng Zhongyun recalled that he and Zhao Shangzhi recognized the gravity of the move, fearing disciplinary repercussions if wrong. Thus, the committee was provisional, pending confirmation from the Central Committee.

Post-conference, according to the Zhutang resolutions, Zhao dispatched Zhu Xinyang—newly elected Standing Committee member—to Moscow as the Beiman Committee's representative. His mission: report to the CCP Delegation (affiliated with the Comintern) and await instructions. *The Resolution on Organizational Matters* explicitly stated: "The Beiman Provisional Committee shall be dissolved only after establishing direct ties with the Central Delegation and reorganizing under new directives."

To ensure Zhu Xinyang could successfully enter Soviet territory and locate the CCP Delegation, obtaining direct instructions from higher Party organizations on critical policies and strategies as soon as possible, Zhao Shangzhi meticulously crafted a passport and letter of introduction for Zhu— both preserved intact in the Central Archives to this day. This underscores how desperately frontline officers and soldiers of the Northeast Anti-Japanese United Army, amid bloodshed and fire, needed correct directives and support from the Central Committee.

With the passport prepared by Zhao and an escort team dispatched by the Fifth Division of the Third Army, Zhu crossed the frozen border from Foshan County (present-day Jiayin) into the Soviet Union after the river froze in late 1936. He was first detained for routine interrogation by Soviet border guards in Khabarovsk and Vladivostok. In spring 1937, Wu Ping (a liaison officer) retrieved him from Vladivostok prison and escorted him to Moscow. Nearly six months later, Zhu finally met Wang Ming. At meetings held from May 17 to 19 that year, Wang Ming chaired discussions on Manchurian work and listened to Zhu's report.

However, Wang Ming and Kang Sheng neither allowed Zhu to return to Northeast China nor responded to the eagerly awaiting Zhao Shangzhi and Feng Zhongyun.

Jidong refers to the eastern part of the former Jilin Province, roughly encompassing present-day Mudanjiang, Jixi, Jiamusi, Shuangyashan, Qitaihe, and parts of eastern Jilin. Although the Jidong Special Committee was the first to receive the directive abolishing the Manchurian Provincial Committee and establishing four new provincial committees, it became the last to formally establish its committee. This delay stemmed primarily from the betrayal of Luo Ying, acting political director of the Fourth Army, which crippled the Jidong Special Committee. It was not until March 14, 1937 that an expanded meeting of Jidong's Party organizations convened at the Fifth Army Headquarters in Sidaohezi, Yilan (now part of Linkou County), near the lower reaches of the Mudan River.

The meeting elected nine individuals—Song Yifu, Zhou Baozhong, Chai Shirong, Chen Hanzhang, and others—as executive committee members of the Jidong Provincial Committee of the CCP. Song Yifu, Zhou Baozhong, Wang Guangyu, and Liu Shuhua were selected as standing committee members, with Song Yifu appointed provincial committee secretary. The Jidong Provincial Committee oversaw the Daonan

Special Committee, the Lower River Provisional Committee, five county committees (including Raobe), the Chinese Eastern Railway Workers' Department, and Party organizations of the Fourth, Fifth, Seventh, Eighth, and Tenth Armies of the Northeast Anti-Japanese United Army.

Song Yifu, born Song Xiaoxian in 1913 in Laiwu, Shandong, joined the CCP in 1933. He had previously served as secretary of the Ning'an County Communist Youth League Committee, secretary of the Daobei Special Committee, and political director of the Fifth Army. When appointed by the CCP Delegation as Jidong Provincial Committee Secretary, he was only 24 years old. [21]

History later proved this appointment a grave error. A year later, during the Western Expedition (for which he held primary decision-making authority), Song deserted his troops and defected to the enemy, inflicting heavy losses on the expeditionary force.

Many cadres in the Jidong Provincial Committee and the Fifth Army found it baffling that Zhou Baozhong—the most qualified candidate for provincial secretary—was distrusted by the CCP Delegation. This stemmed from Zhou's wrongful labeling as a "Trotskyist" during his studies at Sun Yat-sen University in Moscow. Although later exonerated and reinstated in the Party, Wang Ming appeared never to let go of this past incident.

It is admirable that Zhou Baozhong, a Communist with unwavering Party spirit and organizational discipline, faced many comrades' reservations about Song Yifu and patiently conducted persuasion and explanatory efforts before the election. Despite Song Yifu's lack of practical experience and independent leadership capabilities as the provincial committee secretary, Zhou spared no effort to assist and support him. As a result, many authoritative documents currently preserved in archives, issued under the name of the Jidong Provincial Committee of the CPC, bear both Song and Zhou's signatures. Notably, most of these documents were actually drafted by Zhou Baozhong himself.

When interpreting directives from the CCP delegation, Zhou consistently sought constructive angles, much like his earlier response to criticisms of "colluding with upper classes" during his time in the Allied Forces: "He acknowledged the critiques but refused to alter his approach." For instance, while *the New Political Line advocated* "not conflating anti-Japanese and anti-Manchukuo struggles", Zhou interpreted this as isolating Japanese invaders while winning over Manchukuo officials and soldiers. In practice, however, he maintained the dual policy of resisting both Japan and Manchukuo, never implementing the "non-conflation" directive.

In a letter to Liu Shuhua, political director of the Eighth Army, Zhou warned: "However cordial our relations with puppet Manchukuo troops, remember they are Japanese puppets. Never let your guard down—seek tangible gains." He explicitly rejected rigid adherence to Party lines, permitting the disarming and proactive strikes against Manchukuo forces.

The silent historical archives have left us a wealth of vivid and rich materials that provide profound insights into the personalities and conduct of historical figures.

Zhao Shangzhi, outspoken and uncompromising, insisted on strict adherence to principle: he openly challenged flawed directives, demanding corrections, believing even minor policy errors or ill-timed slogans could cost lives on the frontlines. This explains his vehement opposition to compromises with puppet Manchukuo troops and Collective Hamlets.

In contrast, Zhou Baozhong, nearly seven years older than Zhao Shangzhi and seasoned through extensive work in the Self-Defense Army and National Salvation Army (which originated from Nationalist-aligned forces), generally adhered to organizational principles in responding to directives, strategies, and policies from higher authorities. He demonstrated obedience and support, approached them with a constructive mindset and flexible implementation, and never blindly followed incorrect directives, thereby avoiding harm to the revolutionary cause. However, his methods of handling these matters differed significantly from Zhao Shangzhi's.

Zhou Baozhong also voiced his opinions regarding flawed directives from superiors, though typically in diplomatic terms. For example, the statement "disarming and proactive strikes against puppet Manchukuo troops are permitted" was included in a March 31, 1937 letter to the CCP Central Committee Delegation, jointly issued under the names of Song Yifu and Zhou Baozhong. While this stance contradicted *the New Political Line* on Manchukuo forces, Zhou justified it with two arguments:

"Due to the complex combat environment and specific necessary conditions"—implying that puppet troops under Japanese control remained enemies unless disarmed. "Avoid a mechanical interpretation of the policy line"—suggesting *the New Political Line* was not inherently wrong but required flexible adaptation to realities.

Zhou's actions matched his rhetoric. In February 1936, he ordered the Fifth Army's instructional regiment to attack the Wolongtun Collective Hamlet, disarming its puppet police and militia to seize over 20 rifles. Subsequently, they stormed Malianhe collective hamlet, capturing 20 rifles, 2 light machine guns, 3 pistols, and substantial supplies. In April, Deputy Army Commander Chai Shirong led a nighttime raid on Wolongtun, executing a tactical counterstrike that netted 20 rifles, 3,000 rounds of ammunition, and grain stores. By June, the Fifth Army's instructional regiment disarmed an entire puppet company, securing over 100 rifles and 40,000 rounds.

Notes:

[1][2][9] Central Archives, The Second Historical Archives of China, Jilin Provincial Academy of Social Sciences (Eds.). (1991, April). *Selected Archival Materials on Japanese Imperialist Aggression in China: The "Great Suppression" in Northeast China*. Zhonghua Book Company. p. 184, p. 354, p. 119.

[3] Wang, S. (2015, August). *The War of Resistance Against Japan* (Vol. 3). People's Literature Publishing House. pp. 560–561.

[4] Zhang, Z. (2011, April). *Snow Cold, Blood Hot* (Part II). Changjiang Literature and Art Press. p. 35.

[5][11] Central Archives, China Second Historical Archives, Jilin Academy of Social Sciences (Eds.). (1989, Sept.). *Selected Archives of Japanese Imperialist Invasion of China: Major Tragedy in Northeast China*, Zhonghua Book Company,   pp. 52-55, p. 60.

[6] Sun, B. (1993, October). *The Atrocities of Japanese Puppet Regimes*. Jilin People's Publishing House. p. 712.

[7][8] Central Archives, The Second Historical Archives of China, Jilin Provincial Academy of Social Sciences (Eds.). (1993, February). *Selected Archival Materials on Japanese Imperialist Aggression in China: Puppet Manchukuo's Police Rule*. Zhonghua Book Company. pp. 490, 571–572.

[10] Wen, J., & Li, H. (2005, December 9). *How Japan Commemorates the Pearl Harbor Attack*. Global Times, p. 3.

[12] National Museum of Chinese Political Consultative Culture and History (Ed.). (1997, July). *Selected Cultural and Historical Materials* (Vol. 64). China Culture and History Press. pp. 69–71.

[13] [14] [15] Central Archives, China Second Historical Archives, Jilin Academy of Social Sciences (Eds.). (1989, Sept.).   *Selected Archives of Japanese Imperialist Invasion of China: Major Tragedy in Northeast China*. Zhonghua Book Bureau, pp. 66-67, 72, and 71-72.

[16] Shi Yijun (Eds.). (2019, May.). *Chronicle of Feng Zhongyun's Life*, 1st ed. Beijing: National Library Press, pp. 335–336.

[17] Zhang Hongjun (Eds.). (2013, October.). *An Epic Poem of Heroism: Mao Zedong and the Northeast Anti-Japanese United Army*, 1st ed. Beijing: Central Party Literature Press, p. 16.

[18] Northeast Anti-Japanese United Army Historical Materials Compilation Group (Eds.). (1987, December.), *Historical Materials of the Northeast Anti-Japanese United Army* (Vol. 1), 1st ed. Beijing: Chinese Communist Party Historical Materials Publishing House, pp. 355–364.

[19] *Wang Ming and Kang Sheng's Letter to the CPC Central Political Bureau* (No. 4), Central Archives copy, preserved by Heilongjiang Provincial Committee of the Communist Party of China, Party History Research Office; quoted in *History of the Northeast Anti-Japanese United Army Compilation Group, History of the Northeast Anti-Japanese United Army* (Vol. 1), 1st ed. Beijing: Chinese Communist Party History Press, September 2015, p. 504.

[20] Zhao Junqing (2015, August.), *Biography of Zhao Shangzhi*, revised ed. Harbin: Heilongjiang People's Publishing House, pp. 226–227.

[21] Shang Jinzhou (Eds.) (2019, October.). *History of the CPC Delegation to the Comintern*. Beijing: People's Publishing House, p. 195.

Chapter 14

Turn an enemy into a friend

44. When the old hatreds end

On the eve of the 1936 Spring Festival, Wei Zhengmin, Zhou Baozhong, and leaders of the Fifth and Second Army Party Committees and military forces convened a joint meeting at the northern edge of Jingpo Lake to discuss coordinated operations between the two armies and establishing connections with the First, Third, and Fourth Armies.

In accordance with the meeting's resolutions, Li Jingpu, commander of the First Division of the Fifth Army, and Guan Shufan, head of the Political Department, led their troops to assemble first at Lianhuapao (Lotus Pond) near Dongjingcheng. After resolving supply and equi p.ment issues, they planned to advance toward Weihe and Wuchang to link up with Zhao Shangzhi's Third Army forces in Zhuhe.

Lianhuapao was approximately 7.5 kilometers from Dongjingcheng. Li Jingpu arranged for local contacts to purchase 300 pairs of waterproof socks and wula boots (traditional winter footwear) in the city, but they could not be immediately transported out. Through connections with local puppet troops, they planned to have the items smuggled out at dawn the next day during a guard shift change. Consequently, the troops stayed at Lianhuapao for two nights.

Once again, traitors sabotaged the operation.

A collaborator from Zhujiatun village near Lianhuapao informed the Japanese puppet authorities. On the morning of February 28, a detachment of the Japanese garrison stationed in Dongjingcheng, supported by a large force of puppet troops, launched a sudden attack on the unprepared First Division of the Fifth Army. After the enemy vanguard clashed with the Third Regiment's sentry units, Li Jingpu ordered all three regiments of the division to engage, suppressing the enemy's advance. However, due to the enemy's overwhelming numerical superiority, by around 2:00　p.m, the First and Third Regiments were largely encircled, and counterattacks by the Second Regiment repeatedly faltered.

During the intense fighting, Li Jingpu personally led the Second Company of the First Regiment to advance within 20 paces of the enemy, hurling grenades en masse into their ranks and repelling four enemy charges. The frustrated Japanese forces deployed poison gas shells, filling our positions with toxic smoke. While the enemy, wearing gas masks, pressed closer, Li Jingpu decisively ordered all regiments to withdraw, with the Second and Fourth Companies of the Second Regiment covering the retreat.

After the regiments withdrew using their familiarity with the terrain, the Fourth Company of the Second Regiment, led by Company Commander Ma and comprising 19 soldiers, became trapped in the enemy's encirclement due to the gas-induced haze, with some already showing signs of poisoning. Company Commander Ma ordered a cessation of fire and hid the unit in nearby bushes. Lieutenant Colonel Morita, the Japanese commander, believing the battle concluded, recklessly directed troops to search the battlefield. When the enemy drew near, Company Commander Ma fired a single shot, killing Morita. The 19 soldiers then unleashed their remaining ammunition at point-blank range, striking down Japanese and puppet troops with lethal precision until all fell.

The Lotus Pond Battle resulted in the death or injury of over 10 Japanese puppet troops, including Lieutenant Colonel Morita, while the First Division of the Fifth Army suffered heavy casualties. Post-battle statistics revealed over 40 fatalities, 16 wounded, 42 firearms lost, and significant ammunition depletion—a severe setback in guerrilla warfare. Zhou Baozhong attributed the defeat to "complacency and laxity that sowed the seeds of disaster."

Enraged by the Allied Forces' fierce resistance—particularly the sudden deaths of Morita and others during their supposed "victory"—Japanese troops desecrated the bodies of Company Commander Ma and fallen soldiers. After their withdrawal, local anti-Japanese associations recovered 42 martyrs' remains, interring them in coffins with solemn rites. Tragically, many bodies were mutilated, leaving a lasting wound in the hearts of the First Division, immortalized in a poignant poem:

> On the 28th day of February, grief knows no bounds.
> Blood stains the rocks, corpses litter the fields, bones sink into yellow sand.
> Forty-two comrades gave their lives with valor.
> Their noble spirit soars, their bravery etches eternity, striking fear into the enemy.
> The land lies ravaged, invaders run rampant.
> When will new and old grudges be settled? A chorus of sorrow rises from the ruins. [1]

After the Lotus Pond Battle, the First Division of the Fifth Army, following Zhou Baozhong's orders, withdrew northeastward and entered Muling County by March. Fueled by grief and hatred, the troops engaged in multiple fierce battles against Japanese puppet forces near Bamiantong and Xiaojinshan, eliminating mostly puppet troops and capturing substantial supplies: 4 light machine guns, over 200 rifles and pistols, and more than 70 warhorses. These accumulated minor victories bolstered their strength, attracting many local farmers to join the division, which rapidly regained its original combat capacity. In mid-May, the Third Regiment of the First Division, alongside a detachment from the Second Division of the Second Army, clashed with Captain Sato Ryūjirō's Japanese unit near South Jingpo Lake, killing Sato and 10 other Japanese soldiers.

On July 28, 1936, Hideki Tojo, commander of the Kwantung Army's Kempeitai, issued orders under the "Three-Year (1936–1939) Public Security Campaign", designating four key suppression zones: Weihe-Ning'an border. Ning'an-Emu border and Jingpo Lake area. Wuchang-Shulan border (Jilin and Binjiang provinces). Southern/Western Xing'an provinces and Jinzhou-Rehe border. The first two zones overlapped with the guerrilla territories of Zhou's Fifth Army and part of the Second Army, underscoring their formidable threat to Japanese puppet rule.

Hideki Tojo implemented a strategy combining "suppression campaigns" with the widespread establishment of "collective hamlets" and the organization of "self-defense militias," plunging our forces into severe hardship. Previously, the Anti-Japanese Allied Army frequently ambushed enemy supply lines, attacked small towns, and raided enemy outposts. Now, they were often preoccupied with securing provisions and uniforms. After forced relocation into the collective hamlets, even with funds, the resistance forces could no longer purchase essential supplies. Earlier, the struggle was a lack of rifles despite ample manpower; now, rifles were available, but there was no source of troop replenishment. Troops once billeted in villagers' homes now lived year-round in mountains and open fields. From May to July alone, Japanese puppet forces directly assaulted the Fifth Army headquarters nine times, primarily targeting Zhou Baozhong, the army commander.

By August, the enemy threat intensified. Over 400 Japanese troops split into two units to frantically search for the Fifth Army headquarters, with the puppet 27th Regiment fully cooperating in dragnet operations across the old guerrilla zones in Ning'an. The puppet 32nd Regiment also mobilized over 600 troops to join the "suppression," surrounding the Fifth Army's guard battalion by mid-September. Six personnel, including Army Staff Officer Wang Zijun, Adjutant Zhou Shurong, Communications Deputy Zhang Xing, and Second Company Commander Zhang Qingshan of the guard battalion, were tragically killed. The puppet regiment severed their heads and presented them to Japanese forces in Ning'an to claim credit.

Prior to this, the CPC delegation had criticized Zhou Baozhong for "persistently confining operations to fixed guerrilla zones, repeating the errors of the 1934 winter campaigns in East Manchuria and Ning'an." Simultaneously, *the Letter from* the *Central Delegation* urged "careful reconsideration" of the overly dispersed deployment of the Fifth Army's First and Second Divisions.

Amid crises, Zhou remained composed. Years of brutal conflict had forged his resolute and steady character; the graver the peril, the calmer he became. Faced with dual pressures from external enemies and internal dissent (including superiors), Zhou convened a meeting of Party and military leadership in late September to unify strategic consensus.

The meeting concluded that the old guerrilla zones in Ning'an— particularly the Nanhutou area bordering Ning'an and Emu—served as vital communication corridors and strategic hubs linking the Fifth and Second Armies with the First Army. This strategic significance directly prompted Hideki Tojo to designate it as one of the four priority targets for his "annihilation campaigns." Withdrawing from these zones due to harsh conditions would succumb to the enemy's trap. Moreover, if the Fifth and Second Armies fully retreated to border areas such as Boli, Muling, and Hulin (north of the eastern section of the Harbin-Suifenhe Railway), they would not only face concentrated suppression by Japanese border garrisons but also fall precisely into the enemy's scheme to "encircle and eliminate" our forces in one stroke.

The meeting resolved to adopt a dual strategy: The Fifth and Second Armies would leave a substantial main force (including part of the Fifth Army's Guard Battalion, the Third Regiment of the First Division, the Sixth and Seventh Regiments of the Second Division, and the Fifth Division of the Second Army) to operate in the southern sector of the Bin-Sui Railway. Their mission was to sustain guerrilla warfare in Ning'an, Emu, and adjacent areas, ensuring connectivity with the First Army. To strengthen leadership, the CPC Southern Railway Special Committee was established, with Zhang Zhonghua, director of the Fifth Army's Rear Office, appointed as secretary. Meanwhile, Zhou Baozhong, commander of the Fifth Army, would lead the army headquarters and its training unit north of the Bin-Sui Railway to develop guerrilla warfare across a broader territory.

Held in a temporary camp along the upper reaches of Quanyan River northeast of Ning'an, the meeting became historically known as *the Quanyantou Conference*. This was a pivotal strategic planning session. Prior to the meeting, amid dire circumstances, Zhou Baozhong issued *the Appeal to Compatriots for Survival Through Struggle* under the names of the Northeast Anti-Japanese Association, the Second Army, and the Fifth Army of the Northeast Anti-Japanese Allied Army. The document called on compatriots to rise against Japanese aggression and outlined 15 measures, including dismantling Collective Hamlets and subverting puppet troops. The guerrilla strategies decided at the conference later proved crucial, enabling survival amid intense enemy encirclement and even fostering growth through relentless resistance.

Given that the Quanyantou decisions conflicted with directives from the CPC delegation, Zhou Baozhong—a staunch adherent to Party discipline—formally reported the resolutions in a letter dated October 22, 1936, titled *Letter from Zhou Baozhong of the Fifth Army to Comrade 'Song' and the Central Delegation in Manchuria.*

The recipient, "Comrade Song", was Yu Huanan (birth name Yu Shixun, alias "Song"). Born in 1904 in Wendeng, Shandong, Yu joined the CPC in 1932. He held roles including member of the Raohe Central County Committee, liaison officer for the CPC delegation's Vladivostok station in Jidong, member of the Jidong Northern Railway Special Committee, and standing committee member of the Jidong Provincial Committee. After studying at Moscow's Eastern University, he moved to Yan'an in 1938. Post-war, he served as secretary and commissioner of the Boli Prefectural Committee until his martyrdom in 1945.

Following the meeting, Zhou Baozhong immediately led the Fifth Army headquarters, its direct units, the Third Regiment of the First Division, and the Fourth Regiment of the Second Division of the Second Army in a strategic withdrawal. They then advanced northward to the Linkou sector, located north of the eastern section of the Harbin-Suifenhe Railway. True to the ethos articulated in Zhou's *Appeal for Survival Through Struggle*—"Resistance ensures survival; complacency invites death"—he insisted on securing survival and growth through annihilating the enemy, actively seeking decisive opportunities within the dynamic framework of guerrilla warfare.

Intelligence work was not only a critical component of combat effectiveness but also a vital prerequisite for the Anti-Japanese Allied Forces to protect themselves and strike the enemy. A single crucial piece of intelligence could outweigh the strength of an entire battalion. Leaders like Yang Jingyu and Zhao Shangzhi maintained covert operatives in enemy-occupied territories. Among Party committees at all levels, Zhou

Baozhong stood out for his exceptional intelligence efforts. During the establishment of the South Jidong Special Committee, Zhou nominated Su Weimin (Tian Zhongqiao), a courier at the Jidong Secret Communications Station, as a committee member. Su, renowned as a "Heroine of the Resistance", repeatedly achieved extraordinary feats in clandestine operations.

On September 12, 1936, the Fourth Regiment of the Fifth Division of the Second Army and the Fifth Army's Guard Battalion, alongside the "Haishan" mountain forest unit, totaling over 400 troops, ambushed a Japanese military train at Daimagou along the Middle East Railway in Muling. They derailed the train, killing 98 Japanese soldiers, severely wounding 35, slaughtering 70 warhorses, and destroying substantial military equi p.ment [2]—a devastating blow to Japanese forces.

Commanded by Zhang Zhonghua and Hou Guozhong, commander of the Fourth Regiment, the operation exemplified tactical precision: the ambush site was strategically chosen, railway sabotage methods were effective, and the terrain favored surprise attacks. Despite heavy Japanese garrison presence along the railway, Zhang exploited enemy complacency— they never imagined Allied forces would strike a heavily guarded train in a zone flanked by Japanese troops. Employing a "decapitation strike" tactic, the assault began at 9 p.m. and concluded by midnight, with troops withdrawing laden with spoils.

Zhang Zhonghua, born in 1912 in Yongji, Jilin, joined the Communist Party of China (CPC) in 1932. In 1934, he became secretary of the Ning'an County Committee of the Communist Youth League (CYL), later serving as head of the Organization Department of the CYL Jidong Special Committee, secretary of the CPC Ning'an County Committee, political director of the Northeast Anti-Japanese Allied Army's Fifth Army, secretary of the CPC Southern Railway Special Committee concurrently directing the Fifth

Army's Ning'an Rear Office, and member of the Jidong Provincial Committee. An exemplary Party leader and political officer, he sustained severe injuries in combat in 1937, was captured, endured brutal torture without betraying Party secrets, and was executed in prison at the age of 25.

In the "912" train derailment ambush, our forces achieved a lopsided victory—eliminating over 130 enemy troops at the cost of only three fatalities—a success primarily credited to intelligence work. The intelligence, transmitted from Mudanjiang, did not specify the train's troop numbers. However, based on supplementary intelligence assessments, it was inferred that the Japanese puppet forces aboard "would not exceed 400 personnel" [3]. With a derailed train in motion, survivors would be either dead or incapacitated, rendering most combat ineffective. This calculation emboldened Zhang Zhonghua to deploy over 400 fighters to strike the crippled military convoy.

A defining feature of attacks on Japanese puppet military trains was that the Anti-Japanese Allied Forces, operating covertly, struck exposed enemies—a tactic frequently employed to eliminate foes. However, inadequate intelligence work could easily backfire.

In October, Shi Zhongheng, commander of the Fifth Division of the Second Army, led his troops to derail a Japanese military train near Laosong Ridge along the Tumen-Muling Railway in southern Ning'an. Unlike the "912" attack targeting poorly armed Japanese engineers, this operation involved a heavily guarded train. During the assault, Shi Zhongheng sustained severe injuries and later succumbed to his wounds.

Shi Zhongheng, born in 1906 in Yongji, Jilin, had served as a squad leader in the Jilin 27th Infantry Brigade. After the September 18th Incident in 1931, he joined the anti-Japanese uprising led by Battalion Commander Wang Delin, rising to battalion commander of the Jilin National Salvation

Army's supplementary regiment and joining the CPC. He later became commander of the Third Regiment of the National Salvation Guerrilla Army, brigadier of the 14th Brigade, and division commander of the Second Division of the Northeast Anti-Japanese Allied Army's Second Army. He was only 30 years old at his death.

These two train attack cases starkly illustrate the critical role of intelligence. While victory or defeat hinges on multiple factors, intelligence remains paramount— "Know the enemy and know yourself, and you need not fear a hundred battles." The successful "912" operation relied on intelligence "sent from Mudanjiang"—but who provided it?

Su Weimin (Tian Zhongqiao), hailed as a "Heroine of the Resistance," was a key founder of the CPC's Mudanjiang branch, secretary of the Ning'an County Committee, and head of the Jidong secret liaison station. Could she have supplied the intelligence? Or did she relay it to Zhang Zhonghua, secretary of the Special Committee?

These questions had no answers then and remain elusive today. The author revisits them to emphasize that the Northeast Anti-Japanese Allied Forces comprised both battlefield heroes and unsung underground operatives who risked their lives behind enemy lines.

Su Weimin, born Tian Zhongqiao, resided in Bamiantong Town, Muling. Her father, Tian Xiushan, was a wealthy local; both he and his daughters—eldest Tian Zhongqiao and second Tian Mengjun—were underground CPC members. The Tian family bathhouse, which served as a secret liaison station, hosted Jidong Provincial Committee meetings. Tian Xiushan, his wife Xiu Yulin, and their young son Tian Chao (then 5-6 years old) stood guard outside during these gatherings. A man of loyalty and valor, Tian Xiushan was sworn brothers with Korean independence hero Ahn Junggeun. Before Ahn assassinated Japanese Prime Minister Itō Hirobumi in Harbin, Tian Xiushan toasted him with wine for courage. [4]

Tian Zhongqiao was born in 1906. Standing at just over 1.5 meters tall with a slender frame, she was not conventionally attractive. Despite her family's relative affluence, Tian did not marry until the age of 17, to a man named Xun Yukun. At 18, she gave birth to a son who tragically died a little over a year later; she never had children again. From 1936 to 1938, Tian frequently led Sun Cheng—the son of underground Anti-Japanese Alliance operatives Sun Wangui and Ding Zhiqing—posing as mother and son, to gather and relay intelligence across villages and towns in Mudanjiang and Harbin. She maintained contact with leaders like Li Zhaolin, Zhao Shangzhi, and Cui Shiquan, but worked most closely with the Jidong Party organization. At Zhou Baozhong's repeated request, she operated year-round in Harbin (Ha), Jiamusi (Jia), Mudanjiang (Mu), and Qiqihar (Qi). In March 1937, as Secretary of the Ning'an Central County Committee, Tian was dispatched by Zhou to Mudanjiang, where she coordinated clandestine communications between the CCP delegation to the Comintern, Northeast Party organizations, and underground networks of the Fifth and Third Armies.

Petite yet formidable, Tian earned the affectionate nickname "Madwoman Tian" for her fiery temper and decisive efficiency, commanding high respect among Allied leadership. Her "madness" was legendary: during a Second Route Army military meeting, she once slapped Chai Shirong, commander of the Fifth Army, during a heated debate. Remarkably, the good-natured Chai developed a brotherly bond with her afterward.

In spring 1937, Tian infiltrated a Japanese military warehouse and garment factory via an underground contact at a tofu shop, recruiting over 30 workers into anti-Japanese cells. She also established the CCP Mudanjiang

Branch Committee, appointing Wang Qingshan (female) as secretary. To sabotage enemy logistics and support frontline resistance, Tian meticulously scouted Japanese grain and supply depots.

One April night, Tian and Wang infiltrated a grain warehouse, dousing sacks with gasoline and igniting them before escaping undetected. The blaze destroyed nearly 1,000 tons of grain—a devastating blow the Japanese never imagined orchestrated by two women.

45. Life is harder than death

On October 10, 1937, the Northeast Anti-Japanese Allied Forces established the Second Route Army through a coalition of the Fourth, Fifth, Seventh, Eighth, and Tenth Armies. [5] Among the preparatory committee members—comprising army commanders and select division leaders—Tian Zhongqiao (under her alias "Su Weimin") stood as the sole woman, a testament to her pivotal role and contributions.

Despite years of successful underground work, Tian was betrayed by a turncoat and arrested in autumn 1938 while disguised as a beggar near Ning'an City. Her identity, known only to top Party officials, was exposed by Song Yifu—then Secretary of the Jidong Provincial Committee and Political Director of the Fifth Army—who defected to the enemy.

Tian vehemently denied the charges, pleading ignorance: "I'm just a beggar—how could I be a county secretary?" Yet on Song's testimony, Japanese interrogators subjected her to brutal torture: the rack, barrel of nails, and bamboo splints driven under her fingernails. Feigning innocence, she screamed through the tough pain. During electrocution, she nearly lunged at the device to end her life

However, remembering Zhou Baozhong's secret mission: to reconnect with the Central Committee and liaise between Wei Zhengmin (South Manchuria), Li Zhaolin, and Zhao Shangzhi (North Manchuria). "I have no right to die," she resolved. "My death would betray the Party and comrades fighting in the snow."

Yet surviving was infinitely more agonizing than death. The enemy forced chili water into her, causing her nose to run and tears to stream down her face as her belly swelled grotesquely. Then, guards stomped on her bloated stomach, forcing the chili water mixed with bloody froth to gush from her mouth and nostrils. She passed out, only to be revived by icy water dumped over her. Paradoxically, the cold shock sharpened her mind. Feigning helplessness, she pleaded: "You've mistaken me! I'm not the county secretary... I can't endure this... Stop pouring it into me..."

The enemy switched to new torture tools: red-hot branding irons seared her legs, abdomen, and even her most sensitive breasts... In a faint, trembling voice, she gasped: "You must have made a mistake. Could the person you're hunting share my name?"

The frail and disheveled "beggar" wailing in protest hardly resembled a staunch Communist. Enemy interrogators typically applied three to four rounds of torture—enough to either extract confessions (from the weak-willed) or confirm defiance (from the resolute). Tian Zhongqiao proved an exception. The Japanese eased surveillance, transferring her to the Diaoling Japanese Work Unit—a counterintelligence group tasked with subverting Anti-Japanese Allied forces—where she washed clothes and performed menial tasks. As her health gradually improved, Tian was permitted to move within the compound, biding time for escape.

Fate proved both cruel and ironic: what one fears most often arrives uninvited. One day, a familiar voice drifted from a nearby grove, chilling Tian to the core. It was her husband, Xun Yukun, alongside three others—Guo Yuzhou and fellow defectors (all former subordinates of Guan Shufan, the traitorous commander of the Fifth Army's First Division)—reporting to Lieutenant Kobayashi Saito, head of the Work Unit. They detailed how they had been detained during Guan Shufan's execution but later escaped.

Xun Yukun, an opium addict and never-do-well, had long been a liability Tian guarded against—a necessity of underground discipline. Once, while disguised as a noblewoman during a covert rendezvous, Xun discovered and badgered her for answers. To neutralize the risk, Tian sent him to the Fifth Army. During the Western Campaign, he joined Guan Shufan's First Division—only to defect alongside Guan to the Japanese.

Tian now confronted two nightmares: Exposure if Xun identified her. Betrayal of Fifth Army secrets—Xun, having served in the army's logistics, knew supply depots and equipment details. The first threat meant death—a price she accepted. The second, however, filled her with dread.

What to do? He was still her husband. Yet after a moment's hesitation, Tian resolved to eliminate him. Two taels of opium would drive Xun to far greater treachery than either nightmare.

With her seasoned underground expertise, Tian Zhongqiao resolved to expose a secret liaison point to Lieutenant Kobayashi, luring him into a trap to eliminate her husband Xun Yukun and three other traitors. The chosen site was the third crevice in the rock cliff beside the crooked-neck pine tree behind Qian Diaoling—a dead-drop location for encrypted communications between Chai Shirong and Zhou Baozhong, known only to Tian and a few trusted couriers. Before her arrest, Tian had personally placed a coded note from Chai there, inscribed with cryptic symbols: Yuan EN-PO... ending with the signature AK.

The code followed Zhou Baozhong's cipher system: Yuan: Fifth Army Headquarters. EN: Diaoling. PO: Sidaohezi, Mudanjiang. AK: Code name for Commander Chai Shirong. Chai's message indicated the Fifth Army's relocation from Diaoling to Sidaohezi.

Zhou Baozhong, trained in cryptography during his time in the Soviet Union and experienced in underground work, frequently used such ciphers. Codebooks held by sender and recipient ensured intercepted letters remained indecipherable to enemies. [6]

Tian knew this liaison point had become obsolete after her arrest—she could neither retrieve the note nor send another courier. With Zhou maintaining multiple secret contacts, exposing this one to eliminate four dangerous defectors was justified. The note's contents, unbreakable short-term, made the sacrifice worthwhile.

Leveraging her classical education, funded by her affluent father, and forged handwriting skills—a staple of covert operatives—Tian mimicked Chai's script: "Feign surrender to gain Kobayashi's trust for long-term infiltration. Liaison point: Third crevice in the rock cliff by the crooked-neck pine behind Qian Diaoling." —AK

Her next tasks were twofold: Avoid detection by Xun Yukun and the three other defectors. Ensure Lieutenant Kobayashi discovered the forged note and believed its contents. The second task posed the greatest challenge. Kobayashi, after all, was a insignificant agent. Tian could only wait patiently for an opportunity.

The resourceful Tian Zhongqiao soon found her opening. One afternoon, she observed an orderly carrying stacks of laundered uniforms toward Kobayashi's quarters. Suddenly, she recalled her own arrest: the Japanese had confiscated her clothes, meticulously searched them, and only then returned the items. If Kobayashi distrusted Xun Yukun's group—as he surely would—he would subject their belongings to similar scrutiny.

To lay the groundwork for her eventual escape, Tian Zhongqiao had cultivated a rapport with a young Japanese orderly. Skilled in acupressure from her family background, she alleviated his chronic leg cramps. One day, while pretending to sweep floors, she accidentally bumped into him and offered another treatment. Glancing around to ensure no observers, the orderly slipped into her room.

Tian instructed him to lie on the bed, face the wall, and expose his calves. As she pressed acupoints with her left hand, eliciting his muffled groans of relief, her right hand swiftly tucked a pre-written note into the waistband of trousers she had sewn for her husband. She exhaled deeply—first in relief, having neutralized a threat to the Fifth Army, then in sorrow, knowing her husband of over a decade now faced execution.

Sacrificing personal bonds for hundreds of comrades' survival, her heart churned with anguish—like amputating a gangrenous finger to save the body: necessary yet agonizing.

The plan unfolded flawlessly. When interrogators discovered two notes marked "AK" in matching handwriting, Xun Yukun and three others were tortured mercilessly but could not explain the code known only to Zhou Baozhong, Chai Shirong, and Tian. Their silence convinced the Japanese they were Communists. Deeming the defectors useless, the captors executed all four.

Tian later escaped but lost contact with the resistance. Zhou Baozhong secretly tasked Wang Keren, Political Director of the Ninth Army's Second Division and later acting Director of the Fifth Army, with finding her. The typically stoic Zhou lavished rare praise:

> "...The Jidong Party organization deeply respects you as a heroine of
> the anti-Japanese liberation struggle, a disciple of Lenin, and a model
> proletarian Communist. Despite your landlord-bourgeois origins, you have
> upheld the Party's iron discipline and devoted yourself to revolutionary
> hardship, setting an exemplary standard for all members..." [7]

After reconnecting with the resistance, Tian Zhongqiao plunged back into intense clandestine work. Yet in 1941, she was captured for the third time. Enduring unbearable torture, she seized a moment to leap resolutely from a second-floor interrogation room window. Though surviving the fall, she suffered multiple fractures. Aware of her identity and intelligence value, Japanese captors deliberately dressed her in a kimono during her transfer from Mudanjiang to the puppet police headquarters in Harbin.

Paraded through the streets in Japanese attire, Tian suddenly "descended into madness" amid relentless inhumane torture. Frustrated by her refusal to talk, the Japanese puppet regime—initially viewing her as a "prized catch"—now deemed her a useless burden and imprisoned her for four years. She was only liberated after Japan's surrender on August 15, 1945.

Emaciated and frail, the woman who had "feigned madness" for years trekked through mountains and rivers to locate Jiushiwudingzi, where the remnant forces of Wang Yachen, the commander of the Tenth Army of the Second Route Army, still held out, unaware of Japan's defeat.

Historical materials obtained by renowned military historian Mr. Sa Su from Japan prove that Japanese forces consistently marked "Shuanglong Remnant Forces" on their operational maps throughout the War of Resistance until its victorious conclusion in 1945. The designation "Shuanglong" served as the signal of Wang Yachen, commander of the 10th Army of the Northeast Anti-Japanese United Army, demonstrating that the Japanese military never achieved their operational objective of completely eradicating anti-Japanese forces in China. This remnant unit endured a primitive existence in the wilderness for years, refusing to descend from the mountains. They were finally extricated from their hideout in the remote virgin forests when Tian Zhongqiao, liaison operative of General Zhou Baozhong's command, led a rescue mission-as only Tian possessed knowledge of their exact location. [8]

The clandestine operations conducted by anti-Japanese resistance workers involved not only a contest of ideological conviction against the enemy, but also a battle of wits and strategy, compounded by the interplay of contingency and inevitability. These factors collectively rendered underground resistance work an endeavor characterized by intricate and unpredictable mystique. Consequently, even the most astute underground operatives could not escape being misunderstood by comrades while simultaneously falling victim to enemy schemes.

In March 2005, Tian Zhongqiao—a legendary heroine of the Northeast Anti-Japanese Allied Army—passed away peacefully at the age of 99. Surviving decades of hardship, her longevity was nothing short of miraculous, a testament to her unparalleled mental fortitude.

Tian Zhongqiao lived without children or a family. The brutal and bloody struggles of the anti-Japanese war stripped her of everything a woman might cherish, leaving behind only her extraordinary legacy as a resistance veteran.

The dangers faced by covert operatives in the Anti-Japanese Allied Army were no less lethal than those confronting frontline soldiers. Over 14 years, few shared Tian's fortune of witnessing Japan's defeat. Many perished abruptly when a single compromised link collapsed entire networks. Zhang Zonglan and Jin Fengying were among those martyred on the eve of the March 15th Mass Arrests.

Zhang Zonglan addressed Jin Fengying as second sister-in-law. Both were CPC members, recruited by Zhang's elder brother, Zhang Gengye, who joined the Party in 1932. Zhang Gengye served as organizational director of the CPC Jiamusi Municipal Committee and later led the Wutonghe Gold Mine guards' uprising, joining the Sixth Army of the Anti-Japanese Allied Army. Jin Fengying's home had been a secret CPC liaison site in Jiamusi.

Zhang Zonglan joined the CPC in 1935 at age 17, becoming one of Jiamusi's earliest Party members. By winter 1936, she was elected to the

Jiamusi Municipal Committee, overseeing women's affairs. That year, the Party assigned her to infiltrate the puppet Huachuan County Government as a secretary—a critical yet perilous role for gathering intelligence. Had there been no defectors, her position deep within the enemy's ranks might have remained secure.

Fifteen days prior to the March 15th Mass Arrests, the Jiamusi Municipal Committee of the CPC learned of a defector within the Party organization and immediately initiated evacuation and relocation procedures. On March 2, Zhang Zonglan and her sister-in-law, acting on instructions from Municipal Committee Secretary Dong Xianqiao, took in Liu Zhimin— head of the Women's Department of the Xiajiang (Lower River) Special Committee—at their home. Ten days later, they moved Liu to a relatively safer location. On the day of the relocation, the two women hollowed out large radishes, inserted critical documents inside, and passed them to Li Shuyun (Dong Xianqiao's wife), a covert operative disguised as a beggar. Subsequently, Zhang Zonglan secretly destroyed some remaining documents.

Due to a traitor's betrayal, Jin Fengying's home had been under covert surveillance by the enemy, who refrained from apprehending the two women to lure a bigger catch. Guided by her underground operative instincts, Zhang Zonglan sensed imminent danger and coordinated an evacuation plan with Jin Fengying. The household comprised six members: Zhang Zonglan, her younger brother Zhang Zongmin, Jin Fengying, Jin's elder sister Xu Jinshi, Zhang Gengye, and Jin's two young children, Wanling and Wanrong.

Before fleeing, the sisters-in-law undertook two critical actions: Jin Fengying wrote to her husband Zhang Gengye (now with the Anti-Japanese Allied Army), informing him that Fang Xiaofang (alias Gao Guilin), a fellow underground member, had defected, and that she was taking the family back to Shuangcheng. They sprinkled grass ash at the doorstep as a covert danger signal.

When the family boarded a train to Shuangcheng from Harbin, they realized they were being tailed. After checking into a Harbin guesthouse, four agents occupied the adjacent room. Exchanging a knowing glance, the women abandoned plans to return to Shuangcheng—to avoid endangering others—and resolved to seek Party contacts in Harbin the next day.

However, the trailing agents lost patience and decided to arrest them first for interrogation, aiming to extract confessions and capture the "bigger fish" behind them. The special agent believed that two women—burdened with a family and two children—would crack under mere intimidation, sparing the need for torture. Trained in psychological coercion, a core tactic of special agent, they deemed the children their trump card.

That night, Jin Fengying's heart sank as she agonized over her children's peril. Once a source of boundless joy, the siblings now filled her with paralyzing dread. What could she do?

The sisters-in-law froze at the thundering "boom, boom, boom" of approaching footsteps. Jin swiftly retrieved prepared opium from her bag, splitting it with Zhang Zonglan. With a gulp of cold tea, they swallowed the poison in a desperate bid to shield one another from torment.

A violent crash shattered the door. The women hurled teacups and water jugs at the agent. As agents twisted Zhang's arms behind her back, she bit and headbutted wildly. Brutal puppet police slammed their heads against walls, blood streaming down their faces.

Jin's 3-year-old daughter, Wanrong, awoke screaming—only to witness horrors beyond her brief life. In the chaos, the wounded agent viciously stomped and flung her, killing her instantly.

The enemy had fatally underestimated the women's resolve. To preserve Zhang Zonglan for interrogation, they rushed her to a hospital. Yet Zhang, resolved to die, resisted gastric lavage—even as agents pried her jaws open. Her heart stopped mid-struggle. At 20, she died unbroken, sparing herself further humiliation.

Zhang Gengye's youngest brother, 16-year-old Zhang Zongmin—frail and childlike in stature—pulled his nephew Wanling and dashed to hide in a hallway corner as the agent focused on subduing his sister-in-law and sister, who were ingesting opium. From there, he witnessed agents dragging Jin Fengying (his second sister-in-law) and Zhang Zonglan (his sister) out of the room. He later recalled: "Their hair was matted, their faces smeared with blood." [9]

Jin Fengying sacrificed her life in the early spring of 1938. That autumn, her husband Zhang Gengye tragically died in a sudden ambush at Heibeizi, Yilan County. Both martyrs perished heroically, their vibrant lives forever frozen at the age of 37.

Over 14 years, Japanese invaders caused numerous large-scale atrocities in Northeast China, with *Major Atrocities in Northeast China* documenting over 30 such incidents. The March 15th mass arrest on March 15, 1938, was but one of these. Zhang Zonglan and Jin Fengying, sisters-in-law, became among the earliest victims of this particular atrocity.

The March 15th mass arrest was a concentrated persecution targeting the Chinese Communist Party (CCP) and Anti-Japanese Alliance underground networks. Led by the Jiamusi Japanese military police, a six-month covert operation involving surveillance, arrests, bribery, and coerced confessions culminated in synchronized raids across counties in the Lower Songhua River region on March 15, 1938. A total of 328 individuals—CCP underground members, anti-Japanese association leaders, and progressive civilians—were apprehended. [10]

The Japanese puppet regime's secret police subjected detainees to brutal torture. Beyond those murdered during the arrests, such as Zhang Zonglan and Jin Fengying, and others who perished under inhuman torture, 89 individuals received prison sentences: 8 executed, 5 given life imprisonment, 40 sentenced to 10–20 years, and the remainder to 5–8 years. [11] This atrocity nearly obliterated CCP county and district committees in Tangyuan, Huachuan, Fujin, Yilan, and Boli along the Lower Songhua River.

Known as the March 15th Incident, this event marked one of the darkest periods for CCP organizations and Anti-Japanese Alliance underground operatives in Northeast China. Most operatives maintained party secrets with unyielding national integrity, meeting death heroically—including revolutionary couples like Zhang Gengye and Jin Fengying.

A historical account from Harbin Puppet Daoli Prison, narrated by Han Yujie—a 22-year-old prison guard with a sense of justice at the time—and compiled by Tong Shaochen of Daoli District Political Consultative Conference, reveals the indomitable spirit of female Anti-Japanese Alliance warriors through its brief yet poignant testimony.

This women's prison was situated in a corner of the prison compound, far removed from the men's section, with its own enclosed courtyard. It comprised three single-story rooms divided into three cell blocks. By the end of 1937, it held over 300 female prisoners. Among the inmates, political prisoners commanded the deepest sympathy and respect. Figures like Song Lanyun and Han Yongyi demonstrated remarkable fortitude during their incarceration.

Han Yujie recalled a teenage girl named Yang Guizhen among the female political prisoners. Yang often wore boys' uniforms and hid letters in the folded corners of cloth bundles to pass to Communists outside the prison. Once, she begged Han Yujie to deliver a letter to her family, and Han agreed. However, before Han could send the letter after her shift, Yang was reported by a Russian inmate sharing her cell. The prison guards summoned Yang, forced her to kneel, and beat her. A Japanese officer even clamped her little fingers with a pencil.

Han also remembered several political prisoners arrested from the Lower Songhua River region, including Li Guilan, Liu Zhimin, and Zhao Dushi (Wu Xiuzhi). Zhao, who was pregnant upon arrival, gave birth to a daughter in prison, but the child died shortly after. Zhao's husband, Zhao Mingjiu, a Communist Party member barely eighteen or nineteen years old, was executed in prison, shouting "Long live the Communist Party!" as he died.

Another prisoner, Ai Fenglin, had a husband surnamed Feng (his full name is forgotten) who had worked underground with Feng Zhongyun . After her arrest, Japanese soldiers tortured Ai by burning her fingers with large candles until the fat dripped down. Despite this, she never confessed and was later executed. After Han Yujie left the prison, Ai was sentenced to ten years as a political prisoner and died in custody. [12]

This historical account, compiled from firsthand recollections, provides critical insights into the CCP underground and Anti-Japanese Alliance fighters who courageously resisted within this hellish prison. At least two revolutionary couples fought side by side in the same prison: Zhao Mingjiu and Wu Xiuzhi, and Ai Fenglin with her husband surnamed Feng, who had collaborated with Feng Zhongyun (but his name was forgotten).

According to the confession of Japanese war criminal Fujiwara Hiroyuki on August 24, 1954, regarding the March 15th atrocities, Zhao Mingjiu (alternately recorded as Mingjiu), head of the Lower Songhua River

Special Committee's Organization Department under the CCP Northern Manchuria Provisional Committee, was sentenced to death during this massacre. [13]

46. Separate at birth and die at the same point

At this juncture, the author regretfully notes that over 14 years, Communist Party members and Anti-Japanese Allied fighters—including Song Lanyun and Yang Guizhen, the young girl mentioned by jailer Han Yujie, as well as Ai Fenglin whose unnamed husband perished, who herself endured a decade-long sentence before dying in prison—defiantly resisted enemy torture, undoubtedly striking heavy blows against the occupiers. Yet historical records of their deeds remain sparse, some even nameless—a testament to history's cruel omissions. Thankfully, a few survivors allow glimpses into these unsung heroes.

Liu Zhimin, born Liu Chun in 1909 to a prosperous Hailun County family in Heilongjiang, received formal education. After the September 18th Incident, the 22-year-old joined the resistance, working as a textile laborer in Harbin. In 1934, she organized *the Chinese Women's Anti-Japanese Salvation Association* at Harbin's Daowai Yumin Embroidery Factory. Sent to Zhuhe in 1935, she joined the CPC and was appointed Women's Department head of the Lower River Special Committee in 1936.

Li Guilan and Liu Zhimin were fellow inmates, both sentenced to severe prison terms. Li Guilan's impressions and evaluation of Liu Zhimin's life are crystallized in two statements: "Liu Zhimin had a slender figure, fair skin, a straight nose, and large, bright eyes. She was not only beautiful but also cultured." By"cultured", Li meant that Liu Zhimin treated others with kindness, worked patiently, never lost her temper, and carried the gentle grace of a well-bred lady.

Another Statement was :"Liu Zhimin suffered so bitterly. She clung to Lei Yan's photograph her entire life—her existence was one long torment."

This second remark underscores how Liu's life became an elegy of love, marked by lifelong sacrifice.

Liu Zhimin's revolutionary career was deeply intertwined with her husband, Lei Yan. Born in 1911 into a wealthy family in Hailun County, Heilongjiang, Lei's father operated a hospital. Lei entered a traditional private school at age 8 and graduated from Heilongjiang's Second Transportation Secondary School at 21—making him a highly educated intellectual of his era. However, the September 18th Incident upended all Chinese destinies. The handsome and charismatic scholar joined the Anti-Japanese Self-Defense Army. In 1932, as a Communist Party member, Lei left Li Haiqing's volunteer forces to return to Hailun, where he spearheaded the establishment of the local CPC branch in April 1933, becoming its secretary. He then devoted himself to building the CPC-led Hailun Guerrilla Unit, which swelled to over 200 fighters by February 1934. Lei's ferocity and tactical acumen earned him the nickname "Thunder Hammer".

Perhaps because they shared a hometown, education, striking looks, and—most crucially—a mutual passion for national salvation and revolutionary ideals, Lei Yan and Liu Zhimin fell in love and married. Their sweetest days were spent in a place called Pianlianzi in Harbin's Daoli District. Under dim lamplight, Lei Yan engraved wax stencils while Liu Zhimin printed. Together, they completed documents and leaflets, packed them into pastry boxes, and delivered them to designated liaison stations the next day.

These were perilous times, yet also their happiest. When they tenderly wiped ink stains from each other's faces, boundless affection melted their hearts. To call them "star-crossed lovers under the White Terror" would be no exaggeration.

Their happiness was fleeting. Before they could savor intimacy or even welcome a child, Lei Yan was transferred to Shanghai's Armed Self-Defense Corps for revolutionary duties. For these faith-driven youths, the urgency of saving their nation was important than their personal joy. Liu Zhimin silently packed Lei Yan's belongings.

A year later, the Anti-Japanese Alliance, lacking military cadres, recalled Lei Yan to the battlefields of Northeast China to fight Japanese invaders. In 1936, he served as Political Director of the Third Army's Rearguard Regiment under Zhao Shangzhi, later becoming Chief of Staff of the Fifth Division, Political Director of the Ninth Division, and finally Commander of the Fourth Detachment in Northern Manchuria's Anti-Japanese Alliance.

Though Liu Zhimin was assigned to the Zhuhe base area, the couple rarely met—he waged war on the frontlines, while she worked tirelessly in local resistance. They channeled their longing into relentless labor, praying for Japan's defeat and their eventual reunion. In a letter to the Third Army headquarters, Lei Yan wrote: "If I survive this revolution, happiness will be mine." How he yearned to live joyfully with his beloved!

Tragically, during the 1938 "March 15th" mass arrests, despite the Party's efforts to evacuate members—including the life-risking efforts of sisters-in-law Zhang Zonglan and Jin Fengying—Liu Zhimin was betrayed by a traitor. By mid-June, she was arrested, imprisoned in Tangyuan County Jail, later transferred to Harbin's Daoli Prison, and sentenced to life imprisonment in her first trial.

In prison, Liu Zhimin remained composed and resolute. From the moment she and her beloved joined the Party to resist Japan, she had prepared for this fate. She vowed to endure imprisonment until its very end, believing Japan's collapse would come sooner—for her love was leading Anti-Japanese Alliance warriors in fierce combat against the invaders.

No records indicate whether Lei Yan knew his beloved was imprisoned at this time, but as a division-level leader, he likely understood the brutality of the March 15th mass arrests. As commander of the Fourth Detachment of the Third Route Army of the Anti-Japanese Alliance, he led his troops in ambushing Japanese forces near Tieli months after his wife's arrest.

In early 1939, upon learning that a joint Japanese-puppet "punitive force" was advancing upstream along the Jimi River, Lei Yan dispatched nine fighters disguised as peasants to infiltrate enemy-conscripted labor teams carrying ammunition and supplies. They gathered critical intelligence on enemy strength and movements. That night, Lei Yan led his main force to the enemy camp, eliminated sentries, and unleashed concentrated machine-gun fire on six tents housing the troops. Chaos erupted as 30 enemy soldiers were killed in the panicked rout.

Soon after, Lei Yan's cavalry crossed the Binbei Railway (Harbin–Beian) into plains ideal for mounted operations, maneuvering along county borders. Despite enduring harsh conditions, their progress was steady—until betrayal by a traitor shattered their plans.

In mid-February, while encamped at Li Laozhuo Village on the border of Hailun and Wangkui counties, traitor Wang Chengcai alerted the enemy. Over 700 Japanese-puppet troops surrounded Lei Yan's 70 cavalrymen. Fighting fiercely for an entire day, Lei Yan's forces used ridges, trenches, low walls, and haystacks as cover, killing or wounding over 100 enemies. As night fell, Lei Yan ordered a phased retreat. During the breakout, he was struck by a bullet and thrown from his galloping horse. A guard risked his life to hoist Lei Yan onto his own horse and escape the encirclement, but the 28-year-old commander succumbed to massive blood loss. [14]

Years later, veteran soldier Hao Fengwu recalled the battle with profound grief:

> Lei Yan was hit in the abdomen by an exploding bullet during the retreat. We forced him onto a horse, but after galloping ten li, his intestines spilled out—he was gone. There was a river where locals had cut ice holes to fish. We placed his body in one of those holes. Ah, we built a snow grave, if you could call it that. But the enemy would've desecrated it if found. We cleaned the blood, covered it with snow, and by morning, the freeze masked everything. At least his body remained whole. [15]

When Lei Yan sacrificed himself, Liu Zhimin was serving her sentence in a puppet Manchukuo prison. The devastating news, relayed through covert channels, struck her like a thunderbolt, plunging her into a living death. Her beloved's death shattered her hope of his rescuing her from captivity. Gazing through the narrow cell window, she endured countless sleepless nights. Yet this resolute Communist eventually overcame her anguish, emerging stronger, vowing to witness Japan's downfall for her beloved Lei Yan by herself.

In 1944, puppet emperor Puyi issued two amnesties for political prisoners—first to celebrate his successful visit to Japan, then for the birth of a child to his brother Pujie's Japanese wife, Hiro Saga. After six years in prison, Liu Zhimin unexpectedly walked free. Returning to Hailun—her and Lei's hometown—she immersed herself in revolutionary work, as if shouldering her late husband's unfinished mission. By 1947, she served as director of the County Women's Federation and district Party committee secretary in Hailun. After 1949, she became Heilongjiang Provincial Women's Federation's organizational director.

Though only 35 and still youthful upon release, Liu remained alone until her death in 1994—half a century of solitude. Lei Yan had wholly occupied her heart, leaving no room for another. At 85, she passed peacefully, reunited with her beloved in eternity in another world.

Li Guilan, Liu's fellow inmate, was captured not during covert operations but in combat. Initially an underground operative, Li had led women in making military shoes, conducting reconnaissance, and delivering intelligence as head of the Women's Salvation Association. After her cover was blown, she fled home under pursuit and joined the Sixth Army's uniform factory at Yilan's Mao'ershan (Hat Mountain), guided by "Iron-Legged" Li Sheng, a legendary Anti-Japanese figure. Soon, Li Guilan joined the CPC and became director of the Sixth Army's Fourth Division uniform factory.

Her capture followed a brutal battle in early 1938. The traitor Zhao Laoqi (Zhao Hongsheng), broken under torture, led Japanese puppet forces to besiege the factory—which doubled as a rear hospital—where Li Guilan was stationed.

A few months prior, a mother and daughter newly arrived at the clothing factory, drawing particular attention. The mother, known as "Aunt Xia", and her frail daughter, Xia Zhiqing, spoke little, their faces etched with sorrow. Gradually, it became known that "Aunt Xia" was the widow of Xia Yunjie, the recently martyred commander of the Sixth Army, and her daughter was barely 15 years old.

That day, enemy fire raged fiercely. During the retreat, Aunt Xia, Sister Han, Master Li, and others fell one after another. Aunt Xia had been struck in the abdomen by an exploding bullet. When Xia Zhiqing saw her mother collapse, she rushed over and knelt beside her, devastated and helpless as she stared at her mother's unconscious body with intestines spilling out. Noticing this, Li Guilan sprinted to them, grabbed Xia Zhiqing's arm, and dragged her toward a northern ravine. By then, enemy troops had closed in. Li Guilan fired her gun with one hand while pulling Xia Zhiqing with the other, determined to carve a path through. Suddenly, a stray bullet tore through Xia Zhiqing's right shoulder blade, sending her stumbling and crashing into the snow. The momentum knocked Li Guilan down too, and the advancing enemy captured them both.

Unlike other captives, Li Guilan faced both coercion and torture. At just 20 years old, she possessed striking beauty. Zhou Xingwu, the former CCP Tangyuan County Organization Director who had betrayed comrades during the March 15th mass arrests, had become a trusted collaborator. Lusting after Li Guilan, Zhou proposed marriage, deploying bribes of food, money, and promises of status.

Veteran Anti-Japanese Alliance fighter Wang Jun, later deputy commander of Heilongjiang Provincial Military District, confirmed that Li Guilan remained unmoved, furiously denouncing Zhou as a "shameless traitor". In that era, "shameless" was a severe indictment, branding its target as morally bankrupt. Enraged, Zhou Xingwu ripped clumps of Li Guilan's hair out.

Zhou then exacted brutal revenge. He transferred Li Guilan from the puppet police station to the Tangyuan County Japanese military police, where she endured the most savage tortures imaginable. Japanese officers flogged her with wire whips, seared her with red-hot irons, suspended her in stress positions, forced her onto the "tiger bench", and made her kneel on shattered porcelain. These methods repeatedly pushed her to the brink of death, yet her iron resolve never wavered. While the torture spared her severe physical disability, the trauma of bamboo splinters under her nails and gasoline-laced chili water forced down her throat haunted her with pain and illness for the rest of her life. [15]

On October 31, 2007, a documentary crew from CCTV and Central Newsreel Studio, working on *Loyalty*, visited Li Guilan in Hegang. They noted her ten deformed, blackened fingernails. Accompanying historian Shi Yijun was deeply moved: "She was a woman! What conviction sustained her through unimaginable torture? Could this all be true?"

Li Guilan's comrade Li Min replied flatly: "It is true." [16]

After being force-fed gasoline mixed with chili water, Li could no longer tolerate the smell of gasoline for the rest of her life. She also avoided millet rice—a staple she associated with her torture. Japanese soldiers had pried her jaws open with iron rods during interrogations, causing her to lose all teeth before turning 30. Li never spoke of her ordeal or its physical scars, even to media or family. She refused to watch TV scenes depicting Japanese interrogations.

Li's unyielding defiance left her captors impotent. Defeated in the battle of wills, Japanese Kempetai resorted to "proving strength" by breaking a frail woman's body. An 80-year-old enemy archive—*The Tangyuan County Kempetai Detachment's Transfer Document, July 30, 1938*—silently attests to her indomitable spirit, shaming countless men. It states: "Notification regarding the transfer of suspected violations of *the Provisional Law on Punishing Traitors*.

> Li Guilan... wife of Wu Yuguan, political director of the Fourth
> Division, Sixth Army, Northeast Anti-Japanese Allied Army), employee of
> the Sixth Army's uniform factory (Party member). Suspect Li Guilan...
> joined the Tangyuan Taipingchuan Anti-Japanese Association,
> propagandized anti-Japanese ideology to women, engaged in Women's Anti-
> Japanese Association activities, joined the CPC, served as Women's
> Department officer of Tangyuan's Wa District Committee and head of Yilan
> County (or District) Women's Department... Repeated Communist
> indoctrination intensified her anti-Japanese resolve. During interrogation,

despite being a woman, she strictly adhered to Party discipline, obstinately refused confession, exhibited cunning and duplicity, showed no remorse, and warrants no leniency. Sentence: Death... [17]

In July 1938, during the sweltering heat of summer, Li Guilan was transferred to Harbin. Resigned to death, she calmly declared: "So it's death? Nothing to fear!" To her surprise, the Japanese-puppet "high court" sentenced her to 10 years imprisonment for anti-Manchukuo and anti-Japanese activities. Months later, her husband, Wu Yuguang, died in battle.

Wu Yuguang, Political Director of the Fourth Division of the Anti-Japanese Alliance's Sixth Army, had married Li Guilan in mid-July the previous year—immediately after the expanded meeting of the Northern Manchuria Provisional Party Committee. Zhou Baozhong officiated the wedding, where Zhao Shangzhi urged the couple to fight Japan side by side and grow old together. Comrades sang and danced around the newlyweds.

As a military commander, Wu Yuguang departed with his troops the day after the wedding. Though parting pained them deeply, both understood that to secure a future where lovers could thrive, they must temporarily sever their bond until Japan's defeat. What they believed a brief separation became eternal.

With indomitable will, Li Guilan endured six years and seven months of prison life in her wounded state, ultimately witnessing Japan's collapse. Her fleeting marriage to Wu Yuguang left no children, but remarried later, she was blessed with a daughter, Liu Ying—a writer deeply connected to the Anti-Japanese Alliance legacy, whose works focus on its history.

Starting with her mother's story, Liu Ying expanded her research to female heroes like Li Min and broader Anti-Japanese Alliance families. To document their struggles, she traveled from Yilan in Northeast China to Yibin, Sichuan—Zhao Yiman's hometown. Nearly every region where Alliance women once lived bears her footprints. "I rush tirelessly," she explained, "because time is short. I'm over sixty, and our mothers are in their nineties—the war's last witnesses. I fear they'll leave without warning." [18]

Teacher Liu Ying has authored multiple works on the Anti-Japanese Allied Army, including *Journey Through Snow and Wind* and *Loyalty*. When Female Soldiers of the Northeast Anti-Japanese Allied Army was published, she was already in her sixties, yet persevered through illness to chronicle resistance stories late into the night. What drove her tireless writing? Undoubtedly, her veins flowed with the spirit of anti-Japanese heroine Li Guilan. As a fellow writer, I stand in awe: she mirrored Li Guilan's tenacity, documenting history with the same unyielding resolve that defined the resistance itself.

Li Guilan, the battle-hardened veteran, stood like an evergreen pine atop a windswept peak—scarred, bent, yet unbroken. At 90, she made her first personal request to the Party: her daughter Liu Ying was to inter her ashes with those of her late comrade, Wu Yuguang, an Anti-Japanese Allied veteran.

On a day in May 2004, Li Xiaofeng (Li Min)—who had witnessed Wu and Li's wedding decades prior—accompanied Liu Ying to bury the couple's ashes at Mao'ershan (Hat Mountain) in Tangyuan County, where they had fought. With no remains of Wu Yuguang left, Li Yunqiao, a researcher at the Northeast Martyrs' Memorial Hall, collected soil from the Wutong River banks where Wu had battled—a symbolic resting place for the martyr's spirit.

Their tombstone bears eight characters: "War Companions, Eternal Guardians" [19]. Li Guilan, who left the bustle of cities for remote mountains, now rests alongside her beloved comrades, eternally safeguarding this sacred ground of resistance.

47. The Strongest Voice of Consensus to the Outside World

The autumn sun bathed Emei Mountain in warmth, yet Chiang Kai-shek, gazing at its mist-shrouded peaks, brooded. Turning to his aide-de-camp Yan Daogang, he lamented: "Six years of bitter toil, yet the task remains incomplete." Though his armies had chased Communist forces across half of China, driving them into a desolate wilderness deemed certain death, the Red Army had emerged from the perilous terrain. However, Mao Zedong turned out surviving and walked closely to the Shaanbei Soviet.

Chiang's focus remained on "total Communist annihilation"—particularly the Central Red Army led by Mao. The Northwest Bandit Suppression Headquarters in Xi'an, with Chiang as nominal Commander-in-Chief and Zhang Xueliang as Deputy and acting commander, spearheaded this campaign. Chiang assured Zhang: "Once we eradicate Mao's Red Army, you and I shall turn our forces against Japan." [20]

Chiang never imagined that reinstating the headstrong Zhang Xueliang to command the Northeast Army would, within a year, nearly claim his life in gunfire and irrevocably alter China's political trajectory. History proves armies heed their true masters. Seeking to reinvigorate the underperforming Northeast Army by restoring its former leader, Chiang overlooked Zhang's profound personal transformation during his political exile.

Branded a national pariah for losing Manchuria, Zhang first resolved to conquer his opium addiction. He had guards bind him to a bed, placed a loaded pistol by his pillow, and endured daily detox injections from a German doctor. "No matter how I beg," he ordered, "none shall untie me except this doctor. Anyone else approaches—I shoot!" After two weeks of agony, Zhang emerged free of addiction. Such iron will foreshadowed his future defiance—a reality Chiang's arrogance blinded him to.

Chiang trusted Zhang implicitly. Beyond the Northeast Army's core forces, Zhang commanded over 100,000 Nationalist troops from Shaanxi, Gansu, Ningxia, Qinghai, and Shanxi's warlord contingents. Zhang believed Chiang's promise: "Once the Communist Red Army is crushed, we (Central Army) and you (Northeast Army) shall fight Japan together—reclaiming our homeland." In late autumn 1935, Zhang deployed four elite Northeast Army divisions to suppress the Red Army.

Often, erroneous ideologies resist correction by others' sound reasoning. In other words, implanting truth into minds entrenched in habitual, rigid thinking proves exceedingly difficult. Only firsthand experience serves as the ultimate teacher.

General Lü Zhengcao, a confidant of Zhang Xueliang, recalled that the Northeast Army—overconfident against the "weakened" Red Army—suffered devastating defeats between October and November 1935 in Shaanxi-Gansu. Within weeks, the 110th and 109th Divisions were annihilated at the Battles of Dalaoshan and Zhiluo Town, with commanders He Lizhong and Niu Yuanfeng killed. On October 25, the 619th Regiment and a battalion (from the 107th Division) fell at Yulin Bridge; regimental commander Gao Fuyuan was wounded and captured.

Gao Fuyuan became a pivotal figure in resistance history.

A Peking University graduate brimming with anti-Japanese fervor, he volunteered after Red Army re-education to meet Zhang Xueliang. After reading Mao Zedong and Zhou Enlai's handwritten letter, Zhang conversed with Gao all night.

April 9, 1936, marked a watershed in modern Chinese history: Zhou Enlai, the CCP Vice Chairman and Zhang Xueliang the Nationalist Deputy Commander-in-Chief held clandestine talks at a Yan'an church.

By May 1936, an unusual emerged between the Red Army and Nationalist forces (Northeast and Northwest Armies). Skirmishes dwindled; procurement officers exchanged greetings in markets, while Red Army troupes performed in Nationalist-controlled areas. During the play *The Agony of National Subjugation*, Northeast Army soldiers wept openly.

On May 5, 1936, in the name of Mao Zedong and Zhu De, the CCP's Central Military Commission issued *the Circular on Ceasing Hostilities, Negotiating Peace, and Uniting Against Japan*—notably omitting anti-Chiang rhetoric. This shift from "Oppose Chiang to Resist Japan" to "Unite with Chiang to Resist Japan" signaled a seismic policy change.

Thereafter, Zhou Enlai wrote prolifically to Nationalist commanders— at times penning nine letters in a single day. To Song Zheyuan, he implored: "…We, your humble comrades, earnestly hope Your Excellency will uphold your initial resolve amidst trials. We, alongside the entire nation's people, shall never let you shoulder this hardship alone, pledging to exhaust every resource in support…" [21]

To Fu Zuoyi, he declared: "…Defending Suiyuan, the Northwest, and North China is your duty—and that of the Red Army and the nation. Today's choice is stark: retreat spells ruin; resistance ensures survival. Internal strife leads to ruin; united resistance ensures survival… If you resolve to fight, we stand as your rear guard…" [22]

Mao also wrote to T.V. Song Ziwen, a senior official in the Nationalist government: "A decade apart, the nation has been utterly transformed. To save and revive China, we must return to the united front… We urge the Nanjing authorities to alter their domestic and foreign policies. Though some signs of change exist, their core stance remains unchanged, making true joint resistance against Japan exceedingly difficult…" [23]

To Shao Lizi, then Chairman of Shaanxi Province, he appealed: "…There is no reason the CCP and KMT cannot cooperate. As *Romance of the Three Kingdoms* says: 'What long stands united must divide; what long stands divided must unite.' A decade has passed since our parting, yet now a chance for unity arises. Might Your Excellency consider it?" [24]

On August 25, 1936, *the Letter from the Chinese Communist Party to the Chinese Kuomintang* was published. Drafted personally by Mao Zedong and addressed to the KMT Central Executive Committee, it solemnly proposed forming a "solid revolutionary united front." The letter concluded with impassioned vision: "If our united front—yours and ours, and that of all parties, groups, and sectors nationwide—succeeds… Let our enemies tremble before this alliance! Victory shall assuredly be ours! With this, we extend our salutations to the national revolutionary cause!" [25]

This was undeniably a declaration of unity by the CCP, brimming with magnanimity and sincerity. To ensure KMT elites grasped this message, Mao dedicated immense effort to engage figures across society. He wrote tirelessly day and night, sending letters to Zhu Shuliang, Soong Ching-ling, Zhang Naiqi, Tao Xingzhi, Shen Junru, Cai Yuanpei, Li Jishen, Li Zongren, Bai Chongxi, Cai Tingkai, Feng Yuxiang, Yan Xishan, and others. Reading these dozens of heartfelt, intellectually rigorous letters, none could remain unmoved by Mao's broad-minded patriotism and profound concern for the nation.

On September 8, 1936, under the names of Zhang Wentao, Zhou Enlai, Bo Gu and Mao Zedong —four of the Central Politburo Standing Committee members—Mao issued the directive *Resisting Japan and Opposing Chiang*

Cannot Be Raised Simultaneously. It mandated abandoning "anti-Chiang" slogans and calls to "overthrow the Central Army or any Chinese forces," instead advocating "unite to resist Japan." [26]

Despite the CCP's sincere overtures for cooperation, Chiang Kai-shek callously ignored them, mobilizing 260 regiments to suppress Soviet areas. The Red Army retaliated fiercely, annihilating over a brigade of Hu Zongnan's forces at Shanchengbao. Even as hostilities erupted, Mao persisted in writing to Chiang with reasoned appeals. This letter—bearing the signatures of Mao and 18 other Red Army commanders—struck a balance between fierce condemnation and earnest persuasion, addressed "To Mr. Chiang Kai-shek":

> …Though we ordered the Red Army to cease attacks on your forces and retreated step by step, we could not soften your entrenched hostility. For self-defense and to preserve anti-Japanese troops and bases, we had no choice but to engage at Shanchengbao on November 21. While the nation rages at Japan's aggression and fervently supports Suiyuan's resistance fighters, you devote all strength to fratricidal civil war… The debacle at Shanchengbao… stems not from your army's weakness, but their refusal to kill fellow Chinese—choosing instead to surrender arms to us. With hearts and minds so aligned against you, why not reflect deeply on this truth?...

After dissecting the battle's origins and the KMT's loss of popular support, Mao reiterated the CCP's unwavering commitment to national salvation through unity:

> We implore you with utmost sincerity: Act decisively. Grant our plea to save the nation. Transform foes into allies. Joint resistance against Japan benefits not only us but secures China's sole path to survival. Today, you must choose—resist Japan or submit to it. Hesitation will destroy the nation, enslave its people, forfeit all hearts, and condemn you to eternal infamy. We dread history's verdict: "China"s destroyer was none other than Chiang Kai-shek." Instead, let posterity hail you as the hero who repented and saved the

nation. As the sages say: "Fear not to correct errors," and "Drop the butcher's knife, attain Buddhahood." The choice is yours. With calamity at our gates, we await your wise reply. [27]

History has celebrated two legendary texts: Chen Lin's *Proclamation Against Cao Cao* (also known as *Proclamation to Yuzhou on Behalf of Yuan Shao*), which famously "startled Cao Cao into a cold sweat" during the Three Kingdoms era, and Zhuge Liang's *First Memorial on the Expedition*. As a writer, I have read both repeatedly. Yet upon reading Mao's *the Letter to Chiang Kai-shek*, its philosophical depth, incisive rhetoric cloaked in civility, patriotic fervor, and vast magnanimity render Chen's proclamation and Zhuge's memorial pale by comparison.

It can be said that the united front policy was not merely devised but painstakingly forged by Mao Communists through relentless toil. With ant-like persistence, they worked person by person, unit by unit, region by region—engaging Nationalist hardliners, centrists, leftists, and rightists around Chiang Kai-shek—to isolate reactionaries and sway more KMT members toward unity. The Northeast Army and Northwest Army had already befriended the Red Army. Even Hu Zongnan, Chiang's staunch loyalist, confided to aides after receiving a letter from his Whampoa classmate Xu Xiangqian: "Suppressing the Communists is a life sentence." Though he never replied, his words reached Communist ears.

On November 23, 1936, the First, Second, and Fourth Front Armies of the Chinese Workers' and Peasants' Red Army, through coordinated operations, secured a decisive victory at the Battle of Shanchengbao. This marked the first convergence of the three main Red Army forces after the Long March, irrefutably proving that the Nationalist military was fundamentally incapable of annihilating the Chinese Communist Party and its People's Army.

Can the Communist Party's broad mindedness, attitude, and vigorous vitality bring about a response and transformation from Chiang Kai shek? Practice has proven that personality determines destiny. Looking through history, dictator Chiang Kai shek has been rampant in China for many years, and there has never been a precedent for accepting the opinions of others on major issues of principle. He never looks back without hitting the southern wall. This is his personal character flaw and sadness, as well as the misfortune of China at that time.

On October 22, 1936, Chiang Kai-shek flew to Xi'an to personally oversee the sixth "encirclement and suppression" campaign against the Central Red Army, branding it the "final five-minute decisive battle" to crush the Communists. Confident in his 300,000-strong force against 30,000 Red troops, he believed victory was assured within a month.

The idealistic General Zhang Xueliang intended to inform Chiang of his secret talks with Zhou Enlai—hoping to persuade Chiang to halt the civil war and unite against Japan—but Chiang dismissed him outright.

On October 31, Zhang Xueliang, joined by Yan Xishan, again urged Chiang in Luoyang, provoking his fury. The next day, during a military review, Chiang obliquely denounced advocates of Communist cooperation as "worse than traitors like Yin Rugeng."

Zhang, "doused in cold water" with despair, retreated to his quarters, tearfully confiding in Yang Hucheng. Yang suggested "seizing the emperor to command the lords"—a historical allusion to coercing Chiang. [28]

Still clinging to hope, Zhang tearfully pleaded with Chiang at Huaqing Pool in Lintong on December 7, sparking a heated argument that shattered their bond. Both realized reconciliation was impossible.

Unbeknownst to Zhang, Chiang had already moved to replace him: appointing Jiang Dingwen as Northwest Bandit Suppression Frontline

Commander and Wei Lihuang as Border Commander of Shanxi-Shaanxi-Suiyuan-Ningxia. [29]

At dawn on December 12, 1936, the Xi'an Incident erupted. Zhang and Yang detained Chiang, Chen Cheng, Wei Lihuang, Jiang Dingwen, and over a dozen officials, demanding an end to civil war and unconditional unity against Japan.

Chiang's opportunistic allies, feigning outrage, clamored to destroy Zhang and Yang—even at Chiang's peril. He Yingqin, tasked by Chiang to bear the stigma of collaboration, led Central Army forces through Tongguan, forcing Zhang and Yang into a defensive stalemate.

The Communist Party was not aware in advance that the "Xi'an Incident" would occur. This sudden major event demonstrated Mao Zedong's crisis management capabilities. He immediately mobilized troops to assist, fulfilling Zhang Xueliang and Yang Hucheng's request by deploying forces to the Yan'an front to take over defenses, thereby declaring support for Zhang and Yang's stance. Simultaneously, he issued a resolute statement: Chiang Kai-shek's freedom would be restored provided that "the civil war ceases and all unite against Japan," and dispatched Zhou Enlai to Xi'an immediately to assist Zhang and Yang in handling the crisis.

In the December 15th *Telegram to the Kuomintang and National Government Regarding the Xi'an Incident*, Mao solemnly warned pro-Japanese faction members like He Yingqin: "The Xi'an Incident should prompt deep reflection by Nanjing authorities, not reckless escalation into an unprecedented civil war... Just as the snipe and clam grapple while the fisherman waits nearby, Japan now hoists its net aloft. Upon hearing Nanjing's decision to suppress Zhang and Yang, Japan rejoiced, sharpening its weapons and drawing its bow..." [30]

In reality, the captured Chiang Kai-shek faced nationwide demands for execution, but astute politicians understood he must not be killed—precisely because Japan most desired his death.

On December 17th, Zhou Enlai arrived in Xi'an, establishing a tripartite incident resolution committee comprising the Northeast Army, Northwest Army, and Communists.

On December 22nd, Song Meiling and Song Ziwen flew to Xi'an (accompanied by Dai Li and others), with Soong Meiling meeting Chiang Kai-shek.

On December 23rd, Song Meiling engaged in a two-hour discussion with Zhou Enlai. Later, in her *Memoirs of the Xi'an Incident*, she revealed a crucial truth: "Zhou Enlai held the key to resolving this crisis." [31]

On the afternoon of December 24th and the following morning, historic meetings occurred between Kuomintang Chairman Chiang Kai-shek and Communist Party Vice-Chairman Zhou Enlai.

During these talks, Zhou Enlai passionately articulated the necessity of abandoning prejudices and uniting against foreign aggression, detailing the evolution of CCP policies. Ultimately, he secured Chiang Kai-shek's personal pledge to cease civil war against the Communists.

On the afternoon of December 25, Chiang Kai-shek departed Xi'an. Upon arriving at the airport, Zhang Xueliang made a decision that stunned everyone: he insisted on personally escorting Chiang back to Nanjing. When Zhou Enlai learned of this, he rushed to the airport to stop them, but the plane had already taken off. Zhou was both astonished and deeply regretful.

On December 26, Chiang Kai-shek returned safely to Nanjing, averting a renewed civil war crisis. From that day forward, Zhang Xueliang vanished from China's political stage. Chiang never forgot his 12 days of captivity, passing his resentment to the next generation and condemning Zhang to half a century of house arrest.

Zhang Xueliang's voluntary entry into hostile Nanjing was a foregone tragedy, yet he departed with tragic heroism and unwavering resolve—like Jing Ke, the legendary assassin who embraced certain death.

The peaceful resolution of the Xi'an Incident not only reflected the Communists' wisdom, adaptability, and flawless strategy but also fully demonstrated their magnanimity.

From Resist Chiang and Fight Japan to Unite with Chiang to Resist Japan, Coerce Chiang into Resisting Japan, and even Support Chiang in Resisting Japan—what political force could achieve such a transformation? Only the Chinese Communist Party! For it alone possessed the selfless vision to prioritize the nation, its people, and the millions of toiling masses.

A direct outcome of the Xi'an Incident was Zhang Xueliang's handover of Yan'an to the Red Army, prompting Mao's relocation there. From then on, Mao lived and worked in Yan'an for over a decade.

Though impoverished, Yan'an became a beacon of light in the darkness.

Notes:

[1][3] Zhou, B. (2015, January). *Selected Works of Zhou Baozhong* (2nd ed.). PLA Publishing House. pp. 87–89, 93–94.

[2][5] Central Archives, Liaoning Provincial Archives, Jilin Provincial Archives, Heilongjiang Provincial Archives. (n.d.). *Collected Revolutionary Historical Documents of Northeast China* (Vol. Jia 51, pp. 17–18). As cited in Zhao, J. (2015, August). Biography of Zhou Baozhong (Revised ed.). Heilongjiang People's Publishing House. p. 223.

[4][6] Shi, Y. (2016, September). The Most Perilous Hour: A Study of the History of the Northeast Anti-Japanese United Army. CITIC Press. pp. 58, 52.

[7][9] Liu, Y. (2015, August). *Women Soldiers of the Northeast Anti-Japanese United Army*. Heilongjiang People's Publishing House. pp. 187–188, 168.

[8] Sa, S. (2013, June). *The Longest Resistance* (Part I). Xiyuan Publishing House. p. 9 (Foreword).

[13] [14] [15] Central Archives, China Second Historical Archives, Jilin Academy of Social Sciences (Eds.). (1989, Sept.). *Selected Archives of Japanese Imperialist Invasion of China: Major Tragedy in Northeast China.* Zhonghua Book Bureau, pp. 66-67, 72, and 71-72.

[12] Harbin Municipal Committee of the Chinese People's Political Consultative Conference, Cultural and Historical Materials Research Committee. (n.d.). *Harbin Cultural and Historical Materials* (Vol. 5, pp. 126–128). As cited in Shi, Y. (2016, September). The Most Perilous Hour: A Study of the History of the Northeast Anti-Japanese United Army. CITIC Press. pp. 147–148.

[14] Editorial Committee of History of the Northeast Anti-Japanese United Army. (2015, September). History of the Northeast Anti-Japanese United Army (Vol. 2). CPC History Publishing House. p. 837.

[15] Zhang, Z. (2011, April). *Snow Cold, Blood Hot* (Part II). Changjiang Literature and Art Press. p. 259.

[16][17] Shi, Y. (2016, September). The Most Perilous Hour: A Study of the History of the Northeast Anti-Japanese United Army. CITIC Press. pp. 142–143, 143–144.

[18][19] Liu, Y. (2015, August). *Women Soldiers of the Northeast Anti-Japanese United Army*. Heilongjiang People's Publishing House. pp. 372–373, 226.

[20] Wang, S. (2006, September). *The Long March*. People's Literature Publishing House. p. 519.

[21][22][23][24] Central Party Literature Research Office. (1983, December). *Selected Letters of Mao Zedong*. People's Publishing House. pp. 40–41, 43, 45, 54–55.

[25] Central Party Literature Research Office. (1993, December). *Collected Works of Mao Zedong* (Vol. 1). People's Publishing House. pp. 424–433.

[26][27][30] Central Party Literature Research Office. (1993, December). *Collected Works of Mao Zedong* (Vol. 1). People's Publishing House. pp. 438–439, 463–464, 468–469.

[28][29][31] Fang, J., & Zhang, M. (1997, August). *A Century of Spring and Autumn: Personal Accounts of Major 20th-Century Events and Figures* (Vol. 2). Economic Daily Press. pp. 1001, 1042, 1008.

Chapter 15

Internal Strife

48. The Bloody Battle of Motian Ridge

In South Manchuria, decisions seemed to proceed more smoothly. For instance, the dissolution of the Chinese Communist Party's Manchurian Provincial Committee and the establishment of three new provincial committees for South Manchuria (Nanjiao), North Manchuria (Beiman), and East Jilin (Jidong) were swiftly accomplished, with South Manchuria completing its reorganization first in July 1936. Notably, during the representative conference held in Heli, Jinzhou, South Manchuria, a pivotal resolution was adopted: the merger of the Anti-Japanese Allied Forces' First and Second Armies into the Northeast Anti-Japanese First Route Army.

The First Route Army was commanded by Yang Jingyu as both Commander-in-Chief and Political Commissar, with Wang Detai as Deputy Commander and Wei Zhengmin as Director of the Political Department. It comprised the First and Second Armies.

First Army: Led by Yang Jingyu (also as Political Commissar), An Guangxun (later defected to the Japanese) as Chief of Staff, and Song Tieyan as Political Director. It controlled the First, Second, and Third Divisions.

First Army: Led by Yang Jingyu (also as Political Commissar), An Guangxun (later defected to the Japanese) as Chief of Staff, and Song Tieyan as Political Director. It controlled the First, Second, and Third Divisions.

Second Army: Led by Wang Detai as Commander, Wei Zhengmin as Political Commissar, and Li Xuezhong as Political Director. It included the Fourth, Fifth, and Sixth Divisions.

After August 1938, the First Route Army underwent restructuring, abolishing army designations in favor of three Front Armies and a Guard Brigade. Yang Jingyu remained Commander-in-Chief and Political Commissar, with Wei Zhengmin as Deputy Commander and Political Director. The structure now comprised the First, Second, and Third Front Armies, along with the Guard Brigade.

Although the Jidong Provincial Committee was the last to be established among the three (March 1937), the Second Route Army of the Northeast Anti-Japanese Allied Forces, under its leadership, was formed earlier (October 10, 1937) than the Third Route Army.

The Second Route Army Headquarters was commanded by Zhou Baozhong as Commander-in-Chief, Cui Shiquan (Choe Yong-gon) as Chief of Staff, and included the Fourth, fifth, Seventh, Eighth, and Tenth Armies.

The Fourth Army: Led by Li Yanping as Commander, Wang Guangyu as Deputy Commander, and Huang Yuqing as Director of the Political Department. It comprised the First and Second Divisions (November 1937).

The Fifth Army: Led by Chai Shirong as Commander, Song Yifu (later notoriously collaborated with the enemy) as Director of the Political Department. It included the First, Second, and Third Divisions (November 1937).

The Seventh Army: Led by Li Xuefu as Commander and Zheng Luyan (infamously surrendered to Japanese forces) as Director of the Political Department. It comprised the First, Second, and Third Divisions (January 1938).

The Eighth Army: Led by Xie Wendong (ultimately betrayed the resistance) as Commander, Teng Songbai (switched allegiance to the enemy) as Deputy Commander, Yu Guangshi as Chief of Staff, and Liu Shuhua as Director of the Political Department. It included the First to Sixth Divisions.

The Tenth Army: Led by Wang Yachen as Commander, Zhang Zhongxi as Deputy Commander, and Wang Weiyu as Director of the Political Department.

Additionally, the Jiushi Army (Wang Yinwu's unit) and the Volunteer Army (Yao Zhenshan's unit) were also under the command of the Second Route Army.

The North Manchuria Provisional Provincial Committee was established earlier (September 18, 1936), but the Third Route Army of the Northeast Anti-Japanese Allied Forces under its leadership was not formed until May 1939.

From summer to the end of 1938, the Northwest Provisional Command was established to oversee the Third, Sixth, Nineth, and Eleventh Armies, with Li Zhaolin and Li Xishan serving as political and military leaders, respectively. In early 1939, the Northwest Provisional Command reorganized these armies into the First, Second, Third, and 4th Detachments, along with the Independent First and Second Divisions.

On May 30, 1939, the Third Route Army of the Northeast Anti-Japanese United Army was officially established at the Dedu Chaoyang Mountain Rear Base. The general headquarters consisted of Li Zhaolin as Commander-in-Chief, Feng Zhongyun as Political Commissar, and Li Xishan as Chief of

Staff, with subordinate units including the Third, Sixth, Ninth, and Eleventh Armies.

In the spring of 1940, the Third Route Army reorganized its forces into the Third, Sixth, Nineth, and Twelfth Detachments.[1]

Tanggou, Caohezhang Township, Benxi County was one of countless remote valleys nestled in the mountains of eastern Liaoning. Stretching east to west, its northern flank rose sharply into steep cliffs, while a crystal-clear river flowed at its base. By the riverside lay a large bluestone slab, large enough to seat a dozen people.

Seventy or eighty years ago, this place was no different from any other mountain hollow. Today, however, the bluestone bears three bronze characters: "General's Stone". It has since become a pilgrimage site, drawing visitors in steady streams—for it was here, upon this very stone, that Yang Jingyu made the pivotal decision to launch the Western Expedition.

It was mid-May 1936, likely a bright spring morning or afternoon. The air was thick with the fragrance of wildflowers, and the woods echoed with the mating calls of pheasants. The soldiers were in high spirits, having recently annihilated a battalion of Shao Benliang's "Long-Tail Forces". Yang Jingyu gathered division-level officers atop the bluestone to discuss plans for the Western Expedition.

After Wang Ming dissolved the Communist Party's Manchuria Provincial Committee and placed the Northeast's Party organizations and Anti-Japanese Allied Forces under the direct leadership of the CPC Central Delegation, communication between frontline forces and higher Party leadership was nearly severed. The Central Delegation, stationed far from the Northeast's battlefront, struggled to issue timely or practical directives.

The three provincial committees (South Manchuria, North Manchuria, Jidong) and their 11 armies should have operated as a unified force. Yet without the Manchuria Provincial Committee's immediate coordination and leadership, they were left to fend for themselves, fighting in relative isolation. This deepened their urgency to reconnect with the Central Committee for strategic guidance. In a report to the Central Delegation, Wei Zhengmin, Secretary of the South Manchuria Provincial Committee, wrote: "Since the Seventh Congress of 1935 and after receiving Comrade Wang Ming's pamphlet 'Struggle for an Independent, Free, and Prosperous New China' in the autumn of 1935, our ties with the Central Committee were completely severed. We lost all access to Central directives, documents, and communications... We became like a rudderless boat adrift in the ocean, or a blind child stumbling in the dark. Amid the surging tides of revolution, we were trapped behind impenetrable walls, cut off from news of victories elsewhere, left to suffocate in silence." [2]

From Wei Zhengmin's letter, we understand the driving force behind Yang Jingyu's arduous Western Expedition. In truth, Yang had long sought to establish a corridor linking Northeast resistance forces with the Central Committee in mainland China—a goal previously deemed unfeasible.

In the spring of 1936, the Central Committee organized the "Chinese People's Red Army Anti-Japanese Vanguard" to cross the Yellow River into Shanxi. With the publication of the *"Eastern Expedition Declaration,"* the Red Army aimed to advance into Suiyuan (modern Inner Mongolia) to engage Japanese forces directly. This galvanized Yang Jingyu. He believed that pushing westward into Liaoxi and Rehe (Jehol) might bring his forces closer to the Red Army's eastern front. If successful, this could bridge the Northeast's isolated struggle with mainland resistance efforts—a bold strategic vision.

Yang Jingyu meticulously prepared for the Western Expedition. He mobilized over 400 troops from the First Division of the Anti-Japanese Allied Forces, including the division headquarters, the Guard Company, the 3rd

Regiment, and the Youth Battalion. The leadership of the expedition was handpicked for competence: Song Tieyan (First Army Political Director), Cheng Bin (Commander and Political Commissar of the First Division), and Li Minhuan (Division Chief of Staff) were tasked with leading the force. In terms of equipment, the troops carried personal firearms, supplemented by four machine guns, one flat-trajectory cannon, and two grenade launchers—effectively the First Division's core arsenal.

The route was carefully planned to avoid enemy strongholds like Fengtian (Shenyang) and Anshan, instead advancing westward through Liaoyang, Xiuyan, and Yingkou, crossing the Liao River to reach Shanhaiguan or enter northern China via Rehe (Jehol). To conceal their movements, the expedition split into two columns before crossing the Antung-Mukden Railway. The 150-strong 3rd Regiment operated independently, while diversionary tactics were deployed: The Fourth and Sixth Regiments of the Second Division conducted maneuvers on the expedition's flanks to scatter enemy forces. Besides, Yang Jingyu himself led the First Army's headquarters and main forces back to Kuandian and Ji'an, drawing enemy attention away from the westward push.

Once these diversions were in place, the Western Expedition officially commenced in late June. Departing from Shangshipeng, the troops marched through Shawogou and Dadonggou to Caohankou Station, engaging the enemy briefly before retreating north. They crossed the Antung-Mukden Railway between Lianshanguan and Xiamatang, reaching Chaotianbei. Traveling by night and hiding by day, they traversed the rugged Motian Ridge on the border of Benxi and Liaoyang, skirmishing with enemy patrols but avoiding prolonged battles as they pressed westward.

By early July, the expedition entered Xiuyan, where their presence and intent were detected. The Japanese and puppet forces mobilized heavily from Fengtian, Liaoyang, and Haicheng, launching frenzied assaults with aerial reconnaissance and mechanized units in pursuit, determined to annihilate the expedition.

Song Tieyan, the army's political director, suffered a severe relapse of tuberculosis during the march. Already gravely ill before the expedition (coughing blood and weakened), he had insisted on joining despite pleas to stay behind. Torrential rains and forced halts in damp forests worsened his condition. By the time they reached Liaoyang, he was vomiting blood and semiconscious. He was carried back to the Monk's Hat Mountain base in Benxi by Youth Battalion soldiers for recuperation.

The loss of a key leader mid-expedition cast an ominous shadow. Command fell to Cheng Bin, the First Division's commander and commissar, who led the remaining troops onward. Unexpected challenges arose: Local civilians in Xiuyan, unfamiliar with the Anti-Japanese Allied Forces, mistook them for bandits. In contrast to established guerrilla zones where villagers supported the resistance, here, communities either fled or attacked the expedition.

A young soldier from the Youth Battalion, weakened by hunger, approached a village to scavenge for food. Upon knocking on a door, a septuagenarian man burst out brandishing a spear and thrust it into the soldier's chest. Against Japanese and puppet troops, the Anti-Japanese Allied Forces fought fiercely, even at the cost of their lives; yet when confronted by civilians, they had no choice but to withdraw. Compounding the expedition's plight was the near-completion of the Japanese-imposed "Collective Hamlets" policy along their route. Village self-defense militias, now tools of enemy control, became adversaries the troops could not strike back against—ambushing their movements and sounding alarms to aid Japanese pursuers.

Ma Guangfu, commander of the Third Regiment's Eleventh Company, later recalled bitterly: "In southern Liaoning, the enemy's blockade tightened with layers of encirclement. Without local support, villagers—manipulated by the Japanese—stood guard with wooden clubs, sounding alarms at our approach. Enemy forces converged rapidly via roads and railways, trapping us."

The decision to abort the expedition and retreat eastward was made around July 8. Cheng Bin's call was prudent: continuing would have meant annihilation. For the retreat, he organized three routes to minimize detection and ease supply shortages: Cheng Bin and Li Minhuan led the division headquarters and Guard Company. Li Tiexiu (Ci Su), the 3rd Regiment's political director, commanded the regiment. Wang Decai, a battalion commander, guided the Youth Battalion. This dispersal aimed to confuse enemy forces, preventing total encirclement.

The eastward retreat unfolded with brutal intensity. Upon detecting the expedition's withdrawal, Japanese forces launched frenzied encirclements and pursuits. The Youth Battalion was trapped in a heavy siege in Fengcheng County. During a chaotic breakout, the 1st Company lost contact with battalion headquarters. Its commander, Zhang Quanshan, led his men southward, reaching as far as Longtangou in Zhuanghe County before doubling back north toward Haicheng.

Everywhere they turned, enemy forces lurked, forcing the troops to move only under cover of darkness. Starving, they resorted to chewing half-ripe sorghum heads and green corn. Near Tangwang Mountain in Haicheng, they clashed with pursuing enemies after crossing a highway. Zhang Quanshan and his men seized a rocky hilltop, holding their ground from dawn until the next morning. By then, ammunition and supplies were exhausted. Only Zhang, a young soldier named Xiao Cao, and six others remained. Hearing enemy shouts of "Capture them alive!" Zhang and two comrades smashed their rifles and leaped into a 10-meter-deep ravine.

Miraculously, Zhang Quanshan survived—rescued by remnants of Tang Juwu's Volunteer Army operating nearby. After Japan's surrender in 1945 (August 15), Zhang joined the Northeast's anti-bandit campaigns and later served as Logistics Director of the Heihe Military District.[3]

Zhang Quanshan stands among the rare survivors of the Northeast's harrowing resistance, offering us a visceral glimpse into the unyielding courage and sacrifice of the Anti-Japanese Allied Forces.

Motian Ridge, straddling the border of Liaoyang and Benxi, earned its name ("Skyscraping Ridge") from its sheer cliffs and cloud-piercing peaks. Its winding paths, flanked by steep rockfaces, led to a narrow pass traversable by vehicles. The First Division headquarters and Guard Company, hiding by day and marching by night, crossed the pass and rested in secrecy, preparing to breach the Antung-Mukden Railway under darkness.

Fifteen kilometers east of the ridge lay Lianshanguan Town, garrisoned by a Japanese battalion—a key stronghold along the railway. On this day, Captain Konda, commander of the 2nd Squadron, led 49 soldiers and a translator up the ridge. By 2 p.m., under a scorching July sun, the exhausted unit settled on a grassy slope, stacking their rifles to eat.

Unbeknownst to them, scouts atop the ridge had spotted their advance. Had this been during the westward push, the troops might have avoided engagement. But now, humiliated by retreat and hunted at every turn, the sight of Konda's men ignited fury. The Guard Company, the First Division's elite, was armed to the teeth: each soldier carried a Type 38 rifle or carbine and a Mauser pistol (effectively a compact machine gun).

The first shot struck Konda dead instantly. As the stunned Japanese scrambled, a storm of bullets erupted from the forest—leaves shredded, gunfire deafening. Caught unprepared, the enemy fell in droves. In the windless valley, gun smoke lingered. Only a gravely wounded soldier and the translator escaped; the former died days later. The battle claimed 49 Japanese lives without a single Allied casualty, hailed as the "Motian Ridge Triumph." [4]

Enraged by the defeat, the Japanese retaliated with overwhelming force. Cheng Bin and Li Minhuan led their men in a desperate dance of evasion and combat across Motian Ridge. During one skirmish, machine guns proved lethal but drew concentrated enemy fire. When the gunner fell, Li Minhuan, the 23-year-old division chief of staff, seized the weapon—cutting down foes until a bullet claimed his life.

Li Minhuan (also Kim Minhwan or Han Minhuan) was born in 1913 in North Hamgyong Province, Korea. His family migrated to Yanji, Jilin, fleeing poverty. At 15, he joined the Chinese Communist Youth League, and by 17, he was a Communist Party member. In 1933, he formed a 30-strong unit of teenagers, later absorbed by Yang Jingyu as the Independent Division's Youth Company.

The Youth Company (later Battalion) became legendary: its fighters, aged 14 to 17, were lavishly armed and fearless—Yang Jingyu's most prized force. Yet at its inception, they wielded only a few rifles, supplemented by spears and clubs.

Their first weapons raid occurred on a road near San Yuanpu, Liuhe County. Spotting puppet soldiers overseeing roadwork, Li Minhuan devised a ruse. Teenagers disguised as vendors lured the enemy with snacks. At his signal, hidden fighters disarmed the distracted troops, seizing 15 rifles.

Li Minhuan, the first Political Commissar of the Youth Company (organized at a regimental level), stood in stark contrast to his battlefield ferocity. Fair-skinned, scholarly in demeanor, and exuding quiet composure, he was a master of meticulous planning and cunning tactics. One iconic episode occurred during an ambush on a Japanese supply truck near Tonghua.

When unexpected complications arose, Li Minhuan improvised: donning a captured Japanese uniform, he calmly approached the vehicle, engaged the guards in conversation, and swiftly gunned down three sentries—single-handedly turning a botched ambush into a flawless victory.

But it was at San Yuanpu that his ingenuity left an indelible mark. Li Minhuan lured two trucks packed with Japanese and puppet troops onto a highway bridge. As the first vehicle crashed through the sabotaged structure, the second careened after it, plunging both into the ravine below. Over 30 enemy soldiers perished with barely a shot fired. The bridge, sturdy enough to withstand normal traffic, had been secretly weakened days earlier—Li Minhuan had ordered his men to saw through its wooden support pilings. This blend of youthful audacity and tactical genius earned Li Minhuan the unwavering trust of Yang Jingyu. Remarkably, by his early twenties, he rose to become Chief of Staff of the First Division—the backbone of the Anti-Japanese Allied Forces—solidifying his legacy as a "Boy Hero" of the Northeast resistance.

By late July 1936, the surviving forces of the First Division returned to their old guerrilla bases in Benxi, Kuandian, and Huanren. Following the Battle of Motian Ridge, they engaged in repeated skirmishes with pursuing enemies, inflicting over 60 casualties. Yet the division itself suffered devastating losses: many soldiers were killed, wounded, or scattered, leaving barely 100 men upon their return. The Western Expedition had failed to achieve its objectives. Yang Jingyu, known for his deep care for his troops, grieved profoundly over the sacrifices—especially the death of Li Minhuan, whose life had ended at just 23. At a memorial assembly, Yang proposed a tearful three-minute silence for Li and other fallen comrades.

Despite the catastrophic failure, Yang's resolve to reconnect with the Central Committee remained unshaken. In early November 1936, he convened a meeting to plan a Second Western Expedition. The Third

Division was reorganized into a cavalry unit, aiming to exploit frozen winter rivers for a rapid thrust toward Tieling and Faku, then onward to Rehe (Jehol), where they hoped to link with Red Army forces in northern China. The 400-strong force was led by Commander Wang Renzhai, Political Commissar Zhou Jianhua, Political Director Liu Wanxi, and Chief of Staff Yang Junheng.

In late November, the expedition set out from Xingjing County, traversing Qingyuan and crossing the northern section of the South Manchuria Railway. Within two weeks, they reached Shifosi on the eastern bank of the Liao River. Unexpectedly, an unusually warm winter had left the river unfrozen—a bitter irony, as the troops had long cursed the cold as their enemy. By late December, heavy rains flooded key crossing points, all guarded by Japanese forces. Stranded and unable to secure boats, the expedition faced dire straits.

Compounding their woes, Japanese intelligence mistakenly believed Yang Junheng (whose physique and surname resembled Yang Jingyu) was Yang himself. Enemy troops swarmed the area, forcing the division into chaotic retreats. With guides killed and ranks thinned, leaders ordered an immediate withdrawal. By the time they returned to Xingjing, only 100 soldiers remained—the Second Western Expedition had collapsed.[5]

The quest to reach the Central Committee had consumed Yang Jingyu and the First Route Army for years, costing hundreds of lives. Among them was Song Tieyan, the First Army's Political Director.

Born Sun Suxian in Yongji, Jilin (1910), Song joined the Communist Party in 1931. A co-founder of the South Manchuria Guerrillas and Yang's closest confidant, he served as political director at both division and army levels. A graduate of Beiping China University, Song elevated the troops' literacy through self-authored textbooks, literacy classes, and mimeographed newspapers like *Anti-Japanese Masses* and *People's Revolution Pictorial*.

After the September 18 Incident, Song led Beiping student delegations to petition the Nanjing government, enduring imprisonment by the Kuomintang. Years of untreated tuberculosis ravaged his body, yet he insisted on joining the Western Expedition.

Carried back to Monk's Hat Mountain after his collapse, he recuperated until February 1937, when Japanese forces surrounded the camp. Defying his frail health, Song led a desperate breakout but fell to enemy gunfire—his brilliance extinguished at 27.

Countless Anti-Japanese fighters perished similarly: untreated illnesses, unmarked graves, fragmentary records. Even among senior leaders like Tong Changrong (whose sparse archives survive), their stories echo with a haunting, unyielding spirit.

49. The Puppet Manchukuo Army's "Grand Anti-Bandit Campaign"

Tong Changrong, born in 1907 in Hudong, Anhui (modern Zongyang County), joined the Chinese Communist Party in 1924 and later studied at Tokyo Imperial University. After the Jinan Massacre of May 1928, as head of the CCP's Japan Special Branch, he organized anti-Japanese protests, leading to his arrest and deportation by Japanese authorities.

In 1930, Tong was transferred from Shanghai to serve as Secretary of the Henan Provincial Committee. By 1931, to strengthen the CCP's presence in the Northeast, he was reassigned to Dalian as municipal secretary before Luo Dengxian dispatched him to Dongman (eastern Manchuria)—the birthplace of the future Second Army of the Anti-Japanese Allied Forces— where he became Secretary of the Special Committee. In Dongman, Tong spearheaded the creation of anti-Japanese militias, rapidly expanding guerrilla forces in Yanji, Helong, Wangqing, and Hunchun, while establishing over a dozen base areas.

A gifted writer and fluent Japanese speaker, Tong pioneered psychological warfare against Japanese forces during counter-campaigns. His leaflets, written in Japanese, struck a nerve: "Do you remember your mother's tears when you left home?" "Your mothers and children pray daily for your safe return!" These messages, plastered on poles and walls in Japanese-occupied zones, wielded a unique emotional toll.

A document compiled by the Shenyang Military District Political Department recounts an episode from early 1934: after a counter-campaign, guerrillas found two artillery shells on frozen ground in Wangqing, beneath which lay a note: "To the Communist garrison: We are returning to Japan. These shells each contain 300 bullets. Use them to fight Japanese militarism!"

Signed by 12 Japanese soldiers, this act of defiance remains rare in the annals of the Anti-Japanese War.[6]

Fate, however, dealt Tong a cruel hand. The young revolutionary suffered from tuberculosis—a disease ill-suited to Manchuria's knife-like winter winds. For an intellectual from the temperate south, the harsh climate and lack of medical care proved lethal. Yet, like many Communists who had sworn oaths under the Party banner, Tong refused to retreat to warmer regions or seek treatment, viewing such choices as shameful betrayals of duty. This ethos of sacrifice, common among resistance fighters, claimed countless lives to untreated illnesses and premature physical collapse.

Tong's frailty deepened. Even in mild cold, he shivered uncontrollably. One day, numbness seized his hands and feet, rendering him unable to grip a pen. Initially dismissed as exhaustion, the condition worsened until he collapsed while stretching. A doctor diagnosed stroke—astonishing for a man in his twenties, what today might be called a "youthful prime".

Once, the Red Guards reported that the Japanese "punitive force" was approaching. Tong Changrong, frail and ill, ordered the others to retreat to the mountains first. Unable to move quickly, he and Wang, a county committee member, had just left the village when they were spotted by the enemy. Bullets whizzed past their heads and bodies, and Tong was struck by a gunshot. Wang carried him on his back as they fled. Tong shouted, "Put me down! Leave me!" But Wang refused, desperately running over a hill. He hid the wounded Tong, whose arm was injured, in a snowdrift, then removed his old sheepskin coat and draped it over his back to mimic carrying a person, successfully diverting the enemy.

Severely weakened by blood loss and continuous coughing of blood, Tong's face turned as pale as paper. After two days of rest, he resumed writing feverishly under a kerosene lamp, spitting black phlegm and red blood. A comrade risked his life to bring Tong two bottles of cod liver oil to nourish him, but Tong gave them to other wounded soldiers, saying, "If I take these, he'll just risk his life again."

Everyone around him knew that, given his condition, Tong would not survive another winter or two. Yet he stubbornly persisted. A report from the *East Manchuria Special Committee of the Chinese Communist Party to the Provincial Committee* on November 2, 1932, during the bitter winter, stated: "Comrade Rong (Tong Changrong) has miraculously recovered from several near-fatal relapses of his illness. However, movement remains difficult, and full recovery to resume normal work will require another month of rest. The previous letter sent to you was written by Comrade Rong during his critical condition, primarily to request that the Provincial Committee send a replacement (in case of his death, to sustain the work in East Manchuria). Thus, no work report was included, as he was physically unable to compile one at the time..." [7]

From the winter of 1933 to the spring of 1934, Japanese puppet forces launched a large-scale "suppression campaign" against the anti-Japanese base areas in East Manchuria. Despite his emaciated and chronically ill state, Tong led guerrilla fighters through the dense forests of Wangqing, engaging in skirmishes with the enemy. In late March, as enemy forces closed in with a dragnet search, Tong and his comrades were surrounded. During the battle, Tong was shot again and critically wounded. Cui Jinshu, a female soldier who had been caring for him, carried him to a mountain cave. Tong succumbed to excessive blood loss the next day, aged just 27. [8]

It is worth adding that to prevent the enemy from desecrating the body of the Special Committee Secretary (by beheading and public display), the 22-year-old Cui Jinshu refused to evacuate before the enemy arrived. She guarded the cave entrance until her bullets ran out, dying a heroic death.

On an ordinary cold winter day in 1936, an extraordinary event unfolded in Berlin, Germany. Two monstrous ideological aberrations officially intertwined, breeding a virulent "virus" that would claim hundreds of millions of lives worldwide. The date was November 25, when Germany and Japan signed the *Anti-Comintern Pact*. Italy later joined, formalizing the Axis alliance between Germany, Italy, and Japan as the new Eastern and Western epicenters of global warfare.

Hirota Kōki, Japan's 32nd Prime Minister who rose to power over the blood of Prime Minister Saitō Makoto assassinated in the February 26 Incident, accelerated Japan's militarist agenda. By 1937, Japan's military industrial investment surged to 2.23 billion yen, a 2.2-fold increase from 1936, accounting for 61.7% of total industrial investment. The army expanded to 450,000 troops—double the 1931 figure (230,000 troops during the September 18 Incident)—while naval forces grew by over a quarter. [9]

The Japanese military had long planned a full-scale invasion of China for 1937, intending to deploy eight divisions to occupy five northern provinces, five divisions for central China, and one division to seize Guangzhou, alongside naval control of China's coasts and Yangtze River. Confident in their superiority, Japanese strategists believed China would collapse within three months. On July 7, the Marco Polo Bridge Incident erupted, marking the start of Japan's total war of aggression.

On August 25, 1937, the Central Military Commission of the Chinese Communist Party announced the reorganization of the Red Army into the Eighth Route Army under commanders Zhu De and Peng Dehuai. On October 12, southern guerrilla forces were restructured into the New Fourth Army, led by Ye Ting and Xiang Ying. On September 23, Chiang Kai-shek publicly acknowledged the CCP's legitimacy in his *Response to the Chinese Communist Party's Declaration*, formalizing the United Front against Japan.

Thus, China's fragmented resistance coalesced into a nationwide war of survival.

As Japanese aggressors launched massive attacks into China's interior, Northeast China (Manchuria) became a critical rear base for their operations. The anti-Japanese resistance in the Northeast thus emerged as a vital component of the nationwide War of Resistance. Supporting and coordinating with resistance efforts in the interior, harassing and sabotaging Japanese rear bases, and containing Japanese forces advancing into the interior became key strategic tasks for the Northeast Anti-Japanese United Army (Northeast Anti-Japanese Allied Army, or "Northeast Anti-Japan Alliance").

In *Problems of Strategy in Guerrilla War Against Japan*, Mao Zedong pointed out: "Before the nationwide War of Resistance began, the guerrilla warfare in the three northeastern provinces naturally did not involve coordination with interior forces. However, after the outbreak of the war, the significance of coordination became evident. Every enemy soldier killed, every bullet expended by the guerrillas, and every Japanese troop pinned down to prevent their southward advance into the interior contributed to strengthening the overall war effort. Moreover, the psychological blow to the enemy and the morale boost for our troops and people were undeniable." [10]

To align with the national resistance and contain the Kwantung Army's advance into China's interior, the Northeast Anti-Japanese United Army swiftly intensified its campaigns.

On August 20, *the Proclamation by the Commander-in-Chief of the First Route Army of the Northeast Anti-Japanese United Army* called on people across the Northeast to unite, cast aside past grievances, and rise in rebellion against Japan amid the "Sino-Japanese War". The proclamation urged the overthrow of Japanese imperialism and its puppet regime, Manchukuo, to establish an independent, free, and prosperous China.

The First Route Army launched frequent offensives. On September 13, Yang Jingyu led over 300 troops to attack two Japanese-controlled "fortified villages" in Xingjing County. Later, on October 31, he executed a tactical ambush, besieging a point to lure reinforcements, killing 22 Japanese soldiers—including Battalion Commander Mizude Sakei and Squad Leader Rikushima Gensan—and wounding six others. In late October, Wei Zhengmin, political commissar of the Second Army, led a nighttime assault on Huinan County, killing over 20 Japanese garrison troops and seizing massive quantities of grain and ammunition.

On August 25, the Jilin Provincial Committee of the Chinese Communist Party issued an *Emergency Notice on the Current Anti-Japanese National Salvation War Movement* via the Northeast Anti-Japanese National Salvation Association. It urged military and civilian forces to unite and destabilize Japan's rear base in Manchuria, hastening the collapse of its aggression in the interior.

Units of the Second Route Army actively sought engagements. Prior to the army's formal establishment, on August 13, a combined force of 250 troops from the Fifth, Second, Fourth, and Eighth Armies—under the command of Fifth Army Deputy Commander Chai Shirong—launched a fierce assault on 120 Japanese soldiers constructing a military stronghold at Santongdao. After half a day of combat, over 40 Japanese troops were annihilated.

On September 18, the Northeast Anti-Japanese United Army Headquarters issued a directive: "With the full-scale eruption of the Sino-Japanese War, the time has come for the nation to unite in expelling the enemy and achieving liberation. Compatriots must rise swiftly to recover the Northeast and strive for national independence and territorial integrity."

To counter Japanese aggression and bolster national morale, the CCP's Provisional Beiman Provincial Committee organized an anti-Manchukuo uprising in Tangyuan County, a region with strong grassroots support. On September 17, over 1,000 armed civilians in the Gejie River, Wulong River, Heli River, and Tangwang River areas held rallies and demonstrations, condemning Japanese atrocities. Protesters severed telephone lines between Tangyuan County and Lianjiangkou, Erbao and Heli, toppled over 100 utility poles, and burned five to six bridges leading to Jiamusi.

The usually arrogant 20-strong Japanese garrison at Dingjiafenfang in Gejie River District, intimidated by the uprising, barricaded themselves in their stronghold before fleeing in disguise on the night of September 20.

During the National War of Resistance, influenced by the nationwide anti-Japanese sentiment and the efforts of the Communist Party of China (CPC) in Northeast China, a number of Manchukuo soldiers and officers with lingering national consciousness defected to join the anti-Japanese cause. Under the leadership of Zhou Baozhong, the 5th Army's Chief of Staff Zhang Zhenhua, along with underground operatives Wang Jiechen and Feng Shuyan, orchestrated the uprising of Li Wenbin, commander of the Ning'an Three Rivers Forest Police Brigade. On the night of July 12, Li and his forces killed eight Japanese officers, including advisor Tsamura Sho and instructor Katō Naoaki, and disarmed 50 puppet soldiers. Following the uprising, over 150 personnel and their families joined the Northeast Anti-Japanese Allied Army (NAJAA).

Shortly after Li Wenbin's uprising, 118 soldiers from the machine gun company of the 38th Regiment of the puppet army stationed in Yilan also mutinied and defected. On August 21, they joined the Sixth Army of the

Northeast Anti-Japanese United Army, bringing with them one mortar, one heavy machine gun, four light machine guns, and over 100 rifles. [12] On September 10, the 29th Regiment of the puppet army defected and joined the Eighth Army of the Northeast Anti-Japanese United Army. Additionally, puppet troops stationed in areas such as Huachuan, Yilan, Baoqing, and Fujin were in a state of wavering loyalty.

During this phase, the defections and wavering among Manchukuo puppet forces were partially tied to Chiang Kai-shek's public declaration of resistance against Japan. Many puppet troops, having previously served in the Northeastern Army under the Nationalist government, retained a natural affinity for their former command. However, the primary catalyst for their rebellion lay in the Northeast Anti-Japanese Allied Army's (NAJAA) relentless military strikes against collaborationist units.

The NAJAA strategically targeted weaker puppet forces—such as police, militia, and self-defense groups—to dismantle the Japanese army's auxiliary network. By neutralizing these collaborators, the Japanese were left isolated and operationally impaired. Throughout the Northeast resistance (excluding the Soviet Red Army's post-August 15 counteroffensive), puppet forces suffered casualties several times higher than Japanese troops.

In late July 1937, Jin Zhengguo, commander of the 1st Brigade of the Northeast Anti-Japanese Allied Army's Independent Division (predecessor of the 11th Army), ambushed a puppet troop convoy transporting gold from Huachuan to Jiamusi, killing over 10 resisting soldiers. In August, a unit of the 5th Army disarmed an entire company under the puppet Zhang Battalion, eliminating 10 soldiers. Such examples of anti-collaborationist operations were numerous, underscoring the peril faced by puppet forces that continued aiding the Japanese.

However, the overall balance of power in the Northeast remained heavily skewed in favor of the enemy. The Anti-Japanese Allied Army (NAJAA) confronted adversaries vastly superior in numbers and resources. While some large-scale defections occurred—such as Li Wenbin's Forest Police Brigade, driven by nationalistic fervor—they were rare exceptions.

Most defections, like that of He Kuiwu, commander of the puppet 29th Regiment, were opportunistic. Originally swayed by underground Communist operatives from the 5th Army, He instead joined Xie Wendong's 8th Army for personal protection, only to defect back to the Japanese within two months. This exposed the flaws in the Comintern's rigid strategy of "uniting with Chiang Kai-shek" and prioritizing "anti-Japanese resistance" over "anti-collaborationist" action in the Northeast, a policy criticized as dogmatic and detached from reality.

With a population of merely tens of millions, Japan's invasion of China—a nation of hundreds of millions—exposed its strategic weakness: overstretched fronts and insufficient manpower. To compensate, Japan relied heavily on recruiting Chinese collaborators, a policy encapsulated in the "Eastern Border Region Independent Suppression Campaign".

Nominally led by puppet forces, the campaign was actually orchestrated by Major General Sasaki Tōichi, the Japanese military advisor to Manchukuo's puppet regime, and a Japanese-dominated "Guidance Department." Its target was the anti-Japanese forces in Tonghua, a region labeled a "cancer" by Japanese authorities.

The Japanese ostensibly launched the "Eastern Border Region Independent Suppression Campaign" to test the puppet Manchukuo army's capabilities in "suppression" and "pacification." In reality, however, their goal was to force Chinese collaborators to kill their own compatriots, thereby minimizing Japanese casualties. Major General Sasaki Tōichi unabashedly declared: "The Imperial Army continues to bleed across the region, expending immense effort on public security. If we delegate such burdens to Manchukuo's institutions, the Imperial Army can focus on its core missions."

The Japanese, self-proclaimed as a "superior race", believed that the blood of their soldiers had built "Manchukuo" and its puppet army, allowing Chinese collaborators—high-ranking officials and over a hundred thousand puppet troops—to live in luxury while enjoying salaries. Thus, they argued, these collaborators should now "bleed in place of the Imperial Army."

All traitors, like dogs, could not escape their subservient nature. Despite being despised by their Japanese masters, Manchukuo officials and puppet troops obediently followed orders. This ingrained servility allowed the "Eastern Border Region Independent Suppression Campaign" to escalate into an exceptionally brutal operation.

The Dongbiandao, an administrative region established in 1877 during the Guangxu era, became the focal point of this six-month campaign led by Major General Sasaki Tōichi. It targeted northern Dongbiandao, including counties such as Ji'an, Tonghua, Liuhe, Huinan, Jinchuan, Mengjiang, Linjiang, Fusong, and Changbai, as well as parts of Panshi, Huadian, and Antu. The primary objectives were the Northeast Anti-Japanese Allied Army's 1st and 2nd Corps and Wang Fengge's Anti-Japanese Salvation Army. Sasaki's "suppression command" mobilized 27,500 puppet troops for this operation.

All is fair in war. To break the enemy's encirclement, Yang Jingyu devised a plan to expand guerrilla zones in Kuandian. However, the heavily fortified town of Dahuanggou posed a critical threat. Yang ordered a unit from the 1st Army's Independent 11th Division to disguise themselves as bandits, while another group posed as puppet security forces tasked with "suppressing" them. News of this "bandit activity" was deliberately leaked to Dahuanggou's garrison.

To enhance realism, the two disguised forces staged a mock battle outside the town. The "bandits" fled while the "security forces" pursued them. When the fake security forces demanded entry at Dahuanggou's eastern gate, the garrison initially refused. A soldier disguised as a Japanese advisor, Liu, shouted orders in Japanese, with a translator threatening: "The Imperial advisor declares: If you refuse to open the gates, you will be treated as collaborators!"

The gates opened, and the garrison lined up to welcome the "allies". Seizing the moment, the "advisor" berated the garrison for failing to pursue the "bandits" and ordered the disarming of all 30 puppet police officers.

The raid, timed to coincide with the fifth anniversary of the September 18 Incident, carried profound political symbolism. Four days later, the Shengjing Times reported: "Red Bandits Breach Dahuanggou with Lightning Tactics."

Given the Anti-Japanese Allied Army's inferior equipment, Yang Jingyu prioritized overwhelming force and rapid engagements to avoid protracted battles.

After capturing Dahuanggou, he led 300 troops to ambush a Japanese grain convoy in Kuandian in late September, killing 14 soldiers (including Corporal Shirai Ganjirō and destroying nine trucks. In October, his 250-strong unit clashed with 700 Japanese-puppet troops at Waisanbao, killing Major and inflicting 30 casualties.[15]

The simultaneous implementation of the "Eastern Border Region Grand Suppression Campaign", "collective hamlets", and "separation of civilians from resistance forces" policies plunged the Northeast Anti-Japanese Allied Army's 1st Corps into unprecedented hardship. Prior to 1936, basic supplies such as food, clothing, and shelter were manageable. However, after the launch of the "Eastern Border Region Grand Suppression Campaign", troops were forced to camp in open fields, using the sky as their roof and the earth as there be. Summers brought relentless torrential rains and scorching heat, compounded by swarms of mosquitoes, biting flies, and disease-carrying ticks. The hard ticks (scientific name: Ixodidae), known locally as "grass climbers", transmitted deadly diseases such as epidemic meningitis and hemorrhagic fever. Winters were even more brutal. Howling winds and blizzards forced soldiers to huddle around bonfires, lying in a circle with their feet toward the flames and heads facing outward to catch brief moments of rest. To avoid detection, troops often sought shelter in snowdrifts on leeward slopes, but many succumbed to frostbite or illness, leading to severe attrition.

Yang Jingyu, the commander of the 1st Corps, grew increasingly apprehensive.

50. Turning the Japanese into "Lice on a Bald Head"

A competent general understands that a military force's combat effectiveness relies not only on superior weaponry and well-trained soldiers but also on robust logistical support. The sleep and diet of soldiers are crucial components of combat readiness.

Yang Jingyu once told his officers, "If we can't even resolve the issue of where our troops can camp, how can we sustain a prolonged war of resistance? Harsh conditions alone will destroy us before the enemy does." He led soldiers in developing mobile tents. After multiple trials, they successfully created a versatile tent that could accommodate dozens of men, adapt to any terrain, and be easily assembled or disassembled. Resembling a small house, it allowed indoor heating, protected against mosquitoes in summer and cold in winter, and finally solved the problem of open-air camping.

The enemy's "collective hamlet" policy nearly severed the Anti-Japanese Alliance's supply lines, leaving troops without food for weeks. To counter this, as early as 1935, Yang Jingyu began constructing secret camps deep in remote, defensible forests with access to water.

These camps, built in "shed-style" or "underground bunker-style," were hidden under dense foliage and featured earthen beds and smoke vents. They included living quarters, granaries, tailor shops, armories, temporary hospitals, and printing presses. For instance, over ten such camps were established in Laotudingzi Mountain (Huanren County), dozens in Naerhong and Qingjianggang (Mengjiang County), and larger ones in the Longgang Mountains—each stocked with four months' worth of food for 400 soldiers. [16]

Building these camps was grueling. Veteran Wang Hongwen of the 1st Division once led 30 soldiers to construct two secret warehouses in Xianggou (Huangmuyangdong Mountain, Xingjing) and Yanghugou (Jianchang, Benxi).

They dug 10-meter tunnels into hillsides, creating 6.7-meter-wide, 4-meter-high chambers. Excavated soil was dumped into ravines and camouflaged with transplanted trees and grass. Smoke vents were disguised as shallow, kilometer-long trenches covered with wood and soil to disperse fumes stealthily.

The secrecy surrounding these projects was extreme: only top leaders knew their locations, and builders like Wang Hongwen were handpicked.

Tragically, Hu Guochen, the quartermaster who attended the secret planning meeting, later defected after capture, leading to the destruction of many camps—a heartbreaking footnote in history.

During the brutal "Eastern Border Region Independent Suppression Campaign," battles were lopsided and ferocious. In October 1935, Deputy Commander Wang Detai of the 1st Route Army led 200 soldiers against the puppet Manchurian 7th Brigade's 10th Regiment at Dongqinggou (Antu County), killing dozens, including Japanese Colonel Ishizō Ryukichi and Lieutenant Colonel Kawamura. [16]

In late October, the 4th Division surrounded and attacked the puppet Manchurian military camp at Dayangcha, Linjiang, disarming two entire companies. In early November 1935, Wang Detai led over 300 soldiers to operate near Xiaotanghe in Fusong County when they were suddenly ambushed by over 600 cavalrymen from the puppet Manchurian 7th Cavalry Regiment. Despite fierce counterattacks that killed 60 enemies, Wang Detai was fatally struck by gunfire at the age of 29. His death marked a devastating loss for the 1st Route Army.

In March 1937, Zuo Ziyuan, commander of the 11th Independent Division of the 1st Army, led his troops to gather supplies but was encircled by a large enemy force. Though Zuo fought valiantly, his unit suffered heavy casualties during the breakout. After exhausting his ammunition, Zuo leaped off a cliff to his death at the age of 31.[17] On the same day, Wang Fengge, a leader of the Anti-Japanese Volunteer Army, was captured grievously wounded and executed.

The "Eastern Border Region Independent Suppression Campaign" inflicted severe damage on anti-Japanese forces in southeastern Manchuria. According to the confession of Wang Zhiyou, a war criminal of the puppet Manchukuo regime, during the "suppression" from autumn 1936 to May

1937, approximately 20 battles occurred, with anti-Japanese forces suffering over 1,000 casualties each side. Around 100 secret camps were burned, and vast quantities of supplies were seized. The total strength of the Anti-Japanese Allied Forces (including volunteer armies) was reduced by roughly 10,000 men...[18]

Thanks to the secret camps prepared in advance, the enemy failed to locate Yang Jingyu during the "Great Suppression". In February 1937, Yang spent the Lunar New Year at the Laotudingzi Mountain secret camp in Huanren. Later, leading a 150-man training regiment, he maneuvered against hundreds of puppet troops across Matigou, Daojian Ridge, and Yaoqianshu Ridge, inflicting over 70 casualties and ultimately breaking through the encirclement of the "Eastern Border Region Independent Suppression Campaign".

After the July 7th Incident (Marco Polo Bridge Incident) in 1937, Japanese invaders prioritized securing Manchukuo as a rear base for their war in China. The growing activities of the Northeast Anti-Japanese Allied Forces heightened their anxiety. To suppress resistance and maintain "public order", Japanese-puppet authorities relentlessly enforced their "Public Peace and Order Consolidation" plan, intensifying "suppression" campaigns against anti-Japanese forces, particularly the Allied Armies. Dissatisfied with relying solely on puppet troops and police for "independent" operations, Japan deployed main divisions of the Kwantung Army to directly crush resistance.

In 1936, Japanese forces in Manchuria included 4 divisions, 2 mixed brigades, 2 cavalry brigades, and 16 independent garrison units—totaling 120,000 troops. This number surged annually after 1937, exceeding 400,000 by 1939. [19] Japan used Manchuria as a "training ground" for its full-scale invasion of China, rotating domestic divisions into the Kwantung Army for live combat drills against both the Allied Armies and the Eighth Route Army along the Great Wall. Simultaneously, Japan bolstered puppet forces through conscription.

The puppet Manchukuo's *National Military Service Law* mandated that all men aged 19 serve in the military. Those deemed unfit for "national service" were forced into the "Labor Service Corps", toiling on military projects, road construction, mining, and land reclamation.

By 1939, Japan expanded puppet military administration from 6 to 8 districts, reaching 11 by 1941. The puppet army comprised 2 divisions (Jing'an and Xing'an), 7 mixed brigades, 4 infantry brigades, 1 cavalry brigade, 2 independent cavalry regiments, and more—totaling 200,000 troops. [20] Entirely controlled by Japanese officers, their primary task was to "independently" or jointly suppress anti-Japanese forces.

Meanwhile, Japanese-puppet authorities expanded police and gendarmerie forces, trained special agents, and established a pervasive surveillance network across Manchuria. With 100,000 puppet police alone [21], this apparatus, directed by Japanese military police, became a primary target for Allied Army raids.

Sanjiang Province, located in northeastern Manchuria where the Heilong, Songhua, and Ussuri Rivers converge, bordered the Soviet Union. Its remote terrain—featuring the Zhangguangcai and Wanda Mountains and the vast Sanjiang Plain—harbored weaker Japanese control, allowing the Allied Armies to thrive. Units active here included the 3rd, 4th, 5th, 6th, 7th, 8th, 9th Armies and the Independent Division (later 11th Army). Except for the 1st and 2nd Armies in southern/eastern Manchuria and the 10th Army near Wuchang and Shulan, nearly all Northeast Allied Forces operated in Sanjiang, making it a focal point for Japanese suppression.

On July 16, 1937—nine days after the July 7th Incident—the Kwantung Army Headquarters issued the *Second Phase Public Security Pacification*

Plan Outline for the 10th Year of Showa (July 1937–March 1938), launching a full-scale "special grand suppression" in the puppet Sanjiang Province. This operation mobilized approximately 50,000 Japanese and puppet troops, police, gendarmes, spies, and militia, including key units of the Kwantung Army such as the 2nd, 4th, and 12th Divisions and parts of the 4th and 5th Independent Garrison Battalions. By the summer of 1938, Japan further deployed parts of the 8th and 10th Divisions, forcing the Northeast Anti-Japanese United Army (Northeast Anti-Japanese Coalition) into an extremely arduous phase of resistance.

Due to overwhelming enemy numbers, the anti-Japanese guerrilla zones were gradually compressed. Additionally, the "March 15th Mass Arrests" devastated underground Party organizations, leaving the Anti-Japanese Coalition units largely isolated and ill-informed. Continuous counter-"suppression" battles exhausted ammunition and supplies and faced with enemies vastly superior in equipment and manpower, some lost confidence in continuing the fight. A portion of the recruited forest forces considered disbanding or hiding their weapons, while a few even contemplated surrendering to Japanese political enticements through "special task forces." While targeting the main forces of the Anti-Japanese Coalition, the Japanese and puppet troops cynically promoted slogans like "Attack only Communist bandits, spare the Volunteer Armies and forest forces."

Zhao Shangzhi's strategy was clear: break through enemy encirclements, strike their rear lines, avoid static defenses, launch expeditions into weakly garrisoned areas, and establish new guerrilla zones. His goal was to ensure that "not a single stretch of land in Northeast China would lack the footprints of our anti-Japanese resistance forces."

To thwart the enemy's plot to annihilate the main forces of the 3rd and 6th Armies in the Tangyuan base area, Zhao ordered the 6th Army to assault Huachuan and Yilan, while the 3rd Army advanced toward Qingcheng and

Tieli. From there, they would push to the border regions of Heilongjiang and Nenjiang—Hailun, Tongbei, and Xunhe—to establish new guerrilla bases.

To secure the 3rd Army's westward expedition into Heilongjiang-Nenjiang (Hei-Nen), Zhao appointed Li Xishan as commander of the Northern Harbin District, dispatching him to Tieli first. In early October 1936, Li led a vanguard unit from Yidong, joining forces with the 3rd Army's 9th Division in Tonghe County to march west. By early November, they reached Tieli, linking up with the 3rd Army's 6th Division, which had arrived earlier that summer from Bayan and Mulan. Accompanying Li's vanguard were troops from the 5th Army's 1st Division and the 4th Army's 2nd Regiment, both arriving simultaneously. Shortly after, the 3rd Army's 2nd and 3rd Divisions also broke through enemy blockades to reach Tieli.

While the divisions pressed westward, Zhao Shangzhi remained in Tangyuan with the 3rd Army's headquarters, a political security division, and over 500 elite cavalrymen. These mobile forces maneuvered unpredictably, drawing the attention of Japanese-puppet troops and covering the retreat of other units. Only after all divisions had escaped encirclement did Zhao finally withdraw.

During the retreat, Zhao executed a masterful diversion: he feigned an attack on Hulan County by advancing toward Mulan's Mongolian Mountain. The enemy, convinced of the threat, massed defenses along the Bayan-Mulan line. Once their forces were locked in place, Zhao abruptly swung northward, galloping day and night to reach Tieli by December 1936, leaving pursuers far behind.

From autumn 1936 to spring 1937, Zhao's Hei-Nen expedition strategically disrupted enemy suppression campaigns, tying down significant Japanese-puppet forces. During this period, the 3rd Army waged over 100 battles across thousands of li—from Tangyuan, Yilan, Tonghe, Fangzheng,

Mulan, and Bayan along the Songhua River to Xunke and Foshun along the Heilongjiang border, and from Tieli, Qingcheng, and Suiling at the foot of the Lesser Khingan Mountains to Hailun, Tongbei, Bei'an, and Longmen along the Bei'an-Heihe Railway. These operations killed or wounded over 800 enemies, captured more than 300, and raided 20–30 towns. [22]

During this period, the 3rd Army's expeditionary forces also suffered heavy losses, with over 30 military-political cadres and 200 soldiers sacrificing their lives. Their courageous battles and heroic sacrifices shattered the enemy's "Great Suppression" campaign centered on the five counties of Binzhou, Mulan, Tonghe, Tangyuan, and Yilan. Not only did they defend the Tangyuan base area, but they also established new guerrilla zones in Qingcheng, Tieli, Tongbei, and Hailun, laying a crucial foundation for the Anti-Japanese Allied Forces' guerrilla operations in the Hei-Nen Plain during the even harsher phase of resistance after 1938.

While leading the expedition into the Hei-Nen Plain, Zhao Shangzhi engaged in a fierce battle near Zhangpo Maozi Dian (a site in eastern Tongbei's mountainous region). Here, mountain springs had frozen into a glacier at the foot of a hill, locally known as "Bingtangzi" ("Ice Field"). The battle thus became known as the "Battle of Bingtangzi", a renowned example of defeating a larger force with fewer troops, holding significant importance in the history of Northeast Anti-Japanese guerrilla warfare.

Zhangpo Maozi Dian was a vital thoroughfare for carts and horses traveling between the county town and the mountains, featuring several shops where travelers rested. North of the road lay the ice field, while to the south was a low, densely forested ridge. Four sturdy log cabins, once housing lumberjacks, stood nearby. After surveying the terrain, Zhao concluded it was ideal for an ambush: narrow gullies could trap retreating enemies, and the ice field would leave them exposed. "If we lure the enemy onto the glacier," he declared, "they'll be like lice on a bald head—nowhere to hide."

Zhao assigned the task of baiting the enemy to Zhang Guangdi, commander of the 6th Division. On the afternoon of March 7, Zhang and 20 soldiers hid near the southern ridge. Soon, a convoy of horse-drawn sleds carrying over 100 enemies approached. When they entered firing range, Zhang shouted, "Open fire!" Bullets rained down, but the lightly wounded enemy quickly dismounted and returned fire. Realizing the small scale of the ambush, they launched a countercharge.

Zhang Guangdi's unit retreated in stages, luring the enemy into a second ambush by the 3rd Army' main force. Four machine guns erupted, mowing down over 30 Japanese-puppet troops.

Rather than pursuing the survivors, Zhao ordered a swift withdrawal to the Bingtangzi positions.

By evening, Japanese Captain Morita of the Takeuchi Unit, enraged by the earlier defeat, led over 700 troops to retaliate. As usual, puppet soldiers were pushed ahead as cannon fodder. A hesitant puppet unit entered the kill zone, only to have their commander killed instantly. The rest fled in panic. The 200 Japanese troops, disdainful of their puppet allies, charged toward the log cabins but stumbled helplessly on the ice. Six machine guns atop the ridge tore through their ranks, sending survivors scrambling back.

Enraged by the earlier resistance, Captain Morita launched a second and third ferocious assault on the hill, leveraging superior numbers and firepower. It must be acknowledged that the Japanese troops fought tenaciously, fueled by their "bushido" spirit of sacrifice. After brutal close-quarters combat, they managed to seize a wooden fortification on the hill, turning the battle into a stalemate. Losing this position would expose our flank to devastating artillery fire, jeopardizing the entire strategic advantage.

In this critical moment, Zhao Shangzhi (a key commander of the Northeast Anti-Japanese United Army) ordered the Youth Company to retake the position at all costs before the enemy could fortify it. Acting Platoon Leader Zhao Youcai led two squads of young soldiers in a desperate counterattack. The wooden fortification changed hands multiple times in a bloody seesaw struggle, until the surviving Japanese—fewer than 20—were driven out, leaving the rest dead.

That night, fighting raged on. The low walls of the hilltop compound became makeshift defenses, with gunports hastily carved into the wooden structure. The temperature plummeted to such extremes that rifle bolts froze shut, and soldiers' fingers grew too numb to pull triggers. The reclaimed fortification proved vital: oil-drum stoves inside glowed red-hot. Zhao Shangzhi ordered troops to rotate in, thawing their weapons and warming themselves before returning to the fight. Countless rifles spat fire into the enemy ranks.

Stranded on the open, icy terrain, Japanese forces found themselves trapped on slippery ice patches ("bing tangzi"), unable to advance. They focused their fire on the fortification, but pitch darkness neutralized their artillery's accuracy. Mid-attack, their formation was suddenly shredded by flanking fire—Zhao had dispatched a small harassment squad to ambush them from a northern river gully.

By midnight, the merciless cold plunged below -40°C. Japanese troops, frozen in the snow, could barely return fire. Sensing their imminent retreat, Zhao positioned warmed-up soldiers at a narrow gully exit. As the enemy staggered back, a storm of bullets ripped through their densely packed, frostbitten ranks.

Post-retreat, Zhao ordered his men to scavenge the battlefield. The haul was immense, including a discarded Type 92 machine gun and vast ammunition. The battle cost just seven anti-Japanese fighters' lives, while inflicting over 300 enemy casualties: 200+ killed, 100+ wounded or frostbitten. [23] Such a toll—rare in Northeast Anti-Japanese annals—included elite officers like Captain Morita of the Takeda Unit and Fukuda Masao, security advisor to Tongbei County.

After securing the battlefield, Zhao Shangzhi commanded his troops to depart aboard captured horse-drawn sleds (mǎ páli, a traditional winter vehicle used in Northeast China). Laden with seized supplies—rice, meat, clothing, military blankets, and more—the convoy kicked up a whirlwind of snow as it vanished swiftly into the distance.

51. Faint Gunfire Behind the Enemy's Back

Most of the Northeast Anti-Japanese Allied Forces were concentrated in the puppet Sanjiang Province, particularly the Lower Songhua River region (referred to as "Xiajiang"). To crush them, Japanese-puppet forces launched the "Three Rivers Special Suppression Campaign," pushing the Allied Forces eastward from Harbin's southern and eastern flanks while blocking westward movement via the Qiqihar-Heihe Railway. Simultaneously, they tightened their grip using railroads and "collective hamlets" from southern to eastern Jilin, herding the resistance fighters into Xiajiang. Once concentrated, the enemy amassed ground and air forces to encircle and annihilate them in a shrinking perimeter.

This analysis, presented by Zhou Baozhong at a late 1937 Xiajiang Special Committee meeting, underscored the urgency of his proposal: Allied armies must disperse strategically to avoid encirclement.

Compared to other units, Zhou's Second Route Army benefited from superior intelligence networks and his acute grasp of the conflict, enabling preemptive actions. In April 1938, the Jidong Provincial Committee ordered the Second Route Army's main force to expedition southwest toward Wuchang and Shulan—a campaign later known as the "Western Expedition"—to break the enemy's stranglehold on Yilan, Huachuan, Fujin, and Baoqing.

The expedition split into two routes: Western Route: Cavalry from the 4th and 5th Armies, led by Li Yanping (4th Army commander) and Wang Guangyu (deputy commander), joined forces with Chen Hanzhang's 5th Division of the 2nd Army to penetrate Ning'an's northwest, establishing a rear base near Laoyeling Mountain. The 8th Army's cavalry was also expected to participate. Eastern Route: Infantry led by Chai Shirong (5th Army commander) and Song Yifu (political director) advanced toward Wuchang and Yushu, aiming to link with the 1st and 2nd Armies. Song Yifu, as Jidong Provincial Committee secretary, held final decision-making authority.

The campaign faltered from the start. Xie Wendong, commander of the non-aligned 8th Army, refused to contribute troops, while Japanese-puppet forces disrupted mobilizations with repeated ambushes, delaying assembly by over a month.

Forced to revise plans, leaders abandoned the original strategy of first securing Ning'an and redirected all forces directly toward Wuchang. The expedition reorganized into three echelons: Vanguard (150 troops): Led by 1st Division commander Guan Shufan. Second Echelon (260 troops): Commanded by Li Yanping and Song Yifu. Third Echelon (270 troops): Under Chai Shirong and Wang Guangyu. Total strength: 680 troops, with Song Yifu retaining overall command.

Unlike previous "suppressions" led by puppet forces, the "Three Rivers Special Suppression" saw direct involvement of the Kwantung Army's 4th

Division, commanded by Yamashita Tomoyuki (later infamously dubbed the "Tiger of Malaya") and orchestrated by Tojo Hideki (then Kwantung Army chief of staff, later Prime Minister and Class-A war criminal)—both ruthless strategists.

The ill-fated Western Expedition's sole success was the raid on Loushan Town in Weihe County. Located south of the Chinese Eastern Railway, this timber logistics hub was guarded by a puppet Manchurian garrison and a White Russian railway defense battalion. Prior to the attack, the expeditionary force had trekked over 150 kilometers through uninhabited primordial forests, evading enemy detection entirely.

In mid-July 1938, the Allies stormed Loushan, killing, wounding, and capturing dozens of enemies, seizing two light machine guns, nearly 100 rifles, over 40,000 rounds of ammunition, and vast quantities of food and uniforms. They also destroyed forest railways, bridges, and communication facilities. Mistaking the assault for a resurgence of Zhao Shangzhi's 3rd Army, Japanese forces nearly emptied their garrisons across six counties in eastern Harbin. Yet this triumph marked a turning point: the expeditionary force soon found itself heavily surrounded by Japanese-puppet troops.

Amid escalating threats, the expedition fragmented: Chai Shirong and Wang Yinwu's 5th Army Training Regiment retreated to Diaoling. Guan Shufan's 1st Division diverted to Erdaohezi to link with the 2nd Army's 5th Division. Li Yanping and Song Yifu pressed toward Wuchang with the 4th Army and 5th Army's 2nd Division, hoping to revive resistance in old 3rd Army zones.

This optimism proved misguided. The once-friendly Wuchang region was now dotted with "collective hamlets," isolating the troops. Lost in Yanshou County, they clashed repeatedly with enemies but prevailed in the Huanggou counterattack, killing 30 foes. By late July, regrouping in Weihe

County, they merged with Guan Shufan's unit and resumed their desperate push toward Wuchang.

Along the march, coordination between infantry and cavalry faltered, hampering progress. Strict enemy blockades triggered a severe supply crisis—soldiers went over ten days without food, staggering through forests while scavenging wild herbs, grape leaves, and mushrooms. Eventually, they slaughtered their horses, consuming even the bones and hooves after devouring the meat and hides. Without salt, many suffered debilitating diarrhea and edema, their bodies swelling until they collapsed and died in the wilderness.

In late July, desperate for supplies, the expedition attacked another "collective hamlet" but drew relentless pursuit near Yimianpo. Forced to retreat across the Bin-Sui Railway into dense mountains, they faced a catastrophic betrayal at their darkest hour.

Song Yifu, secretary of the Jidong Provincial Committee, political director of the Second Route Army, and the expedition's supreme decision-maker, defected to the enemy.

Born Song Xiaoxian in 1911 Shandong, Song joined the CCP in 1933, rising swiftly from Ning'an Youth League secretary to Jidong's top post. At 27, he became the highest-ranking Party and military traitor in the Northeast.

Generally, people are reluctant to mention the positive contributions of a traitor prior to their betrayal. After the September 18th Incident, Song Yifu had joined the Anti-Japanese Volunteer Army. In the spring of 1933, he served as the political commissar of the Muling Guerrilla Force, working alongside Hu Ren and Zhang Zhenhua to develop this resistance force. Starting with just 21 members, they orchestrated night raids against puppet mine police and rallied defections from puppet security forces, expanding the guerrilla unit to over 100 fighters. Song was later promoted to Secretary of the Communist Party's Muling County Committee. At that time, Song was passionate and revolutionary, earning the Party's trust. Within four to five years, he became the youngest provincial committee secretary in the Northeast Party organization.

However, during the Western Expedition—a critical juncture requiring decisive leadership—Song, who had recently vowed to "shed his last drop of blood to fulfill the Party's mission," abandoned his troops near the South of the Chinese Eastern Railway under the pretext of inspecting sentry posts. He fled with 1,200 yuan of public funds and a pistol.[24]

Just how devastating can a traitor be—especially when it's a high-ranking cadre?

An ordinary defector may only surrender secrets within their limited knowledge, but the betrayal of a senior official exposes all classified intelligence under their authority, plunging resistance forces into military catastrophe and triggering a domino effect of demoralization.

When Song Yifu fled, Japanese puppet authorities launched a widespread manhunt. After discovering he had secretly returned to Harbin, they intensified their citywide search. Soon, Song voluntarily surrendered and "defected," divulging all secrets and top-level intelligence he knew—particularly the Western Expedition plan and the dire state of the troops.

The Japanese puppet regime swiftly mobilized over 500 elite Japanese troops from Harbin and Changchun, along with 2,500 well-equipped puppet soldiers and local garrisons, supported by six or seven aircraft, to encircle the Western Expedition forces. From then on, the troops faced even grimmer conditions. By mid-August, they reached Chonghe in Wuchang County. To avoid annihilation, the Fourth and Fifth Armies split to operate separately.

With their strategies completely exposed, the Fourth Army's situation deteriorated, dwindling to just over 100 survivors. Historical records offer no insight into the mental states of commanders Li Yanping and Wang Guangyu following Song's betrayal, but documents show they continued fighting tenaciously. To reunite with Wang Yachen's Tenth Army—a key objective of the Western Expedition—Li led his troops toward Jiushiwudingzi in Wuchang.

Wang Yachen, upon learning of their approach, mobilized forces to assist. However, near Xiaoshanzi, his troops encountered fierce enemy resistance. Wang was wounded in the battle and forced to retreat to Jiushiwudingzi. Though he later reconnected with the Fourth Army, providing supplies and aid, he could not reverse their overall disadvantage.

Li Yanping, born in 1903 in Yanji, worked as a leatherworker before joining the National Salvation Army after the September 18 Incident. He served as a staff officer, adjutant, and commander of the Suining Guerrilla Detachment, and was sent by the Party to study at Eastern University in Moscow. After Li Yanlu's transfer, Li Yanping acted as acting commander of the Fourth Army before formally assuming the role six months later.

1937 marked a year of expansion for the Northeast Anti-Japanese United Army, which grew to over 30,000 troops across 11 armies. However, historical notes describe the Fourth Army as "weak and underdeveloped" [25], attributed partly to Li Yanping's leadership style: mild-mannered and lacking commanding authority. Compounded by the Fourth Army's origins as loosely organized mountain forest units, early combat losses further eroded morale. The earnest Li Yanping reportedly requested the Party's Jidong Provincial Committee appoint a more capable replacement.

1937 marked a year of expansion for the Northeast Anti-Japanese United Army, which grew to over 30,000 troops across 11 armies. However, historical notes describe the Fourth Army as "weak and underdeveloped" [25], attributed partly to Li Yanping's leadership style: mild-mannered and lacking commanding authority. Compounded by the Fourth Army's origins as loosely organized mountain forest units, early combat losses further eroded morale. The earnest Li Yanping reportedly requested the Party's Jidong Provincial Committee appoint a more capable replacement.

History proved Zhou Baozhong right. Li Yanping maintained excellent relations with other army units and local forces. He was a principled leader who prioritized the broader revolutionary cause, and above all, he remained unwaveringly committed to resisting Japan and sacrificing everything for victory. In the brutal struggle against the enemy, loyalty and conviction proved far more vital than tactical brilliance.

The betrayal of Song Yifu wrought both military and political devastation. Militarily, it enabled Japanese puppet forces to relentlessly pursue and encircle the Fourth Army. By late September, the Fourth Army was overwhelmed, its ranks scattered, and over 60 soldiers captured. Politically, it emboldened wavering elements within the resistance. Demoralization spread, triggering desertions and further betrayals. Among them was Qu Chengshan, commander of the First Division, who coerced three soldiers into defecting with him, stealing rifles and 500 yuan of public funds.

The enemy's dual tactics of ruthless suppression and enticing offers — promising defectors the same comfortable treatment as Song Yifu, sparing them from eating tree bark and sleeping in snow — directly fueled Qu Chengshan's treason. Yet Li Yanping and Wang Guangyu persisted. By November, reduced to nine men (the two commanders and seven soldiers) with no food, shelter, or ammunition, their fighting spirit remained unbroken.

Then came the political aftershock of Song's betrayal. Three soldiers plotted to kill Li and Wang to claim rewards from the enemy. During a nighttime encampment, the traitors opened fire. Li Yanping, struck in the chest, died at age 35.[26] Wang Guangyu, wounded in the arm, grabbed his pistol and returned fire, driving the three assassins into retreat. Burying his comrade in grief, Wang led the four surviving fighters onward through blizzards and bitter cold. By year's end, starving and frostbitten, they engaged the enemy one final time — fighting to the last breath.[27]

Wang Guangyu (born Wang Mingtang, 1911, Dehui, Jilin) joined the anti-Japanese struggle after the September 18 Incident and became a Communist Party member in 1933. Before serving as deputy commander of the Fourth Army, he had distinguished himself as regimental commissar, division political director, and division commander in the Fifth Army, earning recognition as both a skilled strategist and frontline fighter. He died at 27.

The disastrous Western Expedition of the Second Route Army saw catastrophic losses: over two-thirds of the Fourth Army and half of the Fifth Army were annihilated, with equivalent losses in weaponry. While the root causes included the enemy's overwhelming strength and the resistance's fragility, leadership failures — particularly the lack of unity between Song Yifu and Guan Shufan (commander of the Fifth Army's First Division, who openly disdained Song) — compounded the disaster. Yet Song Yifu's betrayal undeniably sealed their fate.

After defecting, Song Yifu became a police inspector in the puppet regime's Binjiang Province, actively sabotaging underground Communist networks. He was arrested and executed in Harbin in 1946, ending his 35-year life of infamy.

The Fifth Army's Western Expedition forces, after separating from the Fourth Army, launched attacks under the leadership of Guan Shufan (commander of the First Division) and Tao Jingfei (political director of the

Second Division). They raided enemy timber camps in Daqingchuan and Chonghe, advanced into Shulan, then retreated to Wuchang. While crossing the Mangniu River, they clashed with Japanese troops, resulting in the First and Second Divisions losing contact.

After the split, Guan Shufan led 110 survivors of the First Division back to their starting point in Diaoling to reconnect with the Fifth Army headquarters. Meanwhile, Tao Jingfei guided a contingent from the Second Division's Fifth Regiment toward the old guerrilla base in Ning'an, aiming to join forces with the Second Army's Fifth Division. Both commanders were seasoned leaders, adept at navigating perilous battles and complex situations.

In late autumn, the First Division camped along the Wusihun River (a Mudan River's tributary north of Linkou). The Manchu-named River, meaning "Fierce Torrent," lived up to its reputation that year. Unseasonal rains had swollen its waters to flood-like levels, churning a hundred-meter-wide expanse of murky rapids. The original ferry crossing was obliterated.

As night fell, the soldiers lit fires for warmth. But the flickering flames drew the gaze of Ge Hailu — a former bandit and ex-adjutant of the Anti-Japanese Ninth Army. That evening, while seeking an old flame, he spotted the campfires from afar. Years of wilderness survival sharpened his instincts. He raced to the Japanese garrison, trading betrayal for profit.

Colonel Kumagai of the Diaoling Japanese garrison mobilized over 30 cavalrymen and rushed to Zhamugang Hill. Under the cover of darkness, the cautious Kumagai waited for reinforcements, planning to strike at dawn. Unaware of the impending danger, Guan Shufan and his troops remained exposed.

After the Battle of Loushan Town, the Western Expedition forces had consolidated over 30 female fighters from the Fourth and Fifth Armies into a Women's Regiment under the Fifth Army. By this point, only eight remained.[28] As the troops approached the river, Guan Shufan ordered Jin Shifeng — a skilled swimmer and staff officer — to test the water's depth. If fordable, the Women's Regiment would cross first. "Women deserve protection," Guan insisted, "especially when only eight are left."

As Staff Officer Jin waded into the river, the First Division troops began moving toward the bank. The female soldiers, having risen earlier, had already gathered by the water's edge — drawn, perhaps, by an innate affinity for the river. Then gunfire shattered the dawn. The men instinctively scrambled toward the hilltop, a defensible position shrouded in dense forest. Hearing the shots, the women retreated into riverside willow thickets — towering clusters of wrist-thick saplings shrouded in waist-high grass. Unseen, they watched as enemy fire rained mercilessly on their comrades.

Crossing the river was impossible; none could swim. They could have remained hidden, waiting for the enemy to chase their comrades away, then slipped upstream or downstream into the woods. Survival was within reach.

Bullets suddenly erupted from the willows — eight rifles, feeble yet ferocious, striking the enemy's rear flank. For any battlefield commander, this was a nightmare: forces pinned between two fronts, however uneven.

The sporadic gunfire from eight rifles, though not intense, immediately drew and diverted the enemy's assault on the First Division soldiers. A locust-like hail of bullets rained down on the willow thickets, setting the dry grass ablaze with artillery shells. The willow branches crackled fiercely as they burned. Seizing the moment when the enemy split their forces, Guan Shufan decisively ordered a charge, breaking through the encirclement. Upon discovering eight female soldiers trapped by the river, Guan turned back to rescue them but failed. He was forced to retreat into the dense forests of Zuomugang with his remaining troops. Seeing the main Anti-Japanese forces withdraw, the enemy concentrated fire on the women's unit, howling for surrender while attempting to capture them alive.

Cornered at the riverbank with no retreat, the eight women exhausted their final bullets. Shouldering their wounded comrades, they linked arms and, under the leadership of political instructor Leng Yun, strode resolutely into the raging currents of the Wusihun River. All perished heroically. [29]

The Japanese shifted focus instantly. A hailstorm of bullets tore into the thickets. Incendiary rounds ignited dry grass, and flames crackled through the willows. In that split-second distraction, Guan Shufan launched a desperate charge, breaking the encirclement. When he realized the women were trapped, he wheeled back — too late. Forced to retreat into Zhamugang's forests, he left the Japanese to converge on the riverside. With ammunition spent, the eight fighters — political instructor Leng Yun at their helm — hoisted their wounded and waded into the Wusihun's raging current. Enemy howls echoed behind them: "Surrender! We'll spare you!"

Leng Yun, originally named Zheng Xiangzhi, was born in 1915 to a prosperous family in Huachuan County. After entering the county's Women's Normal School in 1931, she adopted the name Zheng Zhimin to signify her commitment to serving the nation. Secretly joining the Chinese Communist Party in 1934, she became a teacher at Nanmenli Primary School (later renamed "Leng Yun Primary School" post-1949) after graduation in 1935, conducting underground work under the leadership of the Jiamusi Municipal Party Committee.

Forced into an arranged marriage with Sun Hanqi, a local puppet police lieutenant approved by her father as a "family protector," Leng Yun resisted. To ensure her safety and that of her underground network, she was transferred to the Northeast Anti-Japanese United Army.

Her disappearance left her mother blind from weeping until 1952, when the film *Daughters of China* revealed Leng Yun's identity as the leader of the Eight Heroines who drowned themselves in the Wusihun River. Leng Yun died at 23. [30]

The second among the eight martyrs to enter the river was Yang Guizhen, a native of Lianhua Town, Linkou County. Married at 16, she was widowed within a year. Life as a widow proved bitter—her in-laws plotted to sell her to recoup the five dan of corn spent on her dowry. At this critical juncture, the Fifth Army of the Northeast Anti-Japanese United Army arrived to establish a base. Xu Yunqing, a female soldier and former child bride, persuaded Yang to join. Clutching her face in tears, Yang cried, "My family already ate up all five dan of corn." Women's Corps commander Wang Yushun reassured her: "Is a woman's life worth only five dan of corn? Don't fear—no one can stop you from resisting Japan."

Yang finally removed the crumpled white flower pinned to her hair and followed the Women's Corps into the mountains. Transformed after enlisting, she excelled in every task at the clothing factory and field hospital. By the following autumn, she joined the Communist Party, rising to squad leader and later marrying her beloved Ning Manchang. Their bond began when Yang nursed Ning after a battle injury. Both joined the Western Expedition, but Ning died in combat. No records confirm whether Yang knew of her husband's death, though their sacrifices occurred within six months of each other. Yang was 18 when she perished.

Another pillar among the eight was An Shunfu, a Korean compatriot nicknamed "Sister An." Born in 1915 to a poor family in Xin'an Village, Muling Town, she joined the Communist Party in 1933 and served as director of the Fourth Army's clothing factory. An's entire family resisted Japan— her father, brothers, and younger brother were all Party members. In January 1933, during an enemy raid on Xin'an Village, seven villagers were massacred, including An's father and brother. Their deaths steeled her resolve.

Guo Guiqin, 17 at her death, was an orphaned street urchin who knew constant hunger. Hardship forged her fearlessness, and the Anti-Japanese Army became her family. "For this family, I'll give my life," she vowed.

Wang Huimin was the youngest of the eight martyrs who drowned themselves in the river, sacrificing her life at just 13 years old—practically still a child. She too was from Diaoling Village in Linkou County. Her father, nicknamed "Wang Piyi" (Wang the Fur Coat), served as deputy quartermaster of the Fifth Army headquarters. After he joined the Anti-Japanese United Army, their family home was burned down by Hanjian (collaborator) agents. As the eldest sibling in a large family, Wang Huimin spent her childhood evading danger with her mother and younger brothers and sisters until the age of 11, when she followed her father into the mountains.

Not long after, her father was killed in battle. Though grief-stricken, Wang found solace in the care of her "older brothers and sisters" in the army. Born into poverty and burdened with responsibility as the eldest, she matured quickly. During marches, she stubbornly refused help carrying her pack or rifle, insisting, "I can do it myself!" Her tenacity earned praise. With a wisdom beyond her years, she declared: "The Japanese devils killed my father. My mother and siblings are suffering at home. As the eldest daughter, I must fight hard to drive out the invaders and return to them soon."

This spirited young warrior of the Anti-Japanese United Army never reunited with her mother, younger brothers, or sisters. Among the belongings left in her backpack was a single radish, barely larger than a fist, half-eaten. [31]

The remaining heroines among the Eight Women Martyrs included: Hu Xiuying, 20 years old, a Communist Party member and squad leader, already a battle-hardened veteran of the resistance. She earned fame in the Fifth Army for leading two soldiers to infiltrate an enemy outpost and destroy it with grenades. Huang Guiqing, 20, a soldier. Li Fengshan, 21, of Korean ethnicity. For the latter two, little survives beyond their names and ages, yet the author believes each harbored extraordinary story.

Among the eight martyrs, four were Communist Party members. The eldest was 23, the youngest merely 13, their average age 19. Following their sacrifice, Zhou Baozhong, commander-in-chief of the Northeast Anti-Japanese United Army's Second Route Army, wrote in his diary on November 4, 1938: "The banks of the Wusihun River and Mudanjiang shall hereafter bear eternal witness to the fragrance of these heroines' valor." [32]

Over 40 years later, in 1982, the Memorial to the Eight Female Martyrs was erected by the Wusihun River, its inscription— "The heroic souls of the eight women shall shine for eternity"—glowing under the sun. On the 50th anniversary of their sacrifice, a group sculpture of the martyrs was unveiled in Mudanjiang's Riverside Park. Their figures, cast against the silvery river waves, radiate both solemnity and grace.

A postscript concerns the traitor Ge Hailu, who betrayed the eight women to the Japanese. After the founding of New China, his crimes were exposed. During his transport to trial, his guards executed him en route.

Notes:

[1] [2] The Compilation Group of *Northeast Anti-Japanese United Army Historical Materials*: *Northeast Anti-Japanese United Army Historical Materials* (Volume 1), published by CPC Historical Materials Press, 1st edition in December 1987, pp. 364– 366, p. 199.

[3] Sa Su: *The Longest Resistance* (Volume 2), published by Xi Yuan Press, 1st edition in June 2013, p. 328; Zhang Zhenglong: *Cold Snow, Hot Blood* (Volume 1), published by Changjiang Literature and Art Press, 1st edition in April 2011, pp. 168–169.

[4] Sa Su: *The Longest Resistance* (Volume 2), published by Xi Yuan Press, 1st edition in June 2013, p. 329; Zhang Zhenglong: *Cold Snow, Hot Blood* (Volume 1), published by Changjiang Literature and Art Press, 1st edition in April 2011, pp. 169–170.

[5] Zhao Junqing: *The Biography of Yang Jingyu*, published by Heilongjiang People's Press, revised edition in August 2015, p. 248.

[6] Political Department of Shenyang Military Region: *Blood Sacrifice in Northeast*, published by Baishan Press, 1st edition in October 1993, p. 83.

[7] Central Archives, Liaoning Provincial Archives, Jilin Provincial Archives, Heilongjiang Provincial Archives: Compilation of Revolutionary Historical Documents in Northeast China, Jia 29, p. 279; cited in Zhang Zhenglong: *Cold Snow, Hot Blood* (Volume 1), published by Changjiang Literature and Art Press, 1st edition in April 2011, p. 122.

[8] Zhang Zhenglong: *Cold Snow, Hot Blood* (Volume 1), published by Changjiang Literature and Art Press, 1st edition in April 2011, p. 123.

[9] Xu Tianxin, et al. (eds.): *A General History of the World* (Modern Volume), published by People's Press, 1st edition in April 1994, p. 503.

[10] The Central Committee of the Communist Party of China, Literature Editorial Committee: *Selected Works of Mao Zedong* (Volume 2), published by People's Press, 2nd edition in June 1991, p. 416.

[11] Central Archives, Liaoning Provincial Archives, Jilin Provincial Archives, Heilongjiang Provincial Archives: *Compilation of Revolutionary Historical Documents in Northeast China*, Jia 49, p. 186; cited in The Compilation Group of History of the Northeast Anti-Japanese United Army: *History of the Northeast Anti-Japanese United Army* (Volume 2), published by CPC History Press, 1st edition in September 2015, p. 642.

[12] The Compilation Group of *History of the Northeast Anti-Japanese United Army*: *History of the Northeast Anti-Japanese United Army* (Volume 2), published by CPC History Press, 1st edition in September 2015, p. 643.

[13] [22] Zhao Junqing: *The Biography of Zhao Shangzhi*, published by Heilongjiang People's Press, revised edition in August 2015, pp. 227, 247.

[14] [18] Central Archives, China Second Historical Archives, Jilin Academy of Social Sciences: *The Northeast "Pacification"*, published by Zhonghua Book Company, 1st edition in April 1991, pp. 247, 274–275.

[15] Central Archives, Liaoning Provincial Archives, Jilin Provincial Archives, Heilongjiang Provincial Archives: *Compilation of Revolutionary Historical Documents in Northeast China*, Jia 60, p. 229; cited in Zhao Junqing: The Biography of Yang Jingyu, published by Heilongjiang People's Press, revised edition in August 2015, p. 255.

[16] [17] Zhao Junqing: *The Biography of Yang Jingyu*, published by Heilongjiang People's Press, revised edition in August 2015, pp. 258, 261.

[19] Central Archives, Liaoning Provincial Archives, Jilin Provincial Archives, Heilongjiang Provincial Archives: *Compilation of Revolutionary Historical Documents in Northeast China*, Jia 49, p. 85; cited in The Compilation Group of *History of the Northeast Anti-Japanese United Army: History of the Northeast Anti-Japanese United Army* (Volume 1), published by CPC History Press, 1st edition in September 2015, p. 683.

[20] The Compilation Group of *History of the Northeast Anti-Japanese United Army: History of the Northeast Anti-Japanese United Army* (Volume 2), published by CPC History Press, 1st edition in September 2015, p. 684.

[21] Zhang Fulin, et al.: *Historical Evidence: The Record of China's Education and Transformation of Japanese War Criminals*, published by Jilin People's Press, 1st edition in September 2005, p. 432.

[23] Zhang Xiang: *Memories of the Battle of Ice Trough*, cited in Zhao Junqing: The Biography of Zhao Shangzhi, published by Heilongjiang People's Press, revised edition in August 2015, p. 249.

[24] Zhao Junqing: *The Biography of Zhou Baoshong*, published by Heilongjiang People's Press, revised edition in August 2015, p. 250.

[25] Central Archives, Liaoning Provincial Archives, Jilin Provincial Archives, Heilongjiang Provincial Archives: *Compilation of Revolutionary Historical Documents in Northeast China*, Jia 49, p. 91.

[26] [28] [29] The Compilation Group of *History of the Northeast Anti-Japanese United Army: History of the Northeast Anti-Japanese United Army* (Volume 2), published by CPC History Press, 1st edition in September 2015, pp. 706, 707, 707–708.

[27] Zhao Junqing: *The Biography of Zhou Baoshong*, published by Heilongjiang People 's Press, revised edition in August 2015, p. 252.

[30] [31] Zhang Zhenglong: *Cold Snow, Hot Blood* (Volume 2), published by Changjiang Literature and Art Press, 1st edition in April 2011, pp. 209, 210.

[32] Zhou Baoshong: *Northeast Anti-Japanese Guerrilla Diary*, published by People's Press, 1st edition in July 1991, p. 279; cited in Zhao Junqing: *The Biography of Zhou Baoshong*, published by Heilongjiang People's Press, revised edition in August 2015, p. 269.

Chapter16

Thorns and Trials

52. Women and War

A Westerner once said, trying to prove himself a gentleman: "War should keep women away." This line was blindly idolized by some among us with an infatuation for imitating foreign ideals. In reality, facing the unparalleled brutality of the Japanese invaders, such a notion was nothing but naive wishful thinking.

The poison of war never spares women—nor could it—including their vulnerable children. Female soldiers of the Northeast Anti-Japanese United Army often endured twice the sacrifices and suffering of their male counterparts.

The Diaoling region of Heilongjiang was a key base for the Fifth Army of the Anti-Japanese Alliance. Most Fifth Army soldiers, especially the women, hailed from Diaoling. Over 30 women from the area joined the Fifth Army, yet only Hu Zhenyi and Li Shuzhen survived to the end.

At its peak, the Fifth Army's women's regiment numbered nearly a battalion. Combined with other armies, women constituted a significant proportion of the Anti-Japanese Alliance forces. Yet by 1941, according to

Zhou Baozhong's diary entry on October 9, 1942, only 32 female soldiers remained to retreat into the Soviet Union for paratrooper training.

Hu Zhenyi, a veteran of the Anti-Japanese Alliance who later retired as deputy director of the Chongqing Municipal People's Congress, spent her later years reminiscing about her comrades. Her words pierce the heart: "The Fifth Army's women's regiment once had over 300 members. How many survived? I've counted again and again—about ten." [1]

"War should keep women away" is merely the deluded mantra of those who have never witnessed its bloodshed. Women never left war; instead, war transformed once-gentle and beautiful women into figures as rugged and fearless as men.

In March 1936, an "incident" occurred in Xinglonggou, Diaoling, involving the Fifth Army: "A black brat climbs onto the bride's bed." A scrawny, dark-complexioned "brat" swaggered into the bridal chamber, stared unabashedly at the bride, felt the warmth of the kang (heated bed), then clambered onto it and nestled against her.

The bride, furious, complained to her groom: "Some black brat from the army climbed up and touched me—just like a bandit!" The enraged groom reported the matter to the army leadership, demanding punishment for the "bandit" who dared violate discipline in broad daylight.

The "black brat" was soon identified as Hu Zhenyi. The officer handling the case, Deputy Tao, burst into laughter, explaining to the groom that the "brat" was actually a girl. Hu was ordered to apologize.

When Hu confessed to the bride and unbuttoned her coat to prove she was female, she explained: "It was freezing—my feet went numb on guard duty. I just wanted to warm up." Astonished, the bride pulled Hu onto the kang to thaw her feet.

Hu Zhenyi was born in 1920 in Phoenix Mountain, Dandong, Liaoning. At seven, her family fled famine to Hougang Village in Diaoling. Her lazy father traded her younger sister, then six or seven, for a blind horse. The family protested bitterly. Hu's brother, grieving for his lost sister, whipped the horse until it stamped its hooves in pain. Hu, pitying the creature, said: "This blind horse suffers like my sister. Stop hitting it." Her mother, heartbroken, drank brine in despair. Though saved by forced vomiting, she succumbed to illness soon after.

The village school principal, Guo Zijian, and his wife, Li Suzhen—both underground Communist Party members—ran a secret liaison station for the Anti-Japanese Alliance. They allowed Hu, who tended pigs and horses for her father, to attend classes for free. Gradually, they entrusted her with delivering intelligence.

As the family sank deeper into poverty, Hu Zhenyi's father sought to sell her too. To escape this fate, Hu joined the Fifth Army of the Anti-Japanese Alliance through Guo Zijian's help. For safety, Li Suzhen shaved Hu's head and disguised her as a boy. When registering with the army, Hu explained she had no formal name—her family called her "Xiao Maizi" ("Little Bought One," a superstitious name meant to ensure survival). The officer in charge, Director Wang, declared: "From today, your name is Hu Zhenyi."

Most Anti-Japanese Alliance soldiers carried harrowing tales of suffering—a driving force behind their resilience and courage. For Hu, her resolve to fight stemmed from three searing experiences: Her Second Brother's Execution: Japanese troops forced villagers, including her brother, to build military fortifications. Once completed, all laborers were slaughtered to erase witnesses, including his second brother.

Hu witnessed a Japanese soldier playfully teasing a toddler wearing a bellyband. When the child cried, the soldier—misinterpreting tears as insults—impaled the boy with his bayonet, hoisted him aloft, and marched off singing. The child's agonized wails haunted Hu, who recalled: "My teeth clenched with hatred."

Li Shunqiang, Hu's Party introducer, and his wife Jinzhi were captured after enemy raids destroyed their army's clothing factory and hospital. Stripped naked and bound face-to-face on trees, the couple endured prolonged bayonet stabbings while cursing their tormentors. Their mutilated bodies remained suspended even during burial. Hu wept uncontrollably until her commander snapped: "Stop crying! Dig their grave and lay them to rest!"

Filled with rage, Hu fought with ferocity. During one ambush, she killed two Japanese soldiers and roared: "Director Li! Jinzhi! I've avenged you!"

Another time, while pursuing retreating enemies in Xinglonggou, Hu spotted a wounded Japanese soldier lying in a ditch. Though his coat was soaked in blood, he glared and snarled "Baka!" ("Fool!"). Enraged, Hu bayoneted him on the spot.

When fellow soldiers arrived, they gaped at the lifeless body and her bloodied blade. Hu felt conflicted—killing at close quarters differed starkly from shooting from afar.

Yet once initiated, Hu grew indifferent to bloodshed. The resource-starved Anti-Japanese Alliance relied on scavenging enemy supplies. While looting corpses after battle, comrades once mistook enemy blood on her clothes for wounds. "It's from stripping the devils," she shrugged.

At the brink of national annihilation, the Anti-Japanese Alliance demanded women "adopt masculine discipline, prioritize revolutionary duty, and cultivate political prowess." [2] Women were soldiers first.

These fierce fighters often surpassed men in ruthlessness. When a traitor spying for the Japanese was captured—a capital offense—Fifth Army Commander Chai Shirong ordered: "No guns or blades. Use rope." The collaborator was tied to a tree with a thin cord looped around his neck and trunk, ensuring a less agonizing death. Even for traitors, the Alliance refused Japanese-style cruelty.

When Commander Chai Shirong asked, "Who will carry this out?" the crowd fell silent—many dared not step forward.

"I'll do it!" Hu Zhenyi declared. She took a chopstick, twisted it into the coiled rope around the traitor's neck, and turned it relentlessly until his struggles ceased. Hu later confessed her particular hatred for collaborators: "Traitors did more harm than the Japanese themselves!" [3]

War shattered homes, severed families, and brutalized souls. The meek—especially once-gentle women—were forged into steel. This transformation was no failing of women, but a curse wrought by invaders and war itself.

Yet women are fundamentally different from men. When Nüwa molded humanity, she bestowed upon women a divine gift-the sacred power of motherhood. But this blessing came with its own burdens: the soul-rending agony of childbirth, and the monthly ordeal of blood. In times of peace, women might enjoy meticulous care with endless choices of sanitary products, but war reduces all to bleakness and squalor.

Veteran Li Min recalled: "There were no sanitary pads or paper. We tore rags from worn uniforms, washed them, and reused them. Sun-dried rags turned stiff. In summer, we used dried wild leaves—softened by rubbing— as makeshift pads." Miscarriages or childbirth offered no respite; there was no "confinement" for recovery.

Another veteran, Liu Shuzhen, described: "If your pants got stained, you had no spare. Men would avert their eyes while we washed in streams or springs. Wring out the cloth, let it dry a bit—barely enough—then put it back on. Pure torment!"

These were the better scenarios. During marches or battles—with no water, rain-soaked clothes, or winter's freeze—women endured bloodied legs and icy chills. Older soldiers advised newcomers to bathe in frigid rivers to "shock" their cycles into stopping. Unsurprisingly, gynecological ailments plagued the ranks.

On July 8, 1939, Zhou Baozhong's diary memorialized Li Zhixiong, a 25-year-old intellectual turned soldier who succumbed to untreated uterine disease. A graduate of Beiping's Northeastern University, Li had served as secretary, educator, and political instructor in the Fifth Army. Despite her athletic prowess as a former basketball captain, illness ravaged her body. The army arranged for her to seek treatment in Japanese-occupied Jiamusi.

Her family's tragedy fueled her resolve: Her father died in prison after being jailed for "subversive thought"; her mother hanged herself in despair. In her final letter, Li wrote:

> I would rather die fighting for our nation's liberation, surrounded by
> comrades, than breathe a single day under Japanese fascism. I refuse to
> witness our people enslaved, or risk a woman's fate in enemy hands.

Li perished on July 5, 1939, in a hidden camp, "bereft of proper medicine." Zhou's eulogy lamented:

> Her death robs China's liberation struggle of a brilliant female leader.
> Li once wed Ji Qing, now Fifth Army's political director—a union born of
> revolutionary passion. They dreamed of celebrating victory together. Now,
> as Japan rages, she lies gone. One wonders what thoughts stir in Comrade
> Ji's heart. [4]

Zhou Baozhong's profound admiration for talent and his heartfelt sorrow for Li Zhixiong's untimely death were palpable, particularly his sympathy for Ji Qing's anguish at losing his beloved wife.

A child is flesh of its mother's flesh—the months of pregnancy's toil, the excruciating pain of childbirth—all endured for the sake of life's radiant blossoms and sweetest fruits. But when those blossoms wither too soon, when those fruits fall unripe, the agony is not the fleeting suffering of a monthly cycle. It is a pain that pierces the marrow, a wound that may never heal.

Li Zaide, born in 1918, was the daughter of Jin Chenggang, one of the famed "Twelve Martyrs of Heli." She joined the Tangyuan Anti-Japanese Guerrilla Force in 1934 and later served as confidential secretary to the Government Administration Council, even entrusted with the seals of Premier Zhou Enlai—a testament to her unwavering loyalty as a Communist Party member. Over decades, she held numerous positions, yet her most cherished role was as director of the nursery under the National People's Congress Standing Committee.

Her first child was born in a mountain gully, the fruit of her love with veteran Anti-Japanese fighter Yu Baohe (who later became deputy director of the Radar Bureau under the Central Military Commission's Ordnance Department). The birth took place in a makeshift shelter, and with no food to nourish her, Li Zaide had no milk to give. For two days, the infant managed weak cries; by the third, it fell silent, and on the fifth day, it died.

The harsh conditions left Li Zaide herself swollen and fever-ridden, teetering on the brink of death. An elderly Korean couple tending to her grew desperate. Remembering how in the Sixth Army's clothing factory they had used crow's eye tree bark to treat wounds, Li Zaide urged them to try it—a last resort. Miraculously, the swelling subsided, and she survived.

In the wilderness, where malnutrition reigned, a child's survival was rare, and childbirth itself was a brush with death.

Kim Bong-suk, a soldier in the Sixth Army's clothing factory, went into labor while her comrades were away fetching supplies. Only the young Li Min (who had injured her foot) remained. Hearing Kim's agonized cries, Li Min fumbled to untie her pants, exposing her navel—her mother had once told her babies came from there.

"Help me take off my pants—quick!" Kim gasped, drenched in sweat. As Li Min tugged them down past her knees, a rush of amniotic fluid, blood, and the newborn spilled out.

Weakly, Kim told Li Min to cut the umbilical cord. The girl hesitated, staring at the tiny, wrinkled, crimson infant, afraid of hurting it and unsure where to cut. Soon, Old Wang returned with supplies and, hearing of the birth, barked from outside: "Cut the cord!"

It was a boy. After a long pause, he let out a faint, kitten-like cry. The group scrambled to boil coarse rice grits—the only food on hand—to feed him. Like Li Zaide, Kim produced no milk, and the baby lived just three days. Kim clutched the child, sobbing uncontrollably, refusing to let go. Only after much persuasion did she allow them to bury the nameless infant beneath a tree on the hillside. Thankfully, Kim suffered no lasting illness.

For Kim Bowon, childbirth nearly proved fatal. A Korean veteran fluent in Chinese and former director of the Third Army's clothing factory, Kim was the wife of famed commander Li Zhaolin.

Kim Bowon went into labor while fleeing enemy forces in the dead of winter, with temperatures plunging to -30 or -40 degrees Celsius—a day forever etched in her memory. On the fifth day of the eleventh lunar month in 1940, as the troops marched, her first son was born on the frozen wilderness. Though the umbilical cord was cut, the placenta remained. With the enemy closing in, midwife Sister Park tied the cord to Kim's thigh as the unit began their forced march. Miraculously, the placenta eventually detached. "Had it stayed," Sister Park gasped in relief, "you might have bled to death!"

Kim was fortunate—placental retention often causes fatal hemorrhaging. Even more miraculously, the baby survived. His comrades jubilantly named him "Zhaohua" ("Initiating Glory"), a beacon of hope for both the Anti-Japanese Alliance and the Chinese nation.

From then on, Zhaohua clung to his mother's back as she evaded enemies through dense forests. A year later, when Kim—now nearly paralyzed from the waist down—reached the frozen Heilongjiang River to cross into the Soviet Union, comrades dragged them both across the ice.

The Roman poet Horace once wrote: "All mothers hate war."

War inflicts a double trauma on mothers: the loss of husbands, then children. For mothers in the Northeast Anti-Japanese Alliance, true motherhood was nearly impossible—few children survived, and even fewer remained with their mothers. For these women soldiers, hearing a child call them "Mom" became an impossible dream.

Jin Yukun, a brave soldier and director of a clothing factory, was married to Sui Desheng, a battalion commander in the Tenth Army. In spring 1940, she gave birth to a daughter. With the troops constantly on the move, commanders urged her to leave the baby with villagers.

Tears streamed down Jin's face as she fed her daughter one last time. The child smiled in her sleep, unaware she'd never see her mother again. Jin tore a strip from her jacket and wrote: "Father: Sui Desheng. Mother: Jin Yukun. Born: April 14, 1940. Nickname: Fenglan." [5] As the villager carried the baby away, Jin turned her head—her daughter was too young to even cry "Mama!"

Compared to Park Eun-ju, Jin was fortunate—at least her child left alive. Veteran Hu Zhenyi recounted Park's tragedy:

In autumn 1938, while sabotaging Japanese railways near Ning'an, female soldiers were ordered to retreat first. Pursued by Japanese troops near Jingpo Lake's northern shore, a dozen women hid in lakeside reeds. Park's two-month-old son began crying. She muffled his mouth, released him when he gasped, then muffled again as enemy footsteps crunched on the slope above. Soon, the crying stopped. Hu, hidden meters away in thick reeds, assumed the baby had quieted. When the Japanese left, Park sat motionless, cradling her child—her eyes vacant, tears streaming. The infant had suffocated. [6]

Faced with the inhumanity of Japanese invaders, these women soldiers made choices that shattered the boundaries of human endurance. Such agony surpassed even self-amputation!

Mothers curse war not only for stealing children's lives, but for wrenching the living from their arms.

Li Zaide and Yu Baohe's second child was born on September 28, 1940, at a maternity hospital in Khabarovsk, Soviet Union. That October, as Yu prepared to return to China with General Zhao Shangzhi, Soviet Colonel Anguginov (code name "Wang Xinlin") hosted a farewell banquet. Congratulating Yu on his son, the colonel bestowed the child a Soviet hero's name: "Valery." Zhao Shangzhi interjected, "Let's also give him a Chinese name. Li Genzhi was a Korean-Chinese martyr of the Third Army. Call him 'Yu Genzhi' (Rooted in Yu)."

Later, Yu Genzhi and another child were sent to a Khabarovsk nursery. Li Zaide recalled: "That day, Soviet officer Wu Gang told me another Chinese child would arrive that evening to join my son before both were transferred to the nursery. The boy they brought was sick—vomiting, diarrhea, wailing pitifully. I fed him, rocked him to sleep, but stayed awake all night, tears streaming uncontrollably. Where would they take them? Would they survive? Would I ever see them again?"

In later years, Li reproached herself: "So many of our female comrades had to abandon their children to villagers—or even leave them in the snow— during guerrilla warfare. Some sacrificed their infants to protect the troops. Countless comrades bled out on battlefields. For me to weep over one child… how weak!"

Li Zaide was a mother, tender and vulnerable; but she was first a soldier, duty-bound to the battlefield, and a Communist Party member sworn to liberate her homeland from Japanese occupation. Sacrificing maternal attachment was the price of her faith.

Though still recovering from childbirth, Li underwent training in radio operations, intelligence, and reconnaissance. By summer 1941, she returned to the frontlines in Northeast China. Meanwhile, as the Soviet Union reeled from Nazi invasion, nurseries evacuated deeper into the interior. Li and Yu lost contact with Genzhi forever. Soviet authorities assisted their search, but the boy vanished—his fate unknown to this day.

After the war, especially in retirement, Li often thought of her "Root." Such is a mother's nature.

In truth, Yu Genzhi was among multiple missing children of Anti-Japanese Alliance fighters. Zhou Baozhong once provided Soviet authorities a list of nine children for tracking. [7] Apart from Yang Zhenhua's son Yang Mingshan—marked as "sent back to Boli County in July 1941, then vanished"—the rest left no trace.

Kim Bowon's son Zhaohua, born in the snow, crossed into the Soviet Union with her. Hospitalized, Kim was separated from Zhaohua, who entered a nursery. Upon discharge, she searched frantically. Li Zhaolin finally revealed the truth: weakened by wilderness privations, the boy had fallen ill and died within two weeks of arrival. They'd hidden this to spare Kim, then gravely ill. Later, they had other children.

Yet in the mid-1970s, Kim's son Zhang Like brought startling news: staff at China's UK embassy reported a man claiming to be Li Zhaolin's son sought family reunification.

Kim's daughter Zhang Zhuoya asked, "Should we pursue this lead? Find Zhaohua?"

Kim shook her head mutely. Her children honored her silence but knew she never forgot her firstborn—not merely her flesh and blood, but a living testament to their arduous resistance.

Thus, Zhuoya kept searching. On December 18, 2010, she appeared on CCTV's *Waiting for Me*, a Sino-Russian cross-border reunion program, still hoping to find the brother who haunted her mother's heart. [8]

53. Xiang Lei and The Elegant One by Autumn Waters

To lack tenderness is not true heroism. The passionate, steadfast love of Anti-Japanese Alliance warriors burned as fiercely as their will to fight—a flame both indomitable and unyielding.

Many soldiers were young men and women in the bloom of life, their longing for companionship as natural as spring buds unfurling. Lovers exchanged romantic letters, though paper was scarce; birch bark became their parchment. In the opera Spark of Resistance, a celebrated aria captures this:

Birch barking costs nothing,

Yet priceless when it reaches your hands.

These are the words your brother wrote,

This is your brother's heart. [9]

Amidst unimaginable hardship, romance and humanity persisted. The Alliance's leaders understood: Why fight? For the people—including their own soldiers—to reclaim lives of freedom and love. Thus, while permitting relationships, they upheld traditional Chinese moral codes.

As early as 1935, the Northeast Anti-Japanese Alliance issued *Brief Marriage Regulations*, a ten-article decree. Key principles included: Marriage required organizational approval without compromising military discipline. Soldiers forbidden from romantic entanglements. Remarriage permitted only after three years of severed ties with prior spouses. [10]

War devours love's blossoms. Few couples lived to see victory; growing old together remained a fantasy. Thus, every wedding became a jubilant feast for the troops.

Yu Baohe and Li Zaide's union was orchestrated by Zhao Shangzhi himself. To honor the occasion, he enlisted Feng Zhongyun as matchmaker, served as witness, and tasked Zhou Baozhong with officiating. Soldiers gathered vibrant mountain flowers to deck the venue, while the bride and groom glowed in makeshift finery.

Three generals presiding over two couples' weddings (the other being Wu Yuguang and Li Guilan) symbolized the fighters' defiant hope—a cultural resistance as vital as bullets.

Yet not all ceremonies were lavish. On October 6, 1939, Zhou Baozhong and Wang Yizhi wed in the barest revolutionary fashion.

At a Party cell meeting, they announced their union—already approved by higher authorities—and proposed skipping festivities. The group insisted on ritual: a handshake before comrades, applause, and *The Internationale*. The "reception" lasted minutes before all returned to war preparations.

That day, during the Party cell meeting, Wang Yizhi and Zhou Baozhong formally addressed the group. They first declared their revolutionary camaraderie and intention to form a "revolutionary marital union," emphasizing that their relationship had undergone rigorous scrutiny and received official approval from higher Party authorities. Their initial proposal was to forgo any wedding ceremony entirely, considering the exigencies of war. The cell members unanimously endorsed their partnership but insisted on observing symbolic rituals. "The wedding must proceed, even in simplified form," the group resolved. Comrades demanded the couple publicly seal their vows with a handshake—a revolutionary alternative to traditional rites. Zhou and Wang complied earnestly, their clasped hands trembling slightly as they exchanged solemn glances before the assembly. Applause erupted, soon merging into thunderous strains of *The Internationale*. As the last notes faded, the gathering dispersed without delay—some to draft intelligence reports, others to clean rifles—preparations for the next day's operations already underway.

A handshake substituted for embraces; a communist anthem replaced wedding marches—a testament to the Alliance's austere poetry.

Zhao Shangzhi, ever the matchmaker (he'd recently united Commander Cai Jinkui and Yu Guizhen), remained a bachelor. True to his vow, he refused marriage until Japan was expelled.

Feng Zhongyun's separation from his beloved wife Xue Wen had stretched not merely beyond the three-year threshold stipulated by Party regulations, but fourfold—twelve long years. Through blizzards and typhoid fevers, shrapnel wounds and frigid nights at -40°C, he refused all offers of remarriage, though comrades urged it and female soldiers admired him. In ice-laced caves, delirious with pain, his mind drifted to his family in the south. Between battles, he often sang alone:

> Beloved, will you not return?
>
> We've watched spring wilt to autumn, autumn fade to summer,
>
> Till waters shrivel and stones crumble!
>
> Beloved, will you never return?
>
> For him—our tears have run dry,
>
> For him—our hearts lie shattered.
>
> O clouds shrouding the Nine-Doubt Mountains,
>
> O ripples lapping Dongting Lake—
>
> Do you know where he wanders?
>
> Can you trace his footsteps? [11]

When asked about the song's origin, Feng identified it as Guo Moruo's *Xiang Lei* ("The Exile of Chu"). Comrades remarked that his fidelity to Xue Wen mirrored his revolutionary zeal.

Meanwhile, in the sweltering Jiangnan region, Xue Wen hummed *The Elegant One by Autumn Waters*. On moonlit Mid-Autumn nights, she sang to their daughter Feng Yiluo:

> Green, green the reeds,

White dew turns frost.

Where is she, the one I long for?

Beyond the river's bend.

Young Yiluo didn't recognize these verses from the *Book of Songs*, nor grasp why her mother sang them each autumn before recounting tales of resistance—"always ending with stories of your father."

Years later, Yiluo understood:

By the bank, reeds sway emerald,

Autumn dew crystallizes cold.

Where does my love reside?

Across the waters, far and wide.

Unbeknownst to Feng, battling blizzards in the north, Xue Wen faced her own crucible. After relocating from Harbin to Shanghai, Party connections severed by betrayal, she lost official membership. Her newborn son Jian'er, delivered in a cowshed, soon perished.

Twin devastations failed to break her. With Yiluo in tow, Xue Wen scoured Jiangsu for the Party. In Mao Mountain villages, she taught farmers' children for meals, subsisting on communal charity.

Hearing of New Fourth Army activities, she trekked to their camps— only to be denied reinstatement for lack of witnesses. Undeterred, she lived as a communist sans credentials: smuggling grain, cloth, and weapons to guerrilla units at mortal risk.

Her resolve moved New Fourth Army leaders. Though unable to validate her prewar membership, they honored her as a "veteran comrade" and sent her to Party school. At thirteen, Yiluo joined the New Fourth Army—a decision Xue knew Feng would endorse.

Long separations weave endless longing,

Brief partings birth eternal yearning.

Veterans of the Northeast Anti-Japanese United Army, Feng Zhongyun and his wife Xue Wen, endured 12 years of excruciating separation—a pain only they could fathom. Perhaps heaven finally smiled upon them: the day Japan's invaders collapsed, Xue Wen, after her agonizing wait, received a letter from Feng Zhongyun.

What did Xue Wen feel upon opening it? Decades later, their daughter Feng Yiluo summarized her mother's reaction in five stark words: "She was stunned beyond speech."

Twelve years of war had reshaped countless lives. Feng's letter, brimming with fervor yet tempered by restraint, read:

> My dear Wen,
>
> ...Twelve years apart, yet I've remained faithful—to our Party, our nation. If you've kept your revolutionary integrity, you remain my wife. Whatever trials you've endured, if you choose to return, my arms await...
>
> —Yun [12]

This letter, meticulously crafted and profoundly moving, laid bare Feng Zhongyun's inner conflict. His words trembled between desperate hope for reunion after twelve years and gnawing fear that wartime hardships might have driven Xue Wen to remarry. "If you choose to return, my arms await"— yet this olive branch came with an ironclad condition: her revolutionary integrity must remain unsullied. Here stood a veteran Communist's unbending principle: loyalty to both Party and marriage.

Xue Wen then embarked on her "Journey Beyond the Pass"—a 1,500-kilometer odyssey through postwar chaos. With Japanese forces disarmed but Kuomintang checkpoints now dotting the landscape, she navigated covertly: slipping through night blockades, detouring from Shenyang (under KMT control) to Dandong, crossing into North Korea's Sinuiju by train, then looping back via Tumen River to Mudanjiang. On foot, by cart, train, truck, and boat—twelve years of separation ended in a tearful embrace at journey's end.

How many could preserve such love through twelve blood-soaked years?

The Anti-Japanese Alliance sanctioned love not merely as human necessity, but as vital sustenance for souls battered by sacrifice and starvation—and as hope for humanity's continuity. While steadfast devotion like the Feng-Xue bond earned respect, so did warriors who loved anew.

As Li Min, former vice-chair of Heilongjiang's Political Consultative Conference, reflected: "Lifelong widowhood was rare among our women soldiers. Many remarried fallen comrades, who embraced their stepchildren as their own."

As Li Min, former vice-chair of Heilongjiang's Political Consultative Conference, reflected: "Lifelong widowhood was rare among our women soldiers. Many remarried fallen comrades, who embraced their stepchildren as their own."

Let us return to Kim Yukun's harrowing journey. The winter her infant Fenglan was given away, her husband Sui Desheng—a 30-year-old regiment commander—died covering comrades' retreat. At 21, Kim learned of his death only in Soviet exile.

Jin Yukun, who had lost both her child and husband, sank into deep depression. Later, through an arrangement by the organization, she married Zhao Xilin, a platoon leader of the Anti-Japanese United Army Teaching

Brigade. Though a remarriage, the couple cherished each other deeply. In September 1944, they welcomed a daughter named Zhao Yanfen (Russian name: Lina). Jin's furrowed brows finally relaxed as happiness returned.

Yet war shattered her life again. While crossing the river to carry out a mission in China, Zhao Xilin encountered Japanese puppet troops and died heroically alongside six other resistance fighters.

Widowed once more, Jin was consumed by endless grief – heaven seemed determined to torment her. Only her daughter Yanfen, the fruit of her love with Zhao, kept her going. Emerging from despair, Jin later married Nie Jingquan from the Teaching Brigade. After Japan's surrender in 1945, the couple returned to China where Nie joined bandit-suppression campaigns. He fell at Lianhuapao, Mudanjiang, among eight martyrs. Posthumously, Jin gave birth to their son Nie Wenbo.

A brave soldier who joined the resistance at 15, Jin was famed for dual-wielding pistols – a semi-automatic and a Mauser. Once surrounded at night with a wounded foot, she smeared fallen comrades' blood on her face for camouflage. When enemy flashlights approached, she emptied her magazine at the shadows before escaping through soybean fields, eventually reaching a field hospital.

Jin bore three children, each destined to grow fatherless. Three times she pursued love; three times war tore it apart.

Her romances burned like torches – passionate, vibrant – only to be doused by war's relentless storms. While she endured physical hardships – cold, hunger, injuries – losing three lovers shattered her heart. She passed away at 58.

Jin bore three children, each destined to grow fatherless. Three times she pursued love; three times war tore it apart. Her romances burned like torches – passionate, vibrant – only to be doused by war's relentless storms.

While she endured physical hardships – cold, hunger, injuries – losing three lovers shattered her heart. She passed away at 58.

War creates ruins and orphans but cannot extinguish love or stop life's continuity.

Jin's tragic yet courageous wartime romances bore glorious fruits: her three children inherited their parents' revolutionary spirit, thriving in postwar China.

Her daughter with first husband Sui Desheng, Fenglan, was raised by foster parents Yang Chunlin and Sun Dezhen. Despite their poverty and five biological children, they educated Fenglan.

After 17 years and multiple trips to provincial capitals, Sun reconnected Fenglan with her birth mother. Touched, Jin renamed her "Sui Yanglan" to honor her foster parents.

Zhao Yanfen married Zhang Zhixue, son of veteran resistance fighter Wu Yuqing. Wu's husband Zhang Xishan (deputy commander of the 2nd Route Army) had fought across Mishan, Fujin, and Jianshanzi. This marriage extended the anti-Japanese comradeship to the next generation.

Nie Wenbo, born after his father's death, is traditionally considered a "dream-born" child. Though never meeting his father, he takes pride in local governments renovating the martyrs' monument where Nie Jingquan rests with seven comrades.

Zhao Yanfen, daughter of Jin Yukun and Zhao Xilin, later married Zhang Zhixue — son of Wu Yuqing, a veteran of the Anti-Japanese United Army. Wu Yuqing's husband, Zhang Xishan, served as adjutant of the 2nd Detachment under the 2nd Route Army of the resistance forces. Their son Zhang Zhixue was born in Khabarovsk, Soviet Union. Wu Yuqing herself had joined the Northeast Anti-Japanese United Army at 14, fighting across multiple regions including Mishan, Fujin, and Jianshanzi. As comrades-in-arms, Jin Yukun and Wu Yuqing further solidified their bond by becoming in-laws through their children's marriage — a poignant continuation of their revolutionary fellowship into the next generation.

Nie Wenbo, Jin Yukun's son with Nie Jingquan, was what rural tradition calls a "mengsheng" ("dream-born") — a child conceived before his father's death but born posthumously. Though he never met his father, he knows Nie Jingquan lies buried with seven other martyrs. Today, he expresses profound gratitude towards local authorities for renovating the memorial stele, his heart brimming with reverence for these rev

In September 2012, at Shenyang's August 1st Hotel, Russian WWII veterans and descendants of the "88th International Brigade" gathered. Thunderous applause erupted as Zhao Yanfen received five commemorative medals from Marshal Ivanov – honoring Jin Yukun, Zhao Xilin, Nie Jingquan, Zhang Xishan, and Wu Yuqing. Behind these glittering medals lies the poignant wartime love story centered on Jin Yukun.

The anti-Japanese family arguably deserves one more medal – for regimental commander Sui Desheng, who sacrificed his life before crossing the river to join the Soviet-based Teaching Brigade.

54. Crossing Mountains and Rivers to Reconnect with the Party

From autumn-winter 1937 to spring-summer 1938, the three principal leaders of the Northeast Anti-Japanese United Army—Yang Jingyu, Zhao Shangzhi, and Zhou Baozhong—persistently pursued the same critical mission: reestablishing contact with the Central Committee of the Chinese Communist Party.

By late 1937, the South Manchuria Party organization had completely lost contact with higher authorities. In late May 1938, at the secret camp of the First Army headquarters in Ji'an's Laoling Mountains, Yang Jingyu and Wei Zhengmin convened a joint conference between the First Route Army Headquarters and senior cadres of the South Manchuria Provincial Committee. Nine key resolutions were adopted, including a pivotal decision: "To strengthen the Third Division of the First Army by reassigning personnel, preparing for another western expedition at an opportune moment to establish connections with the Central Committee and the Eighth Route Army in mainland China."

Like Yang Jingyu, Zhao Shangzhi had spent two years dispatching urgent letters and sending key cadres across the Soviet border to report directly to the CCP delegation. Among these envoys were: Liu Haitao, former political commissar of the 1st Regiment and commander of the 1st Division of the Third Army; Han Guang (nicknamed "Xiao Meng"), former acting political director of the Hadong Detachment and secretary of the Zhuhe County Communist Youth League; Zhu Xinyang, former secretary of the Zhuhe County Communist Youth League and standing committee member of the North Manchuria Provisional Provincial Committee. Yet, as Zhao lamented in a letter: "Not a single person we sent has returned."

Zhou Baozhong, too, repeatedly attempted to reach the Central Committee, even sending Fifth Army Chief of Staff Zhang Jiandong into mainland China—all to no avail. Driven by desperation, Zhou ventured across the frozen Ussuri River in late January 1938 to personally meet Wang Ming and Kang Sheng of the CCP delegation. While detained at the Bikin Border Guard Detention Center on the Soviet side, Zhou wrote to Yang Chunshan (Stayanov), head of the CCP liaison station in Vladivostok: "Given my responsibilities, I cannot abandon my post for even a minute amid this urgent national revolutionary war—unless struck dead by enemy fire. The gravity of our situation compels me to risk this perilous journey."

This daring mission nearly cost Zhou his life. Ambushed during his return, he narrowly escaped death.

After two agonizing months at Bikin, Zhou finally received a reply from Yang Chunshan: the Vladivostok liaison station had been dissolved, and the current CCP delegation (led first by Wang Jiaxiang, then by Ren Bishi) no longer oversaw Northeast operations. New connections would be established through domestic channels. Crucially, Wang Ming and Kang Sheng—former heads of the CCP delegation—had already returned to Yan'an from the USSR in November 1937.

Historical records offer no account of Zhou Baozhong's state of mind as he departed the Soviet Union. Yet on his journey back to the Second Route Army headquarters via the Seventh Army, a life-threatening trap awaited him. Leading only six attendants through a mountainous ridge near Li Family Hamlet in Hua'lazi, Baoqing County, a voice suddenly shouted: "Are you from Commander Zhou's unit? We're here to escort him!"

Yang Delong, a cadre from the Lower River Special Committee traveling with Zhou, instinctively replied, "Yes, we're—"

Zhou immediately cut him off, countering sharply: "We're the vanguard of Commander Zhou's forces. His main troops follow behind. Which unit are you from?"

"We're from the Seventh Army," came the reply. "Commander Cui sent us to meet Commander Zhou."

The group instantly recognized the ruse—these were enemies aiming to capture Zhou alive. "Charge!" Zhou ordered under his breath. The seven horsemen bolted southeast like arrows loosed from a bow.

Gunfire erupted as the pursuers yelled: "Take them alive! The tall one is Zhou Baozhong!"

Galloping through a hail of bullets, Zhou's group initially outpaced their attackers by 30 meters. Desperate to widen the gap, Zhou pounded his horse's back. The panicked steed reared, its front legs tangling, hurling Zhou into the snow before fleeing with the other horses. The enemy jeered: "Zhou the Savage! Nowhere to run!"

Bleeding but defiant, Zhou fired while sprinting, dropping one pursuer with two shots. Yet his body—ravaged by prior combat injuries—faltered. Gasping, dizzy, nearing collapse, he clutched a loaded pistol, resolved to die rather than be captured.

At this critical moment, Adjutant Tao Yufeng galloped back, gunning down nearby enemies while shouting: "Commander Zhou! Reinforcements are here!" The bluff caused momentary chaos. Tao thrust his mount at Zhou, then sprinted toward distant woods on foot.

By nightfall, Zhou and his men miraculously broke through the enemy's encirclement ambush (koudai zhen). Tragically, Quartermaster Zhuo Wenyi, wounded and captured, endured brutal torture before being shoved into an ice hole—dying unbroken.

The ambush stemmed from a traitor's leak. At a subsequent Jidong Provincial Party Committee meeting, Zhou faced criticism for "insufficient vigilance and miscalculating risks."

While Zhou narrowly survived, Zhao Shangzhi faced darker fortunes.

Almost simultaneously with Zhou's Soviet crossing, in early January 1938, Zhao trekked across the frozen Heilongjiang River into Soviet territory amid biting winds. Before departing, he had agreed with North Manchuria Party and military leaders on a one-month mission timeline. Instead, Soviet authorities detained him for a year and a half—a cruel twist of fate contrasting sharply with Zhou's harrowing but momentary trial.

In November 1937, Zhao Shangzhi wrote to Marshal Vasily Blyukher, commander of the Soviet Far Eastern Military District, and the Far Eastern Regional Committee of the Communist Party (Bolsheviks), pleading for assistance in contacting the CCP Central Committee and requesting arms, ammunition, and military-technical support. Shortly afterward, Chen Shaobin, acting commander of the 1st Division of the Sixth Anti-Japanese Allied Army, returned from the Soviet Union with a crucial message: Soviet forces were preparing to engage Japan, and Marshal Kliment Voroshilov had invited key Northeast resistance leaders to discuss coordinated operations. Chen emphasized that Soviet authorities insisted "Commander Zhao (Shangzhi) and Commander Dai (Hongbin) must come to the USSR."

This news aligned perfectly with Zhao's ambitions. After deliberation, he resolved to lead the mission personally. Yet upon crossing into Soviet territory, disaster struck. Soviet officials denied ever issuing such invitations, disarmed Zhao and his entourage, and transported them to Khabarovsk, where they were imprisoned at the Far Eastern Army's Internal Affairs detention facility.

One month later, Li Zhaolin (Chief Political Director of the North Manchuria Anti-Japanese United Army) and Dai Hongbin (Commander of the Sixth Army) mobilized over 600 elite cavalry from the Third and Sixth Armies to gather in Luobei County per prior arrangements. Their mission: retrieve Zhao Shangzhi and receive Soviet-supplied weapons.

Fate intervened cruelly. Li Zhaolin's 100-strong cavalry failed to capture Yadanhe and withdrew. Dai Hongbin's 500 troops—the core of the Third and Sixth Armies—also faltered in attacking Zhaoxing Town. During retreat, they clashed with Japanese forces under Captain Itasaka for five hours, killing 18 enemy soldiers (including Itasaka) and wounding six, but suffered heavy losses.

As puppet troops from Suibin closed in, Dai Hongbin, alongside Third Army Division Commander Cai Jinkui, Ninth Army Commander Li Zhenyuan, and Ninth Army Political Director Zheng Hongtao, led their men onto the frozen Heilongjiang River. Their desperate plan: cross into the USSR to rescue Zhao and resupply.

Instead, Soviet border guards disarmed them immediately. Dai was detained, and the Soviets—fearing diplomatic fallout with Japan—later forcibly repatriated Cai, Li, Zheng, and 500 fighters to Xinjiang. Requests to proceed to Yan'an were rejected by Xinjiang governor Sheng Shicai.

Around this time, Qi Zhizhong—Commander of the Eleventh Anti-Japanese Allied Army—crossed into the USSR seeking military aid, only to be disarmed and imprisoned alongside Zhao and Dai.

The prolonged detention of North Manchuria's top resistance leaders— Zhao Shangzhi, Dai Hongbin, and Qi Zhizhong—marked a catastrophic turning point.

Their capture coincided with Japan's brutal "Three Rivers Grand Suppression" campaign, devastating Northeast resistance efforts. With

Zhao—a figure feared by Japanese forces—neutralized, North Manchuria's anti-Japanese forces lost unified leadership and strategic command. By May 1938, the core units of the Third, Sixth, Ninth, and Eleventh Armies under the North Manchuria Headquarters had dwindled to just 3,010 fighters.

Detained in the Khabarovsk prison (his third incarceration in his tragically brief life), Zhao Shangzhi raged like a caged lion—consumed by helpless fury.

His predicament eerily echoed the "butterfly effect" described by American meteorologist Edward Lorenz: "A butterfly flapping its wings in the Amazon rainforest could, through a chain of events, trigger a tornado in Texas two weeks later."

This principle of sensitive dependence on initial conditions applies equally to human affairs. A secret Nazi plot, hatched thousands of miles away, would soon ripple catastrophically into Soviet politics—and ultimately entangle Zhao's fate.

On Christmas Eve 1936, Hitler convened Himmler and Heydrich to devise an audacious scheme. Alongside SS Gruppenführer Berenz, the four men orchestrated Operation Tukhachevsky—a plot to eliminate Marshal Mikhail Tukhachevsky, the youngest and most brilliant of the USSR's founding five marshals. To Hitler, the Red Army Chief of Staff loomed as an existential threat.

Berenz forged letters purportedly from Tukhachevsky and colleagues to German generals, detailing plans to overthrow Stalin with Nazi support. Every detail—writing style, ink aging, paper stock, even the forged seals crafted by Germany's finest engravers—was calibrated to deceive. The forgeries were so flawless they defied forensic detection.

How to deliver the "masterpiece" to Stalin? The Nazi leaders devised an ingenious plot: In late May 1937, a severe "fire" broke out at the German counterintelligence agency, leaving many injured and numerous classified documents destroyed. Amid the chaos, pro-Soviet Czech agents managed to seize a batch of top-secret files. Upon examination, they were shocked to discover Tukhachevsky's classified dossier among them. Soon after, the infamous Tukhachevsky "treason case" unfolded.

On June 4, 1937, Tukhachevsky was arrested alongside seven other senior military commanders. Just five days later, the generals underwent a secret trial. The proceedings were brief, and by 9 p.m. that evening, Tukhachevsky and the seven commanders had all been executed. To prevent any mishaps during the execution, Stalin specifically assigned Marshal Blyukher to oversee the process. Not long afterward, Blyukher himself was also executed. [14]

Over 80 years later, declassified Soviet archives and German historical materials revealed in detail the internal workings of the Red Army's "Great Purge." Following the purge, Hitler boasted triumphantly: "The most outstanding figures among their senior officers have been eliminated. Now, if we just kick at their gates, that seemingly colossal, rotten structure will collapse immediately."

The detention of the three army commanders—Zhao Shangzhi, Dai Hongbin, and Qi Zhizhong—by the Soviet Union was a complex matter, stemming from multiple factors, and was partially linked to the purge of Marshal Blyukher.

Marshal Vasily Blyukher, a pivotal figure in Sino-Soviet relations, had served as: Commander-in-Chief of the Far Eastern Republic Army (1921), Chief Soviet military advisor to Sun Yat-sen's Guangzhou government under the alias Galen (1924-1927), instrumental in founding the Whampoa Military Academy, Commander of the Soviet Far Eastern Military District (1929-1938) and promoted to Marshal in 1935, Blyukher fell victim to Stalin's paranoia. Dismissed in August 1938, arrested in October, and secretly executed in November, he was posthumously rehabilitated in 1956. His removal crippled Soviet military coordination with Northeast resistance forces—a critical factor in Zhao's failed mission and prolonged captivity.

Vasily Blyukher served as the Commander-in-Chief of the Red Army of the Far Eastern Republic in Soviet Russia in 1921. In October 1924, he was dispatched by the Soviet Union to China under the alias Galen, acting as the chief military advisor to the Guangdong Revolutionary Government and assisting in the establishment of the Whampoa Military Academy. Blyukher returned to the Soviet Union in 1927 and became commander of the Soviet Far Eastern Military District starting in 1929. He was promoted to the rank of Marshal in 1935. However, in August 1938, he was dismissed from his post, arrested in October, secretly executed in November, and posthumously rehabilitated in 1956.

Before crossing the border into the Soviet Union, Zhao Shangzhi had written a letter to Blyukher. Unbeknownst to him, Blyukher had already been blacklisted as a purge target and accused of being a "Japanese spy" during the Stalinist repressions. [15] Consequently, Zhao Shangzhi's implication in these events became inevitable. In 2006, Russian historian Gorbunov noted in an article that Zhao's arrest and imprisonment were linked to the Soviet "Great Purge," stating, "This speculation is highly plausible."

The Soviet Far Eastern intelligence apparatus lay in ruins by 1938. Colonel Pokladov, head of military intelligence, along with two deputies and multiple agents, had been executed as "Japanese spies." This purge stemmed from the defection of Lyushkov, chief of the Far Eastern NKVD's military intelligence division, who fled across the Sino-Soviet border to surrender to Japan in June 1938.

Historians widely conclude that the "invitation" to Zhao Shangzhi was a Japanese intelligence ploy, orchestrated through compromised Soviet officials. The messenger—Chen Shaobin (alias Chen Dejun)—had been recruited by Japanese puppet authorities while maintaining ties to Soviet Far Eastern intelligence.

Born in Yongji, Jilin (birthdate unknown), Chen infiltrated the resistance after his 1940 desertion, operating under the alias Shi Xin as a bandit in Kedong until his 1942 death at accomplices' hands.

Unlike overt traitors, Chen's lethality lay in his dual role: a covert saboteur within the Anti-Japanese United Army while holding critical posts like acting division commander and detachment leader

Zhao Shangzhi, during his imprisonment, grew suspicious of Chen's loyalty. After release, he confronted Soviet authorities about Chen's credibility. Major General Ivan Konev replied tersely: "We consider Chen Shaobin a malicious actor…"[17]

Following Zhou Baozhong's near-fatal encounter, the Jidong Provincial Committee concluded Chen had leaked operational plans, decreeing: "All future contact with Chen Shaobin is prohibited. His movements must be strictly monitored." Zhou's swift action exemplified his strategic vigilance.

Covert warfare—a battle of spies, signals, and subterfuge—proved as decisive as frontline combat. Yet the Anti-Japanese United Army, already outgunned by Japanese planes and artillery, faced an existential disadvantage: lacking trained agents, communication networks, or even radios, they were forced to fight shadows with bare hands.

Tragically, many resistance leaders met their end not from enemy bullets to the chest, but from daggers in the back—betrayed by those they once trusted. This asymmetry in clandestine warfare laid bare the cruel paradox of their struggle: to survive a visible war while defenseless against invisible ones.

"Heaven has unpredictable storms, and life is fraught with sudden twists of fate."

By May 1939, the three military commanders—Zhao Shangzhi, Dai Hongbin, and Qi Zhizhong—had been imprisoned by the Soviet Army for nearly a year and a half. However, thanks to a classified telegram (No. 7770) from Moscow dated April 15, they were finally released from detention. The telegram, issued jointly by Soviet People's Commissar of Defense Marshal Voroshilov and People's Commissar of Internal Affairs Beria in the form of a "command," clearly required approval from the supreme leader Stalin.

The main content of this "command" was: To fully utilize the guerrilla forces in China's "Manchuria," assistance in weapons, ammunition, food, medicine, and leadership should be provided upon request from Chinese guerrilla forces.

At the end of May, Major General Ivan Konev (later promoted to Marshal), commander of the Second Independent Red Banner Army, met with the three commanders. Zhao Shangzhi openly criticized the Soviet side for their unjust detention. Konev placated him, conveying that Zhao had been appointed by the Comintern as Commander-in-Chief of the Northeast Anti-Japanese United Army. He encouraged Zhao to return to Northeast China to continue leading the resistance and agreed to Zhao's request to organize a fully armed unit of about 100 men.

One reason for the release of Zhao and his comrades was that the butterfly's wings had once again fluttered—this time not in Berlin, Germany, but in Nomonkan, a remote area bordering China, the Soviet Union, and Mongolia. Though remote, it became the site of a Soviet-Japanese conflict, later dubbed the "war in the world's corner" on the eve of World War II.

The Battle of Nomonhan, lasting from May 4 to September 16, 1939 (135 days), saw the Soviet and Japanese forces deploy all modern military branches except naval units. The Soviets, under General Georgy Zhukov, mobilized 100,000 troops and over 850 tanks and armored vehicles. The Japanese, commanded by Lieutenant General Michitarō Komatsubara, fielded 58,000 soldiers. The Japanese suffered a devastating defeat, with approximately 18,000 killed and countless wounded or missing. Komatsubara later committed suicide. The Soviets also paid a heavy price, with 9,700 dead or missing and 16,000 wounded.

The Battle of Nomonhan was a "strategic litmus test" between Japan and the Soviet Union. By concentrating overwhelming force—100,000 Soviet troops encircling and annihilating Komatsubara's 25,000-strong division (the remaining three Japanese divisions arrived only as the battle concluded)—the Soviets left the Japanese Army Ministry with a psychological scar, declaring it "the first catastrophic defeat in the history of the Imperial Japanese Army."

On June 22, 1941, as Nazi Germany launched its blitzkrieg against the Soviet Union and advanced toward Moscow, Hitler desperately looked to Tokyo, wondering: "Why hasn't Japan attacked the Soviet Union yet?"

Soon, intelligence from top Soviet spy Richard Sorge confirmed: Despite lingering hatred after Nomonhan, Japan would not easily strike the Soviet Union again. [18] True to this, Japan abandoned its "Northern Expansion" strategy and instead launched the "Southern Advance," attacking Pearl Harbor on December 8, 1941.

While the Northeast Anti-Japanese United Army tirelessly sought contact with the Chinese Communist Party Central Committee, the latter also endeavored to reconnect with the resistance forces. To fundamentally resolve leadership issues, between July and September 1937, Mao Zedong repeatedly telegraphed frontline commanders of the Eighth Route Army, deploying troops to advance into Jehol (Rehe).

On July 16, Comrade Mao Zedong and Zhu De jointly telegraphed Peng Dehuai, Ren Bishi, and informed Liu Bocheng and Zhang Hao (Lin Yuyang), ordering: "Organize a guerrilla division of 3,000 troops from the 27th Army, 28th Army, 32nd Army, and the Cavalry Regiment to operate between Rehe, Chahar, and Hebei." Aware of the leadership challenges within the Northeast Party organizations and the Anti-Japanese United Army, the telegram emphasized: "Dispatch more cadres from the Red Army University to accompany the force." [19] Following the formation of the Nationalist-Communist United Front against Japan, on September 25, Mao Zedong telegraphed Zhu De, Peng Dehuai, and others, proposing that the 115th Division under Lin Biao take the lead in coordinating with the Nationalist Northeast Army, Guangxi Clique, and Central Army to form a powerful force. This force would launch raids behind enemy lines in North China and establish base areas. Mao Zedong stated: "If successful, a significant contingent could advance toward Rehe." [20]

After 1938, with the Central Committee completely cut off from the Northeast Anti-Japanese United Army, Mao Zedong prioritized the Eighth Route Army's advance into Northeast China and focused on building the Ji-Re-Liao (Hebei-Rehe-Liaoning) Anti-Japanese Base. On February 8, during a Standing Committee meeting of the Central Politburo, he declared: "Send Yang Chengwu to develop new guerrilla zones in the Wuling Mountains area along the Rehe-Hebei border—a strategic rear of the enemy, where we can coordinate with the Northeast Anti-Japanese United Army in the east…" [21] The next day, Mao Zedong personally drafted a telegram to the Eighth Route Army Headquarters, the Yangtze River Bureau, and the Northern Bureau, outlining plans to establish the Wuling Mountain Base and demanding the dispatch of senior leaders and Northeast-born cadres to the region.

By February 1939, the Advance Army led by Xiao Ke had completed its formation. It played a pivotal role in fulfilling the Central Committee's strategic directive: "Consolidate the Pingxi Base, expand guerrilla warfare into eastern Hebei and Rehe up to Shanhaiguan, and prepare for future advances into Liaoning." By the eve of the war's victory, Mao Zedong's strategy for the Ji-Re-Liao Base had expanded into western Liaoning and Suizhong, becoming a critical anti-Japanese stronghold within Northeast China. This laid the groundwork for Li Yunchang's forces to spearhead the advance into the Northeast and reconnect with the Anti-Japanese United Army.

While dispatching troops to the Northeast was a long-term solution, "distant water could not quench immediate thirst." Alongside military advances, the Central Committee pursued multiple channels to restore organizational ties with the Anti-Japanese United Army.

On January 26, 1939, Mao Zedong chaired a Central Secretariat meeting to discuss Northeast Anti-Japanese United Army operations, stating: "The priority is to establish communication with them—first by sending couriers and attempting to deliver a radio transmitter." [22] He expressed grave concern: "With proper leadership and leveraging mountainous terrain and anti-Japanese sentiment, the United Army could expand. Otherwise, it risks decline."

The plight of the Northeast Anti-Japanese United Army weighed heavily on Mao Zedong's mind. Between August 1941 and January 1943, under the leadership of Mao Zedong and Chen Yun, the Politburo convened three meetings to plan cadre deployments to reconnect with the United Army. They established a Northeast work policy: "Investigate conditions, establish strongholds, and pave the way for future operations," appointing Kang Sheng, Chen Yun, and Peng Zhen to select capable cadres for dispatch.

After 1941, despite years of severed contact, the Party Central redoubled efforts. Han Guang, a veteran of the Northeast Anti-Japanese United Army, was tasked with reorganizing and strengthening the Northeast Work Committee in the Jin-Cha-Ji Border Region near the Northeast. Dozens of cadres were sent to key cities across Manchuria, including Mudanjiang, Jixi, and Hegang, with a primary mission: "Locate the Northeast Anti-Japanese United Army."

Wang Peng, originally named Peng Shennian, was a member of the Northeast Anti-Japanese United Army's 7th Army. In the summer of 1936, he was sent to the Soviet Union for training and returned to Yan'an with Wang Ming, Kang Sheng, and Chen Yun in late 1937. In June 1939, under the direction of Yang Song (Wu Ping), Wang Peng was dispatched back to Northeast China to locate and reconnect with the Anti-Japanese United Army. To ensure his safety, his route was meticulously planned: first to Xi'an, Mianchi, and Yuanqu, then to the Eighth Route Army Headquarters in the Taihang Mountains, followed by Licheng. Given the critical nature of his mission, Chen Guang, acting commander of the 115th Division, personally led a 300-strong escort to accompany him to Yishui in the Lunan Sub-bureau of the CCP Northern Bureau, then to Jiaodong. There, Zhu Rui, political commissar of the Eighth Route Army's First Column, arranged for Wang Peng to disguise himself as a laborer bound for the Japanese puppet state of Manchukuo, boarding a ship in Longkou to enter the Northeast.

After arriving in Northeast China, Wang Peng traveled via the South Manchuria Railway to Harbin, then by boat to Raohe. During the journey, faced with rigorous Japanese military inspections, Wang was forced to destroy the identification documents issued by Zhu Rui. Amidst constant dangers and a grueling thousand-mile trek, Wang spent an entire year before finally reaching Raohe in June 1940, where he located the 2nd Detachment of the 2nd Route Army of the Northeast Anti-Japanese United Army. He became the only Central Committee courier to successfully reunite with the Anti-Japanese forces in years. [23]

The fact that Wang Peng received widespread support—particularly the full escort and meticulous arrangements by Chen Guang and Zhu Rui—underscores the paramount importance Mao Zedong placed on the Northeast Anti-Japanese United Army. Historical records indicate that 11 individuals, including Wang, were dispatched with similar missions. Among them was Li Yiguang, who departed from Yan'an to contact Yang Jingyu, commander of the 1st Route Army. Li later disappeared without a trace. Most of these envoys were lost, highlighting the extreme peril of establishing communication between the Party Central and the Northeast forces. This underscores the immense challenges the Party Central faced in maintaining contact with the Northeast Anti-Japanese United Army during this period!

Wang Peng conveyed the Central Committee's directive to Wang Xiaoming (awarded the rank of Major General in 1955), political commissar of the Second Detachment of the Second Route Army of the Northeast Anti-Japanese Allied Forces: "The Seventh Army must send a loyal and reliable comrade as a representative to accompany him to Yan'an, attend the Seventh Plenary Session of the CCP Central Committee, and familiarize themselves with the communication routes for future liaison."

Wang Peng's arrival greatly encouraged Zhou Baozhong and other Anti-Japanese Allied Forces officers and soldiers, akin to a lone boat adrift in a vast ocean finally glimpsing a distant shore. Zhou Baozhong brought Wang Peng into the Soviet Union, hoping the Soviets would assist his return to Yan'an via Xinjiang. However, the Soviet response was: "This is impossible." Wang Peng was subsequently retained at the Anti-Japanese Allied Forces Teaching Brigade.

It should be noted that between 1940 and 1943, Anti-Japanese Allied Forces personnel who had entered the Soviet Union underwent specialized training—including intelligence gathering, reconnaissance, demolition, chemical defense, and parachuting—under Soviet instructors at the Northern and Southern Khabarovsk camps. Though reduced to 700-800 members, these survivors represented a tempered essence of tested veterans. The Soviet military sought to utilize this politically steadfast and battle-hardened force for its own purposes. Facing Japanese pressure in the north, such an elite special forces unit could prove invaluable for intelligence collection against Japanese deployments.

As the adage goes, "Know thy enemy and know thyself, and victory is assured." Obtaining classified intelligence on enemy troop dispositions, armaments, fortifications, operational routes, and timetables often prefigured battlefield success. Thus, a small reconnaissance unit might wield strategic impact far exceeding its size—sometimes equivalent to entire divisions or brigades.

According to incomplete statistics, from spring 1941 to summer 1943, over 30 reconnaissance teams (cumulatively 300+ personnel) conducted missions behind enemy lines. During summer 1943 alone, more than 30 Anti-Japanese Allied fighters perished, including Third Route Army Secretary-General Zhang Zhongfu. [24]

The prolonged severance of ties with the Central Committee deeply troubled Northeast CCP organizations and the Anti-Japanese Allied Forces. After retreating into Soviet territory, this isolation bred intensifying crisis: the prolonged "suspended state"—"no sky above, no ground beneath"—risked severing Northeast CCP organizations from the broader Party structure.

To reestablish Central Committee connections, Zhou Baozhong proposed multiple solutions to Soviet authorities: providing transit documents for representatives to reach Yan'an via Irkutsk and Xinjiang, or facilitating political refugee crossings into China. Any means to deliver their representatives into China would suffice.

To all such proposals, Soviet replies varied in wording but shared one refrain: "We are striving to assist but currently cannot facilitate your reconnection with the CCP Central Committee."

From late 1940 to early 1941, leading figures of the Northeast CCP organizations in South Manchuria, Jidong, and North Manchuria, along with commanders of the Anti-Japanese Allied Forces, crossed the border into the Soviet Union and gathered in Khabarovsk to convene the Second Khabarovsk Conference.

During this period, the Soviet representative "Wang Xinlin" (a pseudonym for Lyushkov, a Soviet intelligence officer) seized opportunities in private conversations with Anti-Japanese Allied leaders to propose merging the Anti-Japanese Allied Forces into the Soviet military as a reconnaissance unit for operations in Northeast China. He further suggested separating the CCP organizations of North Manchuria, Jidong, and South Manchuria from the Anti-Japanese Allied Forces.

Zhou Baozhong resolutely rejected these proposals, denouncing them as "liquidationism"—an attempt to abolish the CCP's leadership over the Anti-Japanese Allied Forces and erase the very existence of the Northeast resistance. In impassioned tones, Zhou declared: "Every Communist must first be a patriot. We fulfill our internationalist duties under the unwavering premise of resisting Japanese aggression. We cannot walk upside down— feet in the air, heads to the ground!"

Zhou Baozhong sternly declared that the CCP's leadership over its own armed forces was an unalterable principle. Appointing a Soviet officer as commander-in-chief of the Anti-Japanese Allied Forces, he argued, constituted Soviet interference in the internal affairs of the Chinese Communist Party and violated the norms governing relations between fraternal parties of the Comintern. "Wang Xinlin" could only operate within the bounds of fraternal party relations, offering political suggestions and directives rather than imposing decisions.

This stance triggered a fierce debate between Zhou Baozhong and "Wang Xinlin." In a fit of rage, Zhou slammed his fist on the table, declaring that if "Wang Xinlin" insisted on pushing this "liquidationist" agenda, he would personally lead guerrilla forces back to the Northeast battlefield— even if it meant dying in combat against the Japanese. Simultaneously, Zhou wrote letters to Stalin and Georgi Dimitrov to clarify his principled position.

Kim Il-sung, who witnessed the dispute, later recalled in his memoirs: "Zhou Baozhong consistently upheld the principled stance of revolutionary struggle. He possessed a noble spirit and actively safeguarded the Chinese revolution. He would never tolerate any attempt to subordinate the Chinese revolution to the Soviet revolution or reduce it to a mere appendage of Soviet interests." [25]

Due to Zhou Baozhong's unwavering stance and that of other Anti-Japanese Allied leaders, the Soviet side withdrew its proposal to merge the forces. To improve relations with the Northeast Anti-Japanese Allied Forces, the Soviets replaced "Wang Xinlin," appointing Major General Sorkin in place of Lyushkov.

In August 1942, the Northeast Anti-Japanese Allied Forces reorganized into the Anti-Japanese Allied Teaching Brigade, externally designated as the 8461st Special Infantry Brigade and formally incorporated into the Soviet Red Army as the Independent 88th Infantry Brigade. The brigade was structured as follows: commander: Zhou Baozhong, political commissar: Li

Zhaolin, chief of staff: Choi Seok-won (Choi Shi-chun) and subunits: 1st, 2nd, 3rd, and 4th Training Battalions, along with a communications company.

The Northeastern Anti-Japanese Allied Forces accepted military designation from the Soviet Army and were temporarily administered by the Soviet Far East Red Army. However, they maintained their organizational independence internally, preserving their separate organizational system under the leadership of the Chinese Communist Party and continuing to execute their independent combat mission of resisting Japan and saving the nation.

This historical account fully demonstrates that despite being isolated in formidable enemy-occupied territory and foreign lands, far removed from Party organizations and leadership, the Northeastern Anti-Japanese Allied Forces led by Zhou Baozhong never wavered in their unwavering loyalty to the Chinese Communist Party or their ardent love for the motherland—sentiments that only grew stronger.

What defines the steadfast Party spirit and resolute faith of Communist Party members? What embodies national devotion and ethnic consciousness? The officers and soldiers of the Northeastern Anti-Japanese Allied Forces provided the most profound answers.

It must be acknowledged that the Soviet Union's permission for the remnants of the Allied Forces to enter Soviet territory and their reorganization into the Anti-Japanese Allied Forces Training Brigade reflected internationalist assistance to the Chinese people's resistance against Japan. This includes the Soviet Red Army's lightning strike against Japan's Kwantung Army, which helped the Chinese people defeat the invaders—a contribution never forgotten by the Chinese people. However, one critical point must be emphasized: Soviet assistance to China, including its support for the Allied Forces, was never without cost; it consistently prioritized maximizing its own national interests.

Following the collapse of the Soviet Union, declassified Russian national archives revealed that the Northeastern Anti-Japanese Allied Forces' repeated requests to forward reports to Yan'an were never transmitted and instead lay dormant in Soviet archival cabinets. A programmatic pamphlet of Mao Zedong's *Prolonged War* guiding the resistance against Japan, translated into Russian and distributed to select military units for reference, was never provided to the Allied Forces. It was only after the Allied Forces later obtained a Russian copy from Soviet forces, which Feng Zhongyun translated into Chinese, that the document became invaluable material for their struggle.

Was the Soviet Union truly incapable of facilitating communication between the Chinese Communist Party Central Committee and the Northeastern Anti-Japanese Allied Forces? In reality, the Soviet Communist Party and Yan'an had maintained telecommunications links. During the resistance against Japan, the Soviet Union stationed personnel in Yan'an, with its intelligence unit residing behind Yan'an's Zaoyuan (Date Garden). Aircraft also occasionally transported personnel between the two sides. If the Soviets had wished, they could have forwarded the Allied Forces' reports to Yan'an and relayed the Central Committee's directives and documents. The fact that they did not underscores a deliberate obstruction rather than a logistical impossibility.

Notes:

[1]　[6]　Zhang Zhenglong: *Snow Cold, Blood Hot* (Volume 2), Changjiang Literature and Art Press, April 2011, 1st edition, pp. 218, 219.

[2] Central Archives, Liaoning Provincial Archives, Jilin Provincial Archives, Heilongjiang Provincial Archives: *A Compilation of Revolutionary Historical Documents in Northeast China*, Jia 51, p. 439; cited in Zhang Zhenglong: Snow Cold, Blood Hot (Volume 2), Changjiang Literature and Art Press, April 2011, 1st edition, p. 219.

[3] Shi Yijun: The Most Dangerous Moment: Northeast Anti - Japanese United Army Historical Events, CITIC Press Group, September 2016, 1st edition, pp. 151 - 152.

[4] Liu Ying: *Northeast Anti - Japanese United Army Women Soldiers*, Heilongjiang People's Press, August 2015, 1st edition, p. 95.

[5] [9] Shi Yijun: The Most Dangerous Moment: Northeast Anti - Japanese United Army Historical Events, CITIC Press Group, September 2016, 1st edition, pp. 133, 278.

[7] Shi Yijun: The Most Dangerous Moment: Northeast Anti - Japanese United Army Historical Events, CITIC Press Group, September 2016, 1st edition, p. 189.

[8] [11] Liu Ying: *Northeast Anti - Japanese United Army Women Soldiers*, Heilongjiang People's Press, August 2015, 1st edition, pp. 249, 227.

[10] Shi Yijun: The Most Dangerous Moment: Northeast Anti - Japanese United Army Historical Events, CITIC Press Group, September 2016, 1st edition, pp. 275 - 277.

[12] Shi Yijun: *A Detailed Chronology of Feng Zhongyun*, National Library Press, May 2019, 1st edition, pp. 272 - 273.

[13] Liu Ying: *Northeast Anti-Japanese United Army Women Soldiers*, Heilongjiang People's Press, August 2015, 1st edition, p. 348.

[14] [18] Chen Dunde: *Nomonhan 1939*, PLA Press, August 2015, 1st edition, pp. 15, 298.

[15] [17] Zhao Junqing: *The Biography of Zhao Shangzhi*, Heilongjiang People's Press, August 2015, revised edition, pp. 278, 284.

[16] Shi Yijun: The Most Dangerous Moment: Northeast Anti - Japanese United Army Historical Events, CITIC Press Group, September 2016, 1st edition, pp. 119 - 123.

[19]   [21] The Literature Research Office of the Central Committee of the Communist Party of China: *Chronology of Mao Zedong* (1893 - 1949), Revised Edition, Volume 2, Central Literature Press, December 2013, 1st edition, pp. 5, 50.

[20] The Literature Research Office of the Central Committee of the Communist Party of China: *Collected Works of Mao Zedong* (Volume 2), People's Press, December 1993, 1st edition, p. 25.

[22]   [23] Shang Jinzhou: The Central Committee of the Communist Party of China and the Northeast Anti - Japanese United Army, Central Literature Press, May 2010, 1st edition, pp. 38, 39.

[24] Chen Lei: *Unforgettable Past, Deep Memorial, in the CCP Jilin History Party Work Committee: Memories of Zhou Baoshong*, Jilin People's Press, June 1989 edition, p. 131; cited in Zhao Junqing: The Biography of Zhou Baoshong, Heilongjiang People's Press, August 2015, revised edition, p. 377.

[25] Kim Il - sung: *Kim Il - sung Memoirs: With the Century* (8 - 2), DPRK Foreign Language Press, 1st edition, 1998, p. 220; cited in Zhao Junqing: The Biography of Zhao Shangzhi, Heilongjiang People's Press, August 2015, revised edition, p. 337.

Chapter17

Frozen Fingers and Torn Skin

55. Winter, the "Traitor"

In 1938, the Anti-Japanese Allied Forces in North Manchuria faced dire straits. The Japanese puppet regime intensified its "Great Suppression" campaign in the Sanjiang region, threatening to encircle and annihilate the resistance forces. To break free from the enemy's siege, the Provisional Committee of the Chinese Communist Party (CCP) in North Manchuria decided to dispatch the main forces of the Third, Sixth, Ninth, and Eleventh Armies on an expedition northwestward to Hailun and Tongbei. Their goals were to establish new guerrilla zones and, if possible, connect with the Eighth Route Army in China's interior—a campaign later known as the Western Expedition.

In 1938, the Anti-Japanese Allied Forces in North Manchuria faced dire straits. The Japanese puppet regime intensified its "Great Suppression" campaign in the Sanjiang region, threatening to encircle and annihilate the resistance forces. To break free from the enemy's siege, the Provisional Committee of the Chinese Communist Party (CCP) in North Manchuria decided to dispatch the main forces of the Third, Sixth, Ninth, and Eleventh Armies on an expedition northwestward to Hailun and Tongbei. Their goals were to establish new guerrilla zones and, if possible, connect with the Eighth Route Army in China's interior—a campaign later known as the Western Expedition.

The expedition, coincidentally structured like the Second Route Army's forces, was divided into three waves. The first wave comprised 150 troops from the Third Army's Political Security Division and the Ninth Army's Second Division. Commanders included Wei Changkui, a standing member of the North Manchuria Provisional Committee and Director of the Ninth Army's Political Department, alongside Guo Tiejian, commander of the Ninth Army's Second Division, and Chang Youjun, commander of the Political Security Division.

Wei Changkui (1906–1938), born in Shandong, joined the CCP in 1926. He served as Secretary of the CCP's Daowai District Committee in Harbin, Secretary of the Harbin Special Committee, and a standing member and organizational director of the North Manchuria Provisional Committee. As Director of the Ninth Army's Political Department, he remained unwaveringly loyal to the Party until his martyrdom at age 32.

Guo Tiejian (1911–1941), originally named Guo Chengwen, was born in Diaoling, Yilan, Heilongjiang. Joining the CCP in 1935, he initially worked underground under the guise of teaching. Together with his wife Li Shuzhen (using the aliases "Guo Zijian" and "Li Suzhen"), he recruited over 50 people into the Allied Forces within three months, later mobilizing his brothers and 30 students from Diaoling Primary School to join.

A daring strategist, Guo Tiejian once led just two Party members to seize nine rifles and a pistol from a puppet militia in August 1935, forming a 20-strong guerrilla unit that joined Zhao Shangzhi's Third Army as the First Regiment's Guerrilla Company, with Guo as commander. In September, he ambushed a puppet army transport boat, capturing over a dozen rifles and

100 sets of winter uniforms. To strengthen the Ninth Army, Zhao Shangzhi transferred Guo's unit to its ranks. Before becoming commander of the Second Division, Guo served as Political Director of the Ninth Army's First Division.[1]

A daring strategist, Guo Tiejian once led just two Party members to seize nine rifles and a pistol from a puppet militia in August 1935, forming a 20-strong guerrilla unit that joined Zhao Shangzhi's Third Army as the First Regiment's Guerrilla Company, with Guo as commander. In September, he ambushed a puppet army transport boat, capturing over a dozen rifles and 100 sets of winter uniforms. To strengthen the Ninth Army, Zhao Shangzhi transferred Guo's unit to its ranks. Before becoming commander of the Second Division, Guo served as Political Director of the Ninth Army's First Division.[1]

Chang Youjun, born in 1911 in Xiuyan, Liaoning, joined Zhao Shangzhi's Harbin-East Detachment in 1934 and became a CCP member in 1935. A veteran of the Third Army, he served as Political Director of the Third Army's Sixth Regiment and later as commander of its First Division. He was martyred at just 27 years old.

Like Xie Wendong, Li Huatang, commander of the Ninth Army, prioritized self-preservation during this critical juncture. Not only did he refuse to join the Western Expedition, but he also obstructed the Ninth Army's First Division from mobilizing. Consequently, Wei Changkui and Guo Tiejian could only lead the Fourth and Fifth Regiments of the Second Division to join the expedition. After linking up with Chang Youjun, they advanced toward Hailun via Tieli.

The first wave of the Western Expedition began in summer. To avoid clashes with large enemy forces, the troops trekked along rugged mountain paths or hacked through dense forests to forge trails. Upon entering primeval woodlands, fallen trees blocked their way—too high to climb over, too low to crawl under. Detours around the debris caused constant stumbling, shredding their uniforms into rags. Exposed faces, necks, and hands bore bloody scratches.

While the enemy rarely ventured into these vast forests, nature itself became a foe. Fallen logs and "widowmakers"—dead branches hanging precariously from lightning-struck trees—posed lethal hazards. A gust of wind could send these branches crashing down, injuring soldiers.

Another hardship was footwear disintegrating within days. Troops resorted to lashing the remnants to their feet with straw ropes and cloth strips. The journey alternated between mountain trails and waterlogged marshes, under relentless rain. Soldiers waded through knee-deep mud, perpetually soaked.

Starvation compounded their misery. For days, they survived on wild herbs like four-leaf greens, bright-leaf vegetables, and bracken fern, which caused severe edema. When they stumbled upon cornfields or potato patches, they devoured unripe corn cobs or raw potatoes—scant nourishment, but safer than toxic plants.

Wild fruits—stinkberries, mountain hawthorns, and wild apricots— became staples, but their astringent nature led to agonizing constipation, a consequence of fiberless diets. Soldiers, weak with hunger and dizziness, clung to each other to avoid falling behind. Those who collapsed crawled forward with their last strength.

Despite their exhaustion, the troops clashed with enemy forces near Weizigou. During the firefight, Wei Changkui, covering the rear, was struck by a stray bullet. Severely wounded, he crawled onward until enemy pursuers closed in. To protect Party secrets and avoid capture, he burned his documents and slit his own throat in a final act of defiance.[2]

To avoid enemy encirclement, Guo Tiejian and Chang Youjun led their forces separately toward Suiling via Qingcheng and Tieli. During the march, the two units lost contact.

The harsh environment served as a brutal "test of anti-Japanese resolve". Wang (full name unknown), commander of the Ninth Army's Fourth Regiment (a remnant of Li Huatang's forces) operating alongside the Third Army's Political Security Division, exploited the pretext of differing command structures between the Third and Ninth Armies. Claiming to procure supplies, he led over 40 troops away, with only a dozen later returning in remorse. Chang Youjun pressed onward toward the original objective, finally reaching the Third Army's Sixth Division hidden camps in Hailun by late September. Tragically, Chang was assassinated days later by a traitor.[3]

Guo Tiejian, leading 60 survivors, broke through Japanese encirclements only to confront a new foe: floodwaters. At Zhangjiawan in Suiling, torrential rains triggered catastrophic flooding, blocking their path and forcing retreat into mountainous terrain. Skirmishes with puppet militias and Japanese settler brigades ensued. Through Guo's decisive leadership, the troops fought their way to refuge in Pianlianzhang and Gedashan for regrouping.

Prolonged marches in relentless rain left soldiers' feet festering. Starvation and outbreaks of typhoid fever compounded their suffering, while wounds festered without medicine. Guo Tiejian himself fell gravely ill, delirious with fever. Yet in moments of clarity, he rallied his men: "Hold on!"

A former teacher, Guo treated his troops like students. Veteran Song Dianxuan recalled crossing the Greater Hulan River near Taoshan Police Station: Soldiers linked hands in silence as they waded through the current. Midway, two—a man in his twenties and a teenager—were swept away. To avoid alerting nearby enemies, no one dared call out. Under cover of darkness, rescue was impossible. Guo, heartbroken, wept over their loss.

From June 1938, Guo led his division on the perilous Western Expedition to Hailun. Nature and the enemy conspired at every turn, yet their resolve never wavered. By November, only 23 survivors reached the hidden camps in Hailun—each tempered into elite fighters through fire and blood.

Later appointed Deputy Chief of Staff of the Fourth Detachment and Political Commissar of the Ninth Detachment under the Northeast Anti-Japanese Allied Forces' Third Route Army, Guo continued his resistance. In autumn 1941, while leading an expedition from Nehe to Nenjiang, his unit was surrounded at Guonitun on Nenjiang's western bank. Amid torrential rain and gunfire, Guo charged to seize high ground. Struck in the chest, he roared "Advance!" until his last breath.[4] He was 30 years old.

The soldiers of the Anti-Japanese Allied Forces fought to prevent their people from becoming slaves of a vanquished nation, and the people, in turn, risked their lives to support them.

The history of the resistance must remember "Widow Zhang" (also called "Sister Zhang") of Luanjia Shaoguo in Suiling. Her real name was Xu Xiu, an ordinary yet extraordinary rural woman. When she learned that the fighters seeking her help were anti-Japanese guerrillas, this widowed peasant donated her entire harvest of over two shang (approx. 13 acres) of ripe corn to the troops. She then ventured 30 li (15 kilometers) to Shangjichang, a tightly guarded enemy outpost, to purchase medicine under the guise of visiting relatives. To avoid detection, she detoured an additional 40 li (20 kilometers), delivering the supplies under cover of darkness with her son. Later, she returned to Shangjichang multiple times, secretly collaborating with relatives to procure rubber shoes for the soldiers.

Xu Xiu's frequent trips near the mountains aroused suspicion from traitorous police. Once, a puppet officer thrust a bayonet at her, but she calmly showed him a basket of wild herbs. Finding no evidence, the enemy let her pass. As the troops regained strength to continue westward, Xu Xiu scraped together salt through loans and bravely delivered it to them.[5]

This is the true story, documented in numerous historical records, of "Sister Zhang's Daring Aid to the Allied Forces." Xu Xiu's actions embodied the will of the Chinese people, inspiring countless villagers and relatives to assist her in securing supplies.

Throughout the 14-year resistance, countless spineless collaborators, spies, and puppet troops inflicted immense suffering on the Chinese people, especially the Allied Forces. Xu Xiu's bravery shone as a radiant beacon of national righteousness, exposing the moral rot of those who betrayed their country for personal gain. Countless acts of support from people like Xu Xiu became the driving force behind the Allied Forces' unyielding spirit—their willingness to shed blood and sacrifice lives—and the fundamental reason for China's ultimate victory.

The second wave of the Western Expedition, comprising two units, set out in August and September: A 200-strong cavalry led by Feng Zhigang (Chief of Staff of the Sixth Army) and Zhang Chuanfu (commander of the Second Division). A 300-strong force commanded by Jin Ce (Political Director of the Third Army), Hou Qigang (Political Director of the Fourth Division), and Wang Minggui (commander of the Sixth Army's Third Division).

A Historical Analogy: Some scholars argue that the Ming Dynasty's collapse was partly due to rampant plague devastating its armies—a crisis even the famed physician Wu Youke could not resolve. Yet the Qing's 80,000 cavalry allegedly avoided infection because fleas, the plague's carriers, supposedly detested the odor of horse urine. While the scientific validity of this claim remains uncertain, it is true that horses' scent repels certain insects. Fleas may hate it, but bloodsucking mosquitoes and midges thrive on it.

Amid the sweltering summer heat, Feng Zhigang's troops faced their deadliest foe not in rain or mud, but in clouds of mosquitoes and midges.

The windless, dense forests trapped soldiers and horses in a suffocating humidity. Sweat-drenched bodies attracted swarms of long-legged mosquitoes, biting midges, and horseflies, whose sharp proboscises pierced through two layers of clothing. Slapping at the insects left bloodstains on uniforms.

The horses suffered most. Laden with supplies and slogging through mud, their sweat-soaked hides emitted odors irresistible to insects. Despite the troops' efforts—wrapping rags around the horses or swatting relentlessly—the pests attacked in relentless waves, draining blood from both man and beast.

To the soldiers, these horses were more than transportation—they were comrades-in-arms.

A poignant story illustrates this bond: Chai Shirong, commander of the Fifth Army, refused to let his ailing horse be eaten after its death. He buried it with a wooden marker reading: "Rest here, dear friend. We march on, farewell forever." [6]

The soldiers took turns swatting at the mosquitoes and midges assaulting the horses with tree branches. Layer after layer of insects fell, only to be replaced by fresh swarms. The horses writhed in agony, shaking their heads and swishing their tails. Heartbroken, some soldiers stripped off their own clothing to cover the horses' heads or drape over their hindquarters.

Jin Ce's second force departed in early September, each soldier carrying only four ears of corn and scant rations. Torrential rains turned paths into rivers, forcing them into treacherous swamps. Knee-deep in icy water, ten soldiers succumbed to hunger and illness within days, while plague ravaged their horses.[7]

Near Liukuaitun, a 300-strong puppet cavalry from Tangyuan County pursued them. Jin Ce ordered the main force to detour westward while a machine-gun squad ambushed the enemy. Caught off guard, the puppets fled in disarray, leaving 50 corpses. By the time they regrouped, the resistance fighters had vanished.

By October, both units of the second wave had reached Hailun, escaping enemy encirclement at great cost.

Zhang Chuanfu, commander of the Sixth Army's Second Division and a former wealthy landowner who had sacrificed everything to join the resistance, fell in battle at age 36.

The third wave, led by Li Zhaolin (Chief Political Director of the North Manchuria Allied Forces), comprised 100 troops from the Sixth Army's Training Unit and the Eleventh Army's First Division under Li Jingyin. Their expedition began in the dead of winter, confronting unimaginable perils.

Zhang Zhongfu (1911–1943), originally named Zhang Fengqi, was born in Kaiyuan, Liaoning. A graduate of the Law School at China University in Beiping, he joined the Anti-Japanese Allied Forces and served as Secretary-General of the Independent Division (predecessor of the Eleventh Army) and later the Third Route Army Headquarters. A promising young intellect, he was only 27 when he embarked on the Western Expedition. He died at 32 in 1943 while leading a reconnaissance mission for the Anti-Japanese Allied Forces Training Brigade.

Zhang Zhongfu was tasked with maintaining military journals (diaries). One such diary, lost in battle and seized by the enemy, was translated into Japanese and published in the Japanese-puppet compilation Collected Documents on the Manchurian Communist Party and Anti-Japanese Bandit Groups. Later recovered and retranslated into Chinese by Chinese scholars, it reveals the expedition's harrowing conditions: The troops set out in December, enduring temperatures of -30°C to -40°C—cold enough to freeze spit mid-air.

From his diary, we learn the Allied Forces were far from physically robust. Prolonged enemy blockades had left them starved, unclothed, and medically deprived, with many soldiers weakened or injured.

As Feng Zhongyun later reported to the CCP Central Committee: "The Western Expedition was conducted under unprecedented hardship—without funds, food, winter clothing, ammunition, or preparation of any kind. " [8] Survival relied solely on sheer willpower.

On the first day of the march, weakened horses allowed the troops to cover only 20 li (10 kilometers). By December 2nd, five horses had collapsed. With no food for the soldiers, let alone fodder for the horses, the troops halted the next day to mend uniforms and scavenge for supplies.

By December 3rd, veteran scout Lao Xie and his team returned at 4 PM with a dou (approx. 10 liters) of millet and 100 jin (50 kilograms) of potatoes, while Deputy Yang and others retrieved the fallen horses.

On December 18th, as the troops prepared to depart, a soldier's frostbitten foot forced a delay. To avoid slowing the main force, Division Commander Li Jingyin and Political Director Yu Tianfang, along with the injured company commander, stayed behind to assist. They rejoined the troops by 3 PM, and by 4 PM, the entire unit camped in the frozen wilderness.

Zhou Baozhong's diary poignantly describes the scene: "Snow blanketed the earth, a foot deep in the mountains. Towering trees stood draped in white, devoid of beasts or birds—a silence as chilling as the funeral prelude to capitalism's demise. Guerrilla warfare dreaded this landscape most: patriots in thin clothes and waterlogged shoes, threading through enemy lines, their suffering beyond measure." [9]

From Zhou Baozhong's Diary.

Veterans of the Allied Forces often cited camping as the defining ordeal of their resistance. How did one camp in open fields at -30°C to -40°C? After 1938, building fires became a daily survival ritual. Soldiers carried axes and saws—often more vital than rifles in winter. They felled trees, cut them into logs, and split wood for fuel. Certain species like baomazi and cisong (sparking conifers) were avoided to prevent embers from burning skin or clothing; poplar and willow wood, too damp, proved useless.

Fire-building demanded strict technical protocols—violations risked severe burns and disciplinary action.

Sleeping arrangements followed precise rules: smaller groups slept parallel to the fire; larger units formed a radiating circle with feet toward the flames, bodies curled like shrimp to conserve heat. Each fire accommodated only six people—four along the logs' sides, one at each end.

Even so, soldiers woke hourly, numb with cold, to rewarm themselves before collapsing again. To prevent frostbite, hands were tucked under heads or between thighs.

Li Guilin, who joined the resistance at just 14 years old, later reflected on the burdens of leadership: "As an officer, your heart never rests. Soldiers collapsed from exhaustion, sleeping like the dead. We had to shake them awake every hour—a moment's lapse could mean frostbite or death." He recounted the tragedy of Tian Fu, a soldier whose frostbitten fingers turned swollen, purplish-black, and festering. With no medicine or nourishment, Tian endured days of excruciating pain before his rotted fingers fell off, leading to a slow, agonizing death.

Chen Lei (later Governor of Heilongjiang Province) described night watches by the fire: "Our duty was to guard comrades' feet—if they stretched toward the flames in sleep, they'd burn alive." Wang Jun (former Deputy Commander of Heilongjiang Military District) recalled a harrowing 1939 mission: Company Commander Zhu and soldier Ma Wanhai were dispatched to deliver messages to Liangjiajiao. While building a fire at night, Ma accidentally ignited his clothing and burned to death. Zhu, his own feet charred, crawled for two days and nights to complete the mission, only to succumb to his injuries shortly after.[10]

Lu Lianfeng, a teenage horse herder during the Western Expedition under Li Jingyin, survived by sheer luck. He described wula shoes—cowhide boots lined with wula grass. When snow melted against the fire, the leather softened, grass padding slipped out, and heels rubbed raw to the bone. "We walked on tiptoes for thousands of li." Guard Han Chen, whose wula burned, wrapped his feet in horsehide and limped onward.[11]

Beyond footwear and headgear, clothing posed another dire challenge. Marching through dense forests shredded cotton uniforms into rags, leaving soldiers draped in frayed cloth strips. Decades later, Wang Minggui (later Major General, 1955), commander of the Sixth Army's Third Division during the second expedition wave, recalled with tears: "The third wave's fighters wore tattered cotton uniforms gutted by branches, exposing clumps of fiber. Those without uniforms wrapped themselves in torn quilts, burlap sacks, or cloth scraps. Some bound their feet in horsehide; others swaddled their heads in layers of fabric."

Japanese author Gomi Kawarahei, in his wartime memoir *War and Humanity* (1992), detailed Japanese troops' winter gear: woolen underlayers, flannel uniforms, overcoats, fur-lined trousers, double-layered gloves, and face masks leaving only eyes exposed. Despite this, frostbite cases plagued their ranks. Meanwhile, the Manchukuo puppet regime spared no expense equipping Japanese forces for their "Great Winter Suppression" campaigns against the Allied Forces—whose ragtag troops, as noted earlier, resorted to stripping uniforms from fallen enemies.

Gomi Kawarahei, a renowned Japanese author and veteran of the invasion of China, meticulously documented Japanese winter gear in his memoir War and Humanity (Chunfeng Literature Press, 1992): "Soldiers layered woolen undergarments beneath flannel military shirts and trousers, followed by wool-blend uniforms, woolen overcoats, and heavy fur-lined greatcoats made of thick sheepskin. They added fur leggings below the knees, secured with insulated bindings. Feet were clad in cotton military socks and fur-lined boots. Hands wore woolen gloves under oversized fur mittens. Heads were wrapped in wool scarves beneath fur hats, with face masks leaving only eyes exposed. Yet despite this armor against the cold, frostbite reports persisted."

The Manchukuo puppet regime spared no resource to equip Japanese forces with such elite winter gear for their "Great Suppression" campaigns against the Allied Forces. This starkly contrasted with the resistance fighters' dire scarcity—as described earlier, female soldier Hu Zhenyi had to strip uniforms from freshly killed enemies, still bloodstained, just to survive.

Clothing, in such conditions, rivaled weapons in importance. Zhang Zhongfu's diary records an incident on December 23: After seven soldiers carelessly burned their garments, Li Zhaolin declared it a "breach of discipline aiding the enemy". The men pleaded: "After years of resistance, we cannot fail now due to momentary negligence." Li reluctantly ordered 20 lashes each—a punishment he enforced with anguish, knowing such strictness was vital to preserving their scant clothing and survival.

Li Zhaolin, known for his relative leniency among Allied Forces commanders, faced an agonizing dilemma. "Punishing my beloved comrades tore at my soul," he confessed, "but with our rags barely shielding us from the cold, I had no choice but to enforce harsh discipline." His 20-lash order for soldiers who carelessly burned their clothing was a brutal yet necessary lesson: preserving every thread was vital to surviving the frozen wilderness.

Weeks before the Western Expedition, Li orchestrated a daring night raid on Xingshan Town, breaching enemy lines to seize cotton, cloth, and sewing kits from Japanese warehouses. Most soldiers had never held a needle. Li personally stitched a prototype cotton-padded jacket, then with two marginally skilled troops, taught the men stitch by stiffened stitch. Within three days, over half the force wore crude, self-made cotton-padded jackets and trousers—threadbare but life-saving.

While fires staved off hypothermia, smoke risked exposing their position. When enemy "Suppression Units" lurked nearby, flames were forbidden. Hunger could be endured, but -30°C to -40°C cold killed silently. Veterans recalled finding comrades "frozen mid-rest, rifles clutched to chests, backs against trees—eyes closed as if sleeping." Stragglers faced grimmer fates: wolves of the Greater Khingan Mountains devoured the weak. "By the time we found them," one soldier wrote, "only scattered bones remained, skeletal hands still gripping rifles." [12]

The people's deepest hatred was reserved for traitors. Among the Anti-Japanese Allied Forces, a grim consensus emerged: "Winter itself is a traitor"—its ruthless alliance with the Japanese mirrored the sycophantic cruelty of collaborators.

In 1939, Li Zhaolin (using his alias Zhang Shoujian) wrote to Jin Ce: "On the night of March 2nd, Comrade Wang Jizhou (former director of the Eleventh Army's Second Brigade) and five others froze to death."

A February 24, 1940, letter in Tuanjie (Unity) noted: "Last winter, amid enemy raids, lacking proper clothing and food…over 40 comrades perished from wounds, starvation, and bitter cold in two months." [13]

Burial Amid Despair: Veteran Shan Lizhi recalled: "When possible, we buried comrades to spare their bodies from desecration. Graves had to be deep—shallow ones attracted wolves. After 1938, digging even a shallow pit with bayonets and bare hands took hours. We hid bodies in tree hollows, blocked with stones or logs." He sighed: "Few graves of the Allied Forces remain."

Danish fairy tales like *The Little Match Girl* depict freezing deaths as peaceful, but reality was grimmer. Extreme cold induces neurological delusions—victims hallucinate warmth as their organs slowly shut down. "It's not a bullet's mercy," one researcher noted, "but a drawn-out 'lingchi' (death by a thousand cuts) of the body."

For many years, the author believed this to be a fictionalized depiction— how could someone frozen to death pass away with a blissful smile?

It was only after reading numerous historical accounts of the Northeast Anti-Japanese United Army that the author came to understand: many who froze to death indeed died with smiles. This was because extreme cold, beyond the limits of human endurance, caused neurological disarray, inducing hallucinations. As the lungs gradually slowed their intake of oxygen and expulsion of carbon dioxide, and the heart's pumping of blood to the body slowed until both functions ceased entirely—rather than an abrupt end like a bullet to the brain that instantly halts pain—this prolonged agony was nothing less than a "lingchi execution" inflicted by the merciless cold.

Lu Lianfeng recounted that frozen comrades became "stiff as logs," pitiful to behold. During the Western Expedition, hundreds fell on those mountains.

After 1938, more soldiers perished from freezing and starvation than in combat. Some, in their final moments as their blood solidified, stripped off their shirts and clung to red-barked maple-birch trees, dying with smiles—mistaking the tree's crimson bark for flickering flames.

Years later, veteran Wang Jun remained haunted by the image of Comrade Liu Dianfu's frozen corpse. During a food-gathering mission, they found Liu miles from the mountain base clutching a tussock like a brazier, slurring that he'd catch up after warming himself. Despite frantic attempts to massage life back into him and perform resuscitation, they failed.

Similarly, veteran Cao Shuyan could never forget the death of Deputy Commander Sun: "That night, returning with supplies, we noticed Sun missing. We found him at the forest's edge, seated rigidly on a sack, his frozen clothes like armor. His body arched forward, hands outstretched as if warming them by a fire, eyes narrowed in a contented grin—already frozen solid." [14]

Numerous works have attempted to encapsulate the horrors of the Northern Manchuria troops' Western Expedition. Noted historian Zhao Junqing aptly invoked Tang-dynasty scholar Li Hua's *Lament for an Ancient Battlefield*: "Withered reeds snap, frost-dawn chills; Snow buries shins, ice crusts beards. Raptors nest, warhorses falter; Thin cloth offers no warmth—fingers drop, skin splits.

For summer and autumn's trials, Feng Zhongyun described "jagged peaks, impenetrable forests, treacherous paths, torrential rains, raging currents."

Beyond nature's cruelty, the expedition faced relentless pursuit by Japanese puppet forces and desertions among the ranks—ordeals surpassing human limits. Marching past "roads paved with the dead," soldiers buried comrades with tear-streaked resolve, battling death with earth-shaking fortitude.

Their heavy footsteps shattered the silence of Xiaoxing'an Mountains—"where scarce birds fly, no footprints tread." Over six months, the three echelons of the Third, Sixth, Ninth, and Eleventh Armies traversed over a thousand li, finally reaching their destination by late 1938. They broke free of encirclement, achieving the Northern Manchuria United Army's strategic retreat.

It must be noted: this harrowing Western Expedition cost two-thirds of their forces. [15] The survivors—tempered like unquenched torches in tempests, like prairie sparks—soon ignited fearsome guerrilla warfare across Heilongjiang and Nenjiang's plains, striking terror into enemy hearts.

Even more remarkable was the indomitable spirit displayed by the Northeast Anti-Japanese United Army officers and soldiers in the face of lethal cold, starvation, and exhaustion—embodying the Chinese people's fearless sacrifice, unshakable faith in victory, and revolutionary optimism. Led by Li Zhaolin, they collectively composed a magnificent and immortal "Song of Bivouac."

The Anti-Japanese United Army adapted an ancient melody, "Falling Blossoms," into a four-season anthem where each verse revolves around the motif of fire:

Spring: "Gathered round flames in unity, crimson light fills the sky". Summer: "Smoke and fire pierce the heavens, mosquitoes suck through blood-soaked shirts". Autumn: "Withered grass, swift golden winds—frosty dawns with unlit fires". Winter: "Fire warms our chests, while winds freeze our backs"

Titled Camping, this song was recorded in Zhang Zhongfu's December 20th march diary. The full lyrics read:

(I)

Steep cliffs of Tieling, dense with trees,

Storm winds rage, warhorses neigh by desolate shores.

Gathered round flames in unity, crimson light fills the sky.

Comrades! Our resolve fears not Songjiang's evening tides.

Arise! Charge with courage!

Expel the Japanese, reclaim the Northeast—dawn breaks,

A radiance surging ten thousand zhang.

(II)

Canopies blot the sky, wildflowers sprawl,

Damp clouds hang low—sweat-soaked feet, gasping breaths.

Smoke and fire pierce the heavens, mosquitoes suck through blood-soaked shirts.

Warriors! Passion tramples Xing'an's endless peaks.

Strive! The burden weighs on us:

Break blockades, shatter sieges—light arrives,

Sweeping darkness to oblivion.

(III)

Wastelands stretch, white dew veils the sky,

Night fires glimmer—enemy forts tremble, steeds falter.

Withered grass, swift golden winds—frosty dawns with unlit fires.

Brothers! Jingpo's waterfalls rouse us from midday slumber.

Join hands! Face the national crisis:

Wield long reins, bind the tyrants—rivers and mountains shift,

War's flames extinguished in an instant.

(IV)

North winds howl, blizzards whirl,

Steeds hesitate, cold seeps through—sleepless nights.

Fire warms our chests, while winds freeze our backs.

Heroes! With fervor, sweep across Nenjiang's plains.

Great ambitions—how could they perish?

All peoples, all classes, unite—

Take back our rivers and mountains! [16]

It is said even Japanese invaders once expressed admiration for this Song of Camping.

56. A thousand deaths dare we face, yet hunger is unbearable

The catastrophic toll of the Northern Manchuria Anti-Japanese United Army's Western Expedition stemmed not only from the treacherous terrain and relentless enemy encirclement but also—crucially—from starvation. Hunger weakened soldiers, leaving them vulnerable to illness amid extreme cold and heat. Hunger left wounded fighters malnourished, their wounds festering. Hunger sapped the strength of exhausted troops, causing them to collapse in raging rivers. Hunger left fallen comrades dizzy and defenseless, unable to lift their guns as wolves closed in.

Throughout the expedition, soldiers scarcely ate grain. In autumn, they subsisted on wild herbs, berries, and mushrooms. Winter's "staple" was tree bark, occasionally supplemented by pine nuts, wild acorns, or hazelnuts. Horse meat, hide, bones (including hooves) were rare luxuries—reserved only when horses collapsed from exhaustion or illness.

After 1938, tree bark became a primary food source. Soldiers knew elm bark was the most palatable—slimy yet smooth to swallow—but elms grew near water, while the deep mountains offered only pine.

Veteran Lu Lianfeng recalled: "Pine bark was the worst, but we ate it anyway. We'd strip the bark, soak it overnight to remove the resin (which reeked and was indigestible), then roast it on heated stones until charred. We'd grind it into 'flour' for porridge. What kind of 'flour'? Burp, and you'd taste pine resin. Starvation left no choice. The worst part? The bark blocked our bowels. With no fat in our guts, our anuses dried up. We had to dig feces out for each other—using sticks or gun cleaning rods. Many bled, suffered anal fissures, or prolapsed. That's why so many survivors later had stomach diseases… some even colon cancer."

The third wave of Northern Manchuria's winter expedition faced not just a lack of grain but even wild greens. Soldiers developed mouth ulcers, scrotal dermatitis, and night blindness. Their "soup" that winter: chili powder mixed with salt and melted snow.

The cruelest deprivation was salt. Veterans explained: "Too much salt makes you cough; no salt, you cough too—and lose all strength." When salt ran out, they boiled unwashed uniforms—infested with lice, nits, and bloodstains (their own and enemies')—to leach sweat salts for a faint briny taste.

The cruelest deprivation was salt. Veterans explained: "Too much salt makes you cough; no salt, you cough too—and lose all strength." When salt ran out, they boiled unwashed uniforms—infested with lice, nits, and bloodstains (their own and enemies')—to leach sweat salts for a faint briny taste.

In spring 1940, the Northern Manchuria forces, having survived the expedition, reached the Hei'en (Heilongjiang-Nenjiang) Plain south of Keshan County—where Japan's hamlet system had yet to fully entrench. Commander Guo Tiejian, desperate to feed his emaciated troops, ordered them into a village. "As sunset neared," a survivor recounted, "Guo leaned on his cane, gasping for breath. 'Straighten up!' he ordered. 'Throw away the canes! Look sharp! Let the villagers see we still fight—that we'll drive out the Japanese!'"

Veteran Hao Fengwu recalled that a mere half-mile journey took them three hours—pausing every dozen steps to gasp for breath. By the time they entered the village, night had fallen. Following Deputy Commander Guo (likely the Chief of Staff) into a household, he stumbled in the pitch-dark kitchen, knocking his head against a broken clay basin on the stove. Inside was a sticky, half-frozen mush—likely duck or chicken feed. He grabbed a handful and devoured it, savoring its richness, then took another.

In early 1940, during the Second Detachment of the Second Route Army's retreat to Hulin, soldier Wang Fushi fell behind. Cao Shuyan went back and found him motionless in the snow. Checking for breath, Cao first tried carrying him, then dragged him through knee-deep snow until exhaustion forced him to stop. Wang pleaded: "Political Instructor… leave me. I'm done for." Moments later: "Shoot me." Then: "Strangle me."

Decades later, Cao's voice still trembled with grief: "A bowl of hot corn porridge could've saved him. He was right—no one could save him. But as long as he breathed, you stayed. Then, you built him a snow grave."

Hao Fengwu considered himself fortunate. After his first severe injury, his political instructor carried him back. A 40-year-old cook named Wang tended to him, building a shelter on a hillside and digging a two-meter-deep pit nearby, lined with strips of birch bark.

Lying in the shelter, Hao asked Wang about the pit. "Don't ask," Wang replied. Only after Hao recovered did Wang explain: "The division commander said if you died, we'd bury you proper—wrap you in birch bark so the wolves couldn't dig you up. That oily bark resists rot." Hao wondered: "I survived this time. Will I get such a grave next time I die?"

Modern people cherish festivals, especially Lunar New Year, when families prioritize reunion feasts—a tradition unchanged for millennia.

One New Year's Eve, the Third Route Army dispatched a unit to secure supplies. After a night's march, Li Guilin and two others—left behind without horses—awaited the unit's return at a halfway point. Their rations: a horse's head, its hide, and a pound of cornmeal.

In the January wilderness, winds howled through ancient forests devoid of birds or beasts. They singed the horsehide over fire to remove hair, watching it shrink. Camping in -30°C to -40°C cold, hunger gnawed faster. They rationed meticulously, but days later, the horse parts were gone, and the supply unit had not returned. For five days, the trio subsisted on snowmelt, too weak to lift logs, scavenging twigs for a meager fire, huddled tightly together.

Li Guilin and the other two were luckier than Wang Fushi. Just as the "Black and White Impermanence" (a metaphor for death) were about to kick down their door, the supply team arrived first. Each received a small portion of warm corn porridge, allowing the three near-death men to finally stand up. Years later, Li Guilin said he had touched the King of Hell's nose before turning back.

Li Min, who later became Vice Chairman of the Heilongjiang Provincial Committee of the Chinese People's Political Consultative Conference before retirement, was already a four-year veteran of the Anti-Japanese Allied Forces and a Communist Party member by the harsh winter of 1939, despite being only 15 years old. That day, she rejoiced over two things: first, they had unexpectedly found a relatively decent shelter—a rear base at Guokui Mountain where the enemy had burned the roof but left the earthen walls intact. Everyone worked together to clear the snow, block the wind with branches, and build a fire inside. As their spirits lifted, they began discussing what special occasion the day might mark, leading to the second happy revelation. After calculations by Supply Officer Miao, Political Instructor Du Jingtang officially declared that night to be Lunar New Year's Eve.

Supply Officer Miao used an iron bucket to melt snow and boil sections of birch and elm wood for drinking. Instructor Du remarked, "We've eaten this wood many times—it's bitter and unappetizing." Then, he pulled a worn-out wula shoe (a traditional cowhide boot) from his satchel. With no festive food for New Year's Eve, he offered it as their holiday "treat." Though the stinky cowhide wula was unappealing, its protein content made it desirable. Yet the tough leather refused to soften despite hours of boiling. Exhausted but persistent, soldiers kept poking it with sticks, muttering, "Why won't it soften?"

By dawn, the "treat" remained inedible. The supply officer ordered Li Min to take guard duty. In temperatures exceeding -40°C, sentries rotated hourly—female soldiers included. Petite and armed with a carbine, Li Min stood watch while thinking of the simmering wula. Suddenly, she heard noises. When her challenge went unanswered, she fired two or three warning shots to alert the camp.

The attackers were mostly puppet troops, with few Japanese Kwantung Army soldiers. Many puppet soldiers, former bandits, harbored vile intentions upon learning of female troops, aiming to "capture them alive" as wives. At the critical moment, Regimental Commander Bai Fuhou arrived with reinforcements, flanking the enemy and forcing their retreat. Historical records remain silent on whether the protein-rich wula was ever consumed.

To preserve strength for fighting the Japanese, Allied Forces soldiers ate anything that could stave off hunger.

Around 1940, as Allied Forces gradually withdrew into Soviet territory, starvation remained their greatest threat during the retreat. Li Min followed Bai Fuhou, commander of the Seventh Battalion of the Third Division under the Third Route Army. At a mountain pass along the Anbang River, a tributary on the right bank of the Songhua River, the group discovered a large patch of spinach-like wild vegetables. They began grazing like cattle until Bai Fuhou stopped them: "Don't eat them raw—blanch them in boiling water first. We'll set sentries and use half an hour to prepare them properly."

Li Min recalled that Commander Bai (as he was customarily addressed) knew the soldiers had long been eating raw food—wood ear mushrooms, wild boar meat (sometimes even maggot-infested), which had caused intestinal parasites. Once, a young soldier who had just eaten his fill went to the riverbank to fetch water and wipe his sweat, only to be spotted and shot dead by Japanese troops. Platoon Leader Xu was first struck in the leg, then finished off by machine gun fire.

In reality, they had gained no substantial nourishment—just a meal of wild vegetables—yet two Anti-Japanese Allied fighters had perished.

After breaking through the encirclement, the troops wandered to an abandoned field where scallions planted the previous year had grown tall. Starving soldiers dug them up and devoured them ravenously, despite the discomfort of overeating. At that moment, a soldier surnamed Zhu spotted a crow's nest in a poplar tree, containing fledglings with yellow-beaked chicks too young to fly. He climbed up, retrieved them, and roasted them in the fire—gulping down even the intestines.

"One can brave a thousand deaths, but hunger is unbearable."

In the late summer and early autumn of 1941, Wang Xiaoming (formerly political commissar of the Seventh Army and political officer and commander of the Second Detachment of the Second Route Army of the Northeast Anti-Japanese Allied Forces) was ordered to lead over 30 men back from the Soviet Union to reconnect with their original troops and local contacts.

Immediately upon crossing the border, they were pursued by large numbers of Japanese and puppet forces. Under cover of darkness, the unit traversed the Baoqing-Mishan Highway, aiming to cross the Naoli River into Yilan. Unexpectedly, the river had swollen from floods, forcing them to retreat into the mountains and enter Baoqing West Gully. The journey took 27 days—far exceeding their original plan—and their rations ran out. Five comrades starved to death. [17]

The loss of five lives in less than a month seemed preventable. Having returned from the Soviet Union, the troops should have been in relatively good physical condition. The summer-autumn mountains offered wild vegetables, fruits, mushrooms, and rivers teeming with fish, shrimp, and crayfish (Astacus). However, historical records note that under relentless enemy pursuit, even when food sources were available, there was simply no time to forage.

The first to starve to death was Political Instructor Li Zaiming (Democratic). He was a robust man who had served as the vanguard throughout the journey, often scouting and pathfinding ahead, expending the most physical energy. Next to perish were Mess Officer Lao Wang and the cook—both responsible for managing rations.

In those harrowing days when half a bowl of sorghum or a portion of coarse grain porridge could mean survival, the starvation of mess officers and cooks was far from isolated incidents but rather numerous cases. While serving meals, they consistently gave their meager portions to others. Food represented the hope of living, the essence of life itself, yet they prioritized their comrades first.

Since its founding, the Communist Party of China has been a party without resources. The fundamental reason it was able to ultimately defeat its enemies is that, under the leadership of Mao Zedong, the Party consistently adhered to the principles of "independence and self-reliance." During the most challenging period of the War of Resistance, when long-term Soviet support was unavailable, Mao Zedong said, "We very much hope for assistance from the international proletariat and the great Soviet Union. But since various circumstances have prevented such aid, what should we do? As always, the entire Party must unite, rely on ourselves, and overcome difficulties—this is our guiding principle." [18]

After the "August 15th" event, when the Soviet Union, for its own interests, handed Northeast China over to the Nationalist Government and declared support for Chiang Kai-shek, Mao Zedong declared with resolve, "Even if the Soviet Union does not help us, we are not afraid." [19]

It should be noted that throughout the Northeast Anti-Japanese War, the Soviet Union, which maintained so-called "neutrality," never provided the Northeast Anti-Japanese United Army, led by the Communist Party, with assistance sufficient to fundamentally change the situation. In contrast, from October 1937 to February 1938, the Soviet Union supplied the Nationalist forces with major weapons including 297 military aircraft, 290 artillery pieces, 82 tanks, 400 vehicles, and a vast amount of ammunition and spare parts, valued at over 485 million U.S. dollars. [20]

The Northeast Anti-Japanese United Army, operating so close to the Soviet Union, received support that barely amounted to a fraction of what the Nationalist Army received. Moreover, the limited assistance provided by the Soviet Union was conditional, exchanged for the Army's role in containing Japanese forces and providing intelligence. The Northeast Anti-Japanese United Army, which embodied the spirit of the Communist Party's unyielding backbone, consistently adhered to the path of independence and self-reliance from its inception. With immense resilience and effort, it overcame all difficulties through its own strength. When the enemy sealed off supply routes through "group tribes," the Northeast regional Party organizations and the Anti-Japanese United Army dispatched specialized personnel to clear land and farm, ensuring a stable food supply.

In March 1937, Zhang Zhonghua, secretary of the Chinese Communist Party's Daonan Special Committee, reported in a letter to the Central Delegation: Over the past year or two, the Japanese invaders in Northeast China have been constructing "collective hamlets" everywhere to blockade the supply sources of the Anti-Japanese Allied Forces. Therefore, we have decided to dispatch small units to implement a military farming system, planting barley in suitable forested areas as a supply source, resolutely waging a protracted war against Japanese imperialism in Manchuria.

Self-reliance through land reclamation and production had become a consensus among the Northeast Party organizations and Anti-Japanese Allied Forces to sustain resistance. In January 1939, after Gao Yumin, secretary of the Lower River Special Committee, conveyed the Northern Manchuria Provincial Committee's directive on reclamation to subordinate units, he issued a strict demand:

> "The tasks assigned to you must be carried out unwaveringly
> according to plan. Empty talk is absolutely impermissible. The military
> farming plan, in particular, is a matter of survival. Any anti-Japanese force
> in the Northeast that neglects this mission is a sinner of the revolution." [21]

Small units returning from the Soviet Union rigorously inspected local farming efforts. In September 1940, Wang Xiaoming, leading one such unit back to China, submitted a specialized report to Zhou Baozhong on rear-area cultivation:

"The Hulin rear base reported: Deputy Officer Liu's unit cultivated four shang of land, Commissar Sun's unit one and a half shang, and Deputy Officer Zhu's unit one shang. Though sown late, the seedlings thrive. The Raohe rear base has three sites totaling six shang with robust crops. Local villagers farm 87 shang; we may requisition a portion of the autumn harvest. At Daqigan, eight shang were planted, but six were destroyed by the enemy.

At Daxiaolaodengwo, villagers farm six shang. If undamaged, we could obtain 20–30 dan of grain. Yet even this total remains insufficient—we must intensify requisition efforts."

Writing this, I am reminded of Yan'an's "Great Production Movement" during the War of Resistance. However, by then the Second United Front had reduced sabotage risks. In contrast, the Allied Forces' farming faced relentless hardships—crops nurtured by sweat were often destroyed. In later stages, the core mission of Anti-Japanese Allied camps became cultivation, requiring constant vigilance: "Guard against the Japanese, puppet troops, birds, and beasts."

Planting crops deep in the wilderness was nothing like farming on plains near villages. First, they risked their lives to obtain seeds from the Japanese-controlled "collective hamlets." Even after sowing, mountain sparrows pecked at the seeds and chipmunks dug them up. When seedlings finally emerged, they were devoured. They replanted, only to repeat the cycle, resulting in crops of uneven heights, as if multiple generations of plants grew side by side. Just as harvest seemed within reach, wild boars and bears ravaged the fields. Yet the greatest scourges were the Japanese puppet troops, traitors, and collaborationist police.

Wang Yunqing, a veteran of the Fourth Army's Baoqing-Fujin rear base and a company commander at the Tudingzi secret camp, once led a group of five—men, women, and the elderly—to cultivate three shang of corn. By late July, the kernels on the oldest ears had plumped up. One day, while resting in a shack, Wang heard noises outside. The enemy's here! He grabbed his Mauser pistol, kicked open the door, and fired—two enemies fell at the threshold. Others flanked him but hesitated to shoot, fearing they might hit their own.

Wang sprayed bullets left and right, sending the panicked foes diving into the underbrush. Seizing the moment, he bolted toward a jagged cliff nearby—a sheer drop of several meters—and tumbled down. Lying there, he knew the corn was lost, and the secret camp too. The enemy slashed the crops with bayonets and scythes, tearing through the field from end to end.

Wang's heart bled with rage. He had only two bullets left. If I'd had enough ammo, I'd have killed them all! But even that wouldn't have saved the corn. Once the enemy discovered the fields, destruction was inevitable. "Crops don't have legs—they can't run," he lamented.

Wang's heart bled with rage. He had only two bullets left. If I'd had enough ammo, I'd have killed them all! But even that wouldn't have saved the corn. Once the enemy discovered the fields, destruction was inevitable. "Crops don't have legs—they can't run," he lamented.

Yet the Japanese miscalculated. The Allied Forces countered by "camping" to solve shelter and farming to sustain food supplies. After razing secret camps and enforcing "collective hamlets," the enemy resorted to a new economic tactic: scouring the wilderness to locate and destroy Allied crops. This proved devastating. As Wang Yunqing poignantly noted, "Crops don't have legs—they can't run."

In June 1939, Feng Zhongyun, while inspecting operations in the Lower River region, wrote to comrades of the Northern Manchuria Provincial Committee: "Current military activities amount to using force to secure provisions—what we call 'foraging raids.'" Anti-Japanese fighters put it more vividly: "If our guns aren't firing, our stomachs growl."

The Japanese believed cutting off the Allied Forces' "grain routes" would force them to surrender or disband. Yet their ruthless blockade only hardened the fighters' resolve. A saying spread among the ranks: "Better to die fighting than be starved to death! Destroy our crops, and we'll take what's yours!"

In the summer of 1942, six soldiers of the Northeast Anti-Japanese United Army (Northeast Resistance Army) raided an armed Japanese pioneer settlement, striking fear into numerous such settlements. The targeted settlement housed over 40 members, mostly reservist soldiers with substantial weaponry. Yet the six Resistance fighters – described as "the old, weak, and wounded" – achieved this against all odds. The leaders were Piao Jisong, commander of the 12th Detachment of the Third Route Army, who had lost an eye to shrapnel in battle, and Qie Jingfang, a battalion commander known for his Zhao Shangzhi-style decisiveness. Qie had amputated his own infected arm years earlier by strapping it to a tree and severing it with an axe when medical care was unavailable.

The other four fighters included squad leader Zhang Xiang and soldier An Fu, both missing fingers or toes from frostbite. Zhang had served in the Third Army's "Youth Company" under Zhao Shangz. Only Li Guilin and Li Shaogang remained physically intact – teenagers of 18-19 years old, undernourished and slight of build.

Li Guilin later recounted how this ragtag unit exploited nightfall and heavy rain to infiltrate the settlement compound. Complacent guards sheltering from the rain were caught off guard. Six Mauser pistols opened fire through three windows. The veterans Piao, Qie, and Zhang – familiar with battlefield Japanese – shouted commands amid the chaos: "Surrender your weapons and live!" When met with hesitation, Piao roared: "Light the lamps or we throw grenades!" The lights came on, weapons tossed out. Ten Japanese died in the assault. After seizing arms and supplies, the Resistance fighters released the rest.

Emboldened, the unit then mobilized every able-bodied fighter: 12 men stormed the puppet police station in Lidong, Mulan County, followed by the capture of Dagui Town. They burned the puppet police outpost at Shihezi and seized Daluo Town in Qing'an County – all nighttime raids. Puppet police forces, often collapsing at the first gunshot, proved easier targets. After each strike, the guerrillas vanished into mountains, leaving Japanese forces grasping at shadows.

These battles epitomized the Resistance Army's desperate struggle – a weakened remnant force achieving tactical victories through sheer audacity and sacrifice. Every engagement became a life-or-death gamble against overwhelming odds.

Combat resolve stands as a decisive factor in an army's fighting capacity. When soldiers fear no death, they become tenfold warriors. Amidst the overwhelming superiority of enemy forces, the indomitable will and sacrificial spirit of the Northeast Anti-Japanese United Army commanders and soldiers forged an unstoppable combat force.

Yet it must be acknowledged that war ultimately tests the balance of material wealth and resources (including manpower). While the Resistance fighters achieved localized victories, these could not reverse the overall strategic disadvantage. Particularly with the implementation of the Japanese "collective hamlets" policy—a ruthless strategy destroying the Resistance Army's basic survival conditions—the guerrillas were plunged into unprecedented crisis. Starvation remained a lethal weapon against them, yet in the face of death, soldiers consciously prioritized their comrades' survival over their own.

During the winter of 1939, the Seventh Army of the Resistance transferred a group of wounded soldiers to a secret camp in the Shishangdi area for recovery, guarded and provisioned by Wu Yinglong, commander of the army's security company. One day, Wu and three comrades traveled over 200 li (approximately 100 kilometers) to procure grain for the wounded. After receiving supplies—flour, cotton, steamed buns, and a bottle of liquor—from a courier, they began their return journey. Despite extreme hunger and exhaustion, none touched the food or liquor. As they emerged from the forest into open plains, they suddenly encountered over 100 Japanese soldiers advancing toward them.

Wu issued the order: "Deliver the grain immediately. I'll cover the retreat." His men protested, "Commander, we'll die together if we must." Wu barked: "Take the grain back—that's an order!"

Two soldiers shouldered the provisions and tearfully left their wounded commander and another comrade. In the ensuing firefight, they killed three Japanese soldiers before Wu and his remaining companion fell heroically in combat.

Though all humans enter this world crying, few wish to leave it willingly. Regardless of sociologists' or philosophers' interpretations, death remains humanity's most severe test. To die or to live? This question lays bare the authenticity of one's ideals and convictions.

Li Zaide, the sole female soldier in Wang Xiaoming's detachment, witnessed five comrades starve to death. She recalled Quartermaster Wang, formerly a lumberjack, whose appetite typically exceeded two men's rations. As quartermaster, he scavenged for food but never ate first, always distributing it to others. "His massive appetite and the physical toll of searching for food while starving himself—that's how he collapsed, never to rise again," she said.

She also vividly remembered the death of political instructor Li Zaimin. Sent with squad leader Li Zhongyan to investigate an abandoned charcoal kiln near their former base, only Li Zhongyan returned. He reported finding the kiln empty—Li Zaimin had collapsed at its entrance, gasping: "I can't go on. Tell Commander Wang... Even in death, I will never betray the revolution. I remain loyal to the cause to my last breath!"

Quartermaster Wang surely knew the consequences of scavenging on an empty stomach. Li Zaimin undoubtedly understood the risks of reconnoitering in his weakened state. Yet they chose to shoulder these fatal burdens so others might live. They bequeathed hope to their comrades and embraced death for themselves.

Let us remember Quartermaster Wang Xigang, then in his thirties. Let us remember Li Zaimin's final vow: "Even in death, no betrayal—revolution to the end!"

In a November 30, 1938 letter to Huang Yuqing, Resistance leader Zhou Baozhong wrote: "We shall fight till our last drop of blood, resolved that our ashes shall nourish the flower of liberation for all oppressed peoples." [23]

In December 1938, Gao Yumin, Secretary of the Lower River Special Committee, wrote in his report to the CPC Northern Manchuria Provisional Provincial Committee: "Dear comrades: Deep into the night now, fierce winds howl through the trees outside, gusts of icy air rattling our makeshift shelter. The flickering light of an animal-fat lamp casts shadows on walls. Revolutionary fervor burns within us. Soldiers who subsist on horsehide, tree bark, and pine nuts sleep soundly. The coughs of wounded comrades reverberate in my heart, my blood surging wildly... All this sears itself into my memory – I cannot forget, nor will I ever forget. These scenes guide us as we tread through this raging whirlpool... each drop of blood! Forward – slay the enemy – charge!"

In January 1939, the CPC Northern Manchuria Provisional Provincial Committee responded to Gao Yumin in an instruction letter:

"From afar comes the starving moans and shivering voices of our beloved comrades, igniting passion in our veins. Your gaunt, unyielding figures flash before our eyes. Day and night we worry for you, gazing toward the Xing'an peaks where snow-capped cliffs stand like solemn sentinels! Blizzards duel with bitter winds! This truly symbolizes the era of our great cause. We clench our fists, vowing to combat hunger and cold with indomitable spirit, to clash with the vile Japanese invaders! We shall not rest until victory! Comrades, rise and fight! Our motherland and people shall embrace a glorious future!" [24]

This letter from the Northern Manchuria Provisional Committee was likely penned by Feng Zhongyun.

Gao Yumin (1916-1940), born Gao Shengshan in Gaomi, Shandong, joined the Communist Party of China in 1935. He served as Secretary of the Yilan County Committee, Secretary of the Lower River Special Committee, and Political Commissar of both the 9th and 3rd Detachments of the Northeast Anti-Japanese United Army's Third Route Army. In spring 1940, he married with organizational approval but parted from his wife the very next day. That November, during a clash with overwhelming enemy forces at Jiguan Mountain in Arun Banner's Huoerqi Town, he sacrificed himself covering his comrades' retreat, aged just 24. A Resistance fighter brimming with revolutionary ideals and combat passion, Gao Yumin left behind an enduring legacy: the courage to overcome all hardships and an unshakable faith in ultimate victory. His words galvanized comrades: "No matter the suffering or hunger, no matter the freezing cold, as long as blood flows warm in our veins and heads remain upon our shoulders, nothing shall sway our revolutionary resolve." [25]

What is the Spirit of the Northeast Anti-Japanese United Army? What is the Revolutionary Faith of Communists? By carefully reflecting on the revolutionary fervor in the letters of Zhou Baozhong, Gao Yumin, and Feng

Zhongyun, as well as the final words of Wu Yinglong and Li Zaimin before their sacrifices, every true Communist Party member will arrive at the most profound and heartfelt answer.

In 1955, Premier Zhou Enlai issued an invitation to Northeast Anti-Japanese United Army veterans Feng Zhongyun and Xue Wen to attend a conferment ceremony, banquet, and evening reception at Huairen Hall in Zhongnanhai.

When Mao Zedong awarded Feng Zhongyun his honors, he gripped Feng's hand and said, "You are Feng Zhongyun, of the Northeast Anti-Japanese United Army. Your struggle in the resistance was even more arduous than our Long March!"

Tears welled in Feng Zhongyun's eyes as he replied, "Comrade Mao Zedong understands us." [26]

57. The True Geng Dianjun

After 1939, the anti-Japanese guerrilla zones in South Manchuria (Nanjian) and East Jilin (Jidong) entered an extremely arduous phase, while the plains guerrilla warfare led by the North Manchuria (Beiman) Anti-Japanese United Army flourished.

Reasons for the Success of the North Manchuria Resistance: While the Western Expeditions of the First and Second Route Armies of the Northeast Anti-Japanese United Army ended in heavy losses, trapping their main forces within the original guerrilla zones under Japanese puppet suppression, the North Manchuria Army's Western Expedition, despite severe casualties, succeeded in preserving core forces and strength. The North Manchuria forces broke through enemy blockades, avoiding annihilation by concentrated Japanese attacks. Zhao Shangzhi's foresight in establishing guerrilla zones and secret camps during the expedition to the Hei-Nen (Heilongjiang-Nenjiang) Plains proved critical. The Hei-Nen Plains were a relatively weakly controlled area under Japanese puppet rule, where the "collective hamlets" system had not yet been fully implemented.

In early 1939, to combat the enemy more effectively, the North Manchuria Anti-Japanese United Army established the Northwest Provisional Command, with Li Zhaolin as political commissar and Li Xishan as military commander. The Third, Sixth, Ninth, and Eleventh Armies were reorganized into the First, Second, Third, and Fourth Detachments and the First and Second Independent Divisions. Operational zones were divided as follows: Longbei (Northern Dragon) Forces (First, Second, and Third Detachments): Operated in Hailun, Nehe, Nenjiang, Keshan, Dedu, Tongbei, Bei'an, and surrounding areas. Longnan (Southern Dragon) Forces (Fourth Detachment and First/Second Independent Divisions): Active in Suiling, Suihua, Qingcheng, Tieli, Bayan, Mulan, Dongxing, and neighboring regions.

To strengthen Party leadership over anti-Japanese forces in the Nenjiang-Hailun area, the Nen-Hai Regional Delegation was established under the North Manchuria Provisional Provincial Committee, directly accountable to the Provincial Committee and led by Li Zhaolin. This centralized command structure unified resistance efforts.

The North Manchuria Provincial Committee and Longbei Command implemented three pivotal measures to prepare for large-scale plains guerrilla warfare:

The first measure involved enhancing the capabilities of military and political cadres through various means, including the establishment of dedicated cadre training programs—a remarkable effort given the urgent and perilous wartime conditions.

The second measure focused on striking the enemy on both internal and external fronts to solidify the Anti-Japanese United Army's foothold in the Hei-Nen Plains. After meticulous selection and training, seasoned cadres with expertise in local and underground operations were deployed to critical areas. Among them, Yin Zikui (also known as Yin Hongyuan), political director of the Second Division of the Sixth Army, was dispatched to Nehe to establish and lead the Nehe Central County Committee of the Chinese Communist Party. Zhang Wenlian, secretary of the Longbei Work Committee, was sent to Zhaozhou to form and head the Zhaozhou County Committee. Additionally, figures such as Fang Bingyu, former organizational director of the Lower River Special Committee, and Chen Jingshan (codenamed "Female Chen"), director of the Third Army's uniform factory, were deployed deep into enemy-occupied territories.

The third measure saw the North Manchuria Provincial Committee of the Chinese Communist Party, drawing on lessons from counter-"bandit suppression" campaigns and expeditionary experiences, develop a series of guerrilla tactics tailored to plains warfare. These included exploiting enemy weaknesses by "using small forces to defeat larger ones", employing diverse methods such as sabotage, raids, harassment, and ambushes, and mastering the fluid transition between "dispersing into smaller units" and "regrouping for concentrated strikes". Tactics like "decentralized breakthroughs", "gradual expansion of operational zones", and "lightning-fast infiltration by agile units" were also systematically implemented to maximize flexibility and unpredictability.

On May 30, 1939, the Third Route Army Headquarters was officially established, with Li Zhaolin as commander-in-chief and Xu Hengzhi as chief of staff (one year later, Feng Zhongyun would assume the role of political commissar). The formation of this headquarters marked the unification of the North Manchuria Anti-Japanese United Army under a centralized command structure.

The results were swift.

In early 1939, the Second Detachment, led by detachment commander Feng Zhigang and political director Zhao Jingfu, employed flexible tactics to rout a Japanese "suppression force" four times their size. They killed Japanese police officer Meguro Shunichi, captured 25 puppet officials including Liu Risheng, the puppet police director of Dedu County, and seized over 30 rifles.

Around the same time, a combined force of the Second and Third Detachments took advantage of enemy forces being diverted to attack the Second Detachment's rear base. Striking the undermanned Emuer Station, they captured 39 rifles and a cache of ammunition. These two minor victories revitalized morale, reversing the demoralizing aftermath of the arduous Western Expedition.

Geng Dianjun, born in 1903 in Laixian County, Shandong Province, was a towering figure whose ferocious combat style matched his imposing physique. As former commander of the Sixth Army's rear guard regiment, he volunteered during the North Manchuria forces' Western Expedition to lead a vanguard of 30 soldiers, "paving the way through mountains and bridging rivers." After reorganization, Geng was appointed commander of the Sixth Army's Twelfth Regiment.

In August 1939, Geng led his troops in a covert crossing of the Nemor River and launched a daring raid on a Japanese pioneer settlement, seizing over 100 horses. With these horses, Geng transformed his infantry unit into a cavalry force. Emboldened, they struck again, raiding the puppet police substation in Jiujing Village, Nehe County, before withdrawing triumphantly.

However, during their return, Geng's unit clashed with the elite Longjiang Training Unit of puppet forces at Sanmajia Village. Though puppet troops were generally inferior to Japanese garrison forces, this training unit was considered their best. Yet under Geng's relentless assault, the enemy fled in disarray, abandoning 14 rifles, including a light machine gun.

Still undeterred, in late August, Geng stormed Beixing Town in Keshan County, disarming the puppet police and self-defense militia. The raid yielded over 50 rifles, ample ammunition, and critically needed supplies such as cloth and clothing. [27]

A courageous and skilled commander is the soul of a military unit, the decisive factor in its combat effectiveness. Conventional tactics dictated that attackers needed at least double the strength of defenders to assault fortified towns. Yet in the battle for Beixing Town, Geng reversed the odds—defeating an enemy twice his size with half their numbers.

Due to a television drama titled *Thirteen Provinces*, the heroic name of martyr Geng Dianjun became widely known. While real history may lack the dramatic twists of the TV series, it is far more heart-wrenching.

Geng Dianjun came from a poor background. After battles, he would collect items others deemed useless, earning him the nickname "Geng the Ragpicker." Despite the constant threat of sacrifice, the anti-Japanese resistance fighters maintained revolutionary optimism and unwavering faith in victory.

In reality, unlike his TV portrayal, Geng was never captured, tortured, or sent to Unit 731. He died in battle.

In November 1939, Geng led the Twelfth Regiment to split and annihilate a Japanese cavalry unit of over 30 soldiers. After joining forces with the Eighth Regiment of the Third Army, he shared weapons, ammunition, clothing, and horses to bolster their weaker-equipped unit.

In late December, the Eighth Regiment, stationed in Zhangxin Tun, was surrounded. Geng commanded the Twelfth Regiment from Chajia Tun, two miles away, to break the siege. After retaking the courtyard where the Eighth Regiment was trapped, he shouted, "Eighth Regiment, retreat!"—drawing enemy fire that fatally struck him. The Twelfth Regiment's political director, Wang Jun, continued the desperate cover until the Eighth Regiment escaped.

Geng Dianjun, Jiang Furong (the Eighth Regiment's fallen commander), and others were buried by locals. Japanese "suppression forces" in Keshan later exhumed the bodies, photographed them, and brutally severed three heads, including Geng's and Jiang's.[28]

The Eighth Regiment, with only 50 soldiers, paled in size and equipment compared to the Twelfth Regiment. Their joint operations underscored necessity—and the Twelfth Regiment's sacrifice of its commander to save comrades revealed bonds forged in blood.

Reflecting on the Anti-Japanese history, we must draw political lessons not only from artistic interpretations but also from unvarnished truths.

A fortress crumbles most easily from within—a truth both sides exploited through espionage. Though the enemy was stronger, once their weaknesses were exposed, the balance of power could swiftly reverse.

Like Sun Wukong sneaking into Princess Iron Fan's belly, Yin Zikui, Chen Jingshan, and others who infiltrated Nehe County half a year earlier had established a Chinese Communist Party County Committee. They set up Anti-Japanese National Salvation Associations in seven or eight locations, including Sanmajia, Wodutai, and Nanyanggang, forming a 34-member armed force—the Nehe People's Anti-Japanese Vanguard.

To bolster this fledgling force, Feng Zhigang and Geng Dianjun handed over dozens of firearms captured during the Beixing Town battle to the Vanguard. From then on, Geng's Twelfth Regiment frequently collaborated with the Vanguard to strike Japanese puppet forces.

During this period, units of the Third Route Army of the Anti-Japanese Alliance prioritized mobilizing the masses. Li Zhaolin, the Third Route Army's commander, immersed himself in villages, personally fetching water, chopping firewood, sweeping courtyards, and working the fields. Ordinary civilians, long tormented by banditry in the Northeast, had never seen such a benevolent army. After Li Zhaolin's martyrdom, Haritun—a village where he had labored for the locals—was renamed Zhaolin Tun in his honor.

Meanwhile, the Anti-Japanese forged alliances across society. Liu Jingyang, leader of the Nehe Vanguard, hailed from a wealthy landowning family. His elder brother, Liu Yaoting, a former officer in the Northeast Army, joined the Sixth Army of the Anti-Japanese as an adjutant after being inspired by their cause. He fought alongside Wang Jun, the Twelfth Regiment's political director, leading charges in battles until his tragic death during the clash at Tanghuoli in Nehe.

Liu Yaoting was an influential anti-Japanese patriot in the Nenjiang region. His active participation in the Northeast Anti-Japanese United Army

(Northeast Anti-Japanese Allied Army) and leading by example in combat inspired many young people to join the resistance forces.

Liu Yaoting's sacrifice deeply moved Li Zhaolin, who issued a *Directive on Holding a Memorial Service for Martyr Liu Yaoting*. It mandated: "All personnel of the Army's direct teaching corps and the Vanguard shall attend the memorial, wearing black armbands for one month to honor his memory and pledge vengeance for the martyr."

It should be noted that such special commemorative measures were rare within the Anti-Japanese Allied Forces. This not only demonstrated Li Zhaolin's genuine respect for patriots who fought courageously against Japanese invaders for national salvation, but also reflected the determination of the Upper Heilongjiang (Beiman) Anti-Japanese leadership to uphold the patriotic united front and restore the vital connection with local communities that had been severed by Japanese-enforced "collective village" policies.

On September 18, 1939, the eighth anniversary of the September 18 Incident marking China's national humiliation, Feng Zhigang commanded over 270 troops from the Second Detachment of the Third Route Army alongside the Nenjiang People's Anti-Japanese Vanguard. At 11 PM that night, they launched a surprise assault on Nenjiang County town.

The assault forces attacked multiple key targets simultaneously: the puppet county government office, police affairs department, police training institute, and stormed the puppet garrison's Northern Barracks. They eliminated 14 Japanese officials including Deputy County Chief Motokazu Honda, Japanese advisor Mitsurō Sakane, and training instructor Naomichi Morikawa. Over 100 puppet military police were captured, including puppet regiment commander Sun Bingyi, along with the puppet police section chief, intelligence department chief, and police station chief-effectively decapitating the Japanese-puppet ruling apparatus in Nenjiang County. Simultaneously, the troops liberated more than 300 prisoners from the jail, broke into ammunition depots, granaries, and supply warehouses, seizing large quantities of military provisions and matériel. [29]

Nehe is a county located in the central part of Heilongjiang Province. In this battle, the forces captured 130 rifles, 100 Mauser pistols, and 30,000 rounds of ammunition. [30] The capture of Nehe County marked a significant victory for the Third Route Army of the Northeast Anti-Japanese Allied Army after its establishment, and it stood as a major triumph during the resistance forces' most challenging period. This success caused a sensation across Northern Manchuria, inspiring hope among the people in Nehe, Nenjiang, and surrounding areas regarding the future of the anti-Japanese struggle. It also generated strong pro-resistance sentiments among local merchants, wealthy households, and even within the ranks of the Manchukuo puppet army.

On the morning following the battle, the troops organized a public assembly to conduct anti-Japanese propaganda. Overjoyed civilians exclaimed, "The days of Manchukuo are numbered!" Dozens of patriotic youths immediately joined the resistance forces that day.

In the spring of 1940, the Third Route Army of the Northeast Anti-Japanese Allied Army convened a historic meeting at their headquarters along the Nanbei River (Southern-Northern River), presided over by Commander-in-Chief Li Zhaolin and Political Commissar Feng Zhongyun. This gathering became known as the "Nanbeihe Conference."

The conference decided to reorganize the 3rd, 6th, 9th, and 11th Army units operating between the Nenjiang, Songhua, and Heilongjiang rivers into the 3rd, 6th, 9th, and 12th Detachments based on their operational zones. According to veteran soldier Wang Minggui, who attended the meeting and later recalled the event, the most memorable aspect was studying the pamphlet *On Protracted War* by Mao Zedong, which Feng Zhongyun had brought back from the Soviet Union.

The study of *On Protracted War* effectively alleviated impulsive tendencies among some cadres, addressed the lack of preparedness for the prolonged nature of the war, and further solidified their unwavering faith in ultimate victory. Faced with relentless military "suppression campaigns," political enticements, and economic blockades by Japanese puppet forces, the Northern Manchuria Provincial Committee of the Chinese Communist Party responded with fearless revolutionary spirit and flexible guerrilla tactics. They initiated enemy elimination competitions across all units, demonstrating extraordinary revolutionary fervor that proved particularly invaluable under such severe circumstances.

58. The Enemy-Terrifying "Ferocious"

Among the detachments of the Third Route Army of the Northeast Anti-Japanese Allied Forces, the Third Detachment was the most formidable and battle-hardened unit, earning its commander, Wang Minggui, widespread acclaim as a "renowned general" in numerous historical accounts.

Wang Minggui, born in 1910 in Yitong, Jilin Province, joined the resistance in 1934. He rose through the ranks to become commander of the Eighth Regiment of the Third Division of the Sixth Army, later leading the Third Division itself, and ultimately serving as commander of the Third

Detachment of the Third Route Army. After the founding of the People's Republic of China, he was appointed Deputy Commander of the Heilongjiang Provincial Military District and awarded the rank of Major General in 1955.

Though Wang never served directly under Zhao Shangzhi's Third Army, the close cooperation between the Third and Sixth Armies deeply influenced his tactics. His combat style mirrored Zhao's: bold yet cunning, employing unconventional strategies that consistently caught enemies off guard. From April 18 to June 17, 1940, Wang's Third Detachment engaged in 14 consecutive battles during an enemy elimination competition, killing 116 enemy soldiers, capturing 64, and seizing 2 light machine guns, 120 rifles, 5 pistols, over 10,000 rounds of ammunition, and numerous military supplies. By July, the unit had expanded rapidly, adding a new battalion and earning recognition from the Third Route Army as an outstanding unit in the competition.

The Northeast Anti-Japanese Allied Forces adhered to an unwritten tradition: for over a decade of resistance, every September 18th—the anniversary of Japan's invasion of Manchuria (known as the "National Humiliation Day")—units conducted "commemorative actions." For the resistance fighters, this meant renewing their resolve to fight for national salvation. For the enemy, it served as a stark reminder that aggression would not go unpunished. In 1939, the Northern Manchuria Allied Forces marked the day by capturing Nehe County. For 1940's anniversary, the question arose: How would they commemorate it?

On July 20, 1940, the Northern Manchuria Provincial Committee of the Chinese Communist Party issued Guidelines for Commemorating the Ninth Anniversary of the September 18th Incident. The document directed all Third Route Army detachments to prepare attacks tailored to their operational contexts—whether assaulting enemy-occupied towns, military barracks, warehouses, railway stations, or other key strongholds—to honor the occasion with decisive action.

After thorough reconnaissance and planning, the strategic town of Keshan in the Nenjiang Plain became the primary target for the Third Detachment's "county-seizing" operation.

Keshan, adjacent to the puppet Manchukuo's provincial capital of Bei'an, lay in open terrain crisscrossed by roads, railways, and telephone networks. Heavily garrisoned, it was deemed a "model county" by Japanese authorities for its strict implementation of counterinsurgency measures like "villager relocation and household consolidation" and the "collective responsibility system" (baojia lianzuo). The town's defenses included over 1,000 troops: a puppet army regiment, a 200-strong puppet police academy and police station, and a 100-man Japanese garrison. Keshan's walls stood over three meters high, encircled by a 2.5-meter-deep and 2.5-meter-wide moat. The puppet county government compound was further fortified with walls, electrified fences, watchtowers, and sandbag barricades at its entrance.

At the time, Wang Minggui's Third Detachment numbered just over 120 soldiers. Facing such overwhelming odds, most commanders might have abandoned the mission—but Wang insisted on striking, emphasizing the need for cunning over brute force. He argued that by shattering Japan's propaganda of an "ironclad Manchukuo," a "model Keshan County," and the "invincible Imperial Army of the Greater East Asia Co-Prosperity Sphere," seizing Keshan would expose the fragility of the puppet regime's strategic rear and inspire nationwide resistance.

As with Feng Zhigang's earlier capture of Nehe County, underground Communist operatives embedded in Keshan played a critical role. Prior to the assault, Fang Bingyu, head of propaganda for the Nehe Central County

Committee of the Chinese Communist Party, and Gao Mulin (a 14-year-old student doubling as an underground operative) meticulously mapped the layout of puppet military barracks, government offices, watchtowers, and prisons. They also identified concealed assembly points for troops and secured local guides. The sole remaining challenge was the sheer number of defenders.

To lure enemy forces out of the town, Wang orchestrated a series of diversionary guerrilla raids over the following weeks:

August 8: Attack on Nan Town, Nehe County.

August 15: Raid on Daokuan Town, Keshan County.

August 20: Assault on Laha Town, Nehe County.

Additional strikes targeted puppet self-defense units in villages like Jiujing (Nehe) and Caijiawopu (Keshan), netting over 20 rifles and 2,000 rounds of ammunition. These actions were calculated feints, designed to provoke a response.

By mid-September, Fang and Gao reported that Keshan's Western Barracks had finally deployed its puppet troops for a "suppression campaign," leaving only 50 Japanese garrison soldiers, 50 puppet police, and 40 puppet militia in the town. Reinforcements soon arrived: Third Route Army Political Commissar Feng Zhongyun joined forces with Ninth Detachment Commander Bian Fengxiang and Political Commissar Gao Yumin, swelling their combined strength to over 200 elite fighters.

On September 23, Feng Zhongyun, Wang Minggui, and Bian Fengxiang led their troops from Zhang Laodao Wopeng in northern Keshan toward the county seat. After two days of concealed marches, they halted at dawn on September 25 just seven or eight li (2–3 miles) from the town. Ever meticulous, Wang dispatched Gao Mulin for a final reconnaissance. Confirming no changes in enemy dispositions, he ordered the assault.

As dusk fell, a column of "puppet soldiers"—actually Third and Ninth Detachment fighters in captured uniforms—marched boldly through a breach in the northwestern wall. Flying enemy flags and moving in disciplined formation, they advanced along the main street toward key targets: the puppet county government, military headquarters, and bank. A machine-gun squad split off to seize the central crossroads watchtower.

The assault proceeded with remarkable efficiency. The Ninth Detachment disarmed the puppet military headquarters and its mortar company without resistance, capturing four mortars in a single stroke. The Eighth Battalion of the Third Detachment seized the central watchtower, set up machine guns, and swiftly secured control of the main thoroughfare. Only the puppet county government compound posed a challenge, its gates locked for the night. Soldiers scaled the 2.3-meter-high walls using human ladders, cut through electrified fences, and unleashed a barrage of gunfire and grenades. Within 20 minutes, the compound fell. They then stormed the prison, freeing over 300 so-called "criminals."

During the fighting, a Japanese garrison force rushed to reinforce the town in two trucks but was ambushed by a pre-positioned machine-gun squad. Grenades rained down on the vehicles, inflicting heavy casualties and forcing the survivors to retreat.

The raid destroyed the puppet military headquarters and county government, occupied the Manchukuo Central Bank's Keshan branch, and killed, wounded, or captured over 100 enemy personnel. The spoils were substantial: when the arsenal doors were breached, fighters filled their pant legs and sleeves with bullets to carry them. In total, they seized 150 firearms and 20,000 rounds of ammunition.[31]

The fall of Keshan—Manchukuo's "model county"—exposed the puppet regime's fragility, transforming its "ironclad" myth into "paper mache." The victory electrified anti-Japanese sentiment, prompting over 100 locals to join the resistance—a rare and courageous act under the oppressive baojia lianzuo (collective punishment) system.

Though not a top-ranking leader, Wang Minggui became a legendary figure in Japanese accounts. The Manchukuo archival text *Overview of the Northeast Anti-Japanese Movement* slandered his forces: "A bandit gang of approximately 70 under Wang Minggui rampaged through Nehe, Nenjiang, and Dedu counties from June to August, raiding villages, police outposts, and stations, plundering and burning. On September 25, they suddenly attacked Keshan County, thoroughly trampling the county government, Manchukuo military headquarters, and prison."

If a mere 70 guerrillas could "rampage" across multiple counties and "thoroughly trample" a model garrison, how terrifying must their shadow have loomed over the occupiers?

The depth of this fear is laid bare in *Ah, Manchuria* (1965), a memoir by former Japanese "Manchuria-Mongolia Pioneer Group" members. In *Official Forestry Operations and Bandits* (pp. 542–543), Kitazato Tome, a former official of the Hailun-Tangyuan Forestry Bureau, wrote: "When night fell, not only did machine gunners stay awake on full alert, but everyone slept with pistols under their pillows. The office was surrounded by thick earthen walls riddled with firing ports. Day and night, the forest police maintained battlefield-level vigilance."

Kitazato Tome concluded: "Forestry operations could not rely solely on Japanese military 'suppression.' Thus, a specialized 3,000-strong forest police force was established for protection... Yet even with such security, neither the logging teams nor we could ever truly feel 'safe.'"

Why were the Japanese so tense and fearful? Kitazato explained that the area between the Nomin River and Tangwang River was a stronghold of "ferocious bandits" who moved like phantoms, launching nighttime raids. "Wang Minggui—whose ruthlessness defies the term 'ferocious'—led several dozen men based here. Being assigned to develop this region felt like 'snatching chestnuts from the fire.' My life could vanish like dew on the Tangwang River's banks at any moment."

Nakamura Sadanari, a former forestry official of Manchukuo's Binjiang District, echoed this dread in his memoir *Footprints in the Manchurian Railway Forestry Zone: The Greater Khingan Range* (*Ah, Manchuria*, p. 549):

> "The men of the winter Khingan Mountains feared neither Siberian blizzards nor wolf packs. What truly terrified them was the rampage of Wang Minggui's bandits, who emerged around the outbreak of the Greater East Asia War [Pacific War] to sabotage our economic operations. Their presence multiplied the horrors of the winter wilderness, keeping field workers in constant tension."

After 1940, Kitazato noted that volunteer armies and forest guerrillas had largely vanished from the Nomin River forestry zone—except for the Northeast Anti-Japanese Allied Forces. Despite ideological differences, he expressed reluctant admiration for the "ruthless" Chinese commander. In the same essay, he wrote:

> "By the war's end, only a few Communist 'bandits' like Wang Minggui near the Tangwang River remained. But these were masters of survival, weaving through armies with their guerrilla tactics that left [Japanese] forces helpless."

The Japanese perception was astute. Contrary to assumptions that the Northeast Anti-Japanese Allied Forces faded after the deaths of heroes like

Yang Jingyu and Zhao Shangzhi, their resistance persisted in three critical ways:

Sustained Combat Effectiveness Post-1940: While overall numbers dwindled, surviving units like Wang Minggui's honed their guerrilla tactics to lethal precision. A mere few dozen fighters tied down 3,000 puppet forest police, keeping the enemy perpetually on edge.

Cross-Border Raids from the Soviet Union: Even after retreating to Soviet territory, the Allies continuously dispatched small, highly trained squads—often 30–40 strong—to conduct reconnaissance, sabotage, and targeted strikes. Their intelligence on Japanese defenses later proved vital to the Soviet Army's lightning defeat of the Kwantung Army in 1945.

Continued Insurgency Within Manchuria: Secret networks-maintained resistance operations. In his essay The Final Days of Vice County Chief Seiichi Obara in Tonghe (*Ah, Manchuria*, p. 691), Nakamura Kojiro, head of Manchukuo's Colonial Development Research Institute, recalled a large-scale Anti-Japanese uprising in Tonghe County during spring 1945. Rebels briefly seized the county seat, freed imprisoned guerrilla leaders like "Rolling Thunder," and held out against Japanese forces until Japan's surrender.

The organizer of the uprising was the Beiman (Tongfeng) Transportation Hub personally established by Zhao Shangzhi and managed by Yang Chun and his son Yang Zhenying. In reality, resistance fighters on the covert front never ceased their struggle—they simply fought in different ways.

The Beiman (Tongfeng) Transportation Hub was not solely focused on intelligence operations. In 1942, when Japanese forces stockpiled vast amounts of ammunition in a puppet police arsenal to suppress anti-Japanese forces, Yang Chun and underground operatives infiltrating the puppet police station set the arsenal ablaze, inflicting significant losses on the enemy.

To strike at the enemy from within, Zhou Baozhong sent Feng Shuyan and Wang Yadong—a married couple of underground Communists who had incited the defection of the puppet forest police brigade in Ning'an Sandaogou—to the Soviet Union. There, they underwent specialized espionage training in a military camp. By spring 1943, they were secretly redeployed to Muling to gather intelligence on Japanese military deployments in the Mudanjiang region, reporting to the Soviet Union every three months. The intelligence they provided posed a threat equivalent to that of a hundred artillery pieces.

As Japanese forces crumbled, Feng Shuyan and Wang Yadong mobilized local forces to execute a puppet police station chief, incited a puppet police mutiny, and rallied a resistance force that eventually grew to over 2,000 fighters. This unit was later incorporated into the Third Independent Regiment of the Mudanjiang Sub-district of the Northeast Democratic United Army.

Adapting to shifting circumstances, the Northeast Anti-Japanese United Army persisted in combat despite severe late-stage losses while constantly innovating their tactics. Like a vast grassland scorched by fierce flames—charred and desolate—their roots remained deeply embedded in the soil. Once the bitter winter passed, a spring breeze and nourishing rain would revive them, sprouting anew until they flourished into an emerald oasis.

The renowned military historian Mr. Sa Su shared an interesting anecdote: A journalist assigned by his superior to interview veteran general Wang Minggui noticed the old commander's eyes gradually taking on a terrifying gleam-the same gaze that had once petrified Japanese soldiers.

Though Chinese himself, the journalist felt a chill. Upon repeated inquiries, General Wang finally blurted: "Why do I feel you're not here to honor me, but to humiliate me?"

The journalist hastily explained: "How dare I? We just want to document how the Northeast Anti-Japanese Alliance endured such hardships with such tenacity..."

Wang raised his voice: "Why do you keep asking about freezing and starving while being chased by devils? Let me tell you the truth-whatever the Japanese ate, we ate too! Whatever was in the Kwantung Army's warehouses, we took from their trucks! From mountain game to river fish, except for tigers, what delicacies hadn't we tasted? You're a soldier too-tell me, who would join an army that's always starving with no hope of victory? Could I have expanded our forces then? And why obsess over the Kuchu River battle? During my western campaign through the Greater Khingan Mountains, we fought 16 battles-that was the only one where the enemy gained advantage! Why focus on my single defeat? What's your agenda?!"

The journalist was stunned. His assignment had been to highlight the Alliance's tragic hardships and heroic endurance, yet the old general seemed to trivialize those very struggles.

The author notes that while the Northeast Anti-Japanese Alliance's suffering was indeed unprecedented (as Mao Zedong correctly told Feng Zhongyun-their ordeal surpassed even the Long March), what truly commands admiration is their revolutionary optimism. Despite extreme adversity, the fighters never abandoned their pursuit of joy, love, and cultural fulfillment. Through vibrant cultural activities and robust political education, few succumbed to perpetual gloom. Whenever possible, they organized celebrations, performances, and even weddings.

In winter 1936 at Tianqiaogou secret camp, to boost morale, General Yang Jingyu personally wrote and directed a four-act play "Wang Erxiao the Cowherd". He cast his guard Wang Chuansheng as the titular character, with roles including "Mother", "Elder Sister", and "Japanese Officer" played by a machine gunner, another guard, and a political cadre. After the premiere, soldiers demanded an encore performance. [32]

The First Army of the Northeast Anti-Japanese Alliance maintained dedicated drama troupes and propaganda teams, with entertainment gatherings featuring singing, dancing, and diverse performances. Yang Jingyu carried a harmonica with him for years as his personal companion.

Veteran Li Min recalled that before withdrawing to the Soviet Union, troops had buried a gramophone obtained by Geng Dianjun. Post-war attempts to retrieve it proved futile. This machine had brought such joy to female soldiers that Chen Hanzhong immortalized it in his wartime diary. An entry dated April 6 [year] in *Chen Hanzhong's Combat Diary* reads: "Retired around 11 PM. The gramophone's merriment lingered rather late." [33]

Zhao Shangzhi, known for his unkempt appearance, famously quipped "With our homeland fallen, how could my face shine?" to justify his refusal to wash until recovering lost territory. Zhao Yiman bluntly criticized him: "A commander's bearing shapes his troops."

Though three years Zhao Shangzhi's senior, her words struck home- he began paying attention to his appearance and enforcing grooming standards across his forces.

Anti-Japanese Alliance leaders understood revolution's ultimate purpose: pursuing happiness. As basic happiness required joy, they recognized that extraordinary hardships and battles had already deprived fighters of normal pleasures. Thus, they cherished every rare moment of respite.

These commanders also knew a crucial truth: A singing, spirited force versus a sullen, silent one meant incomparable differences in combat resolve. Hence, Alliance units resounded with constant singing and nurtured numerous poets. *First Route Army Song* and *Third Route Army Founding Anthem* were personally composed by Yang Jingyu and Li Zhaolin respectively. Major campaigns marched to verses like *Farewell to Western Expeditions* and *Guerrilla Ballad of Four Seasons*. Zhou Baozhong's Elegy for Martyrs moved listeners to tears, while Zhao Shangzhi's *Black Waters, White Mountains* (set to the *Man Jiang Hong* melody) stirred revolutionary fervor.

This vibrant cultural spirit permeated the Alliance. From 20 million characters of archival materials I've compiled, a substantial anthology of exceptional resistance poetry could be published-verses that truly capture these warriors' indomitable essence.

After reading these revolutionary poems brimming with heroic spirit and optimism, I finally understood one thing: During the 28 arduous years of the New Democratic Revolution and the grueling Long March, how Mao Zedong could compose so many magnificent verses like *Countering the First Encirclement Campaign, Loushan Pass*, and *The Long March*. The blood of revolutional optimism flows through Communists' veins – an optimism rooted in unshakable faith in ultimate victory.

Let me now turn my reluctant pen to a battle that old General Wang Minggui seldom mentioned, considering it inglorious, though it actually contained remarkable aspects. The opponent was the elite Japanese "Pacification Unit" led by Sukuta Tokujiro. When the Third Detachment was scattered, Wang Minggui fought a retreating battle until reaching the

Heilongjiang River with only twenty cavalrymen remaining – only to fall into Sukuta's ambush, suffering further casualties. Seeing the self-proclaimed "ferocious" Wang now a "rat in a bag," Sukuta divided his forces to encircle them. Indeed, Wang's troops faced near annihilation.

Wang often fought with unconventional tactics. Just as Sukuta thought victory assured, instead of breaking through weak points in the encirclement, Wang led his twenty horsemen in a whirlwind assault on the Japanese command post. With death-defying resolve, they launched a fierce attack. Sukuta never anticipated Wang would strike directly at him in such peril! Caught unprepared, all three commanders – Japanese Police Superintendent Sukuta Tokujiro, Deputy Commander Iizawa Toshiichi (Police Lieutenant), and puppet police captain Liu Lin (Police Sergeant) – were killed. Though surrounded by seven-to-eightfold enemy forces, Wang decapitated the enemy leadership first, throwing their ranks into chaos, then seized the moment to break through.

In that battle, Chinese General Wang Minggui taught the Japanese the meaning of "The Thirty-Checkpoint Return Thrust" – a legendary reversal maneuver from Chinese military lore.

The reason General Wang Minggui was reluctant to recall that battle was because of the heavy losses: Of the 24 cavalrymen by his side, 13 fell in combat, with only 11 surviving the breakout – half of them wounded. Those comrades-in-arms forever remained on the battlefield, their sacrifice both tragic and sublime.

Commissioner Nakame Sadanari, who had lived in perpetual dread of Wang Minggui, finally faced his most terrifying moment. In late August 1945, shortly after Japan's surrender on August 15, he wrote in his memoir *Ah, Manchuria* (p.888):

"As representatives of detained Japanese civilians, we were ordered to report to Qiqihar Hall. The military government announced its administrative policies. The speaker was Chief of Staff Wang Minggui (Note: Wang was actually Deputy Garrison Commander). Though fluent in Japanese, he deliberately delivered his speech through an interpreter that day, lecturing us at length about the future path of the Japanese people."

Nakame described his emotions upon encountering the "ferocious" general: "His appearance struck fear into me. This was the very leader branded as 'Bandit Wang' – the man who shattered the tranquility of the Greater Khingan Mountains since the founding of Manchukuo, who repeatedly haunted the South Manchuria Railway Forest zones after 1941, plunging us into a crucible of terror. It was he who disrupted the stable rear base of the Greater East Asia War with his guerrilla tactics... And now I met him face-to-face in Qiqihar..."

Author Sa Su once interviewed former Japanese settler Furukawa Osamu, who recounted that during the winter of 1945, 2,000 Japanese households – mostly women, children, and the elderly (young men having been conscripted into the Kwantung Army) – were stranded in Qiqihar without food or winter clothing. Desperate, two Japanese monks approached the local government for help.

They were received by a "Deputy Commander of the Eighth Route Army" who declared, "Women and children bear no guilt. Now that the war is over, let us all live in peace." He not only provided grain but also 600 cotton-padded coats. Furukawa remarked, "The Chinese showed true benevolence."

That "Deputy Commander" was Wang Mingguo. Decades later, the old general still remembered how they stamped each coat with his personal seal when no official mark could be found – thus every garment bore the imprint "Wang Minggui".

Though feared by Japanese troops for his battle scars and indomitable spirit (he defiantly lived to 95, "annoying even the King of Hell with his combat aura"), it was Wang's tender words – "Women and children bear no guilt" – that Japanese survivors remembered for generations.

As the ancient Chinese saying goes: The benevolent have no enemies.

Notes:

［1］ ［4］ Zhang Zhenglong: *Snow Cold, Blood Hot* (Volume 2), Changjiang Literature and Art Press, April 2011, 1st edition, pp. 278–279, p. 279.

［2］ ［3］ ［5］ The Compilation Group of *History of the Northeast Anti-Japanese United Army: History of the Northeast Anti-Japanese United Army* (Volume 2), CPC History Press, September 2015, 1st edition, pp. 710, 710, 711.

［6］ Zhang Zhenglong, Jiang Baocai: *The Last Anti-Japanese United Army*, People's Daily Press, January 2016, 1st edition, p. 414.

［7］ Zhao Junqing: *The Biography of Li Zhaolin*, Heilongjiang People's Press, August 2015, 1st edition, p. 207.

［8］ ［13］ Central Archives, Liaoning Provincial Archives, Jilin Provincial Archives, Heilongjiang Provincial Archives: *A Compilation of Revolutionary Historical Documents in Northeast China*, Jia 25, p. 131; Jia 57, p. 109.

［9］ Central Archives, Liaoning Provincial Archives, Jilin Provincial Archives, Heilongjiang Provincial Archives: *A Compilation of Revolutionary Historical Documents in Northeast China*, Jia 40, p. 230; cited in Zhang Zhenglong: Snow Cold, Blood Hot (Volume 2), Changjiang Literature and Art Press, April 2011, 1st edition, p. 173.

［10］ ［14］ Zhang Zhenglong: *Snow Cold, Blood Hot* (Volume 2), Changjiang Literature and Art Press, April 2011, 1st edition, pp. 178, 179.

［11］　［12］　Shi Yijun: The Most Dangerous Moment: *Historical Events of the Northeast Anti-Japanese United Army*, CITIC Press, September 2016, 1st edition, pp. 218–219, p. 219.

［15］　Shi Yijun: *A Detailed Chronology of Feng Zhongyun*, National Library Press, May 2019, 1st edition, p. 190.

［16］　Central Archives, Liaoning Provincial Archives, Jilin Provincial Archives, Heilongjiang Provincial Archives: *A Compilation of Revolutionary Historical Documents in Northeast China*, Jia 55, p. 151; cited in Zhao Junqing: The Biography of Li Zhaolin, Heilongjiang People's Press, August 2015, 1st edition, p. 215.

［17］　The Compilation Group of Historical Materials of the Northeast Anti-Japanese United Army: Historical Materials of the Northeast Anti-Japanese United Army (Volume 2), CPC Historical Materials Press, December 1987, 1st edition, p. 662.

［18］　［19］　The Central Committee of the Communist Party of China, Literature Research Office: *Collected Works of Mao Zedong* (Volume 3), People's Press, August 1996, 1st edition, pp. 391–392, p. 77.

［20］　Wang Yao: *Chiang Kai-shek and the Relationships with Great Powers*, Taiwan Strait Press, July 2013, 1st edition, p. 255.

［21］　［23］　［24］　［25］　Central Archives, Liaoning Provincial Archives, Jilin Provincial Archives, Heilongjiang Provincial Archives: *A Compilation of Revolutionary Historical Documents in Northeast China*, Jia 54, pp. 60–61; Jia 53, p. 157; Jia 24, p. 239; Jia 54, p. 104; cited in Zhang Zhenglong: Snow Cold, Blood Hot (Volume 1), Changjiang Literature and Art Press, April 2011, 1st edition, pp. 159, 227, 177, 232.

［22］　［28］　Shi Yijun: The Most Dangerous Moment: Historical Events of the Northeast Anti-Japanese United Army, CITIC Press, September 2016, 1st edition, pp. 209–210, 177–178.

［26］　Shi Yijun: *A Detailed Chronology of Feng Zhongyun*, National Library Press, May 2019, 1st edition, p. 335.

［27］ ［29］　Zhao Junqing: *The Biography of Li Zhaolin*, Heilongjiang People's Press, August 2015, 1st edition, pp. 246–247, 250–251.

［30］ ［31］　Central Archives, Liaoning Provincial Archives, Jilin Provincial Archives, Heilongjiang Provincial Archives: *A Compilation of Revolutionary Historical Documents in Northeast China*, Jia 56, p. 54; Jia 59, p. 35; cited in Zhao Junqing: The Biography of Li Zhaolin, Heilongjiang People's Press, August 2015, 1st edition, pp. 252, 284–285.

［32］　Zhao Junqing: *The Biography of Yang Jingyu*, Heilongjiang People's Press, August 2015, revised edition, p. 258.

［33］　Zhang Zhenglong, Jiang Baocai: *The Last Anti-Japanese United Army*, People's Daily Press, January 2016, 1st edition, p. 221.

Chapter 18

Never Betray the Party

59. Resisting Japan Demands Combating Capitulation

It is said that politicians are the least trustworthy in their words. This, of course, refers to those engaged in conspiracies and political manipulations.

It should be noted that Chiang Kai-shek's abrupt shift from the anti-communist fanaticism of completing the "final five minutes" of "Communist suppression" to allying with his former "enemy" for joint resistance against Japan was as drastic as transitioning from boiling enthusiasm to being doused with ice water. Naturally, this was merely a forced concession---his ingrained anti-communism and passive   resistance against Japan never truly changed.

Observant readers might notice the ten-month interval between Chiang's verbal agreement to cooperate in anti-Japanese efforts during the Xi'an Incident on December 12, 1936, and his official remarks on September 22, 1937 regarding the *Chinese Communist Party's Declaration for the Announcement of Nationalist-Communist Cooperation*, which marked substantive cooperation.

During these ten months, Chiang chaired the Fifth Third Plenary Session of the Kuomintang in February 1937, establishing principles to end civil war and unite against Japan. However, he reiterated the ambiguous policy: "We shall never abandon peace until all hope for it is exhausted; we must resolve to sacrifice when the nation reaches the point of inevitable sacrifice." This revealed his inadequate commitment to resistance, as he essentially postponed rather than abandoned his goals of "communist suppression" and one-party dictatorship. His diary entry from February 5 stated: "Internally avoid civil war. However, never relinquish responsibility to suppress rebellion when internal chaos occurs. Political and military reforms should progress gradually, with unification expected within three to five years." [1]

The most significant event during these ten months was undoubtedly the July 7th Marco Polo Bridge Incident.

Ten days after the incident, Chiang delivered a speech at Mount Lushan. Though still clinging to pacifist illusions, he presented four principles for resolving the conflict - the first clear diplomatic stance against Japanese aggression:

1.No solution shall infringe upon China's sovereignty and territorial integrity;

2.The administrative organization of Hebei-Chahar shall not be illegally altered;

3.Local officials appointed by the central government, including Song Zhe-yuan, Chairman of the Hebei-Chahar Political Council, cannot be arbitrarily removed;

4.The current garrison areas of the 29th Army shall not be restricted.

These four positions represented the minimum threshold for a weak nation's diplomacy. [2]

Published on July 19, two days after the speech, while lacking resolute language and retaining wishful qualifiers (notably using "if" when stating "If war breaks out, regardless of north or south, old or young, all shall share the responsibility to resist"),   Mao nevertheless astutely emphasized the resistance theme. The speech was praised as "establishing preparatory guidelines for the War of Resistance, representing the Kuomintang's first correct declaration on foreign policy in years, thus welcomed by our Party and the nation." [3]

What defines a statesman? Primarily, the ability to thoroughly analyze the comparative strengths and weaknesses of both sides, then formulate appropriate strategies and principles.

Mao understood that in the face of the formidable Japanese invaders, victory in the War of Resistance could not be achieved without the cooperation of the Kuomintang (KMT), China's most powerful political and military group. This constituted the fundamental rationale for establishing the Anti-Japanese United Front. Mao also recognized that building such a united front would be a thorny and arduous path, not something that could be accomplished through mere promises or paper agreements. Throughout the eight years of KMT-CCP cooperation in the resistance war, Mao led the entire Party along a uniquely Chinese path - evolving from opposing Chiang Kai-shek's resistance to allying with, supporting, and ultimately pressuring Chiang to resist Japan - a journey that proved exceptionally challenging yet ultimately successful and glorious.

After issuing the anti-Japanese declaration that had earned Mao's praise, Chiang Kai-shek made no substantive moves to promote KMT-CCP cooperation nor demonstrated any genuine commitment to resisting Japan.

Over the following two months, he focused primarily on one objective: seeking international intervention to achieve peace with Japan through compromise.

From July 21 to 27, Chiang successively summoned ambassadors from Britain, the United States, Germany, Italy, France, and the Soviet Union, hoping these nations would exert influence and pressure on Japan. He also frequently met with foreign correspondents from Reuters, Associated Press, and other agencies, appealing for international support for China. However, responses from foreign powers remained tepid.

Chiang then pinned his hopes on interventions from the League of Nations and signatories of the Nine-Power Treaty. Consequently, the Nanjing KMT government formally submitted an appeal to the League of Nations. Although the League accepted China's petition, its adopted resolution merely offered "moral support" and recommended member states refrain from taking any concrete actions.

Persisting in his efforts, Chiang compared international responses and perceived Germany as relatively more responsive. In late July, he again summoned German Ambassador to China Oskar Trautmann and dispatched military strategist Jiang Baili to Germany, imploring Hitler to mediate with Japan. Surprisingly, Germany agreed. Unbeknownst to Chiang, Germany's enthusiasm for mediating Sino-Japanese peace talks stemmed from strategic concerns: fearing that full-scale war between China and Japan might prompt Japan to redeploy troops from Northeast China to the interior. This could alleviate Soviet military pressure in the Far East, potentially enabling Moscow to shift forces westward and complicate Germany's planned blitzkrieg against the Soviet Union.

When Germany intervened, the effect was indeed different. Unexpectedly, just as the mediation had made significant progress, Japan suddenly escalated its demands for peace talks, including establishing an autonomous government in Inner Mongolia, appointing pro-Japanese leaders in North China, creating an expanded demilitarized zone in Shanghai, and other conditions. Chiang Kai-shek took a sharp breath and stated that if he agreed to these demands, the Chinese government would be swept away by a tidal wave of public opinion, and China would experience a violent revolution. Chiang warned Trautmann that if the Chinese government collapsed, the only outcome would be the Communists gaining dominance in China. This became the historically significant yet ultimately failed "Trautmann Mediation"—Chiang repeatedly implored Trautmann to "maintain absolute secrecy" about the mediation efforts. [4]

History has repeatedly proven that China has never been able to rely on foreign powers to escape its suffering; everything must depend on itself.

Mao observed Chiang Kai-shek's delusion of relying on foreign intervention to achieve compromise and peace with Japan with growing concern. On July 23, Mao published *Policies, Measures, and Prospects for Opposing Japan's Invasion*, proposing a groundbreaking analysis of "two opposing policies," "two sets of methods," and "two possible outcomes" in the resistance war. He explicitly advocated the principle of "resolute resistance against compromise," calling for "total mobilization of national armed forces" and "complete mobilization of the entire population." [5]

Resolute resistance required opposing peace through concessions, necessitating active war preparations to intercept enemy offensives and deplete Japanese combat capabilities. Regrettably, Chiang Kai-shek's reluctance to resist rendered him deaf to these proposals. The precious strategic window for defensive preparations was squandered, allowing Japanese forces to advance southward unimpeded, culminating in catastrophic consequences. On December 13, 1937, Japanese troops occupied Nanjing, resulting in the horrific massacre of 300,000 civilians.

When a political party and national leader bearing responsibility for millions of lives lose their resolve and backbone in confronting formidable enemies, it is ordinary citizens who suffer.

During the eight-year period of allying with, supporting, and pressuring Chiang to resist Japan, Mao provided numerous effective strategic proposals to Chiang. These ideas found expression in seminal works like *On Tactics Against Japanese Imperialism*, *Strategic Issues in Anti-Japanese Guerrilla Warfare*, *On Protracted War*, and *Problems of War and Strategy*. Among these, Chiang showed particular appreciation for *On Protracted War*.

With Chiang's approval, Bai Chongxi—who greatly admired *On Protracted War*—distilled its essence into two strategic principles: "Accumulate minor victories into major triumphs" and "Trade space for time." After securing Zhou Enlai's consent, the National Military Council disseminated these principles nationwide as strategic guidelines for the resistance war.

In evaluating the Nationalist forces during the Second United Front, Mao maintained objective historical assessment: "From 1937 to 1938, the KMT demonstrated relatively determined resistance and maintained comparatively good relations with our Party." [6] More precisely, "Between the Marco Polo Bridge Incident on July 7, 1937, and the fall of Wuhan in October 1938, the KMT government showed relatively earnest commitment to resisting Japan." [7]

Though battles like the Shanghai and Nanjing defenses ended in defeat, the Nationalist troops bloody sacrifices inflicted significant attrition on Japanese forces, shattering Tokyo's ambition to "conquer China within three months." By late 1938, with nearly half of Japanese invasion forces pinned down by Eighth Route Army operations behind enemy lines—

alleviating pressure on conventional battlefronts—the Chinese high command enthusiastically organized guerrilla training programs led by Communist instructors. During that Spring Festival, Wei Lihuang, deputy commander of the Second War Zone, personally paid a New Year visit to Zhu De.

The cooling of the Kuomintang-Communist cooperation began in 1939, particularly after the successive fall of Guangzhou and Wuhan in October 1938, which demoralized the Nationalist forces and shook Chiang Kai-shek's confidence in the war of resistance. "By now, our party is nearly lifeless and utterly silent. Not only do ordinary people lack faith in the party, but they openly show contempt," Chiang declared at the Fifth Plenary Session of the Fifth Central Executive Committee of the Kuomintang in January 1939. This rebuke aimed at KMT senior officials revealed his psychological state and anxieties at the time.

Chiang's anxiety stemmed from the rapid expansion of Communist forces amidst the Nationalist army's collapse. While the KMT regime disintegrated across nearly half of China's occupied territories, the Communists decisively established new anti-Japanese democratic governments, expanding their county-level administrations in Central China to 47 by 1940.

Deep in Chiang's psyche persisted an unshakable conviction over decades: the Japanese were a "skin rash" irritant, while the Communists constituted a "mortal threat to the heart." He would rather see territories occupied by the Japanese than fall into Communist hands.

Thus, the central agenda of the Kuomintang's Fifth Plenum shifted from second-phase war issues to internal affairs. As Chiang stated: "The Communists have their own tactics. They harbor no goodwill toward the Kuomintang—their cooperation with us is merely strategic." [8] The conference formulated a comprehensive set of covert policies and secret documents on "assimilating," "containing," "restricting," and "suppressing" the Communists.

On October 30, 1939, Japan formulated its *Supreme Guiding Principles for Incident Resolution Centered on Establishing a New Central Government*, outlining three modes of inducement to achieve a "Chiang-Wang merger." From November that year, Japanese representatives conducted nearly a year of negotiations with Chongqing's envoys, termed the "Operation Paulownia" by Japan.

Japan's decision to lure Chiang stemmed primarily from two fundamental differences in Chiang's and Mao's proclaimed principles:

First, since the Second United Front's joint resistance began, both Chiang and Mao vowed to "fight to the end," but their bottom lines diverged.

Mao's baseline for victory was: "Fight to the Yalu River, reclaim all lost territories." [9] He clarified that reclaiming all lost lands required not only recovering Manchuria but also Taiwan—not a single inch of Chinese soil could remain under Japanese occupation.

Chiang Kai-shek defined his ultimate objective for victory in the Resistance War as: "To fight until complete restoration of the pre-July 7 Incident status quo." After announcing this baseline at the Fifth Plenary Session of the Fifth Central Committee of the KMT, he explained this was "based on the principle of China as the fundamental reference point." [10]

This comparison reveals a striking divergence between the two leaders' interpretations of "fighting to the end"—particularly regarding Northeast China. Mao's "bottom line" demanded no territorial concessions in the Northeast, while Chiang's "end goal" essentially implied willingness to abandon Northeast China if Japan ceased hostilities.

Secondly, formal declarations of war represent political proclamations of official hostilities between nations. During the Resistance War, both political parties declared war against Japan, but their proclamations were separated by a staggering gap of 9 years and 8 months.

Mao's *Declaration of War Against Japan by the Provisional Central Government of the Chinese Soviet Republic* was issued on April 15, 1932—when Japanese forces had not yet crossed the Great Wall to occupy vast Chinese hinterlands.

The Nationalist government under Chiang Kai-shek finally issued its *Proclamation of the Republic of China's Declaration of War Against Japan* on December 9, 1941: "Hereby formally declares war against Japan, announcing to all nations that all treaties, agreements, and contracts concerning Sino-Japanese relations are hereby abrogated." [11]

Why delay until December 9, 1941?

Analysts suggest two reasons: First, Chiang maintained minimal confidence in victory throughout the war until the United States—a global heavyweight—declared war on Japan on December 8, finally revealing prospects for triumph. Second, avoiding formal declaration kept open diplomatic channels for potential negotiated peace.

This preserved window for negotiation, combined with mutual Sino-Japanese desires for settlement, created particularly perilous conditions from 1939 to 1940. While no conclusive evidence proves Chiang's intent to surrender, historical records confirm that since late 1939, Japanese representatives like Colonel Suzuki Takuji from the Army General Staff Office engaged in multiple contacts with Chongqing's operatives, including Dai Li's Hong Kong station chief Lin Xinheng (using aliases Song Ziliang and Zeng Guang).

From March 7-10, 1940, Chinese representatives Lin Xinheng, Zhang Yousan (former ambassador to Germany and National Defense Council secretary), and Chen Chaolin (Deputy Chief of Staff at Chongqing Headquarters, Lieutenant General) met with Japanese delegates Suzuki Takuji, Imai Takeo, and Shirai Shigeki (Head of the Eighth Section, Army General Staff Office, Colonel) at the Tung Fei Foreign Firm in Hong Kong.

Conducted under absolute secrecy, these talks escalated in June when more "solemn" negotiations moved to a basement in Macau's suburbs. Japanese delegates "presented credentials signed by Prince Kan'in, Chief of Army General Staff," while Chongqing's representatives produced "credentials bearing Chiang Kai-shek's signature on Military Commission stationery, stamped with both the Commission's official seal and Chiang's personal seal." [12]

Mao viewed Chiang Kai-shek's wavering stance and the resurgence of capitulationist factions within the KMT with profound concern. During his June 1939 report titled *Outline Against Capitulation* at the Yan'an Senior Cadre Conference, he warned: "The current situation's critical feature lies in the KMT's potential surrender becoming the gravest danger." "The KMT is already preparing its main groundwork for surrender—anti-communism constitutes the most crucial component of these preparations." [13]

To preserve the Anti-Japanese United Front forged through the Second KMT-CCP Cooperation, Mao maintained principled firmness combined with tactical flexibility. While openly condemning Wang Jingwei's overt surrender, he issued veiled warnings to Chiang's capitulationist tendencies: "These elements lurk within our resistance front, coordinating with Wang Jingwei in a duplicitous performance—some acting in concert, others playing conflicting roles." [14]

A qualified helmsman must first navigate treacherous currents with precise orientation. Where superficial similarities exist, great statesmen discern essential differences through profound analysis.

Mao recognized the KMT's internal divisions, historically split between resistance factions represented by influential figures like Soong Ching-ling, Li Jishen, and Cai Tingkai, and capitulationist elements. Though the KMT's Fifth Plenary Session secretly formulated policies of assimilation, restriction, and opposition to communism—containing elements of anti-communist surrender—the resistance faction's influence ensured the session ultimately maintained the United Front as its primary orientation. [15]

Always treating policy and strategy as the Party's lifeline, Mao drew clear political distinctions between Wang and Chiang:

> Our slogan of supporting Chairman Chiang remains valid—then as now. So long as Chiang leads resistance efforts, we shall continue our support (conditional upon his continued resistance), avoiding any disrespectful expressions toward him.

> However, the possibility of Chiang abandoning resistance under certain circumstances exists. Our response in such eventualities requires prudent consideration... We cannot rashly revive 'anti-Chiang' slogans without thorough deliberation.

> Actively assisting Chiang and urging him toward the correct path remains our policy. Externally, we shall not refer to "Kuomintang capitulation" but instead use "landlord-bourgeois capitulationist faction."[16]

The breadth of one's vision determines the scale of their cause. The United Front in the War of Resistance could persist through such perilous circumstances precisely because the Communists, driven by their commitment to the welfare of humanity and the grand mission of saving the nation from peril, resolutely endured to the end. Without this resolve, victory in the War of Resistance would have been unattainable.

To prevent Chiang Kai-shek from retreating from his public stance on resisting Japan and to sever his tacit connections with capitulationist factions, Mao even praised Chiang's rare anti-surrender actions. He commended that Chairman Chiang solemnly issued a proclamation to the nation, rigorously refuting Japanese Prime Minister Konoe Fumimaro's statements—an excellent rebuttal, and noted Chiang's recent disciplinary actions in expelling Wang Jingwei from the Kuomintang.

In response to Chiang's policies of Communist assimilation, restriction, and suppression, Mao skillfully countered using the Kuomintang's own propaganda apparatus. His remarks during a September 16, 1939 interview with Central News Agency and other media—needles hidden in cotton— soft yet resolute—were less for national consumption and more a message directed at Chiang Kai-shek himself:

> "Wang Jingwei now advocates three slogans: anti-Chiang, anti-Communist, and pro-Japanese. Wang is the common enemy of both the Kuomintang and Communist Party, as well as the entire Chinese people. The Communist Party is not the Kuomintang's enemy, nor is the Kuomintang the Communist Party's foe. Instead of mutual opposition and 'restriction,' we should unite and assist each other.
>
> [...]
>
> Where Wang opposes Chiang, we must support Chiang; where Wang opposes Communists, we must ally with Communists; where Wang embraces Japan, we must resist Japan. Whatever the enemy opposes, we must support; whatever the enemy supports, we must oppose. [17]

The scent of Chiang Kai-shek's post-1939 passive resistance and active anti-Communism was swiftly detected by compromise and capitulation factions, giving rise to the contemptible theory of "National Salvation through a Curved Path"(quxian jiuguo). These elements shamelessly cloaked their cowardice and appeasement in grandiose rhetoric.

The first to propose "curved path salvation" to Chiang was Kuomintang's Hebei Provincial Security Commander Zhang Yinwu. Regarding his subordinate Chai Enbo's surrender to Japanese forces, Zhang wrote to Chiang claiming: "Chai Enbo, caught between irreconcilable conflict with Eighth Route Army forces in Wen'an and Xinzhen while being heavily pressured by Japanese troops, chose nominal surrender to preserve strength for curved path salvation. Appointed as Central Hebei Bandit Suppression Commander by the Japanese, he secretly continues our Party's resistance work. When conditions ripen, he will turn against the Japanese with devastating strikes."

Zhang Yinwu not only theorized but actively practiced this surrender doctrine. His orchestration of the June 1939 Shenxian Massacre slaughtered over 400 Eighth Route Army personnel. Soon after, He Long's 120th Division Northern Expedition Force annihilated Zhang's troops. Escaping under Sun Dianyings protection to Chongqing, Zhang absurdly accused Communists of undermining the United Front.

Chiang Kai-shek was well aware that Zhang Yinwu had instigated the conflicts. With concrete evidence of Zhang's collaboration with Japan provided by the Communists and Zhou Enlai's exposé of the truth to Chen Cheng, Zhang was dismissed and sidelined temporarily. However, Chiang soon reinstated him, appointing Zhang successively as Chief Counselor of the Hebei-Chahar War Zone and Commander of the Beijing-Hankou Railway Northern Section Defense, granting him the rank of full general.

While no historical documents conclusively prove Chiang's endorsement of the "National Salvation through a Curved Path" doctrine, he indeed tolerated—and likely tacitly authorized—such collaborationist actions by hundreds of thousands of Kuomintang troops deployed behind enemy lines.

In 1940, when Pang Bingxun, Commander-in-Chief of the 24th Group Army, was appointed Hebei Provincial Chairman, Chiang personally instructed him: "Your forces must suppress the Communists in Hebei. Beware lest we repel wolves at the front gate only to admit tigers at the rear. Employ the "30% military, 70% political' strategy."

Are the Japanese the wolf at the front door, and the Communist Party the tiger at the back door? Between the Japanese and the Communists, who should be dealt with three parts effort, and who seven? In Chinese officialdom, some things are understood implicitly but never spoken aloud.

Pang Bingxun ultimately defected to the Japanese. By 1942, his forces became an elite unit within the 500,000-strong collaborationist army, peaking at 80,000 troops. Mao bluntly admitted: "The Taihang Mountain Pang Bingxun Army Group was specifically tasked with anti-Communist operations." [18]

When newly appointed Japanese general Yasuji Okamura attempted to mobilize collaborationist forces against KMT troops, he was politely refused. *Okamura's Memoir Records* their explanation:

> We are not traitors—the Communists are China's real rebels. We seek
> to eliminate them alongside Japanese forces. To this day (October 1942),
> we still receive military pay from Chongqing. We regret being unable to
> assist in any operations against Central Government troops. [19]

This "curved path salvation" essentially became a circuitous anti-Communist campaign. Chiang's continuation of payroll to collaborationist forces served dual purposes: binding hundreds of thousands of puppet troops through financial control while directing them against Communists. This strategy, though disastrous for national interests, reflected Chiang's warlord mentality—prioritizing military expansion and personal power consolidation over national survival during existential crisis.

60. The "Explosive Yield" of a Traitor

Human affairs often have coincidences. The "curved path salvation" theory that appeared on the inland anti-Japanese battlefield also appeared on the Northeast anti-Japanese battlefield, and they are so similar.

First, the source is the same, the source of inducement to surrender is all from the Japanese.

The Northeast anti-war lasted for seven or eight years. The Japanese realized that there were too many Chinese people, and they couldn't kill them all, so they changed their strategy, implemented inducement to surrender and disintegration, and incorporated it into the management of special agencies and intelligence agencies. For important anti-union cadres, establish files, analyze their background, hobbies and weaknesses, and carry out inducement to surrender activities targeted.

Second, the time of implementing inducement to surrender is roughly the same, basically all in 1939 to 1940 when the war entered the difficult stalemate stage, the Northeast is a little earlier than the inland battlefield.

Third, both inducements to surrender and surrender were carried out under the banner of anti-communism. In the inland, surrendering to Japan was a curved line to "eliminate communism" and save the country, massacring the Eighth Route Army and the New Fourth Army; in the Northeast, the rebels surrendered to Japan while massacring Communist political workers, clearing obstacles to being traitors, and presenting a pledge to the Japanese army.

Fourth, like Zhang Yinwu and Pang Bingxun in the inland, among the anti-union generals who rebelled and surrendered in the Northeast, a considerable part were old military personnel and landlords; therefore, after the Japanese regime collapsed, these rebels were all reused and promoted by the Kuomintang: Li Huatang was appointed as the commander-in-chief of the First Army Group of the Kuomintang, and Xie Wendong was appointed as the commander-in-chief of the Fifteenth Army Group of the Kuomintang.

China's war against Japanese aggression lasted 14 years, and its hardship and tragedy are rare in the history of world anti-aggression wars. The road to victory in the War of Resistance was built on blood and sacrifice, accompanied by the bones and blood of loved ones, so the will and faith of the people of the War of Resistance were tested and refined like never before. As Mao pointed out: The War of Resistance is a protracted war of attrition, which may lead to many defeats, retreats, and internal splits and betrayals.

Betrayal is an insurmountable topic in the process of China's War of Resistance Against Japan, especially in the Northeast Anti-Japanese War. The emergence of a large number of puppet troops, traitors, and traitors is a painful scar deeply engraved in the hearts of the Chinese people.

It must be acknowledged that while certain elements within the Northeast Anti-Japanese United Army—including former bandits, mountain forest bands, and remnants of the Northeastern Army—produced wavering defectors, this in no way diminishes the glorious legacy of the vast majority of resolute resistance fighters. Like gold refined through fire, their unyielding spirit and national integrity shone brighter amidst adversity.

History repeatedly demonstrates that a national leader's words and actions set the moral compass. The proliferation of traitors and collaborators during this period bears direct correlation to the Chiang Kai-shek-led National Government's 14-year policy of appeasing Japan through territorial concessions and diplomatic capitulation.

Chiang's military appointments revealed complete absence of principle—any warlord willing to pledge forces to bolster his clique received amnesty and promotion. Those commanding substantial troops even gained privileged access to Chiang's inner circle.

A prime example: Zhang Lanfeng, operating under Japanese North China Area Army intelligence since 1935 as "Pacification Commissioner of Eastern Henan," expanded collaborationist forces into Wang Jingwei's 4th Front Army by 1943—comprising 6 divisions across 3 corps plus 3 independent brigades. Despite massacring anti-Japanese forces under Japanese command, Zhang maintained covert ties with Chiang's officials including Jiang Dingwen, Dai Li, and Tang Enbo. By 1944, Chiang formally incorporated him as Newly Organized 3rd Route Army Commander.

In February 1946, the arch-collaborator received astonishing orders: immediate summons to Nanjing. There, Zhang not only obtained Chiang's cordial audience but "privileged" luncheon with the Generalissimo, culminating in commemorative photographs.

Post-Japan's August 15 surrender, Chiang's Order No. 1 granted blanket amnesty to nearly a million collaborationist troops: "All puppet forces in occupied areas shall maintain local order and protect civilians. These units must redeem themselves through good conduct, remaining stationed unless relocated under my direct command." [20]

This policy instantly swelled Chiang's military assets by a million men. As sarcastically observed: "Puppet troops welcomed Chiang—simply switching their flags to his banner, embracing both Chiang and Yan Xishan." [21]

Another critical factor contributing to the emergence of numerous Chinese collaborators was the detrimental role modeled by high-ranking officials within the Nationalist Party.

During the entire Anti-Japanese War, 20 senior KMT military-political officials and Central Committee members, along with 58 KMT generals, defected to the Japanese invaders. [22] As Mao sharply noted:

> Over 800,000 puppet troops (including puppet regular forces and local militias) were largely composed of KMT-led defecting units or organized by KMT turncoat officers. Reactionary elements within the KMT had preemptively supplied these puppet forces with the treasonous fallacy of so-called "curved path salvation", while later providing them spiritual and organizational support to collaborate with Japanese aggressors against liberated areas under Chinese resistance.[23]

This reveals another issue: throughout the Anti-Japanese War, or more precisely, during the persistent implementation of the United Front against Japanese Aggression, combating capitulationism and confronting capitulationist factions remained one of the critical tasks of the war. This was also a primary political objective for Communist Party organizations and anti-Japanese guerrilla forces in Northeast China.

By 1940, the Northeast Anti-Japanese United Army had entered its most arduous phase. While deploying heavy forces for suppression, the enemy intensified efforts to entice wavering members of the United Army. Some defectors were even sent back to their original units as spies, posing severe security risks. Consequently, Communist Party organizations and United Army units in the Northeast strictly prohibited and harshly punished all acts of feigned surrender.

In spring 1937, Zhang Su, then Secretary of the Tangyuan County Communist Party Committee, was captured by Japanese forces. Enduring five rounds of torture by garrison and military police units, Zhang provided "names of deceased, reactionary, or fictitious individuals" and spoke ill of the Communist Party, declaring his "willingness to serve Manchukuo." After escaping and rejoining the Party organization, he was nevertheless expelled from the Party and assigned work "as a revolutionary sympathizer.

In early 1939, following the defection of Lan Zhiyuan, commander of the 2nd Division of the 3rd Army of the United Army, the enemy escalated efforts to lure the 1st Division into surrender. Zhou Shufan, the division's political director, sought approval from Zhang Lansheng, political director of the 3rd Army, to stage a feigned surrender. The plan aimed to assassinate turncoats and spies sent to persuade defections, thereby undermining enemy morale and deterring wavering elements.

Unexpectedly, the enemy dispatched dozens of horse-drawn sleds to escort the "surrendering" troops into the mountains and mobilized students in Qingcheng County to welcome them publicly. Since only a few leaders knew of the ruse, the troops grew restless—some demanded Zhou Shufan's execution, while others plotted to desert. Although the traitors were eventually lured and killed, the 1st Division narrowly averted disaster.

The North Manchuria Provincial Committee of the Communist Party of China believed: Although the surrender was fake, these comrades indeed betrayed the honor of the great revolutionary cause, which was a behavior without national integrity. Zhou Shufan was placed under party probation for 4 months, and Zhang Lansheng for 6 months.

Chinese Communists regard loyalty to the party as more precious than chastity and life; the last sentence of the Communist Party member's oath is "Never betray the party." In the later period when the Northeast Anti-Japanese United Army was in an extremely difficult situation, the characterization of "fake surrender" became increasingly severe, clearly stating that "deceiving the enemy with fake surrender is objectively a betrayal," thereby making fake surrender a high-voltage line that no one could touch.

The party organizations at all levels of the Northeast Anti-Japanese United Army were so strict in punishing fake surrender, so one can imagine their attitude towards true surrender and traitors. Because sometimes the harm caused by a small traitor could be greater than that of hundreds or even more Japanese and puppet troops.

Practice has proven that the higher the official position, the greater the harm. The betrayal of a division commander could lead to the collapse of an entire division; the betrayal of an army commander could lead to the collapse of an entire army: the disintegration of the 8th Army is a sufficient example.

The Japanese army's special agencies carefully studied and analyzed the historical backgrounds, anti-war purposes, and attitudes of each army commander of the Anti-Japanese United Army, and determined that Xie Wendong was the easiest to be recruited and "submit" among all the army commanders, so they used the method known as the "infection chain" for inducement: The special agent Yokota from the Japanese army's special agency was responsible for first inducing the surrender of the 1st Division commander Qin Xiuzhen, then letting Qin Xiuzhen "infect" other division commanders, cutting down the four beams and eight pillars of the 8th Army one by one. In March 1939, Xie Wendong led the remnants to surrender to the Japanese army at Tuchengzi in Yilan County, and the 8th Army collapsed. [24]

As Mao Zedong pointed out above, one cannot surrender without being anti-communist, and killing Communists is to remove obstacles to surrender.

During the process of Xie Wendong's betrayal and submission to the Japanese puppet regime, the party organizations and party members of the 8th Army firmly resisted and worked hard to stabilize the troops, but they were brutally massacred by the surrender faction. Those killed included Director of the Political Department of the 3rd Division Jin Gen, Director of the Political Department of the 4th Division Chai Yinxuan, Chief of Staff of the 8th Army Yu Guangshi, and other excellent Communist Party leadership cadres, all of whom had their vibrant lives frozen in their early 30s.

The most unforgettable is Liu Shuhua, the Director of the Political Department of the 8th Army.

Upon learning that the 3rd Division commander Wang Zifu was going to lead his troops to surrender, Liu Shuhua led a small team of over 20 people, searching through the forests of Hulan County. He wanted to find Wang Zifu, persuade him to change his mind, and finally found him at Qixingduizi. Wang Zifu was determined to surrender and would not listen to any persuasion. Liu Shuhua then turned his persuasion efforts to the grassroots officers and soldiers. He followed this troop without leaving, seizing every opportunity to declare that they must not go down the mountain and must not surrender to the Japanese devils, and exposed Wang Zifu's conspiracy.

Wang Zifu threatened him: "You're ruining my plans; do you want to die?"

Liu Shuhua coldly laughed: "What are you afraid of? Do you dare to show your conscience to everyone?"

Seeing that some people were moved by Liu Shuhua's words, Wang Zifu ordered the disarmament of Liu Shuhua's small team and tied him to a tree. Liu Shuhua shouted loudly: "The Chinese people have only one way out: to fight to the end and defeat the Japanese devils. Everyone must not follow the traitor Wang Zifu down the wrong path!"

Wang Zifu yanked Liu Shuhua's tongue out and severed half of it with a knife. Blood gushed as Liu, unable to speak with the remaining tongue blocking his throat, fixed Wang with a defiant glare—his eyes conveying unyielding resolve to the onlookers. Wang then stripped him naked, slicing flesh from his body in lingchi (death by a thousand cuts), warning his troops: "This is the fate awaiting those who refuse to surrender." [25]

Traitors who willingly betray ancestors and compatriots for personal gain embody ultimate moral depravity.

Liu Shuhua (alias Li Mingxue), born in 1912 in Jinan, Shandong, studied at the Lenin School in Vladivostok, Soviet Union. After returning to Northeast China in 1935, he served successively as: Secretary of Mishan County Committee, Secretary of Muling County Committee, Political Director of the 2nd Division, 5th Army of the Northeast Anti-Japanese United Army, Political Director of the 8th Army, Member of the Daobei Special Committee, Member of the Jidong Provincial Committee. A brilliant political operative, Liu persevered through the 8th Army's direst challenges. Though briefly contemplating withdrawal amid premonitions of the army's fate, he ultimately vowed: "If the Party requires my blood and skull to consolidate revolutionary foundations—or at minimum redeem the 8th Army—I shall fearlessly struggle to the end."[26]

What defines loyalty to the Party?

The unconditional commitment to sacrifice everything for the revolutionary cause. At merely 26, Communist warrior Liu Shuhua poured his fervent blood and young life into the Anti-Japanese United Army's struggle against capitulationists.

61. "Provisional Feigned Surrender" and the Red Line

Mao Zedong, who had always been concerned about the Northeast Anti-Japanese United Army, made a prediction about the anti-surrender situation in the Northeast: "To a certain extent, for a period of time, even if there is a large-scale defection in the Northeast Volunteer Army in the future, the remaining small part can still create a stalemate, as long as they can continuously break through the 'encirclement and suppression', this stalemate situation can be maintained." [27]

As Mao Zedong pointed out, the Northeast Anti-Japanese United Army had numerous traitors and "large-scale defections" from 1938 to 1939, all of which were inseparable from the broader context of the time. On June

15, 1939, the report from the *North Manchuria Provincial Committee of the Communist Party of China to the Central Committee* stated:

> From last May to this May, over the past year, the significant losses in our troops were not mainly due to combat casualties, but rather because many parts defected and fled.
>
> ...
>
> More than fifty members of the Second Division of the Third Army, under the leadership of Lan Zhiyuan (Provincial Executive Committee member, Second Division Commander), assassinated more than twenty of the division's most experienced comrades and then surrendered to Fangzheng.
>
> Last year, the Ninth Army had about 200 members who surrendered in dribs and drabs. [28]

Some troops defected because the main responsible cadres of this anti-Japanese army defected. The reason why more than 200 people from the Ninth Army defected was that their commander Li Huatang defected to the enemy.

Therefore, the main target of the Japanese army's inducement to surrender was still the commanders above the division level of the anti-Japanese army. A leaflet widely distributed by the Japanese army can illustrate this point.

> The Imperial Japanese Army guarantees the safety of those who surrender, introduces them to jobs, and allows them to enjoy the grace of Great Manchukuo... Zhou Baozhong repeatedly obstructs those who wish to surrender, increasing your suffering, and is truly a traitor to Great Manchukuo, an unforgivable criminal. Why do you listen to his deception and ignore your own new life and progress? I hope you will not suffer anymore, strive to remove the oppression of the traitor Zhou Baozhong, and quickly come to surrender... [29]

This is a psychological warfare propaganda leaflet targeted at the generals above the division level of the anti-Japanese army. It shows that in the enemy's pervasive inducement to surrender, as long as the main senior cadres of the Chinese Communist Party and the anti-Japanese army in Northeast China do not defect, they can prevent or delay the trend of large-scale defections. The reason why the puppet regime hated Zhou Baozhong, the secretary of the Jidong Provincial Committee of the Communist Party of China and the commander of the Second Route Army of the anti-Japanese army, to the core was that Zhou Baozhong decisively, promptly, and resolutely dealt with the defection of Guan Shufan, the standing committee member of the Jidong Provincial Committee of the Communist Party of China, the party committee secretary of the Fifth Army, and the commander of the First Division, effectively deterring and curbing the tendency of defection in the Fifth Army.

Guan Shufan was born in Ning'an, Heilongjiang in 1913. He joined the Communist Youth League of China in 1930 and served as the secretary of the Jidong Bureau of the Communist Youth League and the secretary of the Ning'an County Committee of the League. During this period, he joined the Communist Party of China. After 1935, when he served as the director of the Political Department of the First Division of the Fifth Army of the Northeast Anti-Japanese United Army, he was only 22 years old.

Guan Shufan had been arrested by the Japanese and puppets, endured severe torture but did not defect. After becoming the commander of the First Division of the Fifth Army of the anti-Japanese army, he charged at the front in battles, was wounded twice, and showed outstanding military command ability. At the age of 25, he became the commander of the First Division, the main force of the Fifth Army, and became a favorite general under Zhou Baozhong. Zhou Baozhong had great expectations for him and promoted him to be a standing committee member of the Jidong Provincial

Committee of the Communist Party of China and the party committee secretary of the Fifth Army.

During the tragic Western Expedition, when his superior, Song Yifu, the secretary of the Jidong Provincial Committee of the Communist Party of China, the director of the Political Department of the Fifth Army, and the overall person in charge of the Western Expedition, defected to the enemy, he still led his troops to persist in fighting firmly. Unexpectedly, after breaking through the hail of bullets in the Western Expedition, he actually defected. What was the reason for this?

To coerce the feared Guan Shufan into surrender, Japanese military police intelligence agencies meticulously studied his vulnerabilities. They arrested his wife Liu Bingye (a national high school student) and imprisoned her in Harbin. Guan first instructed underground liaisons to verify whether Liu had been executed. Upon learning she remained alive, the love-stricken Guan approached Zhou Baozhong, demanding the underground party secure her release. Zhou, discerning the enemy's scheme, retorted: "Impossible. The enemy didn't arrest her without purpose."

Undeterred, Guan secretly contacted Japanese forces through couriers, feigning hunger: "Our Anti-Japanese troops haven't eaten dumplings in ages," probing whether this might secure his wife's release. Japanese intelligence mobilized civilians to prepare two sacks of dumplings. Though troops feared poisoning and refused to eat, Guan consumed them. Confronted by Zhou, Guan rationalized: "My negotiation aimed to reclaim Liu Bingye. Their dumpling provision signals enemy willingness to parley."

The battle-hardened Zhou immediately recognized Guan's defection tendencies. Soon after, Guan counseled Fifth Army commander Chai Shirong to adopt "temporary feigned surrender," even composing to the

Second Route Army Headquarters advocating "opportunistic preservation of strength."

Despite Guan's wavering, Zhou made desperate efforts at redemption, urgently warning: "Abandon erroneous fantasies! Reject the path of disgraceful betrayal!!! Having shared eight years of hardship and life-and-death struggles on China's national battlefield, I solemnly remind you: Sever all ties with enemy collaborators, resolutely uphold the Anti-Japanese banner!" The letter concluded: "Burn this after reading. My draft is already destroyed."[30]

Zhou's final attempt to save Guan revealed profound painstaking efforts -eliminating excuses for hesitation while maintaining redemption possibilities. So long as Guan hadn't physically surrendered, Zhou clung to hope of his reformation.

But Guan's resolve hardened. Secretly bypassing Chai Shirong, he negotiated with Japanese intelligence chiefs Kobayashi and Saito, then met puppet "Three Rivers Province Suppression Army" advisor Kunio Kita. Their pact centered on reorganizing Fifth Army forces around Mudanjiang into puppet Independent Brigades -consummating his betrayal.

The vigilant Zhou Baozhong monitored Guan Shufan's every move. When Guan returned to Fifth Army headquarters clad in Japanese uniform, he found Zhou sternly seated awaiting him. Zhou's icy remark-"You've finally done the yellow imperial robe"—left Guan visibly shaken.

Guan was subsequently expelled from the Party, relieved as commander of the First Division of the Fifth Army, and sentenced to death. [31]

Saito Yoshio, chief of the Kwantung Army Kempeitai's police department who had invested heavily in Guan's failed defection, developed intense hatred for Zhou. He prioritized destroying the CCP Jidong

Provincial Committee, annihilating the Second Route Army headquarters, and capturing Zhou as primary objectives.

Zhou's decisive handling of Guan's betrayal proved crucial in maintaining troop morale. Concurrently in southern Manchuria, Cheng Bin—commander of the First Division under Yang Jingyu's First Army—initiated similar treasonous actions. Separated from headquarters by Japanese suppression forces and severed communications, Yang couldn't intervene promptly, allowing Cheng's defection to succeed.

This betrayal precipitated catastrophic consequences for southern Manchuria's resistance forces, particularly the First Army, becoming a primary factor in national hero Yang Jingyu's eventual martyrdom.

Cheng Bin was born in 1912 in Yitong, Jilin. In 1932, he joined the Panshi Workers and Peasants' Volunteer Army and became a member of the Chinese Communist Party. Under Yang Jingyu's leadership, he successively served as political instructor of the security company in the Northeast People's Revolutionary Army Independent Division and political director of the First Division—the main force of the Anti-Japanese Allied First Army. In the autumn of 1935, after the successive sacrifices of division commanders Li Hongguang and Han Renhe, Cheng was appointed commander of the First Division at merely 23 years old. Over the following years, it should be acknowledged that Cheng demonstrated resolute anti-Japanese stance and military talent, winning multiple battles. As an outstanding leader of the First Army, he inflicted heavy losses on Japanese "suppression forces" through his command of the division.

To eliminate this persistent threat, Japanese forces shifted their primary suppression target to the First Division of the Anti-Japanese Allied First Army starting early 1938. While intensifying military operations, they amplified political inducements for defection. For this purpose, Shimojima

Jiro, commander of the Tonghua Japanese Military Police, formed the "Shimojima Task Force"—composed of Japanese gendarmes, Chinese collaborators, and spies—to specifically conduct subversion campaigns against the division.

The most perilous development stemmed from the betrayal of two senior First Army officers 1; Hu Guochen, the army's logistics director 2. An Guangxun, the army's chief of staff. [32]

An and Hu accepted the Japanese army's inducement to surrender mainly because they were afraid of death. The Japanese military police special agency believed that Cheng Bin, who held military power, posed the greatest threat, so they instructed An Guangxun and Hu Guochen to send a letter persuading him to surrender, while also applying military pressure.

"At that time, Cheng Bin's determination to resist war was still firm. The regimental commander Hou Junshan spread rumors that resistance was hopeless and they should go home, but Cheng Bin immediately convened a meeting to refute this and executed Hou Junshan. When Changdao work class was at a loss, Hu Guochen, who knew well of Cheng Bin's 'Achilles' heel,' came up with another plan: since Cheng Bin was a filial son, secretly arresting his mother and brother could force him into submission.

In the summer of 1938, the Changdao work class arrested Cheng Bin's mother, Mrs. Cheng Zhang, and his brother Cheng En, and brought them back. Upon learning this, Cheng Bin's resolve to resist began to waver, and pessimistic emotions took over. The Changdao work class then had a traitor take Cheng En up the mountain to persuade Cheng Bin to surrender. The first time, Cheng Bin still talked tough, saying that loyalty and filial piety could not both be fulfilled. The second time, Cheng En asked, 'Are you against Japan or do you want your mother?' This time, Cheng Bin readily agreed: "If I don't resist Japan, I still want my mother."

Having made up his mind to defect, Cheng Bin began to prepare for the defection. He found the political commissar of the Sixth Regiment, Li Zisu, and the political commissar of the security company, Li Qianxing (also known as Jin Zhonghan), to test their attitudes towards surrendering. Li Zisu had already sensed Cheng Bin's plot and argued vehemently, saying: "Even if we don't eat for three days and three nights, we must still revolutionize; surrendering to the enemy is shameful." Cheng Bin took Li Zisu by surprise and shot him dead, then shot at Li Qianxing, who escaped wounded.

After removing the two Communist Party-political commissars who opposed the defection, with the cooperation of the Japanese army, Cheng Bin defected with a total of 115 people in several batches. The defection of the three important responsible cadres, Hu Guochen, An Guangxun, and Cheng Bin, had a very bad influence on the entire South Manchuria Anti-Japanese United Army. This influence not only politically encouraged the reverse flow of escapees to resurface but also, since all three were in important leadership positions in the Anti-Japanese United Army and knew many of its high-level secrets, led to the direct and major loss of the destruction of many secret camps storing grain and supplies, adding frost to the already impoverished Anti-Japanese United Army troops.

Just as Zhou Baozhong did with Guan Yingfan, Yang Jingyu also did his utmost to save Cheng Bin. He sent Zhang Yonghai, a former puppet army who had surrendered, to the enemy camp with a letter for Cheng Bin, the gist of which was Cheng Bin had made a mistake by choosing to "save his mother and brother" and had taken the wrong path out of helplessness; if he suddenly woke up, he could secretly arrange a location, and the military department would send troops to rescue him. [33] When he learned that Cheng Bin had completely sold out his country, Yang Jingyu was filled with contempt and took emergency countermeasures.

In July 1938, Yang Jingyu and Wei Zhengzhu convened a meeting of the senior cadres of the South Manchuria Provincial Committee of the Communist Party of China and the First Route Army of the Anti-Japanese United Army, deciding to implement a wartime system, setting up a provincial committee agency within the First Route Army headquarters to achieve party-army integration. To preserve the underground work force, local cadres were withdrawn to the troops.

After Cheng Bin led his team to defect, his troops were reorganized into the pseudo-Fushen Police Brigade, also known as the Cheng Bin Suppression Brigade, which specialized in disintegrating and killing the military and political personnel of the Anti-Japanese United Army, causing great harm to the anti-Japanese armed forces in southern Manchuria.

It should be noted that in the Northeast Anti-Japanese United Army's struggle against capitulationism, the vast number of true Communists with firm faith and belief in resistance always stood on the front line of the struggle. Under Cheng Bin's deception and coercion, many Communist Party members were unafraid of violence and resolutely resisted.

After Cheng Bin announced his surrender to Japan, more than 30 Anti-Japanese United Army fighters who resolutely refused to surrender, led by Chang Jing, the propaganda section chief of the Sixth Regiment, and Qi Paizhang, resolutely left Cheng Bin. The enemy dispatched troops to encircle and suppress them, but they would rather die than become traitors. Qi Paizhang and more than ten other Anti-Japanese United Army fighters heroically sacrificed their lives.

After clarifying the true face of Army Supplies Department Director Hu Guochen, First Division Army Supplies Department First Squadron Leader Zhen Baocang led more than 30 troops to indignantly break away from Japanese and puppet control. The small teams led by Communist Party members such as Ma Guangfu, the regimental commander of the Fourth Regiment of the First Division, Quan Xiuhua, the special service company instructor, and Li Shuanglu, the guerrilla company, consisting of several, tens, or dozens of people, although weak in strength, disdained to associate with traitors and persisted in fighting in the great mountains of Benxi and Huanren.

It should be particularly pointed out that the cases of Guan Shufan and Cheng Bin, who degenerated and defected, served as negative examples and their outcomes provided a serious education in party spirit for the broad masses of party members in the Northeast Anti-Japanese United Army, especially the leading cadre party members. Apart from the untenable excuses like "temporary fake surrender" and "preserving the strength of the Anti-Japanese United Army," they seemed to have some helpless "reasons." Guan Shufan threw himself into the fire for love, and Cheng Bin was forced to surrender to fulfill his filial duty. Initially, these indeed confused some people, but after extensive discussions and the exposure of the evil consequences of Cheng Bin's surrender, everyone understood:

First, Communist Party members must never defect to the enemy under any circumstances, at any time, for any reason; they must be spotless in terms of party spirit because this is determined by the nature of the party. The last four words of the oath of a Chinese Communist Party member are "never betray the party!"

Second, the road to the great victory of the War of Resistance was paved not only with the lives and blood of Communist Party members but also possibly with the sacrifice of their spirits, emotions, family ties, love, and families. The cruel and perverse enemies would at any time force Communist Party members to make difficult choices between national and family interests, and between the safety of the people and their relatives.

Third, when there is a conflict between the survival of the nation and the safety of family and relatives, Communist Party members should unconditionally make the safety of their families and relatives subordinate to the nation and the ethnic group, as this is stipulated by the purpose of Communist Party members. If one finds this somewhat hard to accept, then please do not raise your hand to take the oath, because the first sentence of the oath is "I volunteer."

China's ancient history has forged a saying: "Loyalty and filial piety cannot both be fulfilled."

Notes:

[1] [4] Zhou Haifeng, *Biography of Chiang Kai-shek*. Beijing: Writers Publishing House, 1st ed., February 2006, 183, 198.

[2] Wang Yunsheng, *China and Japan Over Sixty Years*, vol. 8. Beijing: SDX Joint Publishing Company, 1st ed., April 1982, 233.

[3] [5] [9] CCP Central Committee's Party Literature Research Office, ed., *Selected Works of Mao Zedong*, vol. 2. Beijing: People's Publishing House, 2nd ed., September 1991, 344, 343–350, 571.

[6] [7] CCP Central Committee's Party Literature Research Office, ed., *Selected Works of Mao Zedong*, vol. 3. Beijing: People's Publishing House, 2nd ed., June 1991, 941, 1037.

[8] Yang Kuisong, *The Nationalist Party's "Alliance with the CCP" and "Anti-Communism"*. Beijing: Social Sciences Academic Press, 1st ed., January 2008, 409; quoted in Wang Shuzeng, *The War of Resistance Against Japan*, vol. 1. Beijing: People's Literature Publishing House, 1st ed., June 2015, 71.

[10] Office of the Chairman's Aides (Taiwan), ed., *Selected Speeches of Chairman Chiang Kai-shek*, vol. 5. Taipei: De Guang Press, 16.

[11] Qin Xiaoyi, *Important Historical Materials of the Republic of China: The Anti-Japanese War Period*, series 2, vol. 3. Taipei: Kuomintang Central Committee Historical Commission, 1980, 207–208; quoted in Wang Shuzeng, *The War of Resistance Against Japan*, vol. 3. Beijing: People's Literature Publishing House, 1st

ed., June 2015, 439–440.

[12] War History Office, *Japan Defense Agency, History of Army Operations in the China Incident*, vol. 3, part 2, trans. Beijing: Zhonghua Book Company, March 1983, 49–52; quoted in Wang Shuzeng, *The War of Resistance Against Japan*, vol. 2. Beijing: People's Literature Publishing House, 1st ed., June 2015, 283.

[13] [15] [16] CCP Central Committee's Party Literature Research Office, ed., *Selected Works of Mao Zedong*, vol. 2. Beijing: People's Publishing House, 1st ed., December 1993, 196, 209; 208; 220–221.

[14] [17] CCP Central Committee's Party Literature Research Office, ed., *Selected Works of Mao Zedong*, vol. 2. Beijing: People's Publishing House, 2nd ed., September 1991, 571, 589–590.

[18] [22] [23] CCP Central Committee's Party Literature Research Office, ed., *Selected Works of Mao Zedong*, vol. 3. Beijing: People's Publishing House, 2nd ed., June 1991, 919, 920, 1043–1044.

[19] Inaba Masahiro, Memoirs of Yasuji Okamura. Beijing: Zhonghua Book Company, December 1981, 327.

[20] Wang Shuzeng, *The Liberation War*, vol. 1. Beijing: People's Literature Publishing House, 1st ed., October 2009, 13.

[21] CCP Central Committee's Party Literature Research Office, ed., *Selected Works of Mao Zedong*, vol. 3. Beijing: People's Publishing House, 1st ed., August 1996, 388.

[24] *History of the Northeast Anti-Japanese Allied Army* Editorial Group, *History of the Northeast Anti-Japanese Allied Army*, vol. 2. Beijing: CCP History Publishing House, 1st ed., September 2015, 826.

[25] National Library of China Memory Project Center, *My Years in the Anti-Japanese Allied Army: Oral Histories of Veterans*. Beijing: CITIC Press Group, 1st ed., September 2016, 194.

[26] Central Archives, Liaoning Provincial Archives, Jilin Provincial Archives, and Heilongjiang Provincial Archives, *Collection of Revolutionary Historical Documents in Northeast China*, vol. A52. Beijing, 135; quoted in Zhang Zhenglong, *Snow Cold, Blood Hot*, vol. 2. Wuhan: Changjiang Literature and Art Press, 1st ed., April 2011, 233.

[27] CCP Central Committee's Party Literature Research Office, ed., *Selected Works of Mao Zedong*, vol. 2 (Beijing: People's Publishing House, 1st ed., December 1993), 230.

[28] Central Archives, Liaoning Provincial Archives, Jilin Provincial Archives, and Heilongjiang Provincial Archives, *Collection of Revolutionary Historical Documents in Northeast China*, vol. A25. Beijing, 24–25.

[29] Shi Yijun, *The Most Dangerous Moment: A Critical Study of the Northeast Anti-Japanese Allied Army*. Beijing: CITIC Press Group, 1st ed., September 2016, 159.

[30] [31] Central Archives, Liaoning Provincial Archives, Jilin Provincial Archives, and Heilongjiang Provincial Archives, *Collection of Revolutionary Historical Documents in Northeast China*, vol. A54. Beijing, 18; 34; quoted in Zhao Junqing, *Biography of Zhou Baozhong*, rev. ed.. Harbin: Heilongjiang People's Publishing House, August 2015, 277–278, 279.

[32] [33] Zhao Junqing, *Biography of Yang Jingyu*, rev. ed.. Harbin: Heilongjiang People's Publishing House, August 2015, 301, 303.

Chapter 19

Mastery of both civil governance and military strategy

62. Independence and Autonomy Within the United Front

If one carefully reads the vast number of articles on the *War of Resistance in Selected Works of Mao Zedong* (Volumes 1–4) and *Collected Works of Mao Zedong* (Volumes 1–8), it becomes evident that among these wisdom-laden writings, the term "protracted confrontation" appears with striking frequency. This concept should be regarded as a crucial approach to the prolonged war of resistance, reflecting Zhou's grand strategy of "encircling the cities from the rural areas."

The Japanese, relying on their superior weaponry, had aggressively occupied China's major cities and transportation lines, believing this constituted full conquest—a view shared by Chinese capitulationists. However, the Eighth Route Army, the New Fourth Army, peasant guerrillas, and armed working teams controlled vast rural areas, while the Northeast Anti-Japanese United Army held mountainous regions and remote villages not even marked on maps. Thus, despite their disadvantages, a state of "protracted confrontation" emerged.

Where were China's 400 million people? The overwhelming majority resided in the countryside. Mobilizing the entire population would create an ocean capable of drowning the enemy in catastrophic defeat. Mao illustrated this point: "The anti-Japanese volunteer armies in the three northeastern provinces represent only a fraction of the latent power that China's peasants can mobilize. With proper organization and leadership, China's peasants possess immense potential—enough to keep Japanese troops busy around the clock, exhausting them endlessly." [1]

A cornerstone of Mao's "protracted war" theory was the attrition of enemy resources. Japan, an island nation with limited population, could not sustain a prolonged war against China's vast territory and 400 million people. "Under the long-term attrition of China's resistance," he argued, "Japan's economy will collapse, and its morale will crumble through endless warfare." [2] Regarding the Northeast Anti-Japanese United Army's significance, he noted:

> Before the nationwide War of Resistance began, the guerrilla warfare in the Northeast had no coordination with broader efforts. But after the full outbreak of war, its strategic role became clear. Every enemy soldier killed, every bullet expended, every Japanese troop pinned down from advancing southward—each strengthened the overall resistance. Equally evident was its psychological impact: demoralizing the enemy while inspiring our troops and people. [3]

In late 1937, Wang Ming returned to Yan'an from Moscow bearing Stalin's instructions for Communist cooperation with the Kuomintang in resisting Japan. This marked a rare instance of alignment between Zhou and Stalin's intentions.

As for Stalin, a keen judge of character with sharp insight, Mao had never fully accepted proposals superficially attributed to the Comintern but actually reflecting Soviet interests, recognizing that some of his own policies ill-suited China's realities.

Saying that Mao Zedong and Stalin had consistent intentions refers to the major premise of the cooperation between the Kuomintang and the Communist Party to resist Japan. But how to cooperate? In what way? Specifically, in the cooperation between the Kuomintang and the Communist Party, should the Communist Party insist on an independent and autonomous' anti-Japanese national united front, or should it join the Kuomintang camp and be "assimilated" ("dissolve the Communist Party") by theKuomintang? Wang Ming's opinion was "oppose establishing anti-Japanese bases, do not have ourown army, believing that with Chiang Kai-shek, the world would be at peace." [4]

Because Wang Ming had a certain influence within the Communist Party, especially with the added mystique of Stalin behind him, Wang Ming's arrival once again isolated Mao Zedong.

The candid Peng Dehuai recalled many years later that on a certain evening in December 1937, the Political Bureau held a meeting in Yan'an. At the meeting, Wang Ming spoke, and Mao Zedong also spoke. The common point in the speeches of Mao Zedong and Wang Ming was resistance against Japan, but they differed on how to resist. Wang Ming spoke with an international tone, the basic spirit was that resistance against Japan was above all else, everything must go through the united front,everything must obey the united front, and both parties must jointly undertake the duties of unified regime and unified army. He placed more emphasis on the National Government and the army resisting Japan, and did not value mobilizing the masses to participate in the war: this was a line of capitulationism that abandoned the leadership of the Communist Party.

Peng Dehuai said: "At that time, did not truly recognize the correctness of Comrade Mao Zedong's line, but was influenced by Wang Ming's line, and was fuzzy on these principled issues..."[5]

Peng Dehuai recalled that since the two leaders had differing opinions, they could only go back and convey what Chairman Mao said and what Wang Ming said. As a result, in the following half year or so, the Communist Party's absolute leadership over the Eighth Route Army was somewhat reduced, and the party's political work was also some what weakened, badinage to phenomena such as individual officers deserting and the Kuomintang enticing officers and soldiers of the Eighth Route Army to defect. Through practice, Peng Dehuai gradually realized that Wang Ming's line was unfeasible: Everything must go through the united front, that is, everything must go through Chiang Kai-shek; he would absolutely not allow the Eighth Route Army to expand. By the autumn of 1938, at the Sixth Plenary Session, the Eighth Route Army had already grown to 250,000 people; if this had to go through the Kuomintang, he would not have approved even one person.

Even a steadfast old Communist Party member like Peng Dehuai was once "fuzzy," so what about others?

Regarding Mao Zedong's situation at that time, the famous British historian Philip Short wrote in his biography of Mao: "Mao later commented with a slightly self-pity exaggeration that in such situations, after Wang Ming's return, my authority did not extend beyond this cave of mine'."[6]

From a foreigner's perspective, Philip Short believed that the reason Wang Ming challenged Mao Zedong, apart from his personal ambition, was that he had enormous prestige within the party, although a large part of this prestige came from Moscow.

If one carefully examines the historical trajectory, it becomes evident that Wang Ming, upon receiving Chiang Kai-shek's invitation, departed for Wuhan shortly thereafter. Even before leaving Moscow, he had already prioritized the Kuomintang over the Communist Party—a stance consistent with Stalin's long-held strategic outlook. Consequently, upon arriving in Wuhan, Wang chose to remain there indefinitely.

The most audacious act Wang Ming committed was his unauthorized publication of the *Declaration of the Central Committee of the Communist Party of China* on the Current Situation in Wuhan on December 25, 1937, without approval from the Party Central. In this declaration, he proposed the so-called "Six Tasks for the United Front" (also termed the "Six-Point Program"), which outright repudiated the *Ten-Point Program for Resisting Japan and Saving the Nation* adopted at the expanded meeting of the CCP Politburo (the Luo Chuan Conference) in August 1937.

Wang's "Six Tasks" eliminated key provisions from the Ten-Point Program, such as implementing political-economic reforms and abolishing the Kuomintang's one-party dictatorship. Instead, he advocated for Communist forces to accept "unified command" under the Nationalist government, effectively surrendering the Party's independent leadership in the resistance and its authority over the united front. This triggered a cascade of detrimental consequences both within and outside the Party.

Wang Ming's brazen actions stemmed from his confidence in Stalin's backing. As Mao later remarked at the Chengdu Conference in March 1958: "The Chinese revolution triumphed against Stalin's will. The 'genuine foreign devils' forbade revolution... During the Anti-Japanese War, our debate with Wang Ming lasted from 1937 to August 1938. We advocated the Ten-Point Program; Wang pushed the Six-Point Program. Had we followed Wang's approach—Stalin's approach—the Chinese revolution would have failed. After our victory, Stalin doubted whether we were truly revolutionary. We did not bother to justify ourselves." [7]

Faced with Wang's inexplicable and reckless alignment with Chiang Kai-shek, Mao Zedong adopted a pragmatic stance. Prioritizing unity amid the existential threat of Japanese aggression, he refrained from public confrontation with Wang. Nevertheless, to counteract the ideological confusion and operational disruptions Wang sowed among senior Party leaders and military commanders, Mao quietly steered the course within domains under his influence—particularly military strategy. During this period, he engaged in extensive correspondence and directives, emphasizing in Principles of Red Army Operations: "We must pursue independent, decentralized guerrilla warfare rather than positional or concentrated operations. Tactical flexibility must not be constrained." [8]

Wang Ming repeatedly emphasized that everything must go through the united front and obey the united front, which allowed people in the Kuomintang who intended to eliminate the Eighth Route Army to maliciously order the Eighth Route Army to advance to areas with heavy Japanese troops. For this reason, Mao Zedong solemnly pointed out in *Explanation of Independent and Autonomous Mountain Guerrilla Warfare* that now Jiang Dingwen is still urging Liu Bocheng's department to quickly move to the front lines. Their intention is either that they do not understand that using large forces in a small area is inconvenient for conducting guerrilla warfare, or they harbor malice, intending to force the Red Army to fight tough battles. Mao Zedong emphasized that the Red Army has the freedom to use its forces, and local governments and neighboring friendly armies must not interfere; even Nanjing can only make strategic stipulations.

After the second cooperation between the Kuomintang and the Communist Party, the Kuomintang, under the pretext of "everything going through and obeying the united front," sent military and political officials to some border regions, requesting to join the border regions under the guise of negotiating reorganization, while some leading cadres in our border regions lost their vigilance. For example, He Ming, the secretary of the special committee of the southern Fujian-Guangdong border region and commander of the independent third regiment, was completely unaware of the Kuomintang's plot to eliminate the Red Army through negotiations, resulting in nearly a thousand of his troops being disarmed entirely. The reason He Ming lost his vigilance was closely related to Wang Ming's right-opportunist line of leaning toward the Kuomintang. To eliminate Wang Ming's influence and prevent such problems from occurring again, Mao Zedong clearly required in *The Policy to be Upheld During Negotiations for Reorganization in the Southern Guerrilla Zones* that "the Kuomintang must not insert a single person," and pointed out: "In the united front, local party organizations are prone to falling into right-opportunism, which has become the main danger of the party; please pay close attention."[9]

Practice is the criterion for testing truth. With the simultaneous fall of Guangzhou and Wuhan, and the full unfolding of the Communist Party's guerrilla warfare behind enemy lines, that iron-willed figure from Moscow who had great expectations for the Kuomintang and did not take the Communist Party seriously, due to his great disappointment with the Kuomintang, turned his wide-eyed gaze toward Yan'an.

As Mao Zedong said many years later in "Learn from Historical Lessons, Oppose Great Power Chauvinism," Chiang Kai-shek also "helped" us correct our mistakes. Wang Ming was "dressed up and sent to the door," while Chiang Kai-shek gave "a slap in the face, driving him out the door." Chiang Kai-shek is China's greatest teacher, educating the entire nation and all our party members. He teaches with machine guns, while Wang Ming teaches with his mouth.

In the autumn of 1938, the General Secretary of the Communist International, Dimitrov, had Wang Jiaxiang, the representative of the Chinese Communist Party, bring back two opinions regarding the Communist Party leaders: "one was, for the sake of solving the problem of unity in the party's leadership, the leadership of the Chinese Communist Party should center around Mao Zedong, and there should be an atmosphere of unity and intimacy." [10] And the other was: "Wang Ming should not contend anymore." [11]

Countless facts prove that in interactions between countries, interests are always first, and ideology serves the needs of interests. Stalin, who believed in the principle that might makes right, respected the reality of the Chinese Communist Party, which was a wise choice made by a great man.

Just as he said when he led the entire Soviet Communist Party Political Bureau to welcome Mao Zedong in December 1949: "You are now a victor, and victors are always right. That's the rule."

The broad-minded Mao Zedong allowed comrades to make mistakes and also allowed them to correct their mistakes. In the case where many comrades had differing opinions, Mao did the work and still retained Wang Ming's position as a Central Committee member. Shi Zhe was puzzled and asked Mao Zedong, what is the biggest difference between Wang Ming and other Chinese Communist Party members?

Mao Zedong was silent for a moment and said a sentence: "He thinks too little about his own affairs and worries too much about others' affairs."

In January 1956, Wang Ming traveled to Moscow under the pretext of seeking medical treatment. Before departing, he wrote to the CPC Central Committee requesting to be relieved of his position as a Central Committee member: "Once my health recovers sufficiently for work, the Party may assign me a new role." As it turned out, his "illness" never improved, and he died in Moscow in March 1974 at the age of 70.

A Chinese national who prioritized the interests of another nation, aligned his objectives with those of another country, and subordinated his actions to the directives of another state, Wang Ming could never occupy a place in the hearts of the Chinese people. The day after his death, Pravda hailed him as "a veteran soldier of international communism" and "an old friend of the Soviet Union," declaring that his "image would be forever etched in the hearts of the Soviet people."

63.The Abrupt Termination of "Operation Tung"

During the "Tong Work ' " negotiations, the Japanese army implemented the 101st Operation Agreement, once again bombing Chongqing with 3,000 sorties, intending to create greater panic among the Chinese anti-war central authorities to facilitate the progress of the "Tong Work".

The brutal bombing mentality, as described by the British-Chinese writer Han Suyin, was: "The Japanese seem to have an obsession with Chongqing, as if the continuation of life on the Great Rock Ridge between the two rivers is an insult to their power."

The Soviet Volunteer Air Force had 50 aircraft assisting the weak Chinese Air Force in combat. In Operation 101, the Japanese side had up to 400 aircraft shot down or damaged, [12] but they still frantically bombed without regard for cost.

Chiang Kai-shek suppressed his anger helplessly. As described by American writer Hannah Pakula, in the air-raid shelter, "His facial expression was suppressed... his eyes stared straight ahead, motionless like a mountain."

The Japanese large-scale bombing seemed to have taken effect.

On July 22, 1940, the Chongqing side and the Japanese side reached a conference memorandum, and Chiang Kai-shek met with Itagaki in Changsha. The prerequisite was that the Japanese Prime Minister must write a personal letter to Chairman Chiang, clearly abolishing the previous Japanese statement that did not regard the National Government as an opponent. Therefore, Chiang Kai-shek received a personal letter from Japanese Prime Minister Konoe Fumimaro:

> Dear Mr. Chiang Kai-shek: I have heard that over the past six months, the representatives appointed by you and the representatives of General Itagaki have exchanged opinions in Hong Kong regarding the issues between Japan and China, and recently you will meet with General Itagaki.
>
> I firmly believe that this meeting will lay the foundation for adjusting the relations between our two countries.
>
> Konoe Fumimaro
>
> August 22, Showa 15 [13]

At this very moment, in Chengdu, Sichuan, Chiang Kai-shek's Military Statistics Bureau and the Central Statistics Bureau jointly took action, suddenly arresting dozens of Communist Party members on charges of inciting the public to rob rice, and later, on the grounds of "Communist Party plotting an uprising," arrested Director Luo Shwen of the 18th Group Army's Chengdu Office and more than 30 other Communist Party members.

At this very moment, Chiang Kai-shek received a message that shocked him greatly: the Communist anti-Japanese armed forces launched an unprecedented large-scale offensive against the Japanese army on the enemy rear battlefield in North China. The Japanese side was even more shocked. According to the Japanese-authored *History of Army Operations in the China Incident*, in the middle of June, Showa 15, "At the moment when Japan and China were closest... the Chinese Communist Party, sensing the crisis of peace negotiations between Japan and China, suddenly launched the "Hundred Regiments.""

"The moment when Japan and China were closest," obviously refers to the point where the peace negotiations between Chongqing and Japan were just one step away. At this critical "moment," starting from August 20, 1940, the anti-Japanese armed forces led by the Chinese Communist Party in the Jin-Cha-Ji Military Region, the 129th Division, and the 120th Division of the Eighth Route Army jointly launched a large-scale campaign with the main objective of disrupting the Zhengtai Railway. By the third day of the campaign, the number of participating troops reached 105 regiments, historically known as the "Hundred Regiments."

The Hundred Regiments Offensive was launched by Communist-led anti-Japanese forces under dire circumstances—a campaign intended to demonstrate the unwavering resolve of the Chinese people in resistance, shattering the Kuomintang's illusions of compromise and capitulation to Japan.

The Eighth Route Army troops participating in the offensive attacked Japanese positions with a spirit of self-sacrifice. In North China alone, the enemy deployed 270,000 Japanese troops and 140,000 puppet forces, all highly mobile. Both sides suffered heavy casualties.

Lasting four months, the campaign is documented in Japanese military records: "In fiscal year Showa 15 (1940), the total casualties of the North China Area Army were 5,456 killed and 12,386 wounded." [14]

From a purely military perspective, Peng Dehuai later reflected that had the offensive been delayed by six months—or until after Japanese forces were further dispersed during their assaults on Changsha, Hengyang, and Guilin—the operational outcomes might have been significantly greater.

Yet war is never solely a military matter but intensely political. With Japan's "Operation Kiri" negotiations at a critical juncture, who could guarantee what dark prospects might emerge half a year later? Mao nevertheless expressed satisfaction: "The Hundred Regiments Offensive is truly exhilarating. Could such campaigns be organized once or twice more?"

While Chiang Kai-shek issued commendation telegrams to Zhu De and Peng Dehuai, he simultaneously ordered all frontline commanders to emulate the Eighth Route Army's tactics. One can imagine Chiang's astonishment upon learning the scale of the offensive. Crucially, as the campaign unfolded, Chongqing's secret "Operation Kiri" negotiations with Japan abruptly halted.

On September 17, 1940, Chinese representatives formally informed their Japanese counterparts that the proposed Changsha summit (between Chiang and General Itagaki Seishirō) should not proceed immediately, stating: "China's capacity for resistance remains strong; there is no need today to pursue a submissive peace." The Japanese delegation responded defiantly: "If China believes it can fight, let it fight."

Under Chiang's policies of "assimilating," "restricting," and "suppressing" the Communists, friction between the two parties persisted throughout the war. Hardline capitulationists, in particular, used anti-Communist actions as their "pledge of allegiance" to both Chiang and the

Japanese, provoking continuous clashes while reaping dual benefits from the Kuomintang and Japan.

The Hundred Regiments Offensive inadvertently exposed the Eighth Route Army's organizational size, equipment capabilities, and operational patterns. The rapid growth of Communist forces became Chiang's foremost concern. At a time of national crisis, internal strife between the Kuomintang and Communists only weakened resistance, serving Japan's interests. Mao thus adopted a cautious approach to interparty relations, implementing strategic measures to preserve the united front, such as:

Proposing in the *Anti-Capitulation Outline*: "Cease expanding Party membership within allied armies and withdraw existing Party organizations." Directing commanders like Peng Dehuai, He Long, and Liu Bocheng via telegram: "Do not exploit opportunities to expand into Kuomintang-controlled areas, ensuring Chiang's and Guangxi forces focus on resisting the enemy. Suspend attacks on Han Deqin, Shen Honglie, Yu Xuezhong, and Gao Shuxun's units for now."

After the Hundred Regiments, the Japanese army, which had previously focused on the Kuomintang and paid less attention to the Eighth Route Army, now directed all its efforts against the Eighth Route Army and its bases, escalating the bloody "three alls" policy to its extreme. Strangely, Chiang Kai-shek also took the opportunity to deal with the Eighth Route Army, deploying over 400,000 troops to surround the Communist stronghold in the Shaan-Gan-Ning Border Region.

Faced with this tense and explosive situation, for the sake of the nation and the overall anti-Japanese resistance, Mao Zedong advocated for restraint under the principle of the united front against Japan, stating, "Our task is to do our utmost to ease the situation, avoiding any words or actions that might provoke either side. Our army should strictly guard the defense lines, dig deep trenches and build high walls, be prepared for any eventuality, and endure their military provocations without firing a single shot... Without the central government's approval, no military conflicts should occur." [15]

Mao Zedong also prepared contingency plans for possible frictions, stating that if the Kuomintang army is forced by certain orders to attack us, we should, under the condition that it does not harm our fundamental interests, first take a step back, show utmost goodwill, and seek a midway compromise, speaking in a conciliatory manner... Only when the moderates turn into resolute and unchangeable hardliners, like Lu Zhonglin and Shi You-san, should we adopt a policy of complete rupture, firmly, thoroughly, cleanly, and completely eliminating them. [16]

Mao Zedong was the hardest and most unyielding person, never bowing to tyranny. The reason I have recorded these extremely glaring words of "endurance," "conciliation," "compromise," and even "utmost effort" in the above two directives is to prove that if Mao Zedong was not for the sake of the 400 million ordinary people suffering under the Japanese iron heel, and not for the ravaged mountains and rivers of the motherland, with his strong character, would he have bowed and compromised to the unreasonable Kuomintang?

The greed of capital and the swelling of power finally led Chiang Kai-shek to decide to take action against the Communists. On December 9, 1940, Chiang Kai-shek issued an ultimatum: "All New Fourth Army units south of the Yangtze River must move north of the Yangtze by December 31 of this year. By January 30 next year, they must move north of the Yellow River to fight..." [17]

At the same time that Chiang Kai-shek issued this ultimatum, Gu Zhutong mobilized 7 divisions, totaling 80,000 troops, to surround the New

Fourth Army, which had over 9,100 soldiers. Despite continuous bad news, the New Fourth Army still could not believe that Chiang Kai-shek would issue an order for anti-Japanese troops to fight each other, and they sang the *March of the United Front* as they fell into the encirclement.

Zhou Enlai, who was in Chongqing, was entrusted by the Central Committee of the Communist Party of China to sternly negotiate with Chiang Kai-shek, asking him to "immediately lift the siege." Chiang Kai-shek promised to order the punishment of the generals who attacked the New Fourth Army, but at the same time, he secretly ordered Gu Zhutong to completely annihilate the New Fourth Army.

After eight days and nights of tenacious resistance, the New Fourth Army—once heralded in the *March of the United Front*—found itself exhausted of ammunition and supplies. Political Director Yuan Guoping died in battle; Deputy Army Commander Xiang Ying and Deputy Chief of Staff Zhou Zikun were assassinated by traitors; Army Commander Ye Ting was detained during negotiations. Of the original 7,000 troops, only 2,000 managed to break through the encirclement, with a small number captured and the majority killed. This became the internationally shocking "Southern Anhui Incident" in the history of the War of Resistance.

Following the incident, Chiang Kai-shek tore off the mask of false cooperation, declaring the New Fourth Army a "rebel force," disbanding its designation, and submitting Ye Ting to a military tribunal.

On January 20, 1941, the CPC Central Counterattacked decisively by issuing the *Order to Reorganize the New Fourth Army Headquarters*. The same day, Mao, speaking as the spokesperson of the CPC Central Military Commission, delivered a stern warning: "We still hope those playing with fire will not let arrogance cloud their judgment. Let this be an official caution: tread carefully, for such flames are perilous. Guard your own heads well..."

The devastating losses inflicted on the New Fourth Army left Zhou deeply anguished. Mao briefly considered retaliating militarily against Chiang but ultimately restrained himself. Amid the crisis, he adopted a strategy of "launching a fierce political offensive while maintaining a defensive military posture," recognizing that Chiang's tactical victory had come at a grave political cost.

A tsunami of condemnation engulfed Chiang Kai-shek, not only from Communists but also from national capitalists, left-wing Kuomintang factions, and foreign powers like Britain, the U.S., and the Soviet Union—all critical aid providers to the Nationalist government. Politically cornered, Chiang scrambled to justify his actions through speeches and explanations, eventually forced to declare: "I cannot bear to see so-called "Communist suppression" campaigns continue, nor allow such an ill-omened term to stain China's history." [18] Notably, "Communist suppression" had been a cornerstone of Kuomintang policy since 1927, permeating its political lexicon.

For the sake of China's survival, the Communists exhibited magnanimity by temporarily tolerating this unforgivable betrayal. Yet Mao made their stance unequivocal: "Our concessions have limits; the era of compromise is over. They struck the first blow, leaving a deep wound. If they value their future, they must heal this injury themselves... Should they persist in folly, the people will cast them into the cesspit of history—a regret they will not escape."

In a nation as complex as China—where ethnic and class contradictions intertwined—maintaining an alliance with the Kuomintang throughout the war proved an arduous task.

Regarding the Southern Anhui Incident, facing the indignation of the entire party, Mao Zedong needed to explain to everyone. Mao Zedong told the whole party that not only must we dare to struggle, but we must also be good at struggling, and we must pay attention to the strategy of struggle. Regarding the Kuomintang, on the one hand, we sharply criticize, but on the other hand, we must leave room. In this way, we can negotiate and cooperate, hoping that they will change their policies.

Have we ever said to overthrow the Chairman? No. In my report, I didn't even mention the Chairman once... Regarding this point, the Chairman has also seen it. He has tried several times to provoke us into making such mistakes, to provoke our army to go out and attack Xi'an, to provoke us to propose overthrowing the Kuomintang. Comrades! We must pay attention to these things and be aware of these provocations... [19]

In response to the duplicity of the Kuomintang and Chiang Kai-shek, Mao Zedong set the struggle guidelines for the whole party as "reasonable, advantageous, and restrained," "not firing the first shot," "not being the first in the world," confronting sharply but not breaking off relations. Mao Zedong metaphorically described it as the "face-washing policy," where for Chiang Kai-shek, it is "asking him to wash his face, not cutting off his head." Mao Zedong summarized, saying: "For the past eight years of the war of resistance, our policy has been to make Chiang Kai-shek unable to surrender and unable to 'suppress the Communists.'" [20]

64. I Cannot Survive a Single Day Without the

Party

On a late summer night in 1939, under a sky ablaze with stars and a warm breeze, Heilongjiang lay in profound silence. A Soviet gunboat sliced through the river, ferrying a force of over a hundred men to the western bank. Nearly a year and a half had passed since Zhao Shangzhi's retreat to the Soviet Union amid frozen rivers and snow—now returning to turbulent waters, his heart surged with urgency. Having not fired a single shot at the Japanese in eighteen months, he was determined to reclaim lost time and strike ruthlessly.

The next day, he delivered his first blow at the Wulaga Gold Mine, a critical pain point for the enemy. Under cover of darkness, Zhao divided his troops into two columns to storm the mine compound. Over 30 puppet police guarding the site were disarmed; all but one fleeing Japanese were killed, including two radio operators obliterated by grenades. The puppet mine police captain and five to six officers who refused to surrender were executed.

The raid yielded substantial spoils beyond weaponry. Zhao ordered the mine's warehouse opened, distributing flour to impoverished miners while rallying them to resist Japan. When the miners realized the fiery, diminutive commander was the legendary Zhao Shangzhi, over 20 immediately enlisted.

Yet a grave mishap during the battle marked a dark turning point in Zhao's resurgence. Decades later, Li Zaide, then deputy Party branch secretary, recalled:

"That night, we split into two teams to attack the mine: Dai Hongbin led one, Qi Zhizhong the other. Dai's group struck the west, Qi's the east. When the fight began, Dai broke through, but Qi hesitated. Zhao shouted,

'Qi Zhizhong, why aren't you moving?!' then charged into the mine himself with his men." [21]

Post-battle, Li recounted hearing reports that Qi had grumbled to old comrades: "Zhao doesn't trust me—sending me in first was a death sentence." Suspicion spread through the ranks, with troops speculating Zhao doubted Qi's loyalty. Alarmed, Zhao convened a Party branch meeting, abstaining to allow candid discussion.

Divisions emerged: some proposed sending Qi to Soviet camps for "reeducation"; others feared he'd escape en route or preemptively retaliate. Most agreed drastic measures were necessary in crisis. Ultimately, Zhao ordered Qi's execution. [22]

This decision proved a severe political error. As noted in a CCP Northern Manchuria Provincial Committee report: "Comrade Qi Zhizhong, commander of the 11th Army, retained some naive habits and backward notions, yet his innovative spirit warranted further education and redemption." [23]

At that time, Qi Zhizhong's combat operations were slow, he did not execute the attack orders, and he also spread words of dissatisfaction with Zhao Shangzhi. The comrades in the troops, under the pressure and influence of the severe environment, found it hard to tolerate his actions, but he did not go as far as Song Yifu, Xie Wendong, and Li Huatang. Later developments proved that this wrong decision was exploited by infiltrated traitors, putting Zhao Shangzhi in a very passive position and leading to setbacks.

After capturing the Wulaga Gold Mine, Zhao Shangzhi successively eliminated two Kwantung Army surveying teams, seizing a batch of the latest surveying reports, maps, and surveying instruments (new-style sights, rangefinders). These were urgently needed by the Soviets. After praising and congratulating, the Soviet side hoped to quickly send these seizures back to the Soviet Union. Zhao Shangzhi dispatched a small team of 5 people, including Liu Fengyang (squad leader) and Shang Liansheng, to send the seizures back to the Soviet Union.

At the end of summer, Zhao Shangzhi met with Jiang Lixin, the former commander of the Third Army's garrison regiment of the Anti-Japanese Alliance, and learned of many changes that had occurred in the year and a half since he left: Jin Ce had become the secretary of the North Manchuria Provincial Committee of the Chinese Communist Party, the main forces of the North Manchuria Anti-Japanese Alliance had transferred from the lower reaches of the Songhua River to the western foothills of the Lesser Khingan Mountains, most of the Lower River bases had been lost, and many people, including Xie Wendong, the commander of the Eighth Army, had defected to the enemy... The most unexpected news for Zhao Shangzhi was that shortly after his imprisonment, the North Manchuria Temporary Provincial Committee of the Chinese Communist Party had launched a campaign to correct "leftist" sectarianism, with Zhao Shangzhi as the main target.

In April 1939, the North Manchuria Temporary Provincial Committee of the Chinese Communist Party made a disciplinary decision against Zhao Shangzhi. Within the party, his position as an executive member of the North Manchuria Temporary Provincial Committee was revoked, and he was given a severe warning; in the allied forces, his positions as commander-in-chief of the allied forces and commander of the Third Army were revoked. [24]

In the "anti-tendency" struggle, some comrades who had previously agreed with Zhao Shangzhi's views were identified as "tendency elements" and were implicated and punished. This internal struggle took place during a period when the enemy situation was extremely perilous, damaging unity within the party and the army and diverting energy from the struggle against the enemy.

Regarding the reasons for this "anti-tendency" struggle, the more common view is that at that time, under the conditions of dispersed guerrilla warfare, the enemy struggle was very complex, party life was not sound, and leaders lacked experience in internal party struggles, which should be taken as a historical lesson.

More than 40 years later, the Heilongjiang Provincial Committee of the Chinese Communist Party, based on the opinion of the Organization Department of the Central Committee of the Chinese Communist Party regarding the re-examination of Zhao Shangzhi's party membership, issued the *Decision of the Heilongjiang Provincial Committee of the Chinese Communist Party on Restoring Comrade Zhao Shangzhi's Party Membership*, which stated that Zhao Shangzhi "only criticized some issues in the letters from the Jidong Special Committee, the central representative, and the directive letters from Wang Ming and Kang Sheng, and there was no issue of opposing the central leadership or the anti-party 'leftist' sectarian line ......"

At the outset of the "anti-deviation" struggle in Northern Manchuria, despite the influence of "leftist" tactics marked by "ruthless struggle and merciless blows," some comrades were branded with labels like "splittist," "anti-Central Committee," "conciliationist," and "conspirator." Yet two facts remain clear: First, Zhao Shangzhi, accused of "anti-Party" activities, was still addressed as "comrade" and retained Party membership. Second, though criticized for promoting a "left-deviationist closed-doorism" line, none denied his status as "the most resolute anti-Japanese fighter with the greatest military achievements."

Upon hearing Jiang Lixin's report, Zhao initially reacted bitterly: "Why voice criticisms only in my absence, when I was dispatched to the Soviet Union as the Northern Manchuria Provisional Provincial Committee's representative?" Yet he soon regained composure. Recognizing the catastrophic losses suffered by troops and base areas, he insisted on convening Northern Manchuria's top Party and military leaders to devise new strategies. With the Japanese threat looming, internal disputes had to be sidelined. Thus, still unaware of his "severe Party warning" and "administrative dismissal," Zhao issued the *General Order of the Northeast Anti-Japanese United Army Headquarters (No. 16)* on July 1, 1939:

> By order, Zhao Shangzhi is hereby appointed Commander-in-Chief of the Northeast Anti-Japanese United Army. All units under the Third, Fifth, Sixth, Seventh, and Eleventh Armies shall obey his command. This appointment, sworn into effect at the end of June, is hereby promulgated to all relevant parties.
>
> Zhao Shangzhi, Commander-in-Chief

Evidently, Zhao's urgency to resolve crises blinded him to the impropriety of summoning Party and military leaders under his self-assumed title. Nevertheless, Kim Ch'aek, CCP Northern Manchuria Provincial Committee Secretary, responded cooperatively. In a letter to Third Route Army Commander Li Zhaolin, he wrote: "Forward Commander Zhao's directives to all anti-Japanese units west of the Lesser Khingan Range. Ensure immediate dissemination upon receipt."

By late December, Li Zhaolin further instructed subordinate Xie Guanghai to relay Kim's endorsement: "Unreservedly uphold Commander Shangzhi's authority and faithfully accept his leadership."

It must be acknowledged that despite Zhao's disciplinary penalties, Northern Manchuria's leadership had largely reconciled with and accepted his command. Yet at this critical juncture, Chen Shaobin—the same figure who had deceived Zhao into Soviet detention for 18 months—resurfaced, now accompanied by Shang Liansheng. A ship nearing safe harbor was thus steered toward treacherous reefs.

Before their downfall, the Japanese military police intelligence agencies not only ruthlessly slaughtered imprisoned Communist Party members but also frantically destroyed classified and top-secret archives in an attempt to cover up their crimes. These documents reportedly contained schemes to reestablish their presence in China, leaving numerous complex historical mysteries unresolved to this day.

Zhao Shangzhi had persistently demanded explanations from Soviet authorities regarding the source of Chen Shaobin's false intelligence. However, the Soviets only branded Chen as "a bad element" while refusing to disclose further details. This secrecy stemmed from a national scandal – Lyushkov, the head of the Soviet Far Eastern Interior Ministry's intelligence bureau, had been successfully bribed by the Japanese.

Logically, Chen Shaobin should have avoided Zhao Shangzhi after his return to Northeast China. Paradoxically, since Zhao's homecoming, Chen began haunting Zhao's periphery like a persistent ghost.

When Zhao learned that Japanese puppet forces were constructing railways deep into Xiaoxing'an Mountains, having reached Tangli River, his alarm escalated. The enemy's penetration into this strategic area posed an existential threat to the North Manchuria Anti-Japanese Allied Forces operating there. While awaiting senior Party and military leaders from North Manchuria, Zhao dispatched Dai Hongbin with 80 troops to attack the White Russian guards protecting the railway construction team at Tangli River.

Dai Hongbin had assumed command of the 6th Army after its commander Xia Yunjie's sacrifice. Known for his tactical acumen, Dai had previously led 500 elite cavalrymen to attack Zhaoxing Town one month after Zhao's coerced entry into Soviet territory. This operation failed catastrophically when 38 of 40 mortar shells proved to be duds. Utilizing the two functional shells strategically – one repelling Japanese reinforcements and the other provoking Soviet warning artillery fire across the river – Dai ingeniously exploited the international incident to facilitate his troops' escape.

Despite leading 80 well-armed fighters against inferior White Russian forces in the Tangli River operation, Dai suffered unexpected defeat with scattered troops and personal injury. Whether this resulted from intelligence leaks or internal sabotage remains a historical enigma.

Simultaneously, Zhao's deployment of Liu Fengyang with 20 men to establish guerrilla forces in Suibin met similar failure. Pursued by enemy troops at Fuxing Village, Liu's unit was forced to retreat to Soviet territory. This wasn't Liu's first setback – during a previous mission delivering maps and instruments to the Soviets, Chen Shaobin had disarmed his team, confiscated funds, and forcibly returned them to Soviet territory while retaining Shang Liansheng in the unit.

Li Min later recounted the disarmament incident, expressing shock at Chen's betrayal of comrades: "After confiscating Captain Liu's pistol, Chen ordered me to keep it. I hesitated – how could I take my commander's weapon? Liu glared at me and growled through gritted teeth, "That's an excellent firearm – use it against the Japanese!""

Liu Fengyang, born in 1906 in Gaiping, Liaoning, joined the Seventh Army of the Anti-Japanese United Army in 1936, joined the party in 1937, and served as the commander of the Military Department's Guard Regiment.

From Chen Shaobin's unusual behavior, he had already sensed that Chen Shaobin had problems. He had Li Min take the gun to shoot the Japanese, meaning the gun cannot be given to "others". Chen Shaobin confiscated his gun because he thought he was Zhao Shangzhi's accomplice.

Many years later, Chen Lei, an old Anti-Japanese United Army fighter who had retired from positions such as governor of Heilongjiang Province, recalled that after they completed their mission and returned to the country, they went to the Soviet military camp in Blagoveshchensk. Before crossing the border, they contacted the Soviet army. Liu Fengyang was carefree, and coupled with hunger and fatigue, he was dazed and his reaction was a bit slow. The Soviet sentry shouted the password and told him to stop. Liu Fengyang answered the password but continued to walk forward, and was shot by the sentry, hitting the hand grenade on his waist. His lower body was blown off, and he sacrificed at the age of 34.

How much damage can a traitor do? How much destructive power can a traitor turned spy have?

After the teams of Dai Hongbin and Liu Fengyang suffered losses, there were few people left around Zhao Shangzhi. Chen Shaobin once led sixty or seventy people from the First Division of the Sixth Army to the location of Zhao Shangzhi's headquarters, intending to disarm Zhao Shangzhi, with dozens of people forming a semi-surround from one side.

Everyone was worried about the safety of Commander Zhao, and wanted to strike first. Zhao Shangzhi said that the troops brought by Chen Shaobin are not enemies, we cannot fire on our own people. He sent Yu Baohe, Chen Lei, and Li Zhende to bring some venison and half a bag of flour to comfort Chen Shaobin's troops, pretending not to know that Chen Shaobin was coming to disarm them. Zhao Shangzhi sent these three because Li Zhende was originally from the Sixth Army, Yu Baohe had stayed in the First Division Hospital of the Sixth Army, and was very familiar with the people of the Sixth Army, and Chen Lei was a local cadre with no contradictions with the Sixth Army.

When they arrived, Chen Lei shouted loudly: "We brought venison for you. Comrades, we don't fight our own people, our guns are for the devils." Li Zhende saw Company Commander Wei and Commissar Du, and everyone was very affectionate. When they met Chen Shaobin, the three of them gently told him that Commander Zhao welcomed him to talk, but Chen Shaobin did not answer with a straight face, but instead arranged guards in the direction from which the three came. After returning to report, Zhao Shangzhi saw that Chen Shaobin did not dare to come, so he asked Yu Baohe to go again, asking Chen Shaobin that if he didn't want to come, could he send a company-level cadre to see Commander Zhao? Chen Shaobin had no reason to refuse, and sent six or seven company commanders, commissars, and regimental cadres to see Zhao Shangzhi.

Zhao Shangzhi was very happy to see them, and said kindly: "Did you come to disarm me? To tell you the truth, I have a radio here, and the Soviet Union has telegraphed that you have disarmed Liu Fengyang and want to disarm me too. I am the commander-in-chief of the Anti-Japanese United Army who fights the devils, disarming me is wrong. You are also troops of the Anti-Japanese United Army, why don't you go fight the devils, but come here to disarm your own people, that's not right." He spoke so convincingly that everyone was convinced and said that they could not disarm their own people.

Some cadres asked Zhao Shangzhi if he still wanted to kill the leaders of the North Manchuria Provincial Committee. He was very angry and said that the North Manchuria Provincial Committee is the party's leading organ, and the commander-in-chief is also under the leadership of the provincial committee, how can we kill the party's leaders? Killing them is not counter-revolutionary? This is pure rumor, everyone should not believe it.

Close call! Had it not been for Zhao Shangzhi's formidable reputation against the Japanese invaders and his psychological campaign of outreach and communication that won over Chen Shaobin's subordinates, the consequences would have been catastrophic. Through negotiations, Zhao had already thwarted Chen's conspiracy to personally disarm, kidnap, and assassinate him, forcing Chen to lift his siege.

As Chen Shaobin withdrew with his troops, morale within his ranks began to shift. Walking beside Regimental Commander Bai Fuhou, Li Min overheard Adjutant Sun Guodong whisper to Bai: "What kind of operation is this? That old man (Chen Shaobin) seems suspicious. Should we eliminate him?"

Bai glanced around and replied quietly: "No. Without orders from above, my mission is to deliver these troops to Political Commissar Zhang (Zhang Shoujian, later known as Li Zhaolin). We'll address this there."

Just then, Chen Shaobin summoned Sun Guodong.

Some soldiers questioned Bai Fuhou: Was the decision to attack Zhao Shangzhi based solely on Shang Liansheng's testimony? Something felt off. Others recalled how Chen, as division commander, had earlier encouraged troops in Shuangyashan to "return home and fend for themselves with their weapons"—effectively advocating disbandment.

Bai Fuhou, Li Min's regimental commander, later proved pivotal. Decades later, Li Min reflected that without Bai, the unit would have faced grave peril—not only due to Bai's tactical brilliance but also his unshakable resolve to resist.

When Chen proposed disbanding, Bai rallied the troops: "Comrades! Those unafraid of hardship, follow me! The revolution cannot be abandoned midway—we fight to the end!" His leadership stabilized the unit. Through relentless enemy assaults and near-annihilation, Bai guided them to reunite with Third Route Army Commander Li Zhaolin, preserving the core of the Sixth Army's First Division. Bai Fuhou would heroically perish in battle in 1941 at age 28.

Chen Shaobin summoned Sun Guodong to assign him, Yan Xibao, Che Tingxing, and two others a treacherous mission: infiltrate the Wutong River Gold Mine or Xingshan (modern Hegang) to contact Japanese puppet forces and betray Zhao Shangzhi's whereabouts—under the pretext of "preventing Zhao from assassinating Provincial Committee and Third Route Army leaders." Sensing treason, all five defectors refused and fled to the Soviet Union instead.

Sun Guodong, born in 1916 in Daming, Hebei, was a member of the Chinese Communist Party. He served as the commander of the independent battalion of the Third Army of the Anti-Japanese United Army, deputy officer of the Ninth Detachment of the Third Route Army, among other positions. In 1941, he was assigned to a small team led by Yu Tianfang (then the special commissioner of the Third Route Army of the Northeast Anti-Japanese United Army) for a mission to return to China. Unfortunately, he was captured in a battle. On the eve of the Japanese invaders' surrender—on August 14, 1945, at 3 PM—Sun Guodong was cruelly executed and should be considered a hero who sacrificed himself just before dawn.

On July 4, 1956, Goukou Yoshio, who had served as a prosecutor in the Harbin Higher Prosecution Office of the puppet Manchukuo, confessed: "According to the laws of the puppet Manchukuo, the execution of a death sentence must be approved by the Minister of Justice. However, when I killed Sun Guodong, the judgment had not yet been approved." "At that time, I thought that Japanese imperialism was bound to fail. If Sun Guodong and other members of the Anti-Japanese United Army and other anti-Japanese salvation personnel were allowed to continue living... if I did not kill Mr. Sun Guodong, my life would be in danger."

In *Du Xigang's Accusation Book*, there are two scenes that the author believes should be recorded here.

One scene is when the Japanese judge asked Sun Guodong in Chinese why he was resisting Japan. Sun Guodong answered: "On Chinese soil, foreigners are not allowed to run amok, kill and set fires, kill young people and children, and rape women." Du Xigang said, "At that time, we debated with them for about an hour, and they, like wolves, fiercely demanded the death penalty for us. A week later, the sentence was pronounced: death penalty for Sun Guodong, me, Yu Lancab, and Zhao Wenyou."

The other scene is of Sun Guodong's execution: "I heard the guard shouting, 'Sun Guodong, the higher court has come to execute you." Sun said: "No hurry!" and then loudly said: "I want to say a few words to my fellow prisoners. The Soviet Red Army has been fighting the Japanese bandits for a week, and the Japanese bandits are about to be finished. In the future, you will be able to live good lives as Chinese people. I am sacrificing myself to help the Chinese people get rid of the dark days, and my sacrifice is glorious..." The Japanese guard pushed him, but he again loudly sang the *Song of National Salvation* and shouted: "Long live the Chinese Communist Party!" "Down with Japanese imperialism!" "Many people in the prison shed tears." [25] This firm anti-Japanese hero and loyal Communist Party member fell in the dawn light at the age of 29. How painful!

The reason why the author has detailed the above stories of grassroots officers and soldiers of the Anti-Japanese United Army is to illustrate that the Northeast Anti-Japanese War was able to form a magnificent prairie fire, and even after a downpour, the sparks did not go out. This was not only because of the exemplary organizational leadership of commanders like Yang Jingyu, Zhao Shangzhi, Zhou Baozhong, and Li Zhaolin, but also because of the conscious and active bloody battles fought by tens of thousands of known and unknown ordinary officers and soldiers of the Anti-Japanese United Army. In other words, the heroic deeds of Yang, Zhao, Zhou, and Li conformed to the wishes of the officers and soldiers of the Anti-Japanese United Army. Therefore, conspiracies like those of Chen Shaobin repeatedly failed.

As China's War of Resistance entered its middle-late stages, exhausted Japanese invaders, unable to subdue the Northeast Anti-Japanese Allied Army (NAJAA) through military force, intensified espionage campaigns alongside widespread defection inducement. Beyond exploiting White Russian exiles in Manchuria—training them to infiltrate the Soviet Union— they dispatched fake underground operatives and NAJAA impersonators to receive Soviet military-political training before returning to assume leadership roles in Manchuria.

Chen Shaobin had arrested a "Red-aligned Russian" named Ivan in July 1937, detaining him for five months.[26] During this period, Chen himself defected after capture, only to be inexplicably released back to NAJAA ranks. Shockingly, in December of that year, Chen traveled to the Soviet Union with Ivan.

Was Chen a double agent? Multiple sources claim Chen was killed as a bandit after being hunted by NAJAA leaders Li Zhaolin and Feng Zhongyun. Was this due to internal disputes over spoils? Or a silencing act? The historical truth remains obscured. Yet considering Chen's unprecedented access to Soviet territory—unthinkable for a NAJAA division-level commander—the catastrophic implications of his betrayal demand scrutiny.

Georgi Dimitrov of the Comintern, sympathetic to the Chinese Communist Party (CCP), maintained top-secret telegraphic communications with the CCP Central Secretariat and Mao Zedong, attempting to reconnect the CCP Central Committee with Manchurian resistance forces. A April 3, 1942 cable from the Comintern Executive Committee Secretariat warned:

> "We lack precise intelligence on Manchurian guerrilla base locations. Warnings indicate extensive spy infiltration. Advise your operatives to avoid immediate contact with guerrillas. First vet local collaborators thoroughly before establishing Party connections."

Shang Liansheng, twice arrested and defecting to Japanese gendarmerie, was disguised as a NAJAA straggler and sent to the USSR as a spy. After returning with Chen Shaobin, Shang falsely testified that he had personally heard Zhao Shangzhi plotting to assassinate North Manchuria Party-military leaders. Lacking access to Manchurian Provincial Committee leadership, Shang's accusations were channeled through Chen Shaobin and Zhou Yunfeng (Political Director of NAJAA Sixth Army's Third Division, captured and defected in 1940). Their jointly submitted *Report to Directors Feng and Gao by Shaobin et al*. devoted nearly one-third to "Comrade Shang Liansheng's testimony":

> We have obtained Comrade Shang Liansheng's secret deposition exposing Zhao's conspiracy. Shang states: "I was previously deceived by Zhao's facade. Now hearing Shaobin's (Chen Shaobin) revelations, I pledge loyalty to the Party-army to break Zhao's spell." Full deposition follows:

> I attended Old Zhao's meeting as an auditor. Among the attendees were Lu Yangchun's deputy, Baohe, and others. Zhao said that Comrade Chen Chun was previously deceived by Shao Bin and was drawn to his side. ... Among them, Zhang Shoubin, Feng Zhongyun, Zhou Baozhong,

Xie Wendong, Li Huatang, and others all joined the Trotskyist faction specifically to oppose Zhao Shangzhi who was fighting the Japanese. Currently, only Feng Qunshoubin from the 57th Army, 8th Army, and 4th Army has collapsed and defected to the enemy. I will definitely arrest and behead him. I gave Shang Liansheng the task: tell him to go to Feng Yun and say that there is a central representative coming from the grassland to ask Comrade Feng Yun to make contact, to deceive him into coming, and absolutely do not mention Zhao Shangzhi's name; this will be your achievement. After Shang arrived, he saw that Comrade Feng Yun showed a desire to automatically go and contact Zhao, and also asked Shang Liansheng to cross the river to send a letter to Gao Yumin, and completely revealed the mission he was carrying, which was to return to Zhao's place. Because of my work error, he was killed without being questioned. I, Shang, am a young person with aspirations to save the country, and at the moment of death, I could only say "Long live the revolution." Tears flowed freely, extremely painful. Now, hearing the division commander's words, I suddenly awakened, offer my loyalty, and hope for guidance. [27]

With the "testimony" from two Anti-Japanese United Army leaders above the rank of division, and with Qi Zhizhong having been killed beforehand, coupled with the old rift from past 'anti-tendency' issues, the leadership of the North Manchuria Provincial Committee of the Chinese Communist Party canceled their original plan to meet with Zhao Shangzhi.

In 1939, winter seemed to arrive early; the Lesser Khingan Mountains were already icy and snowy. Zhao Shangzhi was anxiously waiting to meet with the responsible persons of the North Manchuria Anti-Japanese United Army. Situations of being out of food for a week occurred from time to time, and Chen Sen, who was sent to procure supplies, rebelled and defected to the enemy. During this period, there was also an instance where the troops were pursued and attacked by over 200 Japanese soldiers from the Nishimura unit. Zhao Shangzhi selected 9 fighters who could still fight and engaged in a fierce battle with the enemy. If it weren't for Zhao Shangzhi's excellence in command and combat, the consequences would have been unimaginable. By the end of that year, Zhao Shangzhi led the remaining troops across the frozen Heilongjiang River and crossed into the Soviet Union.

In the Soviet Union, Zhao Shangzhi met with Zhou Baozhong, the long-separated Secretary of the Jidong Provincial Committee of the Chinese Communist Party and Commander of the Second Route Army, and Feng Zhongyun, a member of the Standing Committee of the North Manchuria Provincial Committee of the Chinese Communist Party, who was ordered to cross the border to request Soviet assistance in establishing contact with the central party. Thus, the three jointly participated in the joint meeting of representatives from the Jidong and North Manchuria Provincial Committees of the Chinese Communist Party.

Since the meeting was held in Blagoveshchensk, it is historically known as the "Blagoveshchensk Conference."

The Blagoveshchensk Conference was an important meeting in the history of the Northeast Anti-Japanese United Army. In reality, it was a meeting attended by Zhou Baozhong, Zhao Shangzhi, and Feng Zhongyun. The first stage of the meeting mainly consisted of individual conversations, which can also be considered the preparatory stage for the meeting. After all, such debates had been going on for a long time, and both sides had many understandings that needed to be unified.

The Blagoveshchensk Conference was formally convened on January 24, 1940. Before the meeting, through individual conversations and correspondence, Zhou, Zhao, and Feng communicated the situation and deepened their mutual understanding, laying the foundation for the convening of the meeting. The meeting was conducted in the form of a "three-person discussion," carrying out serious and solemn criticism and self-criticism. The first stage lasted 12 days, and finally, they reached a consensus on major issues, and all three were very happy.

Under normal circumstances, such critical disputes should have been resolved through higher authorities' adjudication and guidance. Amid severed communication with superior command, the Jidong and North Manchuria Party organizations demonstrated commendable unity, strategic foresight, and revolutionary responsibility through their independent combat operations, arduous explorations, and proactive problem-solving. This historical initiative deserves full recognition. The conference produced three pivotal documents: *Summary Outline for Discussing Intra-Party Struggles in Jidong and North Manchuria; Conclusion of North Manchuria Intra-Party Discussions: Opinions on Evaluating Leading Comrades; Draft New Program for the Northeast Anti-Japanese National Salvation Movement.*

The second document, *Conclusion of North Manchuria Intra-Party Discussions*, contained "evaluative assessments" of Zhao Shangzhi, Zhou Baozhong, Feng Zhongyun, and other Party-military leaders in North Manchuria, formulated through rigorous debates among the three principals. As a Party member with 50 years of service, I am profoundly moved by the NAJAA veterans' commitment to truth-seeking, accountability, and sincere criticism and self-criticism.

The successful Boli Conference marked the unification of the Northeast Party and NAJAA under the political line of the Anti-Japanese National United Front, achieving consensus on operational principles, policies, and strategies. All three leaders anticipated greater anti-Japanese achievements while securing Soviet military aid through newly established ties with the Far Eastern Regional Party Committee and Red Army.

Yet a lurking specter distorted reality, plunging Zhao Shangzhi into political oblivion. Infiltrators-turned-traitors within Party ranks exploited Zhao's vulnerability: his existential dread of losing Party affiliation. During the Boli Conference, the North Manchuria Provincial Committee—relying solely on Chen Shaobin and Shang Liansheng's testimonies in Zhao's absence—permanently expelled him from the CCP.

The blow proved catastrophic. Learning of the expulsion two months later, Zhao urgently petitioned: "Party membership is a communist's lifeblood. Having devoted 15 years to revolutionary struggle, my entire existence is bound to Party work. I implore reinvestigation. Expulsion equates to a death sentence. With utmost urgency, I beg for organizational reinstatement and continued Party leadership—I cannot endure a single day severed from the Party."

Feng Zhongyun and Zhou Baozhong voiced dissent, demanding re-examination of Zhao's expulsion. Their appeals, however, could not pierce the veil of intrigue that had already sealed Zhao's fate.

During his political exile, Zhao Shangzhi agonized over comrades implicated by his case. On May 31, 1940, he pleaded in a letter to the North Manchuria Provincial Committee: "I implore the swift resolution of Party reinstatement for other comrades expelled due to their association with me."

Outsiders saw clearer. Soviet advisors, ruthless in their own purges, perceived Zhao's predicament with startling clarity. Far Eastern Army representative Wang Xinlin urged the North Manchuria Party: "Zhao Shangzhi's Party membership must be resolved and communicated to us… Do not discard our veteran cadres—they hold immense value for our future endeavors."

Yet Chen Shaobin's sabotage ran too deep. The Provincial Committee's reply to Zhao stated: "Comrades [name redacted] and Chen

Shaobin contacted us west of the ridges, revealing your anti-Party conspiracies during last year's Xiajiang operations… While respecting Comintern proposals, the majority vote maintains your expulsion, removing only the "permanent' designation." [28]

By August 1940, the Provincial Committee and Third Route Army Headquarters issued a warrant: "Chen Shaobin, repeat offender… spreading rumors and deserting with arms, stands condemned as a wartime fugitive. All units and civilians must report his whereabouts. Captors shall deliver him for judicial punishment." [29]

The false charges orchestrated by infiltrator Chen Shaobin lingered unresolved until 1982. The *Heilongjiang Provincial Committee's Decision on Reinstating Zhao Shangzhi's Party Membership* declared: "No evidence supports claims of Zhao plotting against North Manchuria leaders… His expulsion constituted a historical injustice." [30]

Zhou Baozhong extended trust by appointing Zhao Shangzhi as Deputy Commander of the Second Route Army (NAJAA), even permitting his participation—as a non-Party member—in Party assemblies of the headquarters' direct units and assigning him to deliver reports. Grateful yet humiliated, Zhao dedicated himself to military collaboration with Zhou despite his compromised status.

The Second Boli Conference should have offered Zhao reconciliation with North Manchuria Party-military leaders. Like the first conference, where all united under the Anti-Japanese National United Front with minimal ideological discord, this gathering could have clarified misunderstandings and renewed solidarity. Tragically, entangled historical complexities barred Zhao from attending while stripping him of his deputy commandership. This plunged Zhao back into the political isolation of 1933 following his first expulsion—a veteran revolutionary rendered solitary once more.

Though initially despondent, Zhao rallied defiantly: "If none will join me, I'll carry the revolution alone."

A polymath warrior-poet, Zhao channeled his nadir into verses of unyielding resolve during his second expulsion. His poetry crystallized the indomitable spirit of China's resistance:

> To die resisting Japan brings true glory,
> Defying the invaders' savage cruelty.
> Though countless heroes have perished in this story,
> A decade's bloodshed demands final victory.
>
> Mock not our tattered uniforms in battle,
> Nor scorn our wounded, aged, or infirm.
> Unyielding resolve outshines mere chattel—
> A decade's bloodshed demands final victory.
>
> Factional strife breeds disintegration's seed,
> Sabotage poisons like a traitor's creed.
> Purge every turncoat, crush their vile deed—
> A decade's bloodshed demands final victory.

......

Notes:

[1] [2] Central Committee Literature Research Office. *Selected Works of Mao Zedong* (Vol. 1). 1st ed. Beijing: People's Publishing House, December 1993, p. 406, p. 406.

[3] Central Committee Literature Compilation Committee. *Selected Works of Mao Zedong* (Vol. 2). 2nd ed. Beijing: People's Publishing House, June 1991, p. 416.

[4] [7] Central Committee Literature Research Office. *Selected Works of Mao Zedong* (Vol. 7). 1st ed. Beijing: People's Publishing House, June 1999, p. 121, p. 371.

[5] Peng Dehuai. Reorganization of the Red Army into the Eighth Route Army. Quoted in A Century of Spring and Autumn: Personal Accounts of Major 20th-Century Events (Vol. 2). 1st ed. Beijing: Economic Daily Press, August 1997, pp. 1126–1128.

[6] [10] Short, Philip (UK). *Mao Zedong: A Biography*. 1st ed. Beijing: China Youth Press, January 2004, p. 294, p. 297.

[8] [9] Central Committee Literature Research Office. *Selected Works of Mao Zedong* (Vol. 2). 1st ed. Beijing: People's Publishing House, December 1993, p. 1, pp. 13–14.

[11] Xu Yan. *Soviet Military Intervention in Northeast China*. 1st ed. Beijing: PLA Publishing House, August 2015, p. 102.

[12] [14] War History Office, Japan Defense Agency. *Army Operations in the China Incident* (Vol. 3, Part 2). Translated in *Historical Materials of Republican China: Translated Series*. Beijing: Zhonghua Book Company, March 1983, pp. 41, 59; quoted in Wang Shuzeng. *The War of Resistance Against Japan* (Vol. 2). 1st ed. Beijing: People's Literature Publishing House, June 2015, p. 285, p. 306.

[13] Compilation and Review Committee of Historical Materials of the Chinese People's Liberation Army. *Reference Materials on the Eighth Route Army* (Vol. 2). Beijing: PLA Publishing House, p. 300; quoted in Wang Shuzeng. *The War of Resistance Against Japan*. 1st ed. Beijing: People's Literature Publishing House, June 2015, p. 274.

[15] [16] Central Committee Literature Research Office. *Selected Works of Mao Zedong*(Vol. 2). 1st ed. Beijing: People's Publishing House, August 1996, p. 279, p. 284.

[17] [18] Wei Hongyuan. *Chronicle of the Republic of China: The Anti-Japanese War Period* (Vol. 6, Part 2). Shenyang: Liaoning People's Publishing House, pp. 76–77, p. 82; quoted in Wang Shuzeng. *The War of Resistance Against Japan* (Vol. 2). 1st ed. Beijing: People's Literature Publishing House, June 2015, p. 347, p. 353.

[19] [20] Central Committee Literature Research Office. *Selected Works of Mao Zedong* (Vol. 3). 1st ed. Beijing: People's Publishing House, August 1996, p. 325, p. 388.

[21] China Memory Project Center, National Library of China. *My Years in the Northeast Anti-Japanese Allied Army: Oral Histories of Veterans*. 1st ed. Beijing: CITIC Publishing Group, September 2016, p. 23.

[22] Zhao Junqing. *Biography of Zhao Shangzhi*. Revised ed. Harbin: Heilongjiang People's Publishing House, August 2015, p. 290.

[23] Central Archives, Liaoning Provincial Archives, Jilin Provincial Archives, Heilongjiang Provincial Archives. *Collection of Revolutionary Historical Documents in Northeast China* (Series A, Vol. 26), p. 77; quoted in Zhao Junqing. *Biography of Zhao Shangzh*i. Revised ed. Harbin: Heilongjiang People's Publishing House, August 2015, p. 290.

[24] Resolution of the Second Plenary Session of the Provisional North Manchuria Provincial Committee to the Third Army Party Committee: Political Responsibility for "Leftist Sectarianism" and Bolshevik Iron Discipline (April 12, 1939); quoted in Zhao Junqing. Biography of Zhao Shangzhi. Revised ed. Harbin: Heilongjiang People's Publishing House, August 2015, p. 286.

[25] Central Archives of China, Second Historical Archives of China, Jilin Academy of Social Sciences. *Selected Archives of Japanese Imperialist Invasion of China: Major Tragedy in Northeast China,* Zhonghua Book Company, September 1989, 1st ed. p. 707-708.

[26] Heilongjiang Provincial Archives, File 14-2-8: *Jiaxian High Court Document No. 520 (August 17, 1938)*; quoted in Zhao Junqing. *Biography of Zhao Shangzhi*. Revised ed. Harbin: Heilongjiang People's Publishing House, August 2015, p. 311.

[27] Central Archives, Liaoning Provincial Archives, Jilin Provincial Archives, Heilongjiang Provincial Archives. *Collection of Revolutionary Historical Documents in Northeast China* (Series A, Vol. 56), pp. 263–264.

[28] Central Archives, Liaoning Provincial Archives, Jilin Provincial Archives, Heilongjiang Provincial Archives. *Collection of Revolutionary Historical Documents in Northeast China* (Series A, Vol. 26), p. 182, p. 187.

[29] Shi Yijun. The Most Perilous Hour: Critical Examinations of Northeast Anti-Japanese Allied Army History. 1st ed. Beijing: CITIC Publishing Group, September 2016, p. 119.

[30] Zhao Junqing. *Biography of Zhao Shangzhi*. Revised ed. Harbin: Heilongjiang People's Publishing House, August 2015, p. 355.

Chapter 20

Deathless Life

65. A Frozen Sentinel Still Stares at the Enemy

Trapped in Khabarovsk, Zhao Shangzhi yearned ceaselessly to return to the anti-Japanese battlefields of Northeast China. Yet, stripped of his Party ties and troops, he could not freely leave the Soviet "workhouse" where he was confined.

For nearly ten months, he had pleaded, petitioned, even raged. To their credit, the Soviets respected him as a Chapayev-like hero. No matter his outbursts, they treated him kindly, providing ample food and shelter. But for Zhao, each day dragged on like a year.

By October 1941, autumn's bleak winds swept the land. Yet Zhao's heart burned with fervor—the Soviets had finally agreed to let him lead a small team back to China. Though the group numbered fewer than half a squad—just four men besides himself: Jiang Lixin (former commander of the Third Army's rear guard), Zhang Fengqi (former regimental commander of the Third Division), Zhao Haitao (a Sixth Army veteran), and Han You (a soldier from the Second Route Army)—it was still better than his first expulsion from the Party, when he'd been utterly alone.

What defines a warrior? A warrior may fall, but unlike the weak, he rises again—no matter how many times he is struck down.

When Zhao had fallen in 1932, the Japanese scarcely knew his name. Even the lowest bandit in Sun Chaoyang's militia could mock him. Now, he haunted Japan's nightmares. His every move triggered top-priority intelligence alerts. The April 14, 1939, puppet regime document *1939 Public Security Maintenance Outline* (Appendix to Manchukuo Operational Order No. 13) listed him as the second-most-wanted "insurgent leader," with a bounty matching Yang Jingyu's at 10,000 yuan.

The Soviets' concession came as Hitler invaded the USSR. Fearing a Japanese pincer strike in the Far East, they tasked Zhao's team to sabotage Xingshan (present-day Hegang) Power Plant and key railway bridges between Jiamusi and Tangyuan if war erupted. They also ordered him to prepare hidden airfields in the Xiaoxing'an Mountains' depths.

Though framed as a strategic special ops mission, the Soviets demanded Zhao's return within three months—a deadline he secretly vowed to ignore. "Better to die fighting in Manchuria than crawl back to the USSR," he resolved.

Though it was unconventional for a commander-in-chief to lead a special operations squad, Zhao Shangzhi had his own convictions: "I'd rather die fighting on the Northeast's anti-Japanese battlefield than return to the Soviet Union." He knew that if he crossed back into Soviet territory again, he might never get another chance to fight the Japanese invaders. His resolve was unshakable—he would start anew, rebuild his forces, and strike the enemy once more. By mid-January 1942, three months after returning to China, Zhao dispatched Zhang Fengqi, Zhao Haitao, and Han You back to the Soviet Union to report, while he himself remained in the Northeast. During this time, he recruited a young fur-gathering man named Wang

Yongxiao into his ranks, slowly piecing together a new guerrilla force to reignite the flames of resistance.

In reality, Japanese intelligence agencies had long deployed spy networks to track the feared Zhao Shangzhi. Former puppet Xingshan Police Special Affairs Director Masao Tōjō later confessed that in late November 1941, to establish an intelligence network in the Wutong River mountainous area, he "issued mountain entry permits to 35 hunters led by a man surnamed Ruan." By year's end, Zhao's movements were pinpointed. A spy posing as a hunter, Feng Jiede, reported to the puppet Heli County Police Department that around late December, Zhao and five others had suddenly appeared at a mountain cabin belonging to hunters Wang Yongjiang and Feng Jiede—approximately 100 li (50 km) northwest of Wutong River in Heli County. There, they inquired about two individuals: Dai Hongbin and Chen Shaobin... Concurrently, intelligence from Tangyuan County claimed: "On December 23, Zhao Shangzhi—wearing a Japanese military uniform—along with subordinates Jiang Lixin, Zhang Fengqi, and three others, abducted hunter Wang Yongxiao 64 km north of Wudeku Police Station in Tangyuan County." [1]

It should be noted that when recruiting new fighters, the Anti-Japanese Alliance often staged "abductions" in public view to protect recruits' families from retaliation—Wang Yongxiao's case likely followed this pattern. Both reports were immediately deemed "verified intelligence," classified as Category A, and forwarded to Xingshan Puppet Police. Crucially, the *Sanjiang Provincial Police Department Report on the Shooting of Former NEAJUA Commander Zhao Shangzhi* contains a critical addendum: "Spy Wang XX used by Heli County was captured by Zhao Shangzhi while hunting north of Wutong River in mid-November. After entering the USSR with Zhao in January and returning, Wang feared reprimand from his handler for crossing into Soviet territory. We ordered his immediate withdrawal from the mountains. His debriefing will clarify Zhao's group's movements." [2]

The Japanese spy Wang XX had actually crossed the border into the Soviet Union with Zhao Shangzhi and returned unscathed—a chilling revelation. Was there a Soviet collaborator? Had Zhao's movements during his time in the USSR, especially after re-entering Northeast China, already been mapped by Japanese intelligence? Without historical evidence, these questions remain unanswered. One fact is clear: When overwhelming military force failed to capture or kill Zhao Shangzhi, the enemy pivoted to infiltrating the Anti-Japanese Alliance with "elite" spies to sow discord. Their strategy bore fruit through Chen Shaobin. According to the confession of Japanese war criminal Hisajirō Tai (a police lieutenant and former chief of the puppet Xingshan Police Department): "Even mobilizing an entire Japanese division couldn't capture Zhao Shangzhi. The only way was to covertly plant disguised agents into his ranks, lure him into police-controlled territory, inflict critical injuries, and then arrest him." [3]

In early 1942, the puppet regime meticulously selected agents for this "suicide mission" from Xingshan Police's spy pool.

The prime candidate was Liu Deshan (alias Liu Haifeng), a 42-year-old hunter from Yimianpo, Zhuhe County. Renowned for his marksmanship as "Liu the Sharpshooter," he had previously led security for the puppet Wutong River Gold Mining Company before becoming a Japanese spy. Posing as a hunter, he gathered intel on the resistance, earning full trust from Chief Tai and Special Operations Director Masao Tōjō. Liu was designated Spy No. 1 for the assassination infiltration.

Spy No. 2, Zhang Xiwei (recorded in Japanese files as Zhang Qingyu), a 34-year-old opium addict, was tasked with logistics. Formerly of the puppet Jiamusi Police, Zhang posed as a mountain porter while conducting espionage, earning the nickname "Little Porter Zhang."

In mid-January, Liu Deshan entered the mountains disguised as a fur trader. To support his mission, puppet Heli County police officer Takeo Anazawa led 16 men to reinforce surveillance in the Wutong River area. By late January, 25 additional agents—including Wang Xiufeng—were deployed to tighten the intelligence net. A deadly trap was closing in on Zhao Shangzhi.

A dozen days later, Liu Deshan finally located Zhao Shangzhi and his small unit. Zhao remained highly suspicious of Liu's sudden appearance, but the spy's scheme succeeded due to Jiang Lixin—a man whose loyalty unwittingly became the fatal flaw. Jiang Lixin, nicknamed "Crippled Jiang" or "Clawless Jiang", had lost all fingers except his thumbs and most of his toes to frostbite, leaving him to walk "like an old woman with bound feet." Yet his unyielding anti-Japanese resolve had earned Zhao's absolute trust.

Here lay the tragic irony. Jiang and Liu were old acquaintances. Relying on Jiang's personal endorsement and Liu's impassioned vows to "fight the devils," Zhao accepted the spy into his ranks. Jiang, unaware of Liu's betrayal, vouched for the man he'd known in better days—a mistake that would doom them all.

Though "even the wise err at times," hard-won protocols exist for a reason. Zhao abandoned standard vetting procedures, trusting Jiang's word over caution. This lapse—allowing a comrade's assurance to override principles—proved catastrophic. A bloody lesson: No bond, however deep, should ever supersume vigilance.

Spy No. 2, Zhang Xiwei, arrived in early February. Unlike Liu's rugged guise, Zhang's gaunt frame and sallow complexion screamed "opium addict." Zhao deemed him a spy and ordered execution. But Liu intervened with cunning lies: "He's my sworn brother—came looking 'cause he feared I'd died!"

One misstep leads to another. Zhao Shangzhi, who had lost his Party membership and his vast army to traitors in the past, was no stranger to vigilance against infiltration. Yet during this critical period, his famed alertness inexplicably wavered. Was it desperation to rebuild his forces? No historical records confirm this. After absorbing Liu Deshan into the ranks, Zhang Xiwei also joined the unit. Zhao armed both men with rifles and ammunition, expanding his troop from four to six—a numerical ratio of 2 enemy infiltrators to 4 loyal fighters. Though outnumbered, the spies held lethal advantage: a fortress crumbles fastest from within. Thus, the Japanese intelligence agency's "elite operatives" set their sinister plot into motion.

Snow fell heavily, blanketing the world in silent white. On the very night Zhang Xiwei arrived, Liu Deshan fed Zhao Shangzhi a fabricated tip: "The Wutong River police outpost is lightly guarded. They're still lax after the New Year—a perfect target." His true aim was to lure Zhao toward Takeo Anazawa's puppet police ambush.

Zhao Shangzhi remained noncommittal. This was his strategic and deliberate habit, never revealing plans prematurely. Three days later, shortly after midnight on February 12, a six-member squad, including two traitors, reached the isolated hut near the Lü Family Vegetable Garden, two kilometers north of the Wutong River, preparing to raid a puppet police outpost. Liu Deshan suggested to Zhao, "We should send someone to scout the Wutong River area." Zhao agreed, deciding to dispatch someone familiar with the fortified villages. Zhang Xiwei, seizing the opportunity, volunteered. Following Liu's instructions, Zhang instead rushed to alert the puppet police.

Liu Deshan, who had been walking ahead of Zhao, seized his moment. Pretending to need a bathroom break, he stepped behind Zhao, raised his rifle, and fired at point-blank range. The bullet struck Zhao's lower back, dropping him instantly.

The gunshot revealed Liu's treachery. Despite excruciating pain, Zhao, with superhuman resolve, grabbed his pistol and shot Liu—who was already turning his rifle on Wang Yongxiao—twice in the head and abdomen, killing him on the spot. Wang, however, was critically wounded.

Hearing the gunfire, Jiang Lixin, trailing behind, rushed forward. In the dim moonlight, he saw Zhao's blood-soaked torso. Knowing his fate, Zhao ordered Jiang and a newly recruited comrade (surname Bian) to flee. Overwhelmed with guilt for having vouched for Liu, Jiang tearfully carried Zhao into the Lü Family's hut.

The midnight commotion woke the vegetable garden's owners. Terrified by the bloodied men in Japanese uniforms, Zhao reassured the family: "We're anti-Japanese fighters. Don't fear—we mean no harm…" The matriarch and her daughter applied flour paste to his wounds and bandaged them. As Jiang insisted on carrying him away, Zhao handed over documents and repeated his order: Leave. Now.

Guided by Zhang Xiwei, Japanese officer Anazawa Takeo and a large force cautiously surrounded the hut. Finding no resistance, they stormed in, loaded the unconscious Zhao and Wang onto sleds, and hauled them to a nearby shed for interrogation, hoping to extract last-minute intelligence. Zhao's defiance never wavered. When offered food by puppet officers, he snarled, "I will not eat the rice of Manchukuo!" As Japanese and collaborators neared, he spat, "Stay back—your stench sickens me!" He endured agony in silence. When Wang Yongxiao cried out in pain, Zhao growled, "Does wailing ease the pain? Stand firm, soldier." [4]

Over a decade later, war criminal Tanoi Hisajiro confessed in a written statement: "During the interrogation, the general roared, 'I will say nothing to Japanese imperialism!' He adamantly refused to answer any questions." A report from the puppet Sanjiang Provincial Police Department noted: "Zhao Shangzhi survived for about eight hours after his critical injury. During this time, he identified himself as Zhao Shangzhi and rebuked the police officers: 'Are you not also Chinese? Now you betray your nation. My death alone means little—why interrogate a dying man?' He then fell silent, glaring sidelong at his captors. He uttered no sound of pain, embodying the unyielding defiance of a legendary commander." [5]

From the moment Zhao joined the anti-Japanese resistance, he had prepared for martyrdom. During his stay with "Old Mother Lü" (Lü Liangshi), a matriarch of the resistance, he taught her daughter—child league member Lü Fenglan—songs like *The Soldier's Ballad* and *Release the Swine.* He once told her: "Learn these well, little sister. We may not live long, but you will. Sing these songs far and wide. Preserve them for posterity—they are history itself." From Yang Jingyu to Li Yanping and Zhao Shangzhi, countless high-ranking commanders perished directly or indirectly at the hands of traitors. One cannot help but ask: Why were there so many collaborators in China?

When the king favors a slender waist, the court starves.

The aforementioned account of Chiang Kai-shek providing pay to Japanese-collaborating puppet troops, hosting Zhang Lanfeng—the leader of the largest pro-Japanese puppet force—for meals and photographs, pardoning nearly a million puppet soldiers with a single order after Japan's surrender, incorporating them into the Nationalist Army, and even promoting traitors like Xie Wendong and Li Huatang (former commanders of the Eighth and Ninth Armies of the Northeast Anti-Japanese United

Army who surrendered to Japan) to the rank of general... Does this not reveal certain truths?

Zhao Shangzhi's death was extraordinarily brutal. At approximately 9 a.m. on February 12, 1942, his heart ceased beating at the age of 34. His life was marked by relentless hardship. In his short years, he was arrested and imprisoned three times by the enemy, enduring a total of five years and four months behind bars. He once faced a mock execution at a killing ground, was wrongly expelled from the Communist Party twice, stripped of his positions and authority three times, suffered three severe combat injuries that left him blind in one eye, and ultimately met a gruesome end: his head was savagely sawed off by the enemy, his body dumped into an icy river, leaving his remains dismembered. [6]

Though brief, Zhao Shangzhi's life was legendary and glorious. His fearless combat prowess struck terror into enemy hearts, while his heroic deeds inspired the people. He epitomized the ideals of the Chinese Communist Party and stands as a hero of the Chinese nation. Though his physical form departed too soon, his unyielding national spirit remains etched in the people's hearts. Though his Party membership was unjustly revoked for years, his boundless loyalty to the Party and unwavering faith will forever be recorded in history.

I have long wished to pen a few words mourning Zhao Shangzhi's heroic sacrifice, yet struggled for days to find adequate expression. Suddenly, I recalled the eulogy Zhao himself wrote on January 28, 1938, to honor martyrs of the Third Army Headquarters of the Northeast Anti-Japanese United Army. Its words resonate profoundly with his own life, so I excerpt them below:

> My beloved comrades, there are those who perished in battle by
> charging ahead fearlessly into the fray, and those who fell due to

miscalculations of military strategy. All these are but heroic sacrifices for our nation and people! With drops of hot blood staining the battlefield, they extinguished the ambitions of the Japanese invaders, steadfastly striving to recover the four northeastern provinces to fulfill their lifelong aspirations. How magnificent! Their might shook all of Manchuria. How valiant! They sent the Japanese foes fleeing in terror. May their fragrant names endure through eternity, while their vanguard sacrifices blaze the path for comrades. How admirable is the great man who lays down his life for his country! We vow to fight for the liberation of the Chinese nation, wielding an indomitable spirit that sweeps across Manchuria. How bitterly grievous! Our comrades' courageous deeds on the blood-soaked battlefield. Ah, the pain! The nation remains unredeemed as they depart first, their unfulfilled vows lingering beneath the springs of the netherworld. How tragic! Though our stalwart warriors have nearly all shed their lifeblood, their frozen corpses still glare at the enemy. Yet the martyrs' fragrance of honor shall never fade... [7]

66. The Greatest Threat Lies Within

The history of the Northeast Anti-Japanese United Army (Northeast Anti-Japanese United Army) proves that, in a sense, its most dangerous enemies were not the Japanese puppet troops armed to the teeth on the battlefield, but the traitors within its own ranks. These turncoats, having long operated inside the organization, knew exactly where the resistance forces were most vulnerable and how to strike in ways the Anti-Japanese United Army could hardly withstand.

From the winter of 1937 to the summer of 1938, during the brutal years of relentless enemy encirclement campaigns, Hu Guochen, An Guangxun, and Cheng Bin defected to the enemy one after another, plunging Yang

Jingyu and the First Route Army into grave peril. As the chief of staff, An Guangxun possessed intimate knowledge of the army's equipment and military strategies. Hu Guochen, the head of the logistics department, knew the locations of countless hidden supply depots. With the widespread establishment of Japanese-controlled "collective villages", the destruction of these depots severed the lifeline of the Anti-Japanese United Army.

Yet compared to Cheng Bin—former commander of the First Division of the First Army—the threats posed by An Guangxun and Hu Guochen paled in comparison. Cheng Bin's treachery was catastrophic because he knew every route, operational pattern, and tactical style of the commanders within the First Army. Merely sitting at a desk, he could predict which division or regiment commander would take which path and what tactics they would employ. For this reason, Yang Jingyu swiftly reorganized the military structure, transforming divisions into front armies, and immediately led the main force northward. This decisive strategic move proved both bold and correct.

As Yang Jingyu led the First Route Army headquarters and its Guard Brigade through the regions of Ji'an, Mengjiang, Huadian, and Changbai, they were relentlessly pursued and ambushed by large forces of Japanese puppet troops. Enemy airplanes circled overhead, while motor vehicles and cavalry units charged wildly on the ground. The journey was marked by constant skirmishes. When the enemy detected the First Route Army's intent to advance northward, they mobilized 13 enemy units totaling nearly 10,000 troops, encircling Yang's forces—numbering just over 400 soldiers—in the mountainous terrain of Linjiang's Chagou Valley. The inner ring of the encirclement comprised four units led by commanders such as Fusen and Niu Tian, totaling over 1,500 soldiers, who boasted of setting up an "iron wall" formation to ensure total annihilation.

The Battle of Chagou raged from dawn until dusk. The valley's highest peak, held by the First Front Army of the First Route Army, served as a strategic stronghold. Whoever controlled this vantage point could dominate the battlefield, sparking ferocious clashes between the two sides. Enemy aircraft conducted reconnaissance and directed ground assaults, while at the height of the fighting, combatants were separated by as little as 50 meters.

During the battle, turncoat Cheng Bin led his defector unit in the attacks. In truth, without Cheng Bin's intimate knowledge of the Anti-Japanese United Army's tactics, the enemy could never have trapped the guerrillas in Chagou. When Cheng's forces launched psychological warfare by shouting surrender appeals, Yang Jingyu ordered the "Iron Blood Youth Corps" to select over 20 singers to form a counter-propaganda team. The young soldiers climbed atop rocky outcrops, chanting slogans like "Chinese don't fight Chinese!" and "Save your bullets for the Japanese!" while singing patriotic resistance songs. Their solemn and impassioned voices echoed through the valley, shaking Chagou to its core. Soon, the surrender cries from Cheng's ranks fell silent, and gunfire dwindled.

As the battle for the valley's strategic peak intensified, Yang Jingyu instructed his troops to hold fire until the enemy closed within 100 meters, maximizing defensive efficiency. During the 13th enemy assault, Commander Park Xianfeng of the Third Regiment of the Guard Brigade was fatally struck by gunfire. Yang Jingyu rushed through artillery fire to the Third Regiment's position, cradling Park's body in anguish. He urged his soldiers to hold the line, avenge their commander, and slaughter as many foes as possible. The heroic Third Regiment ultimately held the vital high ground, securing the fate of the entire army.

As night fell, the gunfire ceased. Bonfires lit up the surrounding ridges, gully mouths, and peaks like Sifangdingzi, signaling that the enemy had tightened their encirclement. The Japanese boasted that "all units are maintaining surveillance within 50 to 150 meters of the enemy front," foreshadowing an even fiercer assault at dawn. The southeastern flank showed fewer fires, while the southern direction lay eerily silent. Based on the enemy's combat patterns observed that day, Yang Jingyu deduced that heavy forces lay in ambush there. To the northwest, where the terrain was steepest, bonfires blazed most densely, accompanied by sporadic gunfire—a ruse to mask their weakest point.

Yang Jingyu declared that breaking through the encirclement required action in the predawn hours, hinging on two words: "Ferocity" and "Speed." They must carve a path through blood and fire. The troops were ordered to abandon all non-essentials and advance light.

Yang Jingyu assembled an assault team from elite members of the Guard Brigade and the Iron Blood Youth Corps. Led by Huang Haifeng, political commissar of the First Regiment (who spoke Japanese), and Park Sung-chol, commander of the Machine Gun Company, the team was tasked with breaching the enemy's northwestern defenses. A platoon from the Machine Gun Company and a squad from the Iron Blood Youth Corps would then suppress the second enemy line, while the remaining forces formed the third echelon, with the First and Third Regiments covering the rear.

The Iron Blood Youth Corps—a unit within the First Army composed entirely of teenagers aged 14 to 17—had been personally mentored by Yang Jingyu since its formal establishment in mid-August 1938. Despite their youth, these 50 fighters displayed unmatched bravery, becoming a core force of the army. Decades later, Wang Chuansheng, then the corps' political instructor, recalled: "After a day of encirclement and half a night of bluster, the enemy thought all was quiet and fell asleep. Our assault team crept close. At Commissar Huang's signal, we fanned out, bayonets fixed, and lunged at the sleeping foes. Within minutes, dozens were stabbed to death. The rest fled in panic, firing wildly. We raked them with machine guns as they scrambled. The enemy camp descended into chaos—soldiers ran amok, trampling their own lines. Two platoons charged in separate directions, widening the breach. The Machine Gun Company and the Iron Blood Youth Corps broke through first, followed by the main force in orderly ranks. We raced over 20 li (10 kilometers) without stopping."

The Battle of Chagou Breakout stands as one of the most perilous and fiercely contested engagements in the history of the Northeast Anti-Japanese United Army, a legendary case study in guerrilla warfare. Even the enemy grudgingly admitted: "The stubbornly resistant and composed 'Yang Bandits' [Yang's forces] calmly directed their troops while plotting an escape." This battle shattered the enemy's meticulously crafted 20-day campaign to annihilate the First Route Army headquarters and its core units, turning imminent disaster into survival. The fight claimed the life of one enemy regimental commander, killed or wounded 80 enemy soldiers, and seized over 20 rifles [8], showcasing Yang Jingyu's military genius. The baffled Japanese lamented: "Had Yang Jingyu sprouted wings and flown away?"

After the traitor Cheng Bin's unwavering defection to the Japanese, Yang Jingyu found himself repeatedly cornered. Determined to punish this collaborator, in November 1938, Yang led his troops to camp near Dongganfanpen ("Dry Rice Basin"). Cheng Bin's "suppression force," tracking their movements, attempted a sneak attack on the First Route Army headquarters. Yang dispatched a small detachment with strict orders to feign defeat convincingly. True to plan, the unit "fiercely" engaged Cheng's troops before "retreating in disarray," luring Cheng into pursuit toward Dongganfanpen.

The "Ganfanpen" was a labyrinthine primal forest where travelers often lost their way and perished, earning it the local nickname

"Mengganfan" ("Suffocating Rice Pot"). Eager for glory, Cheng Bin chased recklessly until he noticed anomalies: the "retreating" former comrades had abandoned nothing of value, and their withdrawal, though chaotic, followed a hidden order. Realizing this was Yang Jingyu's trap, Cheng broke into a cold sweat, abandoned several corpses, and fled in haste [9].

The greatest fear in warfare is facing an opponent who knows you inside out, and for the Northeast Anti-Japanese United Army, the worst threat was betrayal by their own. Cheng Bin's defection was like stepping in dog shit that couldn't be wiped clean for the First Route Army—a lingering hazard that might trip them up at any moment. Thus, even a minor victory over Cheng Bin should not be underestimated, as it at least forced him to keep his distance temporarily.

Whether Cheng Bin had leaked Yang Jingyu's whereabouts remained unclear, but in December, when Yang led his troops to Huadian's Dashuhezi, a combined force of 500 Japanese soldiers from the Kikuchi Unit and puppet Jing'an Army closed in. On the first day, the enemy, confident in their superior numbers and firepower, pitched tents and slept soundly, planning to resume their "mopping-up" campaign the next day. Yang Jingyu decided to strike first, launching a nighttime raid dubbed the "Touching the Fire Piles" operation in historical records—a name derived from the 12 bonfires lit in front of each enemy tent.

Organizing his men into 12 groups of 10 soldiers each, each armed with a machine gun, Yang emphasized his usual tactics: "ferocity" and "speed." The assault began at midnight. Night combat and close-quarters fighting were the Anti-Japanese forces' specialties. Twelve machine guns unleashed a barrage of fire on the sleeping enemy. As flames engulfed the tents, Yang led his troops onto the river embankment, launching a pincer attack from the elevated position. The battle left over 100 enemy troops dead. The First Route Army seized one machine gun and various supplies, suffering 15 casualties. The next day, humiliated and vengeful, the enemy sent a reconnaissance plane to scour the area. Yang Jingyu ordered his men to train over a dozen machine guns skyward. When the aircraft swooped low, they opened fire in unison, sending it plummeting into the Songhua River with a trail of black smoke. [10]

After establishing Changbai Mountain as a stronghold, Yang Jingyu led his troops in launching relentless strikes against the enemy. His flexible and unpredictable tactics left the Japanese and puppet forces in constant disarray. The staggering losses inflicted on the enemy sowed terror among their ranks. In March 1939, Yang's forces dealt a devastating blow at the Muqihe Lumberyard. The assault wiped out over a dozen puppet forest police officers, including their commander Li Haishan, and forced nearly 100 enemy soldiers to surrender. The lumber stockpiled for enemy transport was set ablaze, burning for an entire day and night. The First Route Army seized over 30 rifles, more than 200 horses and cattle, and vast quantities of supplies such as grain, salt, and cloth. Additionally, over 70 lumber workers joined the ranks of the resistance. Enraged, the enemy vilified Yang Jingyu as "the cancer of Manchukuo's security." [11]

Meanwhile, other divisions of the First Route Army achieved significant victories:

The First Front Army, under Cao Yafan and Yi Junshan, advanced into the former base areas of the martyred Wang Fengge and along the Yalu River. During the spring-summer transition of 1939, they engaged the enemy over 20 times, eliminating more than 100 troops.

The Second Front Army, commanded by Kim Il Sung, annihilated over 50 Japanese soldiers, including a high-ranking officer, in June 1939. They captured 4 light machine guns and over 100 rifles.

The Third Front Army, established later under the leadership of Chen Hanzhang (commander of the Fifth Division of the Second Army), distinguished itself through multiple campaigns. In August 1938, Chen's forces killed or wounded over 200 Japanese and puppet troops in the Battle of Tokyo City (Dongjingcheng)—a rare feat in the history of Northeast China's resistance. [12]

In July 1939, the Third Front Army was formally organized under the guidance of Wei Zhengmin, with Chen Hanzhang appointed as its commander. The following month, Wei and Chen orchestrated an ambush against the Japanese "Mopping-Up Unit" led by Miyamoto and the puppet "Jiandao Special Forces." The battle claimed over 80 enemy lives, including Miyamoto himself, and yielded substantial spoils: 2 grenade launchers, 3 light machine guns, 40 rifles, and other military supplies.

In September, Chen Hanzhang ambushed the Japanese Matsushima Unit, killing over 80 soldiers, including Captain Matsushima. Among the casualties were more than 10 Japanese officers. Nine enemy trucks were incinerated, and the Third Front Army seized one heavy machine gun, two light machine guns, three grenade launchers, and a cache of other firearms and military supplies. The Third Front Army suffered over 20 casualties in the operation. [13] The enemy, deeply shaken by Chen's prowess, labeled him and his forces as "the most active and formidable insurgents in the Dongbiandao region during this period." [14] Local civilians celebrated, chanting: "When the Japanese devils venture out, they meet Chen Hanzhang—that's their curse!"

Chen Hanzhang, born in 1913 in Dunhua, Jilin Province, joined the Jilin National Salvation Army after the September 18 Incident and became a member of the Chinese Communist Party in 1932. A man of unyielding resolve, Chen once sustained a gunshot wound to his left leg during combat. With no medical supplies available, he ordered a medic to probe the wound with a cloth strip. Hesitant to cause further pain without anesthesia, the medic refused. Chen then took matters into his own hands: gripping a chopstick, he threaded a strip of white cloth through the through-and-through wound, pulling it out the other side as dark blood gushed. Not a groan escaped him, though sweat poured down his face. After repeatedly dragging the cloth to remove necrotic flesh and pus, he instructed the medic to cleanse the wound with hot water and bandage it, declaring: "A festering wound fears the resolute. Show it no mercy, and it'll surrender. This little injury is nothing."

Chen Hanzhang kept a diary, which fell into Japanese hands after his death. Among its entries:

> April 21: Rose early. My leg is swollen and throbbing with pain.

> Began marching to the rear after 6 a.m., resting at 2 p.m. Covered only 20 li (10 kilometers) on foot. Light rain soaked through, the cold biting deep._

Despite his agonizing leg injury, he had trudged 20 li—how could the cold not seep into his bones? Yet, as Chen himself declared, "A festering wound fears the resolute."

True to his words, his diary entry from May 14 reads:

The wound has fully healed. Only the bullet hole's scar remains.。

By May 29, he noted:

> The bandage was removed today. The grievous injuries sustained in the struggle for the people's liberation are glorious revolutionary scars. Today marks my full recovery. This chapter is closed.

> Sixty-three scars stand as eternal memorials. (He bore 63 wounds over his lifetime.) [15]

In December 1940, Chen Hanzhang was encircled by enemy forces. During the battle, his right hand and chest were severely wounded, yet he leaned against a tree and continued fighting with his left hand. When the enemy closed in and wrested his gun away, Chen glared at them, hurling furious curses. The brutal Japanese soldiers gouged out his eyes with a dagger, ending his life at the age of 27. The enemy severed his head and sent it to "Hsinking" (present-day Changchun). [16]

Earlier, on April 18, 1939, the commander of the Kwantung Army's Second Independent Garrison issued orders to prioritize the "extermination" of Yang Jingyu and his forces. The garrison's Pacification Guidelines emphasized:

Under the direct command of the defense headquarters, pursue Yang, the bandit leader, relentlessly. Eliminate him without territorial restrictions. Employ swift, flexible tactics, prioritizing night raids and surprise attacks to ensure his capture. Four days prior, Japanese-puppet authorities had listed Yang Jingyu as the "top target" in their Pacification Guidelines, offering a bounty of 10,000 yuan for his death—an astronomical sum reflecting both their bone-deep hatred and soul-shaking fear of him.

To the Japanese, Yang was not just a nemesis to be destroyed but a spectral terror to be exorcized for their own peace of mind.

What made Yang Jingyu most hated and feared by the enemy was his ruthless targeting of Japan's most vital and vulnerable interests—its plunder of Northeast China's resources.

After the September 18 Incident, Japanese "national resource survey teams" scoured the Dongbiandao region to map mineral deposits, particularly iron, coal, and rare metals critical for wartime production. Their reports exclaimed: "Dongbiandao—Manchuria's treasury!"

How could the resource-starved islanders have imagined such abundance? The mineral riches of the Northeast—from the century-old Korean pines of Changbai Mountain to the coal veins of Hegang and Liaoyuan, the golden soybeans, and pearl-like rice—were stripped away via railways to Korea, then shipped to Japan.

These were China's treasures, stolen at bayonet-point without a single penny paid. When Yang Jingyu arrived in Ji'an, the Japanese were feverishly constructing the Tonghua-Ji'an Railway, designed to connect with the Pyongyang-Manpo line in Korea to the east and the Siping-Meihekou Railway to the north. This artery would accelerate their looting.

In March 1938, Yang Jingyu deployed what the enemy deemed "using a butcher's knife to slaughter a chicken": leading over 500 troops from his headquarters, he launched a three-pronged assault near the Laoling Tunnel, 71 kilometers from Tonghua. The targets included the construction site of the East Asia Civil Engineering Corporation at the tunnel's western entrance, the Shiyidaogou Power Station, and the Shierdaogou Supply Depot.

The raid killed or captured 12 Japanese garrison soldiers and puppet railway guards. Twelve buildings—including the engineering office—and vast quantities of construction materials were incinerated. Machinery, electrical systems, and infrastructure were obliterated. All forced laborers were liberated, while 12 sacks of rice, 800 bags of flour, and other supplies were seized. The Japanese-puppet regime suffered losses totaling 200,000 yen, branding the attack "the most colossal chapter in Dongbiandao's pacification history."

Before the Japanese could recover from their wounds, Yang Jingyu launched a relentless series of attacks along the Tonghua-Ji'an Railway and its surrounding areas. From early June to late July 1938, he mobilized over

600 troops in a large-scale operation divided into three columns. They simultaneously struck the construction site of the East Asia Civil Engineering Corporation at the Tuzikou Tunnel, as well as bridge construction sites at the 11th and 12th Laoling River sections. The assault killed 10 enemy guards, captured 80 others, and reduced the facilities to ashes. Dozens of liberated laborers joined the Anti-Japanese forces, inflicting direct losses of 220,000 yen on the enemy. Japanese-puppet authorities lamented this as "the bloodiest and most tragic day in the Tonghua-Ji'an Railway's construction history." [17]

Originally slated for completion in March 1939, the Tonghua-Ji'an Railway was delayed until September due to Yang's relentless sabotage— a six-month setback. Six months of uninterrupted rail transport could have shipped countless resources to Japan. The impact was not merely economic but also military and political. This blow grew even more critical in July 1939, when the United States terminated the Treaty of Commerce and Navigation with Japan, freezing Tokyo's access to American strategic supplies. Japan's desperation to plunder resources from Northeast China intensified, making Yang's railway sabotage campaigns a strategic masterstroke—a glorious chapter in the history of Northeast China's resistance.

Yang Jingyu himself recognized the significance of his forces' disruption. As Wei Zhengmin, Secretary of the South Manchuria Provincial Committee of the CCP and Deputy Commander of the First Route Army, reported to the CCP Central Delegation:

"By severing the Manchuria-Korea border and launching ceaseless assaults, we forced the Japanese invaders to fight on two fronts. In response, the enemy diverted approximately 10,000 troops from their main forces to our operational zones, aggressively targeting us." [18]

Under the orders of Japanese Commander Miura to "eliminate the bandit leader Yang", Wang Zhiyou, commander of the puppet Eighth Military District, mobilized 10,000 troops—including the puppet Mixed 1st and 3rd Brigades and the 6th Infantry Regiment—under the supervision of Japanese advisor Colonel Ritsu Mitsu. Their mission: to annihilate the First Route Army operating in the Andong and Tonghua regions. The situation escalated rapidly.

67. Split Forces, Split Again, Split Once More

Yang Jingyu and Wei Zhengmin convened a meeting to strategize. Some comrades proposed retreating to Soviet territory to preserve their forces, given the overwhelming numerical superiority of the enemy. Yang rejected this outright: "We are the Northeast Anti-Japanese United Army. If we flee to the Soviet Union, what right do we have to keep that name? Will the Japanese devils just pack up and leave if we run away?"

Others suggested relocating the First Route Army headquarters deep into Changbai Mountain while dispersing remaining troops to harass the enemy. Though acknowledging their concern for his safety, Yang firmly refused: "How can we call it 'resistance' if we abandon the fight? Hiding in the mountains won't drive out the Japanese. By holding our ground here in Huinan, Huadian, Mengjiang, and Fusong, we tie down enemy forces, easing pressure on the national resistance effort inland. Even our small force can pin down part of their strength."

The debate grew heated, Yang's voice rising with conviction. Ultimately, consensus was reached: No retreat to the Soviet Union. No hiding in the mountains. They would stand firm in the heart of enemy territory.

Yang Jingyu's strategic thinking and decisions were closely linked to his deep study and understanding of Mao Zedong's series of resistance war theories, particularly the concept of containing the Japanese Kwantung Army through Northeastern resistance. According to recollections by his aide Huang Shengfa, Yang Jingyu always carried a mimeographed booklet titled *On Protracted War* and frequently read it with great interest. Especially during his recovery from a gunshot wound to his right leg in the spring-summer of 1939, he gained profound insights into the treatise's arguments: "Every enemy soldier killed, every bullet expended, and every hostile force pinned down prevents them from advancing southward through strategic passes..." This period of convalescence deepened his comprehension of these strategic principles.

A leading cadre of the Communist Party, isolated behind enemy lines and severed from the Party's central leadership, Yang Jingyu nonetheless conscientiously studied the Party's principles and policies, prioritizing the revolutionary cause above his own safety. His profound political consciousness deserves deep reflection and emulation by every Party member and cadre.

In short, Yang Jingyu was not merely a fearless warrior willing to shed blood, nor simply a commander of exceptional military talent. What truly distinguished him was his unwavering political dedication and strategic vision for the broader revolutionary struggle.

How significant was this containment effect?

Following the betrayal of Cheng Bin, the First Route Army was reorganized into a structure directly under the Route Army command, comprising three Front Armies: The 1st Front Army: Approximately 250 troops (August 1938) [19]; The 2nd Front Army: Around 350 troops (November 1938) [20]; The 3rd Front Army: Roughly 300 troops (July 1939) [21]. The Route Army's direct units included the Guard Brigade (over 500 troops in August 1938) [22], army headquarters units, the Youth Iron-Blooded Detachment, and others, totaling around 1,500 troops. By May 1939, the Third Route Army of the Northeast Anti-Japanese United Army had a total strength of just over 800 troops [23], and the Second Route Army's situation was no better than the First or Third. By 1939, the entire Northeast Anti-Japanese United Army numbered only a few thousand troops, scattered across isolated regions without coordination. Yet this modest force of 2,000–3,000 soldiers—with Yang Jingyu's contingent of roughly 1,500 as the core—managed to contain a staggering number of enemy troops. During the Nofu Major Suppression Campaign from October 1939 to March 1940, the Japanese mobilized 75,000 troops [24].

Do not assume that the Northeast Anti-Japanese United Army (NEAJU) contributed only politically and spiritually. In reality, its military and strategic role in containing enemy forces was equally monumental—this was the NEAJU's profound contribution to China's War of Resistance.

Though small in number, we struck at the heart of your occupied "Manchukuo," like Sun Wukong infiltrating the belly of Princess Iron Fan, targeting your most vulnerable core. Though poorly armed, we fought fearlessly—outnumbered yet undaunted, trading ten lives for one. With our blood and defiance, we shattered your imperial ambitions. We were battle-hardened veterans, each skilled as commandos, waging guerrilla warfare on home terrain where every river and ravine served as our ally. We severed your logistical arteries, incinerated plundered resources—timber, grain, strategic supplies—leaving your war machine crippled.

Even when driven into the Soviet Union, we crossed back to strike, to surveil, to expose your every weakness. We stung like relentless hornets, sacrificing ourselves to torment your occupation forces, denying you rest or respite. You were a rabid wolf, but we harried you into exhaustion. This was Mao Zedong's vision of guerrilla warfare.

In their decades of colonial rule over occupied territories, the Japanese had "accumulated rich experience," relying heavily on collaborators (hanjian) while employing a core tactic: "decapitation"—targeting symbolic leaders to crush resistance. The Northeast Anti-Japanese United Army (NEAJU) was a blood-stained banner of defiance, with figures like Yang Jingyu, Zhao Shangzhi, Zhou Baozhong, and Li Zhaolin as its standard-bearers. Yang Jingyu stood as the foremost among them. To eliminate the First Route Army and capture Yang, the Japanese Kwantung Army's 669th Division commander, General Nofu Koshichiro, concentrated over 75,000 Japanese and puppet troops—triple the force deployed in prior "suppression campaigns"—against Yang's forces. This operation, dubbed the Nofu Major Suppression Campaign (also known as the Southeastern Pacification or Three-Province Joint Suppression), aimed squarely at Yang Jingyu.

It must be acknowledged that the greatest threat during the campaign was not the ruthless Japanese troops—who were largely blind and deaf without collaborators—but the 10 puppet police battalions (each 200–300 strong) under the command of Kishitani Ryūichirō, a "China expert" and chief of the puppet Tonghua Province Police. These units, including the notorious Cheng Bin Battalion, were composed of former NEAJU fighters, defectors from guerrilla groups, or volunteers—traitors who knew the resistance's inner workings. Authorized to pursue across provincial borders, they executed Nofu's strategy: dividing three puppet provinces into five zones for systematic "stomping" and "combing" searches. Air reconnaissance, tracker dogs, surrender-inducing "propaganda squads," and spy networks operated in tandem. The campaign demanded a relentless, "tick-like" tactical style—clinging, biting, and draining the enemy's resolve.

The tick (Ixodidae), known colloquially in Northeast China as the "grass crawler" (caopazi), has a notorious trait: it silently buries its head into human skin. The more you strike or pull at it, the deeper it digs, preferring to have its body torn apart rather than retreat. As a vector for pathogens, it transmits debilitating or fatal diseases like forest encephalitis and hemorrhagic fever. One must grudgingly admire the Japanese military's grotesque imagination in likening their tactics to this parasite. Any unit deemed insufficiently aggressive in pursuing the Anti-Japanese United Army (NEAJU) faced harsh reprisals.

At a meeting in Huadian, General Nofu berated commanders for their lackluster suppression efforts. Mori Yutaka, the puppet Jilin Province police chief, collapsed from a heart attack induced by the stress and died on the spot.

For the NEAJU—adept at maneuvering like "fish in a forest sea"—neither the "tick-like" harassment nor the "combing" tactics posed the gravest threat. They could still outmaneuver confused enemy units dragged through the wilderness. The real crisis lay in the destruction of their hidden supply caches by traitors like Cheng Bin and Hu Guochen. History has proven time and again: severing supply lines severs an army's lifeline. Alongside the Nofu Major Suppression Campaign, the Japanese imposed draconian policies in NEAJU-active regions: daily necessities were banned from markets, and purchasing over 3 jin (1.5 kg) of salt, 2 bags of flour, or 5 pairs of rubber shoes required permits issued by puppet police stations.

Among the ten puppet police units composed of traitors and collaborators, another formidable threat was the Cui Zhoufeng Battalion. After the September 18th Incident (1931), Cui Zhoufeng had once fought alongside the First Army of the Northeast Anti-Japanese United Army (NEAJU) and collaborated with Wang Fengge to resist the Japanese. After defecting to the enemy, he, like Cheng Bin, became a lethal adversary with intimate knowledge of the NEAJU's operations. Kishitani Ryūichirō deployed both Cheng Bin's and Cui Zhoufeng's units as spearhead forces tasked specifically with hunting Yang Jingyu.

It must be acknowledged that the Japanese strategy of using NEAJU defectors to combat the NEAJU was devastatingly effective. In early December 1939, Yang Jingyu had barely shaken off pursuing enemies when Cui Zhoufeng's unit caught up, trailing a full battalion of puppet troops. Yang's forces engaged Cui's unit in a fierce five- to six-hour battle, suffering six fatalities and one captured soldier.

The situation grew increasingly dire, primarily due to starvation. Shen Fengshan, a surviving NEAJU veteran, recalled that the enemy rotated pursuit teams—resting by day and night shifts—leaving the guerrillas no respite. Soldiers could not lie down to sleep, managing only 20–30 minutes of fitful rest. Fires were forbidden to avoid detection. Worse still, traitors like Cheng Bin had destroyed their hidden grain stores, forcing troops to subsist on tree bark. Even with money, supplies were unobtainable. Exhausted and starving, many soldiers collapsed mid-march, never to rise again.

In early January 1940, Yang Jingyu made a critical decision. He divided his forces once again: Han Renhe, political commissar of the Guard Brigade, and Huang Haifeng, political commissar of the 1st Regiment, were tasked with leading 60 troops northward, while Yang himself remained in the Xigang area with over 200 soldiers from the machine gun company's

1st Platoon, the Special Guard Platoon, the 4th Company of the Guard Brigade's 1st Regiment, and the Youth Iron-Blooded Detachment. Clearly, Yang's repeated divisions of troops aimed to shield other units from danger.

Yang had stayed in Xigang to rendezvous with Quan Guang, the First Route Army's supply director, to resolve urgent shortages of food and winter clothing. However, after 20 days of waiting, Quan Guang never arrived. Prolonged confinement in this narrow, perilous zone left Yang's forces trapped in a strategic death trap—a tactical misstep. Quan Guang's absence stemmed from his wavering loyalty; he soon defected to the enemy.

With supplies severed, Yang dispatched small units to forage for food, but their movements exposed their tracks, drawing encirclement by puppet police suppression units and puppet cavalry regiments. Days of relentless combat ensued. Amid this crisis, Fang Zhensheng, commander of the Guard Brigade, was captured and executed while gathering provisions. Shortly after, in late January, Ding Shoulong, staff officer of the Guard Brigade's 1st Regiment, was captured and betrayed Yang, divulging all military plans to the enemy.

If Cheng Bin's betrayal in the summer of 1938 had severely disrupted the First Route Army's operations, Ding Shoulong's treason now plunged it into existential crisis. Han Renhe and Huang Haifeng's northward diversion initially succeeded in luring enemy forces, but Ding's confession nullified the strategy. The Japanese ceased pursuing Han and Huang, instead concentrating all forces to annihilate Yang Jingyu. This underscores how a single traitor privy to high-level secrets could inflict damage equal to two elite diversionary forces.

The enemy marshaled elite Japanese units under commanders such as Daihara, Arima, Obama, and Arimasa, alongside the puppet army's 1st Brigade and 3rd Infantry Regiment, as well as "spearhead forces" led by traitors like Cheng Bin and Cui Zhoufeng, to encircle Yang Jingyu's troops in a tightening noose.

By late January 1940, the valleys lay shrouded in icy fog, visibility reduced to mere meters. Amid the haze, Yang's forces clashed with the enemy in chaotic combat, inflicting casualties but suffering heavy losses— around 70 killed or wounded. Through repeated skirmishes, Yang identified a weak point in the encirclement and fought his way out.

The enemy understood the stakes: Yang Jingyu's prestige within the Communist Party extended far beyond Manchuria. As early as 1938, at the Seventh National Congress of the Chinese Communist Party, Yang had been elected as one of 25 Central Committee members, ranked 24th—after Chen Yi but ahead of Gao Gang [25]. His prominence was further cemented at the Sixth Plenary Session of the Sixth Central Committee, where Comrade Mao Zedong proposed sending a tribute message to Yang and the Northeast Anti-Japanese United Army (NEAJU), a move that rattled Japanese occupiers. Toppling this towering banner of resistance, they reasoned, would achieve more than annihilating legions of troops, sparing the need for recurring large-scale "suppression campaigns." If Yang escaped now, they feared, his mere call to arms would rally thousands anew under the anti-Japanese flag.

Political Instructor Wang Chuansheng of the "Iron-Blooded Youth Corps" proposed selecting over 20 robust young soldiers equipped with one or two machine guns to escort Yang Jingyu to a safe hiding place, insisting that preserving this symbolic leader was crucial not just for Yang personally but for the entire Northeast Anti-Japanese United Army.

Yang Jingyu immediately criticized the suggestion, demanding why Wang would have him abandon his troops. Wang hastily explained that Japanese forces had invested heavily in targeting headquarters that year:

"Our sacrifices matter little. With you alive, there's hope for the resistance." Visibly displeased, Yang retorted, "You fear no death—do you think I do? We share life or death alike. My presence binds this army together. Without me, it would scatter. Only by staying can we sustain this fight against the Japanese."

Thereafter, no one dared suggest Yang's withdrawal. By late January 1940, after a skirmish left Wang Chuansheng with a shattered right calf bone, Yang sighed and ordered a soldier to evacuate him to safety. Yang's forces then dwindled to fewer than 60 men.

The unrelenting crucible of war tested their resolve. In early February, Special Guard Platoon Chief Zhang Xiufeng defected to the enemy, surrendering firearms, confidential documents, and funds—a betrayal that exposed Yang's whereabouts. The next day, Japanese forces under commanders Watanabe, Yoshimori, and Uhatake, alongside puppet police units led by traitor Cheng Bin, launched an air-supported assault. Despite overwhelming odds, Yang miraculously broke through the encirclement. Enraged, Cheng Bin spearheaded the pursuit, leveraging his intimate knowledge of Yang's tactics to rediscover the unit. After another bloody clash, by February 7 (Lunar New Year's Eve), only 15 fighters remained at Yang Jingyu's side.

It must be acknowledged that amidst overwhelming enemy encirclement, Yang Jingyu repeatedly broke through sieges with his outnumbered and ill-equipped forces—a testament to both his masterful guerrilla tactics and command brilliance. Yet tragically, even as Japanese forces reeled in confusion, the traitor Cheng Bin managed to track him down again. By February 12, only seven men remained with Yang, four of whom were wounded. Decades later, Yang's former bodyguard Huang Shengfa still vividly recalled how Yang insisted the four injured men leave:

"The Commander said, 'The situation is critical. We must split up.'"

68. The revolution will always triumph!

None agreed to abandon him, pledging to live or die together.

Yang patiently reasoned: "Every survivor strengthens the revolution—what good comes from dying together?" He ordered Huang Shengfa to escort three wounded soldiers—Liu Futai, Old Sun, and frostbitten Hong Ruitai—back along their path to seek refuge and recover. Yang himself would press forward with guards Zhu Fanjian and Nie Donghua to regroup with troops.

Huang understood the cruel calculus: retreating offered relative safety as enemy forces surged ahead, while advancing meant near-certain peril. At this life-or-death juncture, Yang once again steered survival toward the wounded.

Clasping each man's hand in farewell, Yang declared: "Comrades, for the revolution's sake, we must endure to the end. Even in death, never yield! However dire, the revolution will prevail!" [26]

In truth, Yang's decision to divert enemy pursuit from his injured comrades marked his acceptance of martyrdom. The solemnity of those final handshakes and earnest exhortations revealed his resolve—he knew this parting was final.

No one wishes to die. When Yang Jingyu sacrificed himself, his two children were already over ten years old—meaning he had not returned home for more than a decade. Yang was a man of deep emotion and love for life. In quiet moments, he likely yearned for his wife and children, as evidenced by the harmonica found among his belongings. Yet in his heart, the mission of resisting Japan and saving the nation always took precedence.

He understood that the flower of victory demanded blood to water it and ashes to nourish its roots. On this perilous path to liberation, strewn with traps and minefields, someone had to lead the way through danger—and that someone, he believed, must be a member of the Chinese Communist Party. Did Communists suffer losses? Kangzhen veteran Jiang Dezhou often recalled Yang's answer: "The Commander always told us, 'Don't fear death in battle. If we die for our country, the next generation won't be enslaved. If we don't fear death, why fear hardship? If we all wait for others to act, who will save the nation? Once we drive the Japanese devils from China, we'll finally be masters of our own land." [27]

On February 15, Yang Jingyu—who had seemingly vanished from Japanese surveillance—was tracked down by collaborators like Cui Zhoufeng. Noticing fresh footprints, they speculated "bandits" might be found within half a mile, and their guess proved correct. Hundreds of enemy troops soon gave chase. Japanese puppet records chillingly describe Yang's final moments:

"Though starved for days, he ran astonishingly fast, arms swinging overhead, legs pumping like an ostrich in flight." In this desperate flight, Yang's superhuman endurance became both legend and epitaph—a final defiance against the machinery of oppression. [28]

By 3:00 PM, over 600 enemy troops had cornered Yang Jingyu and his two bodyguards on a mountain peak. A gunfight erupted at a distance of 300 meters. At this critical moment, Japanese Police Assistant Inspector Ito attempted to persuade Yang to surrender, shouting that escape was impossible and urging him to submit.

Yang feigned interest, demanding an immediate ceasefire and insisting Ito approach alone for negotiations. As the overconfident Ito stood up, Yang fired three rapid shots, grievously wounding him.

Cui Zhoufeng, eager to prove his loyalty to the Japanese, charged forward only to be struck in the thigh by Yang's bullets and collapse. In this clash, Yang's Mauser pistol killed one enemy and wounded six others before he broke free once more—though not without taking a bullet to his left arm.

Night fell. Exhausted from pursuing Yang since dawn, the 600-strong "suppression force" dwindled through attrition: 300, then 200, then 100 men. By 2:00 a.m. on the 16th, only 50 pursuers remained. Yang himself neared collapse—battling severe illness, starvation, and his wounded arm. What superhuman will drove him to defy such physiological limits remains unimaginable. [29]

The enemy's strategy ultimately prevailed. On February 18, when Yang sent guards Zhu Fanjian and Nie Donghua to procure food from a nearby village, traitors alerted the puppet police station. Both men died heroically in the ensuing firefight. Enemy troops recovered Yang's personal seal among their belongings.

That both guards left their fever-stricken, wounded commander simultaneously defies logic unless compelled by Yang's direct order. Amidst a landscape permeated with lethal threats, Yang likely refused to risk sending either man alone. Their dual departure—despite the heightened danger—speaks to his protective resolve, even as it sealed his isolation.

February 22 marked China's Lantern Festival. Yang Jingyu spent the night in a dilapidated shack, ravenous, his agonizing arm wound throbbing, his vision blurred. He knew he needed food to steady his hands on the rifle and sharpen his failing sight to align the gun's sights.

On the morning of the 23rd, Yang encountered four peasants gathering firewood. He spoke to them about resisting Japanese aggression. Recognizing the disheveled giant before them as a fighter against Japan, they urged, "You should surrender. 'Manchukuo' no longer executes those who yield."

Yang replied: "I am Chinese. My conscience forbids it. To surrender would betray the people." [30]

Though Yang often emphasized Communist ideals and revolutionary duty within the Party, he tailored his words to these peasants. Faced with their pragmatic plea to submit, his refusal rested not on political dogma but on universal principles: "I am Chinese—I cannot surrender to foreigners." He repeated "conscience" and "the people" as his anchors, framing resistance as a moral imperative.

The simplicity of his reasoning— "Chinese," "conscience," "the people"—strikes with profound force. In these words, lay no grand ideology, only the unyielding essence of a man who chose martyrdom over compromise, embodying the dignity of a nation refusing to kneel.

As soldiers, our fundamental duty is to safeguard our homeland and protect our people from foreign oppression and tyranny. When our nation is invaded and our compatriots suffer in misery, how can you abandon this sacred obligation? Where is your conscience? Your comrades fell under enemy gunfire, yet you exploit their blood to stain your "official cap of betrayal" – where is your conscience? You consume the grain grown by civilians, wear the shoes and cotton coats made by them, and recruit their precious sons into your ranks – how dare you surrender to the enemy for high positions and wealth? Have you no shame before our people? Has your conscience been devoured by dogs?

The very word "surrender" brings burning shame. Historical records recount how Yang Jingyu, the anti-Japanese resistance commander, maintained calm composure while patiently explaining patriotic principles to local farmers. Yet when the word "surrender" escaped their lips, his demeanor shifted abruptly. Visibly agitated, he passionately delivered these rebukes.

For centuries, "conscience" has served as the bedrock of moral judgment among ordinary Chinese people, intertwined with the sacred duty to honor one's promises.

Among the four farmers present, the leader was Zhao Tingxi, a puppet army squad leader. He initially agreed to Yang Jingyu's requests. However, upon encountering Japanese-collaborationist spy Li Zhengxin during his return, Zhao broke his pledge. Lured by substantial reward money, the pair betrayed Yang by reporting his location to a collaborationist police substation. This act of treachery would seal the fate of the legendary resistance fighter.

Based on Zhao Tingxi's description, the enemy concluded that the man in question was none other than Yang Jingyu. They dispatched five waves of "suppression squads," totaling nearly 200 men. Hearing the rumble of approaching vehicles, Yang realized the enemy had arrived. Later, during a post-capture "discussion forum" about Yang Jingyu, it was noted that the man who eight days prior had been described as "running with astonishing speed... like a sprinting ostrich" now bore no trace of that vigor. He was a gravely wounded man—his left arm shot through, his hands, feet, and face severely frostbitten, battling severe illness. Most crucially, he was on the brink of collapse from starvation. To maintain his ability to stand, he stuffed exposed cotton wadding from his padded coat into his mouth, chewing and swallowing it with mouthfuls of snow to trick his empty stomach into feeling full. Amid waves of surrender demands, Yang Jingyu answered only with gunfire.

At this "forum," the Japanese claimed they had not initially sought Yang Jingyu's death, hoping instead to "utilize his talents for beneficial purposes" through surrender. However, the *Tonghua Provincial Police Department Report on the Circumstances of Yang Jingyu's Shooting* states:

> "During the engagement, the suppression squads repeatedly eased their attacks to urge his surrender, but he showed no intention of compliance. Wielding a Mauser C96 pistol and a Colt Model 1903 pistol (types identified post-mortem), he persisted in fierce resistance." [31]

Yang Jingyu leaned against a large tree, firing at his assailants until he was struck approximately 20 minutes into the exchange. Crimson blood seeped into pristine snow. As the gunfire ceased, the snow of Mengjiang fell soundlessly.

At 16:30 on February 23, 1940, Yang Jingyu's heart stopped beating.

Enemy soldiers encircled the body of this "colossal bandit" who had once struck terror into their hearts. After a moment of bewildered silence, they erupted into cries of "Banzai!"—only to then break into muffled sobs.

A lingering question plagued them: Since February 15, when Yang had been essentially surrounded, and February 18, when his food supply was cut off—what had sustained him through those final days?

The enemy ordered an autopsy on Yang Jingyu's body. To their shock, his stomach and intestines contained no trace of food—only undigested grass roots, tree bark, and cotton wadding. Dr. Kim Won-sang, director of the People's Hospital, who was forced to perform the dissection, was deeply moved and secretly shed tears. [32]

What defines a true warrior? It cannot be measured by fleeting victories or defeats.

Under Yang Jingyu's command, the First Route Army of the Northeast Anti-Japanese United Forces waged an eight-year bloody struggle from 1932 to 1940. During this period, they engaged in 348 major battles, seizing 10 mortars, 11 grenade launchers, 8 heavy machine guns, 90 light machine guns, 12 submachine guns, 5,002 rifles and pistols, and 3 military radios. They killed or wounded 2,329 Japanese soldiers and 4,919 puppet troops, while capturing 2,324 enemies. [33]

In a sense, Yang Jingyu's psychological impact on the enemy surpassed their military losses. His unyielding will and indomitable spirit struck both fear and awe into their hearts. In early March, following orders from General Yoshifuru Amano, the Japanese held a memorial ceremony for Yang Jingyu at the Guan Di Temple on Mengjiang County's West Mountain. Kōkoku Iwayama personally inscribed "Tomb of Yang Jingyu" on a wooden plaque, erected at a hill west of Bao'an Village. [34]

What defines a true warrior? One who terrifies the enemy yet commands their respect. Notably, Japanese invaders had a history of honoring formidable adversaries.

The phrase "nine deaths, one life" is often used to describe the cost of struggle, but it fails to capture the sacrifice of the Northeast Anti-Japanese United Forces. At its peak, the forces numbered over 30,000. By 1945, however, a Soviet Far East Command report dated August 25 recorded only 1,354 personnel in the Instructional Brigade: 373 Chinese, 103 Koreans, 416 Nanais (Hezhe people in the USSR), and 476 Russians. [35] Excluding the Nanais and Russians, only 476 Chinese and Korean fighters remained— a stark testament to their near-total annihilation.

It should be noted that in late July, to coordinate with the Soviet Army's blitz against the Kwantung Army, the Northeast Anti-Japanese United Forces had already dispatched 340 officers and soldiers from the Instructional Brigade as advance teams to guide Soviet troops or carry out special missions. Many of them perished in the Soviet offensive against the Japanese Kwantung Army. Additionally, some fighters remained in China on missions or had not joined the Soviet-based Instructional Brigade.

By any calculation, of the original 30,000 Anti-Japanese United Forces fighters, fewer than 1,000 remained in the end. They had been lost to battle, starvation, illness, desertion, defection, or languished in enemy prisons. Yet these survivors—forged through unimaginable trials and relentless attrition—persisted like the last flickering sparks of resistance amid a blizzard of tyranny. In time, these embers would ignite into a raging fire of anti-Japanese resistance that swept across the land.

Following the "August 15th Liberation" in 1945, over 330 Anti-Japanese United Forces officers and soldiers, led by Zhou Baozhong and Li Zhaolin, assisted Soviet forces in reclaiming 57 towns and strategic locations across Northeast China. They swiftly expanded the Northeast People's Self-Defense Army, which grew to over 40,000 troops by October 20. The forces confiscated vast quantities of Japanese-puppet weaponry, including 60,000 rifles, 2,000+ light machine guns, 800+ heavy machine guns, 500+ grenade launchers, 20+ mortars, and 12 million rounds of ammunition. [36] Meanwhile, Nationalist forces seeking to claim the fruits of victory remained stranded in the distant southwest, near Mount Emei.

On November 4, 1945, Mao Zedong issued *The Deployment for Reinforcing Northeast China*, stating: "Lin Biao has now been appointed Commander in Chief of the Northeast People's Autonomous Army, with Lü Zhengcao, Xiao Jinguang, Li Yuncheng, and Zhou Baozhong (leader of the Volunteer Army) serving as First, Second, Third, and Fourth Deputy Commanders..." [37]

With this, the Northeast Anti-Japanese United Forces were formally integrated into the Northeast People's Autonomous Army, marking a critical transition in consolidating Communist-led military power during the postwar struggle for control of the region.

Even more exhilarating for the Northeast Anti-Japanese United Forces was an earlier milestone: at 18:00 on September 25, Zhou Baozhong, representing the Northeast Committee of the Chinese Communist Party, formally transferred the organizational leadership of the Northeast Party to Peng Zhen and Chen Yun of the Northeast Bureau. The Anti-Japanese United Forces and countless Communist Party members in the Northeast had finally reunited with the Central Committee—they were home at last!

Yet it was deeply poignant that two leaders who had desperately sought this moment—Yang Jingyu and Zhao Shangzhi—did not live to witness this triumphant reunion.

Among the first generation of 11 Anti-Japanese army commanders, only Li Yanlu and Zhou Baozhong were fortunate enough to see Japan's defeat and experience the joy of New China's founding. Of the three original route army commanders, Zhou Baozhong and Li Zhaolin survived to witness their brutal enemies lay down arms, though Li Zhaolin himself would not live to see the formal establishment of the People's Republic. Their fates stand as a bittersweet testament to the immense sacrifices underpinning China's liberation.

Among the many commanders of the Northeast Anti-Japanese United Forces, Li Zhaolin was known as the "Lucky General." Despite countless perilous battles, not a single hair on his head had been harmed by the brutal assaults of Japanese invaders. Over the 14 grueling years of resistance, the greatest threats to his life came not from enemy fire but from starvation. On one occasion, he survived over 20 days without food, teetering on the brink of death. Yet tragically, this hero who had defied Japanese aggression met his end not at the hands of foreign invaders but at those of his own countrymen. On March 9, 1946, Nationalist intelligence agents stabbed Li Zhaolin seven times (leaving eight wounds), felling the indomitable commander who had withstood Japanese artillery and machine guns—only to succumb to the knives of Chinese reactionaries.

Li Zhaolin's assassination robbed the Chinese Communist Party and its military of a seasoned, exemplary leader. The mountains and rivers seemed to mourn his loss. Here was yet another hero who survived foreign tyranny only to fall victim to domestic treachery—a bitter testament to the complex fractures of China's wartime and postwar struggles.

On March 25, 1949, during a military review ceremony at Beiping's Xiyuan Airport, Mao Zedong made a point of meeting Li Zhaolin's widow, Jin Bowen—a veteran of the Anti-Japanese United Forces. The People's Daily recorded: "As Mao Zedong shook hands with General Li Zhaolin's wife, the entire assembly fell silent, hundreds of eyes fixed on the moment." [38] This gesture reaffirmed Mao Zedong's profound respect for all Anti-Japanese United Forces soldiers who had endured 14 years of bloody struggle and his solemn remembrance of those who perished.

What defined the spirit of the Anti-Japanese United Forces? What kind of army was this?

In October 1941, Zhao Shangzhi—once a commander of thousands—was reduced to leading a squad of just five men, including himself. Yet he remained undaunted, content so long as he could fight the invaders. Three months later, his unit appeared to number six (though only four were genuine fighters—two recruits and two traitors). Still, Zhao boldly led them to attack a puppet police substation.

Yang Jingyu, after entering Mengjiang in late 1939 with over 400 troops from the First Route Army headquarters, endured relentless combat, dispersal, casualties, desertions, and betrayals. By February 15, 1940, only three fighters remained by his side. Even then, he killed one enemy and wounded six. After February 18, he stood utterly alone. To the cacophony of surrender demands, he answered with gunfire—fighting until his last breath.

The Northeast Anti-Japanese United Forces were an army guided by unwavering principles: to stand unflinchingly with the Chinese people and fight wholeheartedly for their liberation.

"Under this principle, this army possessed an unyielding spirit—to overwhelm all enemies and never submit. No matter how dire the circumstances, even if only one soldier remained, that soldier would fight on." [39]

Notes:

[1]   The Sanjiang Provincial Police Department: Report on the Shooting of Zhao Shangzhi to the Director of the Police Department of the Security Bureau, Taniguchi Akayama (March 1942), Heilongjiang Provincial Archives; cited in Zhao Junqing: The Biography of Zhao Shangzhi, Heilongjiang People's Press, revised edition in August 2015, p. 341.

[2]   [3]   The Central Archives, China Second Historical Archives, Jilin Academy of Social Sciences: Selected Materials on the Archives of Japanese Imperialism's Aggression Against China   The "Great Punitive Expedition" in Northeast China, Zhonghua Book Company, 1st edition in April 1991, pp. 484,

[4]   Oral Account by Huo Zhanhui: The Sacrifice of Zhao Shangzhi (1961); cited in Zhao Junqing: The Biography of Zhao Shangzhi, Heilongjiang People's Press, revised edition in August 2015, p. 346.

[5]   The Central Archives, China Second Historical Archives, Jilin Academy of Social Sciences: Selected Materials on the Archives of Japanese Imperialism's Aggression Against China   The "Great Punitive Expedition" in Northeast China, Zhonghua Book Company, 1st edition in April 1991, p. 483.

[6]   Zhao Junqing: The Biography of Zhao Shangzhi, Heilongjiang People's Press, revised edition in August 2015, Preface p. 2, main text p. 349.

[7]   Zhang Zhenglong, Jiang Baocai: The Last Anti-Japanese United Army, People's Daily Press, 1st edition in January 2016, p. 36.

[8]   The Central Archives, Liaoning Provincial Archives, Jilin Provincial Archives, Heilongjiang Provincial Archives: Compilation of Revolutionary Historical Documents in Northeast China, Jia 60, p. 240; cited in Zhao Junqing: The Biography of Yang Jingyu, Heilongjiang People's Press, revised edition in August 2015, p. 324.

[9]   Liu Xian: The Battle of the First Route Army of the Anti-Japanese United Front in Mengjiang, in The First Route Army of the Anti-Japanese United Front in Mengjiang, Jilin University Press, 1st edition in November 1990; cited in Zhao Junqing: The Biography of Yang Jingyu, Heilongjiang People's Press, revised edition in August 2015, p. 334.

[10]   Jiang Dianyuan: My Anti-Japanese United Front Life in Huadian, in Huadian Party History Materials Volume 1; cited in Zhao Junqing: The Biography of Yang Jingyu, Heilongjiang People's Press, revised edition in August 2015, p. 335.

[11]   The Central Archives, China Second Historical Archives, Jilin Academy of Social Sciences: Selected Materials on the Archives of Japanese Imperialism's Aggression Against China   The "Great Punitive Expedition" in Northeast China, Zhonghua Book Company, 1st edition in April 1991, p. 563.

[12]　[16]　The Compilation Group of History of the Northeast Anti-Japanese United Army: History of the Northeast Anti-Japanese United Army (Volume 2), CPC History Press, 1st edition in September 2015, pp. 769, 927–628.

[13]　The Central Archives, Liaoning Provincial Archives, Jilin Provincial Archives, Heilongjiang Provincial Archives: Compilation of Revolutionary Historical Documents in Northeast China, Jia 58, p. 178; cited in The Compilation Group of History of the Northeast Anti-Japanese United Army: History of the Northeast Anti-Japanese United Army, CPC History Press, 1st edition in September 2015, p. 774.

[14]　Jilin Provincial Archives: An Overview of the Anti-Japanese Movement in Northeast China, Jilin Literature and History Press, 1st edition in October 1986, p. 88.

[15]　Chen Han Zhang's Battlefield Diary (Excerpts), in Zhang Zhenglong, Jiang Baocai: The Last Anti-Japanese United Army, People's Daily Press, 1st edition in January 2016, pp. 223–224.

[17]　South Manchuria Railway Co., Ltd., Mengjiang County Construction Works Chronicle (November 1942), stored in Heilongjiang Provincial Archives; cited in Zhao Junqing: The Biography of Yang Jingyu, Heilongjiang People's Press, revised edition in August 2015, p. 295.

[18]　The Compilation Group of Historical Materials of the Northeast Anti-Japanese United Army: Historical Materials of the Northeast Anti-Japanese United Army (Volume 1), Central Party History Materials Press, 1st edition in December 1987, pp. 201–202.

[19]　[20]　[21]　[22]　[23]　The Compilation Group of Historical Materials of the Northeast Anti-Japanese United Army: History of the Northeast Anti-Japanese United Army (Volume 2), CPC History Press, 1st edition in September 2015, pp. 756, 760, 771, 749, 841.

[24]　[29]　Zhao Junqing: The Biography of Yang Jingyu, Heilongjiang People's Press, revised edition in August 2015, pp. 353, 365.

[25]   The Resolution of the Central Political Bureau of the Communist Party of China on Convening the Seventh National Congress (December 13, 1937), in The Central Committee of the Communist Party of China, Literature Research Office, Central Archives: Selected Important Documents Since the Founding of the Party (1921–1949), Volume 14, Central Literature Press, p. 737.

[26]   Huang Shengfa: Fighting in Hard Times, in Jilin Party History Materials Issue 2, 1986; cited in Zhao Junqing: The Biography of Yang Jingyu, Heilongjiang People's Press, revised edition in August 2015, pp. 367–368.

[27]   Bodyguard Jiang Dezhou's Recollection of General Yang Jingyu (September 19, 2001), in An Eternal Monument, Jilin Literature and History Press, published in 2005, p. 409; cited in Zhao Junqing: The Biography of Yang Jingyu, Heilongjiang People's Press, revised edition in August 2015, p. 354.

[28]   The Central Archives, China Second Historical Archives, Jilin Academy of Social Sciences: Selected Materials on the Archives of Japanese Imperialism's Aggression Against China   The "Great Punitive Expedition" in Northeast China, Zhonghua Book Company, 1st edition in April 1991, p. 569.

[30]   Shi Yijun: The Most Dangerous Moment: Northeast Anti-Japanese United Army Historical Events, CITIC Press Group, 1st edition in September 2016, p. 12.

[31]   The Central Archives, China Second Historical Archives, Jilin Academy of Social Sciences: Selected Materials on the Archives of Japanese Imperialism's Aggression Against China   The "Great Punitive Expedition" in Northeast China, Zhonghua Book Company, 1st edition in April 1991, p. 559.

[32]   Liu Xian: Forever Yang Jingyu (December 18, 2006); cited in Zhao Junqing: The Biography of Yang Jingyu, Heilongjiang People's Press, revised edition in August 2015, p. 372.

[33]   The Central Archives, Liaoning Provincial Archives, Jilin Provincial Archives, Heilongjiang Provincial Archives: Compilation of Revolutionary Historical

Documents in Northeast China, Jia 60, p. 248; cited in Zhao Junqing: The Biography of Yang Jingyu, Heilongjiang People's Press, revised edition in August 2015, p. 374.

[34]   Shi Yijun: The Most Dangerous Moment: Northeast Anti-Japanese United Army Historical Events, CITIC Press Group, 1st edition in September 2016, p. 14.

[35]   Report by Yuen Chih Lin, Chief of the Far Eastern Supply Department, on the Composition and Distribution of the 88th Division (August 25, 1945); cited in Zhao Junqing: The Biography of Li Zhaolin, Heilongjiang People's Press, 1st edition in August 2015, p. 372.

[36]   Zhou Baoshong: Northeast Anti-Japanese Guerrilla War and the Anti-Japanese United Army, in Selected Works of Zhou Baoshong, Yunnan People's Press, published in 1985, p. 429; cited in Zhao Junqing: The Biography of Zhou Baoshong, Heilongjiang People's Press, revised edition in August 2015, p. 406.

[37]   The Central Committee of the Communist Party of China, Literature Research Office: Collected Works of Mao Zedong (Volume 4), People's Press, 1st edition in August 1996, p. 63.

[38]   Liaoning Academy of Social Sciences Local Party History Research Institute: A Singable and Moving Poem: Mao Zedong and the Northeast Anti-Japanese United Army, Central Literature Press, 1st edition in October 2013, p. 157.

[39]   The Central Committee of the Communist Party of China, Literature Editing Committee: Selected Works of Mao Zedong (Volume 3), People's Press, 2nd edition in June 1991, p. 1039.

Tribute and References

The September 19th Changchun Anti-Japanese War Historical Materials Compilation, compiled by the Changchun Municipal CPPCC Committee on Historical and Literary Materials and the Changchun Municipal Archives, September 2015.

A Century in Review: Major Events and Celebrity Narratives of the 20th Century (Volume II), edited by Fang Jianwen and Zhang Ming, Economic Daily Press, August 1997, 1st Edition.

Benxi County Historical and Literary Materials (Volume II), compiled by the Benxi County CPPCC Committee on Historical and Literary Materials Research, December 1987.

Benxi Heroes (Volume I), compiled by the CPC Benxi Municipal Party History Office and the Benxi Municipal Civil Affairs Bureau, Publication Registration Number (Internal) 0131, August 1988.

The Long March, authored by Wang Shuzeng, People's Literature Press, September 2006, 1st Edition.

Changchun County Gazetteer, compiled by the Changchun County Local Gazetteer Compilation Committee, Liaoning Nationalities Publishing House, December 2003, 1st Edition.

Infectious Diseases, edited by Zhejiang Medical University, People's Health Publishing House, May 1980, 1st Edition.

Dai Xu on the First Sino-Japanese War: Political Reasons for Dynastic Defeats as Seen from the Late Qing Dynasty, authored by Dai Xu, People's Daily Press, December 2018, 1st Edition.

Hell Ship: 'Living Coffins' in the Asia-Pacific War, authored by Mitchener (US), translated by Ji Wen, Chongqing Publishing House, December 2015, 1st Edition.

Northeast! Northeast!, compiled by Tong Qinglin, People's Publishing House, September 2015, 1st Edition.

A Compilation of Revolutionary Historical Documents from the Northeast Region (Jia 1-66, Yi 1-2), compiled by the Central Archives, Liaoning Provincial Archives, Jilin Provincial Archives, and Heilongjiang Provincial Archives, 1988–1991.

Overview of the Communist Anti-Japanese Movement in Northeast China (1938–1942), compiled and translated by the Jilin Provincial Archives, Jilin Literature and History Publishing House, October 1986, 1st Edition.

The Spirit of the Northeast Anti-Japanese United Army, authored by Zhang Hongxing, Baishan Publishing House, August 2010, 1st Edition.

Women Soldiers of the Northeast Anti-Japanese United Army, authored by Liu Ying, Heilongjiang People's Publishing House, August 2015, 1st Edition.

The Fourth Army of the Northeast Anti-Japanese United Army, authored by Gong Hui and Ma Yanwen, Heilongjiang People's Publishing House, May 2005, 2nd Edition.

History of the Northeast Anti-Japanese United Army, authored by the "History of the Northeast Anti-Japanese United Army" Compilation Group, CPC History Publishing House, September 2015, 1st Edition.

History of the Northeast Anti-Japanese United Army, authored by Zhu Shuxian and Yue Siping, PLA Publishing House, January 2014, 1st Edition.

Historical Materials on the Northeast Anti-Japanese United Army, compiled by the "Historical Materials on the Northeast Anti-Japanese United Army" Compilation Group, CPC Historical Materials Publishing House, December 1987, 1st Edition.

Biographies of the Northeast Anti-Japanese Volunteers, edited by Tan Yi, Liaoning People's Publishing House, January 1987, 1st Edition.

History of the Northeast Anti-Japanese Volunteers, edited by Wen Yonglu, Heilongjiang People's Publishing House, April 1987, 1st Edition.

The Northeast Anti-Japanese War in Practice, authored by Li Shuyuan and Wang Mingwei, Changchun Publishing House, May 2011, 2nd Edition.

History of the Northeast Anti-Japanese War, authored by Wang Mingwei, Changchun Publishing House, August 2016, 1st Edition.

The Tokyo Trials, authored by L. N. Smirnov and E. B. Zaitsev (Soviet Union), translated by Li Zhizhong, Shi Qihua, and Lin Shuhua, Military Translation Publishing House, August 1987, 1st Edition.

The Long Biography of Feng Zhongyun, organized by the National Library of China's Memory Project Center, written by Shi Yi-jun, National Library of China Publishing House, May 2019, 1st Edition.

Betrayal at the Top: US Betrayal of Its Allies Exposed, authored by James MacKay (New Zealand), translated by He Linrong, China City Publishing House, October 1998, 1st Edition.

Joining the Nation in Hardship, authored by Li Junhu, Bei Yue Literature and Art Publishing House, December 2014, 1st Edition.

The Memoirs of Wellington Koo, authored by Wellington Koo, translated by the Institute of Modern History, Chinese Academy of Social Sciences, Zhonghua Book Company, 1983, 1st Edition.

The Inner Story of Traitors, authored by Shen Zui, Xu Zhaoming, et al., China Literature and History Publishing House, January 2010, 1st Edition.

North China Security Warfare, compiled by the Japanese Defense Agency's War History Section, translated by Fan Youping and Zhu Jiaqing, Unity Publishing House, December 2015, 1st Edition.

River and Mountain in the Yellow River: The Memoirs of Ray Huang, authored by Ray Huang (US), translated by Zhang Yian, The Commercial Press, February 2007, 2nd Edition.

A Compilation of Important Documents Since the Founding of the Communist Party of China (1921–1949), compiled by the Central Compilation and Translation Bureau and the Central Archives of the CPC, Central Literature Publishing House, April 2011, 1st Edition.

The Cambridge History of Late Qing China (1800–1911), edited by John King Fairbank and Albert Feuerwerker (US), translated by China Social Sciences Press, February 1985, 1st Edition.

Chiang Kai-shek, authored by Brian Crozier (US), Inner Mongolia People's Publishing House, July 1995, 1st Edition.

Biography of Chiang Kai-shek, written by Zhou Haifeng, Writers Publishing House, February 2006.

Unveiling Chiang Kai-shek's Diaries, compiled by Zhang Xiuzhang, Unity Press, January 2007.

Chiang Kai-shek and the Great Powers, written by Wang Yao, Taiwan Strait Press, July 2013.

Chiang Kai-shek and Japan: Entangled History, written by Weng Youwei and Zhao Wenyuan, People's Publishing House, January 2008.

Chiang Monlin's Autobiography: Tides from the West and New Currents, written by Chiang Monlin, Unity Press, October 2004.

The September 18th Incident, compiled by the Jilin Provincial Archives, Archives Press, September 1991.

The Chrysanthemum and the Sword, written by (US) Ruth Benedict, translated by Yi Bing, Wuhan Publishing House, June 2009.

The War of Resistance Against Japan, written by Wang Shuzeng, People's Literature Publishing House, June 2015.

An Epic Poem: Mao Zedong and the Northeast Anti-Japanese United Army, written by the Institute of Local Party History of the Liaoning Academy of Social Sciences, Central Party Literature Publishing House, October 2013.

Glory in Adversity, written by Jin Yinan, Huayi Publishing House, January 2009.

Biography of Li Zhaolin, written by Zhao Junqing, Heilongjiang People's Publishing House, August 2015.

The Other Half of World War II History: 1945·Great Power Game, written by Ding Xiaoping, Huawen Publishing House, July 2015.

China and Japan in the Past Sixty Years, written by Wang Yunsheng, SDX Joint Publishing Company, July 2005.

General Ma Zhanshan, compiled by the Editorial Team of General Ma Zhanshan, China Literature and History Press, October 1987.

Biography of Mao Zedong, written by (UK) Philip Short, translated by Tong Xiaoqiu, Yang Xiaolan, and Zhang Airu, China Youth Publishing House, January 2004.

Chronology of Mao Zedong (1893-1949), revised edition, compiled by the Party Literature Research Office of the CPC Central Committee, Central Party Literature Publishing House, December 2013.

Selected Letters of Mao Zedong, compiled by the Party Literature Research Office of the CPC Central Committee, People's Publishing House, December 1983.

Collected Works of Mao Zedong, compiled by the Party Literature

Research Office of the CPC Central Committee, People's Publishing House, August 1996.

Mao Zedong's Military Strategy, written by Hu Zhefeng, People's Publishing House, May 2001.

Selected Works of Mao Zedong, compiled by the Editorial Committee of the Party Literature of the CPC Central Committee and the Editorial Committee of the Selected Works of Mao Zedong, People's Publishing House, June 1991.

National Soul: The Northeast Anti-Japanese United Army, edited by Zhuang Yan, Jilin Publishing Group Co., Ltd., August 2014.
The Rape of Nanking, written by (US) Zhang Chunru, translated by Tan Chunxia and Jiao Guolin, CITIC Press, January 2013.

Nomonhan 1939, written by Chen Dunde, PLA Press, August 2015.

Selected Archival Materials on Japanese Imperialism's Invasion of China: The September 18th Incident, jointly compiled by the Central Archives, the Second Historical Archives, and the Jilin Provincial Academy of Social Sciences, Zhonghua Book Company, August 1988.

Selected Archival Materials on Japanese Imperialism's Invasion of China: Puppet Manchukuo Police and Gendarmerie Rule, jointly compiled by the Central Archives, the Second Historical Archives, and the Jilin Provincial Academy of Social Sciences, Zhonghua Book Company, January 2001.

Selected Archival Materials on Japanese Imperialism's Invasion of China: The "Great Suppression" in Northeast China, jointly compiled by the Central Archives, the Second Historical Archives, and the Jilin Provincial Academy of Social Sciences, Zhonghua Book Company, April 1991.

Selected Archival Materials on Japanese Imperialism's Invasion of China: Major Massacres in Northeast China, jointly compiled by the Central

Archives, the Second Historical Archives, and the Jilin Provincial Academy of Social Sciences, Zhonghua Book Company, September 1989.

Secret History of the Japanese Gendarmerie: Murder, Violence, and Torture in the Asian Theater of War, written by (UK) Mark Felton, translated by Ji Wonu, proofread by Fan Guoping, Chongqing Publishing Group Chongqing Publishing House, November 2017.

Atrocities of the Japanese-Puppet Regime, edited by Sun Bang, Jilin People's Publishing House, October 1993.

Historical Evidence: A Record of China's Education and Reformation of Japanese War Criminals, written by Zhang Fulin, Tian Jingbao, Xia Mang, and Zhang Yanfeng, Jilin People's Publishing House, September 2005.

A Modern History of the World (Modern Volume), edited by Xu Tianxin, Xu Ping, and Wang Hongsheng, People's Publishing House, April 1997.

The Soviet Union's Expedition to Northeast China, written by Xu Yan, PLA Press, August 2015.

Taierzhuang Nirvana, written by Xu Jingeng, People's Daily Press, August 2015.

The Pacific War (Three Volumes), written by (Japan) Shōkō Iwahama, translated by Xing Yuan and Jin Zhe, Jincheng Publishing House, July 2011. A Fourteen-Year History of Manchukuo, written by Qiu Shuping, compiled by the Cultural and Historical Learning Committee of the Changchun CPPCC, April 1998.

Why Mao Zedong, written by Ren Zhigang, Guangming Daily Press, May 2019.

Selected Historical and Cultural Materials (Volume 64), compiled by the Cultural and Historical Materials Research Committee of the Chinese People's Political Consultative Conference National Committee, Cultural and Historical Materials Publishing House, July 1997.

My Years with the Northeast Anti-Japanese United Army: Oral Histories of Veterans, compiled by the China Memory Project Center of the National Library, CITIC Publishing Group, September 2016.

The First Half of My Life (Full Edition), written by Puyi, People's Publishing House, January 2007.

Cold Snow, Hot Blood, written by Zhang Zhenglong, Changjiang Literature and Art Publishing House, April 2011.

Biography of Yang Jingyu, written by Zhao Junqing, Heilongjiang People's Publishing House, August 2015.

Embracing Defeat: Japan in the Aftermath of World War II, written by (US) John Dower, translated by Hu Bo, SDX Joint Publishing Company, September 2008.

Zhang Xueliang's Oral History, oral account by Zhang Xueliang, written by Tang Degang, China Archives Publishing House, July 2007.

Collected Works of Zhang Xueliang, edited by Bi Wanwen, Xinhua Publishing House, 1992.

Biography of Zhao Shangzhi, written by Zhao Junqing, Heilongjiang People's Publishing House, August 2015.

Biography of Zhao Yiman, written by Li Yunqiao, The Commercial Press, June 2018.

Truth: Hirohito and the War of Aggression Against China, written by (US) Herbert Bix, translated by Wang Liping and Sun Shengping, Xinhua Publishing House, September 2004.

The CPC Central Committee and the Northeast Anti-Japanese United Army, written by Shang Jinzhou, Central Party Literature Publishing House, May 2010.

History of the CPC Delegation to the Communist International, written by Jin Shangzhou, People's Publishing House, October 2019.

China 1946, written by Zhang Zhenglong, Baishan Publishing House,

January 2014.

Chinese Idiom Dictionary, Shanghai Lexicographical Publishing House, August 1987.

History of the Communist Party of China in Liaoning Province·Volume I (1919-1949), written by the Party History Research Office of the CPC Liaoning Provincial Committee, Liaohai Publishing House, June 2001.

China's Secret War: A Record of the CPC's Intelligence and Security Work, written by Hao Zaijin, Jincheng Publishing House, January 2015.

Historical Materials of the Republic of China: Translation Manuscripts on the Northeast Anti-Japanese United Army, translated by Li Zhu, Jia Yuqin, Gao Shuquan, et al., Zhonghua Book Company, January 1982.

Preliminary Compilation of Important Historical Materials of the Republic of China: The Period of Anti-Japanese War (Prologue), edited by Qin Xiaoyi, compiled by the History Committee of the Central Committee of the Chinese Kuomintang, September 1981.

Sino-Japanese Secret War, written by Hao Zaijin, PLA Press, August 2015.

Compilation of Old Sino-Foreign Treaties, edited by Wang Tieya, SDX Joint Publishing Company, March 1962.

Biography of Zhou Baozhong, written by Zhao Junqing, Heilongjiang People's Publishing House, August 2015.

The Last Northeast Anti-Japanese United Army, edited by Zhang Zhenglong and Jiang Baocai, People's Daily Press, January 2016.

The Longest Resistance, written by Sa Su, Xiyuan Publishing House, June 2013.

The Most Dangerous Moment: Historical Research on the Northeast Anti-Japanese United Army, written by Shi Yijun, CITIC Publishing Group, September 2016.

Author's Postscript

With the book now completed, the author should step back and leave all judgment to the readers. What follows are merely superfluous reflections.

To undertake such a voluminous work in my septuagenarian years was perhaps overambitious—a realization that struck me midway through the writing, yet retreat was no longer an option.

Over twenty million words of archival materials and historical texts filled half my study. A significant portion, including numbered files from provincial archives, was delivered to my doorstep by the Jilin Provincial Party History Research Office. They arranged transportation for me to attend meetings, connected me with descendants of Anti-Japanese fighters to gather firsthand accounts, organized visits to revolutionary sites, and hosted multiple expert symposiums where I absorbed invaluable insights... Mr. Chen Chen, my publisher, solemnly advised me to focus my "limited energy" (my interpretation — he phrased it as "prioritize") on this monumental subject. He sent crates of reference materials to my home and assigned two senior editors to help organize notes, summaries, and indexes...

Thus, for nearly a thousand days and nights, I immersed myself in this sea of documents. I dared not fall ill or be distracted. Even when plagued by toothaches or leg pains, I limited my outings to pharmacy runs. To manage worsening eyesight, I fractured my sleep into two or three segments nightly, forcibly resetting my circadian rhythm with Estazolam (a sedative). Exhaustion and anxiety gnawed at me. Yet as I delved deeper, the work became its own reward—holidays blurred, seasons passed unnoticed. Past seventy, I'd grown stoic, but these historical accounts repeatedly brought me to tears: my nose would sting, my eyes moisten, my heart surge with indignation and sorrow. It was the indomitable spirit of the Northeast Anti-Japanese United Forces—their earth-shaking courage, their unwavering loyalty to nation and people—that sustained, inspired, and drove me forward. The writing ceased to feel arduous; instead, it became a source of exhilaration and joy. Upon typing the final character and peeling the medical tape from my swollen right middle finger, I realized with relief that my planned hospital visits (except for eye treatment) could be canceled. The martyrs had taught me how to endure physical suffering. My deepest gratitude extends to the leadership of the Jilin Provincial Party History Research Office and Mr. Chen Chen for granting me this spiritual baptism.

I dare not claim this work as definitive history. Truthfully, it synthesizes fragments of brilliance from the works of countless experts, writers, and scholars (with sources duly credited), interspersed with my own humble observations. Imperfections and errors abound—this is no false modesty. To all who contributed, I bow in gratitude and respect.

It is said that those with half a century of Communist Party membership will receive a commemorative medal this year. I count myself fortunate.

Passion

Authored after extensive research into modern historical archives—particularly materials on the Northeast Anti-Japanese United Army—this 700,000-word, twenty-chapter work chronicles the Chinese Communist Party's leadership in uniting diverse resistance forces and mobilizing ethnic groups across Northeast China to sustain a grueling anti-Japanese campaign following Japan's invasion, highlighting the patriotic resolve, unyielding integrity, tenacious heroism, and ideological loyalty of Communist figures like Yang Jingyu, Zhao Shangzhi, Zhou Baozhong, and Zhao Yiman, who embodied defiance against foreign aggression through their sacrifice and strategic perseverance, while also exploring the army's broader role in coordinating with national resistance efforts and cementing its legacy within China's collective struggle for sovereignty and dignity.